Our Family Album

The Unfinished Story of the Christian Reformed Church.

JAMES C. SCHAAP

CRC Publications is grateful to the Archives, Hekman Library, Calvin College and Theological Seminary for their assistance in supplying most of the photographs in this book and for granting us permission to use them.

Other photos © David De Jonge: pages 13, 23, 79, 161, 393-396; SuperStock: pages 66, 78, 215, 235, 269, 270, 289; Hulton Getty Images: page 255; Edwin de Jong: pages 331 (for Rehoboth Christian Schools), 375, 378-379 (for *The Banner*), 404 (For Christian Reformed World Missions)

Our Family Album: The Unfinished Story of the Christian Reformed Church. © 1998, CRC Publications, 2850 Kalamazoo Ave. SE, Grand Rapids, MI 49560.

Library of Congress Cataloging-in-Publication Data
Schaap, James C., 1948-
    Our family album: the unfinished story of the Christian Reformed
Church/James C. Schaap.
      p.   cm.
      ISBN 1-56212-361-0
      1. Christian Reformed Church—History. I. Title.
BX6816.S33 1998
285.7'31'09—dc21   98-36521
                                            CIP

10 9 8 7 6 5 4 3 2 1

ACKNOWLEDGMENTS

The story of a denomination is a family story. It can be told from many different perspectives.

James C. Schaap is the primary storyteller in this book. With warmth and wisdom he takes us into a past filled with glory and shame, triumph and failure, joy and sorrow—the past of a small part of God's church at work building his kingdom in this world.

The stories in sidebars and pictures throughout the book come from other storytellers. Herbert J. Brinks (HJB), William D. Buursma (WDB), and Tymen E. Hofman (TEH) spent many hours selecting pictures and writing the stories that appear in boxes on these pages. These warm, sometimes humorous, always informative sidebars add a richness to the story—the kind of richness that comes from listening to many different voices and seeing things through many different eyes.

Because the story of the Christian Reformed Church is so complex and involves so many details, we also needed experts to review the story and to offer suggestions for correcting and enriching it at times. The members of the Historical Committee of the Christian Reformed Church took on that important role, volunteering many hours of their time to make our book more accurate and complete.

We're grateful to all these people—both the storytellers and the reviewers—for helping us understand what it means to be Christian Reformed as we stand together on the threshold of a new century.

This history is not complete. Like most family albums, this book skips over many important names and events and movements. There simply isn't room to include mention of all of those who have lovingly led and served this church. It's likely that each person who reads this book could add names and even chapters that would enhance the story. Perhaps reading these chapters will inspire all of us to tell the stories of our past that are worth telling and to accept the challenges facing the CRC in the future.

CONTENTS

No one should assume that this book is entirely the product of a single person or a single mind. It is not. The writer whose name appears on the title page inherited much of this manuscript from an unfinished project designed to be completed somewhere around the 125th anniversary of the Christian Reformed Church in 1982. For a variety of reasons that project was never fully completed, but the most significant legwork on that manuscript was accomplished by two individuals—Dr. Herb Brinks, a historian and the keeper of the CRC archives at Calvin College, and Mr. A. James Heynen, who was at that time the Executive Director of the Board of Publications of the CRC.

Most of the credit for putting together this history, for its original design and substance, belongs to those two individuals. They did the hard work of trudging through sources and old histories and carving from all that weight the important stories here told. Many of the colorful renditions of the denomination's early fathers you will find in this book come originally from the pens of Heynen and Brinks.

Jim Schaap is not a historian. I am, by profession, a teacher; when you hear lecturing, it's very likely in my voice. Blame me, if you will, for many of the asides and much of the subjectively drawn association you'll discover throughout your reading. You will hear me often, but you'll also hear—not so clearly identified—the voices of Herb Brinks and Jim Heynen.

What about my part? When Synod 1996 instructed the denomination's Historical Committee to create materials through which the denomination can come to better know its own history, that committee came knocking on my door. CRC Publications, they told me, already had a significant manuscript somewhere in its offices, an unfinished narrative that needed considerable updating and a consistent voice throughout. What they wanted was a storyteller. They asked me to breathe new life into the manuscript and pull the whole story together.

In the event that you want to pick a fight with something here recalled and narrated, I'll take some comfort in hiding a bit; after all, the manuscript is not all my work. It may well be someone other than myself with whom you want to draw swords. But then, should you like what you read, I suppose I can't very well take credit either. For all the strengths and weaknesses of this effort to tell the story of the Christian Reformed Church in

North America, I am deeply indebted to what was passed along into my hands.

Much of the credit, for good or ill, belongs to the two individuals I've already mentioned. Herb Brinks has done, in quiet obscurity, a yeoman's task in keeping track of this story. From his desk in the archives, he has, for years, held on tenaciously to the historical record of the denomination and its people. Historians rarely get headlines, but we'd be in bad shape without someone to file those headlines away so that others, like me, can read them and attempt to configure the real shape of the story. My friend Herb Brinks deserves great credit for doing that work, as well as contributing tons of copy to the project itself.

My friend A. James Heynen was, twenty-some years ago, the appointed storyteller. As I said, much of the color of the portraits you'll read here comes from his ability to collate the historical record and mold and shape it into a narrative full of style and grace, humor and pathos—a narrative fully as true to our humanity as the story itself. Both of these men deserve great credit for accumulating the story and telling it graciously.

A third individual also played an important role. Along with my dictionary and thesaurus, always ready on the desk throughout my own work on the manuscript, stood—and still stands—James Bratt's *Dutch Calvinism in Modern America.* It is unlikely that anyone in the CRCNA has read through more old *Banners* and *De Wachters* than James Bratt, and that immersion is what makes his study so central to the story's telling. I am deeply indebted—we all are—to Jim Bratt for both the extent and the wisdom of his work on Christian Reformed Church history.

I want to thank the Historical Committee for giving me the opportunity to be a part of this project. As my own writing has long illustrated, I'm sure, I do respect my Christian Reformed Church heritage greatly. I don't think I am entirely blind to its weaknesses, but I've come to believe that the loyalty my own grandparents held to the denomination into which I was born was created out of a love for the theological and cultural heritage they themselves had received from being nurtured in its particular and sometimes quite peculiar world.

I could dedicate this book to them, to all of those ancestors who loved and respected the Christian Reformed Church; but they're gone. In the environment of their own eternal present, they have no need for my thanks or ours.

So it is to my children that I dedicate this book—specifically, to Andrea and David. Like all of us who are parents, I have no idea where their lives' pilgrimages will take them, where they will someday worship the Lord. I only hope—and pray—that they will. And when they do their worship, both within the church and outside of the church, I hope and pray that they do it with the deep conviction their own ancestors had, a conviction not initially to the denomination called Christian Reformed, but to God Almighty, Creator of heaven and earth, and his Son, Jesus Christ, who pulled on what was undoubtedly a tight and binding suit of human flesh so that his beloved but fallen creatures might eventually reach a good and perfect community so much greater than the one we chose not to be a part of way back in Eden.

At this point in my children's lives, I have no idea what the Lord has intended for them in his world. But I want them to know that they aren't simply free agents, disconnected to anything but the immediacy of American popular culture. I want them to know they have a faith heritage, a goodly heritage of belief and custom. They've come from something worth knowing and respecting. I want them to know what their grandparents, their great-grandparents and even earlier ancestral generations came from—what those people valued, what they felt worth living and dying for, what they loved, and why.

This book is for the living, for those who are now recipients of a heritage that comes with membership in one small band of God's family, those people of all colors and backgrounds who today call themselves the Christian Reformed Church in North America.

Soli Deo Gloria.

CHAPTER ONE

Why This Story?

Not so very many years ago in the town where I live, an old woman died and, presumably, went to be with her Lord. She left behind a few pieces of furniture and some assorted households goods, a bit of real estate, an old car, various garden tools, and, her pride and joy, a host of kids and grandkids.

When those children looked over their mother's belongings, they came across a pile of scrapbooks and photo albums, a museum of personal and familial artifacts, all of it collected and collated into a wordless, priceless history. She had not thrown much away. So, with her untimely death, the inevitable task someday awaiting most of us fell to her children. They had to sort through the goods, decide what each of them wanted, keep what might be valuable to others for an auction, and toss the rest.

One scrapbook didn't make the cut. It was fat and ungainly, thick with pasted-in pages. For years and years, their mother had kept—religiously, I'd say—a scrapbook of mug shots taken from a particular annual edition of *The Banner*, the magazine of the Christian Reformed Church.

What Grandma had put together was a family album of the candidates for ministry in the CRC. Each year in early summer, when she'd get the *Banner* that posted photos of preachers-to-be, she'd dutifully cut them out and paste them on the pages of the annually thickening scrapbook. What she created was a photo-by-photo record of all those men who'd become preachers of the Word in the Christian Reformed Church, the hope of the denomination.

For those of us who've been around people who call themselves Christian Reformed for any considerable length of time, this story will resonate with a kind of quaint charm that is unmistakably nostalgic. For those of us—like me—who remember a CRC world that was much different than it is today, nostalgia comes easily, sometimes too easily. As someone once quipped, "The good old days are good all right—because they're not here."

But it's not difficult to wax a bit nostalgic about a story like this. The image is so defined: this woman adored her denomination so deeply that she kept photos of its fresh young preachers amid her own family remembrances.

My own children would find the attention their grandparents paid to denomination affairs, well, weird; they'd be nonplussed to know that Grandpa and Grandma used to watch *The Banner*'s lists

of calls accepted and calls declined with as much attention as they gave local news. My children would find it quaint to know that their grandparents and great-grandparents once looked up to Johanna Veenstra the way people today look at media superstars. Or that not too long ago many, many CRC folks listened to Rev. Peter Eldersveld's radio sermons because his words carried more authority than most anything said in North America. My children would be as surprised as this old woman's kin to discover that one of the ruling passions of

Worship service in a small church during the Synod of Dort.

their ancestors' life was the minutia of CRC denominational life.

Petty, insular, inbred, stifling, even silly—that level of devotion to a community (for *community* is what the denomination was in those days) is all of those. I have no doubt that Oma (my grandmother) is likely to have spent her time attending to denominational affairs when she might better have been serving the poor in her neighborhood or doing door-to-door evangelism.

I have no doubt that at one time CRC scrapbook-keeping seemed more important than creating a Christian political presence in North America. Oma probably never protested racism or nailed down shingles on a Habitat for Humanity project. Her sense of righteousness was, in part, created by her time and place, and, for better or for worse, what was good and noble and fitting for her included devotion to her denomination, the Christian Reformed Church.

We can argue endlessly about the propriety of her attention to those ministerial candidates, even speculate on the sociological reasons for her attention. We can call it a characteristic of an ethnic tribe finding its way in a North American landscape variegated by colors and races and national backgrounds. We can call that scrapbook evidence of her quest for identity, typical of individuals in dozens of American ethnic subcultures trying hard to stay afloat in a melting pot.

But whether we admire her attention or dismiss it as silliness, most of us know that the degree of devotion she gave to "her people" has gone. It no longer exists. Look where you might in the Christian Reformed Church in North America today, you'll not find that doggedly attentive care. Each year, fewer and fewer of us care to define ourselves by denominational affiliation. For some of us, being CRC is an embarrassment.

Not long ago, one of my best and brightest students, a young woman, a member of an ethnic minority in fact, told me that she'd had her denominational affiliation changed when her parents, afraid of increasing liberalism, left the Christian Reformed Church for a more orthodox fellowship. I'd never considered her that "conservative." I was surprised that she'd gone along with her family. Now she would be affiliating with a church that might well define itself most specifically by the fact that in its midst women did not hold church office.

"I'm shocked, I guess," I told her. "I just didn't think you were that type."

"Ah, Dr. Schaap—you don't understand," she said with typical forthrightness. "Nobody in my generation cares about 'being Christian Reformed.' Nobody cares about denominations anymore."

If she's right, then I guess I am probably closer to the Grandma of the scrapbook than I am to my student's generation.

A couple of decades ago Jimmy Carter, a one-term President of the United States, lost big to Ronald Reagan. Some say that his loss was, in part, attributable to his honesty. Inflation soared during Carter's administration, and the gas crisis created aggravating lines at gas pumps. But when Carter talked to the nation, he used a particular word—*malaise*—to describe the

major problem America faced. According to my dictionary, *malaise* is a "vague discomfort or unease."

While Reagan likely wouldn't have denied President Carter's assessment, he brought his unique brand of unbridled optimism out to attack it, and thereby grabbed the presidency from Jimmy Carter. Few people appreciate naysayers.

In a way, I feel like Jimmy Carter as I begin this history, because it seems that the place to start is with an assessment of the condition of "things CRC" that might look uncomfortably similar to what Carter saw and called a "malaise." For the Christian Reformed Church in North America—which is a long way from being the church it was to the Grandma of the scrapbook—is not in particularly good shape. The hemorrhage of members who've departed for what they consider more orthodox fellowships is obvious—we've lost thousands in the last twenty years. Less visible, perhaps, but noteworthy nonetheless, are those who've departed to what we might call more "mainline" denominations, more progressive fellowships, or what our friends on the right would call more liberal churches.

We've also lost many to what is called "the religious right"—fellowships more inclined to fundamentalism and a view of Scripture that defines itself with the word *inerrancy*. These folks are quite sure that the CRC has no teeth left, at least not when compared to Jerry Falwell or organizations like the American Family Association, our own Christian brothers and sisters who more regularly make the evening news.

The old caricature of Christian Reformed people—folks with soulful seriousness in such ample supply that they too often seemed dour and cheerless—isn't entirely inaccurate. But today it's not a theological doctrine that erases smiles from people's faces, not a deeply held conviction of our own depravity; instead, what makes for long faces in many CR churches is something sometimes sadly akin to the rodent's sense of a sinking ship. Some, who assail the denomination for being far too stoic and bumbling in its ability to change, leave for fellowships where the tent painlessly stretches wider. Others vilify the denomination for chasing American cultural trends like feminism or for chumming with Darwinists or those campaigning for homosexual rights. Others, sick unto death of constant bickering, simply wander down the street to big, sweet fellowships where smiling faces greet them every Sunday morning. They're tired of the fighting.

I sometimes wonder how it is that any of our kids remain in the CRC today. For as long as our college-aged kids have lived, there's been an acrimonious war in the denomination. The debate on women in ecclesiastical office and the difficult questions of how we read the Bible have been around that long. A quarter century's worth of our young people have not known peace in the pews.

But there's more to this malaise, and anyone close to the denominational offices knows it. What we used to call quotas—now ministry shares—have remained static in the past few decades, instead of rising to reflect inflation and the growing prosperity of the denomination. No agency in the CRC is working at what they would like to consider full staff. There are mission

Calvin Theological Seminary, 1892-1916, known then as Grand Rapids Theological School. (Below) Calvin Theological Seminary, built 1962.

positions open and wanting, both here in North America and abroad. The Christian Reformed World Relief Committee (CRWRC) could do much more than it does to alleviate suffering and meet the needs in places where disaster strikes. The Back to God Hour's enviable track record in broadcast evangelism around the world could be even more astonishing. But the money isn't there.

Why not? It's entirely too easy to say that denominational giving has leveled off because of a church adrift, listing left or right. Certainly, some have withheld their denominational offerings for reasons of protest. But there is another significant reason. Today we are, as individual churches, much more taken with our own pet projects—our food pantries, our support for kids going on SWIM or SERVE or to Youth Unlimited conventions, our own special needs for evangelism and local witness. Who can question the propriety of such decisions? Creating a place for neighborhood kids has made some congregations much more visible on the city map, more vibrant and alive.

When the denomination's evangelistic efforts take second place to witnessing in the very neighborhood we worship, who can fault the church? Such an attitude toward the denomination may seem more like simple indifference than disenchantment.

There may be some bona fide, mustachioed, black-hatted villains here, but much of the cause for the malaise lies in change which is, in part, inevitable. The Council of Iowa Teachers of English, a statewide organization, has trouble gathering new members, as does the national American Legion, the Republican and Democratic parties, and the local bowling league. Today North Americans seem more interested in their personal affairs than they do in professional, civic, or ecclesiastical organizations, whether those organizations be local, regional, or national. That the CRC would suffer in that kind of shift in values is almost unavoidable. As we approach the turn of the century and the millennium, what seems clear is that many old-line institutions of significant size and national breadth and scope are on the wane. The spirit of individualism is alive and well in North America. The ravenous appetite of a consumer culture doesn't simply gobble up consumer goods; it devours organizations as well.

What's more, one doesn't need to read tea leaves to know that ethnic communities eventually dissolve. Grandma's CRC was much more homogeneous, much more Dutch than the CRC today. Her devotion to the annual crop of CRC preachers was based on the fact that she considered them family—which some of those young men may well have been. One of the eccentricities of denominational life even today, according to some of our newer members, is *The Banner*'s listing of the anniversaries and deaths of its members, as if we were a neighborhood newspaper.

We are not what we were in Grandma's day—nor would we want to be. But who are we? What we're facing today is a denominational identity crisis, a need to define the principle that sets us apart. To replace the family spirit of our former ethnic community, we must discover an alternative—say, doctrinal unity. But are we, as a denomination, unified doctrinally? Have we ever been? What is it that holds us together anyway?

For the last two decades, organizations all over the continent, from Fortune 500 multinational corporations to the local Lions' Club, have determined that one of the most significant tasks they face is goal-setting—determining a vision and then creating realizable objectives and working hard to meet them. Fifty years ago, nobody thought much about goal-setting; today it's a job we all do. We have to know where we're going. We have to set goals. We have to accomplish them.

Several years ago, the Christian Reformed Church established a goal of 400,000 (members) by the year 2000. Not long ago, that goal was officially abandoned. Malaise.

Recently a financial scandal of immodest proportions hit the denomination. Now agencies and institutions suffer, not simply because substantial sums of money seem to be lost, but because most of us not in the loop on such matters wonder who on earth is in charge over there at 2850 Kalamazoo Avenue.

And always there is the siren call of dozens and dozens of para-church organizations. Take the Promise Keepers. No single force has brought as much revival to evangelical Christendom's male spirit as

Coach McCartney and stadiums full of high-fiving men. Scores of CRC men and their pastors swear by the organization, testify what joy and strength their participation has brought not only to themselves but also to their relationships to wives and churches. Who ever could have guessed that a football coach could drag millions of men into huge arenas, keep them on their Nikes with a dozen gospel songs, feed them with hot dogs and two days of energetic chalk-talk inspiration, break them into small groups for intimate prayer—intimacy, between men!—then send them back home on a mission, pumped up to be better husbands, better fathers, and better human beings? The Promise Keepers phenomenon is a miracle, really, and if it weren't Christian, it would receive far more media attention than it does.

Consider Fred, a member of your local CRC. He goes to Promise Keepers, attends with his son-in-law. They pray together, sing together, and feel the whispering currents of the Holy Spirit in ways Fred hasn't for years. When he leaves, he exits the stadium the way he used to leave his high school locker room—he's up for the game. His hands are fisted. He's ready to take on Satan in a series of dazzling moves that will leave the wily one behind. When he gets back, real life hits him. A week passes, and work hasn't changed, even though he has. His marriage glows for awhile, but old problems sneak back into late-night disagreements he thought he and his spouse wouldn't have anymore. The local church doesn't give him the high that Coach McCartney did. Life gets tedious.

Fred goes back for another rally, climbs back up again. Everything seems bright and right. It's a great day. And then, the tough stuff sloughs back in—work is a grind, his wife doesn't really want to move to that acreage, his teenage daughter harrumphs in voluble silence when he suggests she stay home one weekend night a week and build family togetherness. And as for the church—the minister's not that hot, and there's war in the liturgy committee because some stick-in-the-muds won't change music styles—First Church of the Iceberg if he ever saw it.

There's a wonderful fellowship just down the block, glowing like a perfect dawn, drawing people in from all walks of life, full every Sunday, full to overflowing. People are happy there—you can see it. Things are happening. The Spirit is alive and well at Pleasant Valley. People leave the place excited, ready to live the Christian life.

But Fred is loyal. He's got this sense that he shouldn't really abandon everything he's grown up with. He tells himself that there's enough good stuff in the CRC to stay with it, even though sometimes on Sunday he wonders whether he isn't sacrificing his own spiritual life for something that seems pretty much silly or dead.

He stays. But he keeps attending the rallies that give him the high it takes to enable him to stay with Iceberg CRC. If he can't or won't or shouldn't leave for another church, he can at least experience these great moments in Soldier Field—fifty thousand guys swaying and sweating, holding hands, singing to Jesus. He starts to live, really, for those moments. He's on fire for the Lord, he tells himself, but his commitment to the CRC is negligible, at best, and his scrapbooks are filled with photos of football stadiums.

Consider Lori, another member of the CRC. She marches with the pro-life activists. She's been to jail. She's stood at the medical center where abortions are done and watched young women walk in and end a baby's life. She loves her children. It makes her nauseated to watch those young kids go in there and kill their babies. It also makes her angry, and more and more committed to righteousness.

On Sunday in the CRC Lori attends, the preacher says that being a Christian means climbing into other people's tragedies, bearing their burdens, knowing their pain. He says that before we criticize those who abort their children, we have to love them. Lori has seen those women, and not all of them look lovable. Some of them have raised a middle finger to the crowd of pro-lifers. How do you love someone like that? she wonders.

On the way to the marches that Lori attends, the whole bus sings "Amazing Grace," "We Shall Overcome," and "Shine, Jesus, Shine," and she feels something she never feels at her church, something rich and deeply satisfying, a kind of community of spirit with those who have given themselves totally for the babies, the children this country massacres. When she gets back to her church on Sunday, she doesn't see that kind of determination, that willingness to fight evil. What she sees around her are comfortably complacent Christians who drive up in their expensive cars and assume they qualify for righteousness on the basis of having punched the church clock. What do they know about what it's like to suffer for the sake of Christ and the babies he called to him?

Fred and Lori stay Christian Reformed—sometimes it's hard to say why. But neither of them studies this year's crop of new seminary graduates and pastes them into a scrapbook. Instead of tuning in to "The Back to God Hour," they have their own favorites—Dobson, maybe. Fred gets the Promise Keepers' magazine; Lori reads a dozen pro-life newsletters; neither gets *The Banner.* Neither cares a whole lot about

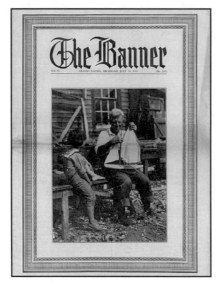

the issue of women in office, about evolution, about homosexuality or homosexualism. If they think about those things at all, they get a shaky feeling in their stomachs because they know very well that what those things mean is just more infighting. And they're tired of infighting, not only because of the havoc it brings but because the constant bickering and endless arguing don't have to be. If more people experienced what they have with Promise Keepers or the pro-life movement, they say, if more people knew what it was like to feel that God was using you, they wouldn't want to argue constantly. Are Fred and Lori wrong?

So fraught with divisions and old-time wars has this denomination been that even CRC Home Missions churches often soft-pedal the use of the word *Reformed.* Few in suburban America understand the word anyway. Take your typical seeker—what does he or she know about *Reformed?*—unless it's a school where bad kids go to get their lives hammered straight.

The people at Home Missions may well be reflecting what the denomination as a whole believes about the nomenclature traditionally used to separate Christians. How many people really care whether followers of the Lord Jesus are Lutherans or Baptists or Roman Catholics? Aren't the biggest churches today—the ones showing real growth—pretty much nondenominational? In a world that seems more and more to deny the existence of God, doesn't it make sense to transcend the old boundaries and divisions and simply praise the Lord? Who cares whether there's a triangle in a cross on the sign on the front lawn? We're trying to attract people who don't even know the meaning of the cross itself.

We live in a new age, an age of image and moment, of perception and media, an age where reading, like nineteenth-century music, is something nobody does, right? You want to attract people today, you've got to put on shows. Nobody's got the time or inclination for study, for doctrine. You've got to sell the good news. Look at Willow Creek and what they're doing for

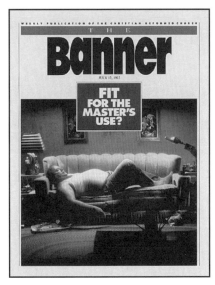

the Lord. Don't they put all of us to shame, with our constant wrangling about this or that or the next issue? Our problem is that we don't simply preach the gospel, the plain and simple truth; we don't deliver the good news in an inviting package, we don't praise the Lord enough. To a people today who don't even recognize sin when they do it, what good is the Heidelberg Catechism? Who on earth really understands sin/salvation/service, other than a few Neanderthals who keep scrapbooks?

Get with it. Lift your hands and sing, brothers and sisters! Hear the drum, feel it in your gut, and blast away in praise to the Lord until the Spirit lays you cold, and you finally know and feel the peace of the Lord.

Who are we? Today, on the front step of the twenty-first century, what does it mean to be *Reformed*? More important, does anyone really care?

That's what I wonder as I begin this story, the story of the Christian Reformed Church in North America. I know there's reason for concern, but I also am confident that any despair—mine or yours—is flat wrong. God Almighty works in our midst. There are, after all, good, sound reasons to

(Top) Allendale Christian Reformed Church, organized in 1881 with many prominent CRC leaders among its first pastors: W. Heyns, L. Berkhof, H. Keegstra.

(Right) Sunshine Ministries Center.

rejoice in what God is doing in the CRC. Take California, for instance. While, recently at least, no single area of the country has suffered as devastating a loss in denominational membership, the central work of Christ's church in the sunny west continues unabated. In a recent *Banner* news article, Ruth Donker cites a score of good examples of growth and heady reasons for excitement—new church efforts undertaken by Californians in places like Hawaii and Nevada; three new Korean congregations; new church plants in Tracy, Folsom, Carson, and even Bellflower; the reappearance of Crenshaw CRC smack dab in the middle of the "City of Angels," a fellowship that officially closed its doors several years ago and is now being restarted by Evangelist Ron Black and a small core of people under the sponsorship of Community CRC, Los Angeles; a new Hispanic congregation in Long Beach; five new families in Love Song Community CRC in Fresno, and many more new faces in other churches.

As I write, if any region of the country has reason to feel real doom-and-gloom about things CRC, California does. But the work of the gospel goes on—and it's full of promise.

But many of us—not just in California, but denomination-wide—feel uncomfortable about things. There are even godly reasons for what some might feel to be the sad state of the denomination; after all, good people on both sides of the hot-button issues of our day leave our churches for what some might feel are very good reasons.

So what's left for the rest of us? How can we learn to rejoice in our communal bless-

ings when it's so easy to feel that something important about who we are, something at the very heart of the denomination, has somehow come undone? How can we avoid wondering whether someone, someday, is going to be the one to pull the string on the last light at 2850 Kalamazoo Avenue? And, is there something unique about us, something worth keeping alive? Today, almost 150 years after a rather inauspicious emergence as a denominational fellowship, who have we become? Who are we anyway? We're not what we were—that everyone can agree on; but then who are we? And where, pray tell, are we going?

History is no crystal ball. The story of the CRC will not somehow reveal the nature of the horizon we see before us. A look at who we were will not bring into focus who we shall become. But a sense of our history can reveal something about why we react as we do to the new; it does reveal something of how we've looked at problems in the past, something about what we've come from. An investigation into our roots can be enlightening, even stupefying. An awareness of our own story can explain something about how we think and feel.

History can also empower us. Think of the Israelites. There were times in their history when they seemed unsure of themselves, hesitant, even skeptical. Often, when they felt a malaise threatening, they would rehearse their story. Let's remember Moses, they'd tell each other, and one of the storytellers would run through the narrative, from the flies to the bloody water to the miracle of the Red Sea and the omnipresence of the Lord God Almighty along the path through the wilderness. It was the story—their grand narrative—that brought them together.

We too have a grand narrative—the same narrative as the Israelites. Moses is ours, as are David and Samson and Ruth and Habakkuk. Our grand narrative includes, at the very center, Immanuel, the God who pulled on a suit of human flesh for our sin. He is our story. His is the story that shapes us and gives us life. His story is the gospel, the greatest love story ever told.

But there is another part of our story too, one that begins even before the special revelation of the Bible ends. It starts with the apostolic church, moves slowly through what historians used to call the Dark Ages, is refreshed by the Reformation, then moves into the European lowlands and finally discovers the New World. Its most obvious patriarch is Simon Peter, the upon-this-rock Peter; and it includes Saint Augustine and John Calvin. Among its particular celebrities, in addition to the ones I've already listed, are Abraham Kuyper, once Prime Minister of the Netherlands, and Johanna Veenstra, the early twentieth-century missionary to Nigeria. It has moments of sheer brilliance, a record of activism and social concern that is remarkable. The CRCNA has brought North American evangelicalism some of its finest minds and a system of private, Christian education that predates and even ignores most everyone's dissatisfaction with public schools.

All our heroes are human, none of them divine. Some of our most crucial decisions

Lydia Ladies Aid Society of the Grandville Ave. Christian Refor[m]
June 8: 1949

were hybrid offspring of contrary personalities and persnickety platitudes. Our story is not more glorious than a sunset. It is fraught with human frailty. But it is a story worth telling, I believe. What we are today is, at least in part, formed by what we have been.

Some of you may have heard an old story that emerged from the deep lakeshore forests of the original colony of Dutch Reformed folks in western Michigan. Long before roads were laid, in the days when paths through the hardwoods and pines were few and far between, it was altogether possible for people to get lost in the wide woodlands that spread along Lake Michigan. It happened, and when it did the new settlers found the experience terrifying. But sometimes, in the darkness or simply in the maze of huge trees centuries old, some wandering souls found their home by suddenly stumbling on the throb of the old psalms being sung in a church or a home on a newly cleared acre of land. The music brought them home.

There's sentimentality in that story, of course, but I hope that the joy and strength of its message transcends its own time and place. We may not be floundering in the American wilderness or even singing those ancient plodding psalms a capella as our ancestors did, but that scene from our past still offers us something good, something of substance and conviction.

It is my hope that this history, the story of the Christian Reformed Church, will help us understand the past we've come from, so that we can better know the today we see around us and the tomorrow of the new millennium. With this scrapbook of sorts, let me try to tell you our story.

1949 Grandville Ave. CRC Ladies Aid Society (below). Contemporary small group (right).

Revelation to Reformation to Revolution

Where to begin? Why not with Adam? "With Adam's fall, we sin-ned all," or so states the *New England Primer*, the first book on a student's required reading list in Puritan New England. Adam's fall would seem a logical place to start, given the caricature of Calvinism as a version of Christian doctrine seemingly obsessed with human depravity, the dark state of the human soul.

Whether or not the caricature is accurate, Adam's fall is not fiction. He and the First Wife undoubtedly altered the course of humankind by their choice of fruit in the garden, but the fact that they changed things for all time implies that there was a preexisting different way—and there was. Their fall was not the opening act.

In the most incredible show ever staged, God Almighty had created a perfect world with nothing more than a few well-chosen words. With no computer enhancement and no special effects, God made everything out of nothing, including the First Husband and his First Wife. God said the word, and it happened. The creation of the world makes Stephen Spielberg look like a kid making mud pies.

But the Creator of heaven and earth laid down the law to the first two earthlings. God said the world would be a good place for them—a beautiful garden. God said things could go well in this place; the two of them could enjoy each other and their Creator. God said they could have a harmonious relationship with this garden too. Together, Adam and Eve, God, and nature would weave an ecology perfectly balanced and transcendent—no rape and pillaging, no major quarrels, no long periods of icy silence, no typhoons or quarter-mile-wide tornados. The First Couple could be happy—truly happy, eternally happy—*if* they'd simply obey. The big *if*.

They didn't. They opted for what they couldn't have and grabbed forbidden fruit from the only tree in the garden that their Maker had placed off-limits. Was it human curiosity that made them do it? Or was it that slithering wretch, Satan? Maybe it was simply their aspiration—their desire to be more than what they'd been created to be. Maybe their choice of that single variety of fruit was nothing more than the first edition of the American dream.

Whatever their imperfect motive, they disobeyed God's command, and the world has never been the same. God had created it all good and perfect, a remarkable world of harmony and blessedness and self-sufficiency that, thanks to Adam and Eve, no

Martin Luther nails his 95 theses
to the door of Castle Church, Wittenberg, Germany.

human being ever since has been able to imagine.

Chapter one, then, was creation—everything in the world itself fashioned out of nothing, from morning glories to nightingales, from wonderful wetlands to shimmering mountain lakes, from the very atmosphere above our heads—lumbering cloud formations, a gazillion stars, and untallied galaxies whose size and distance are still unimaginable—to clay and loam and quartzite. But creation—before the fall—found its crowning glory in the most astounding work of all, humankind, a perfect marriage of style and function, each given a body equipped with its own remarkable perpetual-motion machine—a single pound of muscle that circulates blood down passageways so microscopic that believing they even exist requires a leap of faith. Hearing—an unlikely juxtaposition of bones and cartilage that enables us to tune in to a Bach sonata or the rattle of a diamondback. Muscles sufficient, when in sync, to permit some of us to run sub-four-minute miles. A mind that can process information like a megacomputer, yet is capable of imagination and real wisdom. And all of this comes packaged in a container that can be, with little more than ordinary upkeep, drop-dead gorgeous. All around, what we see and are—black holes to toenails, mud puddles and endless oceans, the lion and the lamb—all of the world singing in tuneful harmony. That was the status quo at creation. That's the beginning of our history.

Leaders of the Reformation:

Back (l to r): John Calvin, Martin Luther, Philip Melanchton, John Huss, Ulrich Zwingli.

Front (l to r): Johannes Bugenhagen, Gustaaf Adolf, Ulrich Van Hutten.

Chapter two. The fall. Weeds and old age. A sun that's too hot and nights that freeze almost every living thing. Work. Sweat. Boredom. Body odor. Pesky brothers. Family feuds. Headaches. Heart disease. AIDS. Highway accidents. Cancer and a million other paths to the big one, death—the only thing more sure than taxes, people say.

We messed up. In Adam's fall, we sinned all.

Creation. The fall. Our world and all its problems. Seven deadly sins—pride, envy, wrath, sloth, lust, greed, and far too much food and drink—all of it leading to death. Death—yours, mine, and ours.

And then chapter three: redemption! Only a God who loved us could take us back after we turned our backs. Only a God who loved us would offer the sacrifice of his own child, the Word-made-flesh, to bring us back to him, our fallenness and the world's disharmony brought somewhat in tune again by the blood of the Lamb of God, God's only Son. His death for ours. His life for our sin. His divine pain for our eternal happiness. Jesus Christ came to earth to take us—and it—back to the impeccable bliss we might have had before we messed it all up, to bring us life eternal, to end the groaning of the world all around us.

The beginning of the story of the Christian Reformed Church comes in three monumental installments—creation, fall, redemption. Nothing that happened in our lowly saga makes any sense without it. If we are to understand the history of our own continuing desire to create a better church and a better world, we need to recognize in ourselves our collective motive—

to make things right, to bring all sinners (including ourselves) back to faith, to make justice roll down. We need to remember that we've been trying for thousands of years to undo what we did ourselves when "we sinned all."

But we also need to remember the state of our souls, which isn't good. We are descendants of Adam and Eve, children of lousy decision-makers; and like them, we mess up—not only when we fully intend to, but even when we don't. Even our best deeds, the Bible says, are as filthy rags when placed beside the works of the God of heaven and earth.

Still, God loves us and empowers us. God makes us his. With God's love we—believers and non-believers alike—can do great good in the world. We can cure tuberculosis and prevent a hundred exotic varieties of influenza. We can bring the grief-stricken a tuna casserole or hot apple dumplings. We can take an hour out of our lives to listen to and pray with someone whose hands are full of balled, wet handkerchiefs. We can free the prisoner. We are redeemed, and we can do a world of good. We can tell others the blessed good news that never stops thrilling us.

Nothing in this history makes sense without these first three chapters—creation, fall, redemption: first, "Let there be light"; then, the treacherous serpent's horrendous whispers; and finally, and gloriously, the birth, death, and resurrection of our Savior, Jesus Christ. And the end: He's coming again. He may be tarrying, but he's coming again. Count on it.

That's biblical history, and while it is the genesis of all believers, and while there is no story more significant or crucial to understanding our identity as God's own family, there are many other lesser chapters. Everything else, however—all the rest of our history—is only an appendix.

But what an appendix! Two millennia have passed since Christ's ascension, two thousand years that include, among other events and epochs, the apostolic church and Emperor Constantine, who forced the world he ruled into a species of belief. The appendix includes the Crusades, the Middle Ages, and the church's own apostasy, whoring as we did after wealth and prestige. It includes Saint Augustine, from whose visions John Calvin formulated his own; it includes monumental architecture like the cathedral at Canterbury, a place to which pilgrims made annual treks that granted them a stronger sense of purpose and devotion. Geoffrey Chaucer is part of our history too, his portraits of those pilgrims a museum, in effect, of human character both in his time and ours.

Broadly stated, the grand narrative of the Christian Reformed Church includes much of what is suggested by the phrase "Western culture," for it is within that broad designation of the sweep of human history where we most evidently locate our own past.

To do that history justice would require a multivolume study of a past that extends from Athens to Rome to Geneva to Toronto, an entire course in Western civilization—its history and literature, its art and agriculture. That history would include, among other things, a detailed look at the long succession of popes and prelates, a study of the role of the church in the life of thirteenth-century peasants, and a chronicle of the seemingly unending power struggle between church and state. Economics. Art. Politics. Cooking. Kid's games. Theater and sport.

But if discretion is to be the better part of valor here, if what you're about to read won't demand years of your lives, then we have to summarize, not so much to cut to the chase as to pick and choose among those events and eras most pointedly relevant to the story of the Christian Reformed Church in North America.

THE REFORMATION

Many Protestant historians, I think, would likely begin the appendix—everything after creation, fall, and redemption—with the Reformation. That's true not only because some of the most memorable names appear in its annals—Calvin, Luther, Knox—but also because the departure the Reformers undertook from the Roman Catholic Church when they "protested" (hence, Protestants) against its errors and extravagances created one of the most memorable splits in the history of Christianity.

The Reformers, after all, weren't simply starting something new. Their vehement anger at the state of things was, in fact, a reaction to the abuses of the medieval church. What the Reformers wanted was something closer to what they saw to be the church's own original apostolic design. They wanted to return to something good and pure (hence, Puritans).

So let's begin just before the Reformation with a church council of the Roman Catholic Church, our own mother church. In 1415, almost six hundred years ago, the Council of Constance was convened to deal with matters of importance to the church, one of which was heresy. *Heresy* is a tough word; its implications are deeply divisive. It assumes that we can know the Truth—capital T—an assumption our age shies away from with some horror. Heretics, you see, aren't invited to the party. If they show up, they're directed to the door with direct dispatch. In an age when inclusion and diversity are often considered the virtual pillars of righteousness, *heresy* is a dirty word. It suggests discrimination and divisiveness. In North America today, where some consider censorship the most hideous of sins, the accusation of *heresy* is a torch we've too often used to incinerate the ideas of people, no matter how well-meaning, who demur from what is considered good and orthodox.

But one of the agenda items for the Council of Constance was heresy, and it's fair to say that the church fathers of that time (and rest assured they were fathers, not mothers) didn't have the hesitancy we might feel today in calling certain individuals *heretics.* One of those so judged was John Wycliffe (c. 1330-1384), a man whose major sins included translating the Bible into English, training laypeople for evangelism, and, the most capital of offenses, opposing papal authority. If you've noticed the name "Wycliffe" before, it may be because today a whole organization of missionary linguists have taken his name to describe exactly what they do when they enter a region of the world where no one has yet brought the good news in the language of the people. When they get there, they "pull a Wycliffe"and begin to translate Scripture into a language it's not appeared in before.

John Huss is burned at the stake.

But when the name Wycliffe came before that fifteenth-century council, it had none of those positive associations. To that august gathering of church leaders, *Wycliffe* was synonymous with *heretic,* and the church of that day didn't deal with those it judged to be heretics by simply bidding them to leave the premises. The Roman Catholic Church sentenced heretics to death (as the Protestant seceders themselves would do in the not-too-distant future). Heresy was judged a capital offense, a sin against the Almighty—what could be worse? Death to the heretics.

Unfortunately for the Council of Constance, Wycliffe had already died (of natural causes) thirty years earlier. So to dramatize their unholy horror at Wycliffe's heresy, the council ordered his body dug up and burned—a task which, quite valiantly, was accomplished.

But one of Wycliffe's disciples, a man named John Huss (1372 or 1373-1415), was still very much alive. His heresy included spreading Wycliffe's teachings throughout what is now the Czech Republic and Slovakia. The case against Huss, who was still around and even present at the Council, offered even higher drama than the case against John Wycliffe. Since Huss was present, the Council accused him publicly of his heretical sin, and when he refused to recant his beliefs, they watched him burn at the stake.

These two early reformers—and their stories—are part of a history of repression and persecution that characterizes much of the early history of Protestantism and the Christian Reformed Church. We've come a long way. Today, some members of the Christian Reformed Church are among the wealthiest in the United States. Today, members of the Christian Reformed Church occupy significant political offices. Today, interest groups composed of members of the Christian Reformed Church attempt to bring a witness—often effectively—to government legislation. From the vantage point of Huss and Wycliffe, we've arrived. In recent history, at least, no member of the CRCNA has been burned at the stake.

It may be difficult for us to conceive of a church brought together by hardship, persecution, and martyrdom; but that is the church we've come from time and time again—first with the apostles, then with the Reformers, and even (although less horrendously) into the nineteenth-century European lowlands. *Fox's Book of Martyrs,*

for a long time thought to be required reading for Protestants, lays out a detailed account of the brutality and barbarism of those who, from positions of power and authority throughout the centuries, have sought to rid themselves of the radical followers of Jesus. Although it may seem like another world altogether, the persecution, ignominious death, and martyrdom that characterized the early church make up significant initial chapters of our history.

MARTIN LUTHER

Just about seventy years after Wycliffe's body was exhumed and burned, and after Huss, convicted by views we would likely share, became a fiery spectacle at the Coun-

Martin Luther (1483-1546).

cil of Constance, a German mine owner named his son Martin—Martin Luther. Because Hans Luther, like many fathers of his day, was, by his son's own account, rather handy with a whip, historians and psychologists have had a field day psychoanalyzing his famous son, blaming Martin's reforming instincts—his passionate oratory and deeply convicted soul—on everything from lousy toilet training to his troubled relationship with a stern father. But there's more to Martin's story and crusade than an authoritarian father. There is, after all, the sad state of the church as Martin Luther came to know it—a church that, sometimes with the best of intentions, dealt with heresy by flames.

Luther was brilliant and colorful, a charismatic leader, an odd and always energetic combination of scandalous earthiness and radiant spiritual visions. If Luther's father had had his wish, his son would have gone to law school, but young Martin disappointed him by opting instead to enter a monastery. Within ten years he had a doctorate in theology and was teaching.

The story of Martin Luther's life-changing insight into the apostle Paul's "The just shall live by faith" is already well known. But the Roman Catholic Church of his day was not the only target for his anger: his invectives against Jews have been studied as a precursor of the anti-Semitism in Hitler's Germany. So Luther was not perfect, but it is quite possible that without him there would have been no Reformation. We have much to thank him for, and every time we sing "A Mighty Fortress," his skills and devotion are apparent, as are

---

Katie Luther

In 1525 Luther married the ex-nun Katherine von Bora. Katie, as he called her, had responded to Luther's teaching and escaped, with Luther's help, by hiding with eight others in the smelly wagon that delivered fish to the convent. Luther tried unsuccessfully to find her a husband and then, on her suggestion, married her himself. By this public act he confirmed the right of clergy to marry. Later he said he married Katie to "please his father, rile the Pope, and make angels laugh and devils weep."

It was a good marriage. It changed Luther's initial view of marriage as "chains" to "the greatest sphere for good works, because it rests on love." Katie presented Luther with six children and sustained him in his frequent times of stress so that he said, "I would not change Katie for France or for Venice" or for the "riches of Croesus."

—*To All Generations: A Study of Church History* by Frank Roberts (Grand Rapids, MI: CRC Publications, 1981) and *Women of the Reformation in Germany and Italy* by Roland Bainton (Boston: Beacon Press, 1971).

---

his ideas about the church. Some historians rank him with Shakespeare as a writer.

Luther's utter disgust at the condition of the church finally brought him to the door of the Castle Church in Wittenberg, where, on October 31, 1517, he hammered his way into history with his own Ninety-Five Theses. The theses, which were almost immediately translated into several other languages, carried sizzling attacks on the papal church and lit fires of Reformation across Europe. If, as Emerson says, "an institution is but the lengthened shadow of one man," then it is the shadow of Martin Luther, perhaps more than any other human being, that looms over the myriad institutions in Europe and America that are the legacy of a movement known as the Reformation. Martin Luther too is a major character in our story.

In 1530, Luther offered his new beliefs to another church meeting, the Diet of Augsburg, in a fashion that wasn't contentious or mean-spirited but did seriously question the positions and authority of the church. The result was a split in Christian Europe, a split that gave rise to the churches commonly called Protestant or evangelical. Three main traditions emerged from the Lutheran platform: in Germany and Scandinavia, the Lutheran tradition; in Switzerland, France, the Netherlands, and Scotland, the Calvinist or Zwinglian traditions; and in England, the Church of England.

ULRICH ZWINGLI

In Zürich, Switzerland, during Luther's time, a young priest named Ulrich Zwingli had begun his own reform movement. Zwingli, like Luther, was a keen student. He once claimed, or so it is said, that he felt as if he were being pulled by the very hair of his head when he heard passages from the Word of God that had been neglected for over a thousand years.

While he had occasionally taken on the church in minor skirmishes early in his life, in 1523 Zwingli came out firing with his "Sixty-Seven Articles." Zwingli maintained—very dangerously, of course—that it was the Bible, not the pope's declarations, which offered real authority for Christians. Jesus Christ, he maintained, was the only head of the church. Vigorously he insisted that no priest could atone for anyone's sins by the celebration of the mass and that Christ's crucifixion was, and

Ulrich Zwingli
(1484-1531).

is, the only sacrifice for our sin. Using his Sixty-Seven Articles as his platform, Zwingli began a protest against the church almost as potent as that brewed in Germany by Martin Luther.

As united as these two men were against their common antagonist, the Roman Catholic Church, they weren't capable of much teamwork. Zwingli had a different view of Scripture's authority than did Luther, who placed primary emphasis on his judgment that the Roman Church had strategically neglected justification by faith, the basic teaching of gospel.

Zwingli, who became a powerful preacher with a loyal following, went farther than Luther, claiming that the Bible he'd recently discovered offered not only the truth about salvation, but also the basis of church organization. (Luther considered matters such as liturgy much less important than the doctrine of justification; quite simply, he allowed lots of individual differences in lesser areas of the faith.) Zwingli rejected whatever he believed the chapters of the Bible itself did not condone. He felt strongly, for instance, that fast days be discontinued, that images be destroyed, and that music in the church be silenced. Even though he was a musician himself, Zwingli dismantled organs, not because he disliked them but because he felt that God should be worshiped in spirit and without sensory aids. That's what the Scriptures say, he would have argued.

Sadly, the two men seemed unable to work out their differences. In a famous 1529 meeting at Marburg, Luther and Zwingli sat down to try to come to some consensus. What began as a discussion of theology and the place of Scripture ended in a battle that created personal animosity between the two Reformation giants and led them to dislike each other immensely. Aides from both camps tried to work through Zwingli and Luther's disagreements and patch together a purely political alliance to counter the power of Rome, but even those attempts failed. That two minds so united by a critical view of the practices of the Roman Church could not themselves see eye to eye is not only sad, but tragic.

When a civil war erupted in Switzerland between Protestants and Catholics in 1531, Zwingli, serving as chaplain for his evangelical troops, was killed. Since Luther generally did not believe in using force to defend the gospel, he felt Zwingli's participation in a civil war was reprehensible. When Zwingli's death was reported to Luther, the German theologian, who was capable of great passion and deep emotion, is reported to have told acquaintances quite coldly, "Those who live by the sword, die by the sword."

THE ANABAPTISTS

Along with Lutheranism and Zwinglianism, another "reform" movement emerged early in the sixteenth century from Zwingli's own followers. The movement, Anabaptism, had a number of leaders and took a variety of different forms: In 1525, a group led by Conrad Grebel, the son of a prominent family in Zürich, began worshiping in private homes and rebaptizing those judged to be "true believers." In Moravia, Jacob Hutter became the leader of a group whose views on infant baptism differed radically from those of other Protestants. In the Netherlands, the leader of the move-

---

Fanatical Anabaptists

It's likely that one of the reasons Anabaptists were persecuted by other Christians had to do with the actions of a few fanatic extremists in the movement. The more balanced Anabaptists found it difficult to live down the reputation created by these visible and sometimes violent radicals. The famous Münster experiment is an example of the kind of negative press some Anabaptists gave to the whole group:

Believing the world was about to end, Jan of Leyden led an uprising that took over the city of Münster in 1534. Proclaiming the New Jerusalem, an Anabaptist kingdom, he invited all true believers to come; and "they came, Frisians and other scoundrels," by the thousands. In preparation for Christ's glorious return to this city, Jan established a "holy government"—but this kingdom of heaven on earth soon turned into a living hell. Jan declared that all private property must be surrendered. Those who refused were executed or, if they were lucky, driven out of the city. Polygamy was made mandatory, with Jan setting a marvelous example by taking sixteen wives. Finally, after the behavior of this group had become even more bizarre, a coalition of Protestant and Catholic armies attacked and reconquered Münster.

—*To All Generations: A Study of Church History*
by Frank Roberts (Grand Rapids, MI: CRC Publications, 1981).

---

ment was a man named Menno Simons—from whose name comes the term "Mennonites." In Germany, the reform leader was Melchior Hoffmann.

Wherever they went, the Anabaptists opposed infant baptism, argued against state involvement with the church, and attempted to maintain what they called "pure" churches, congregations from which all sin and practicing sinners were to be "banned." Their view of many

Protestant churches was simply that all that glitters is not gold. They were convinced that even the new protesting churches were filled with people who were, at best, social believers, and, at worst, non-Christians—a criticism that neither Zwingli nor Luther denied, by the way. But the Anabaptists' ardent opposition to infant baptism made them enemies among both the Protestants and the Roman Catholics, and their politics (stubbornly anti-government) pushed them into opposition with just about every society they lived in. What's more, some of them practiced polygamy (based as it was upon the practice of the Old Testament patriarchs), which was considered barbaric and distasteful by Protestant and Catholic alike. What all of this added up to is a long and sad history of Anabaptist persecution by all elements of the church—Lutheran and Zwinglian Protestants, as well as Roman Catholics.

JOHN CALVIN

The man whose name has not appeared yet—except perhaps as an adjective—is probably most central to the history of the Christian Reformed Church in North America. Though French by birth and nationality, he lived most of his life as a Swiss pastor. His theology, expounded in the *Institutes of the Christian Religion,* spread from Geneva to the Netherlands, where thousands of lowlanders became disciples of his views—lowlanders whose descendants eventually would immigrate to America in the mid-nineteenth century. That man, of course, is John Calvin.

Calvin's first book, written while he was finishing his studies at the University of

Paris, was published the same year that Zwingli became a casualty of the Swiss civil war (1531). Five years later, Calvin completed his first edition of the *Institutes,* a book once described to me as so full of

John Calvin (1509-1564).

wisdom that it serves as a compendium of everything worth knowing in the mid-sixteenth century. With the *Institutes of the Christian Religion,* John Calvin altered the shape of Christian and world history.

Born in Noyon, France, in 1509, Calvin was raised in a comfortably wealthy Catholic family. He was a gifted student who studied languages, arts, theology, literature, and philosophy very successfully. But he was never capable of the passion he coveted in others. To please his father, Calvin studied the law. And even after reading Luther's works, he remained loyal to the papacy.

But in Paris in the early 1530s things changed. This is how he himself described the conversion in his life:

> And at first, whilst I remained thus so obstinately addicted to the superstitions of the papacy that it would have been hard indeed to have pulled me out of so deep a quagmire by sudden conversion, [God] subdued and made teachable a heart which, for my age, was far too hardened in such matters. Having thus received some foretaste and knowledge of true piety, I was straightway inflamed with such great desire to profit by it that although I did not attempt to give up other studies, I worked only slackly at them. And I was wonderstruck when, before the year was out, all those who had some desire for the true doctrine ranged themselves around me to learn, although I was hardly more than a beginner myself.

—Preface to *Commentary on Psalm.*

Soon enough this "sudden conversion" brought Calvin into the very heart of the conflict between the Reformers and the papacy. As a result, things changed drastically for him in 1534, when Francis I, the

French king, decided to eradicate Protestantism from his country. Among those he had in mind most specifically was the young intellectual upstart John Calvin, whose views he found dangerous to the Roman Catholic Church. Calvin spent two brief stints in prison but, unlike his own brother, avoided execution.

Eventually, he planned a move to Strassburg for more study and writing.

Farel threatens Calvin with God's judgment if Calvin does not remain and carry on the reforming of Geneva.

And therein lies one of the little twists that charm the best-laid plans of mice and men into the will of the Lord God Almighty. In order to get to Strassburg, Calvin, then only twenty-seven years old, needed to pass through the city of Geneva, where he planned to spend the night. There he was nearly kidnapped by William Farel, a local preacher who had read Calvin's writing and appreciated his views. Farel begged the young Calvin to stay in Switzerland to help him establish a genuinely Reformed city and church. Calvin told Farel that he wasn't interested in being a social activist; besides, he said, such a change in his plans was out of the question. Then Farel begged God to curse Calvin's retirement and dis-

rupt whatever peace Calvin hoped he'd have for study and contemplation.

John Calvin changed his mind, and the rest, as they say, is history.

CALVINISTS

A quick joke. Some Grand Rapids native is visited by a friend from, say, New Jersey. The GR native, ever thrilled with what the CRC has done in that fair city, gives his friend a tour that includes all of the highlights. "This," he says, pulling along the curb at an elementary school, "is Calvin Christian School." Another few blocks, and he pulls over again. "And this," he points out, "is Calvin Junior High." A few right turns and once again he slows down. "This is Calvin Christian High School." His friend is speechless. Then, up Burton Street a ways, he points to a huge campus. "This is Calvin College—and right in there is our own Calvin Seminary."

The friend seems bewildered. "So what is it with all this Calvin stuff?" he says.

The GR native stiffens angrily. "Don't you read your Bible?" he says.

Just exactly how Calvinist we are—or were, for that matter—is a question that could be disputed for decades. But what is clear is that a goodly number of folks in our collective past felt it was John Calvin who left the most indelible mark on our theology and culture. My middle name is Calvin, like my father's first name. For many years we called our Girl Scout-type organization Calvinettes; our boys' group, Calvinist Cadets. An annual rally of the denomination's young people was once called the Young Calvinist Convention.

We certainly have adopted the Frenchman's name, although it seems less appeal-

A Grant from Heaven

Today, four hundred years after Calvin's *Institutes* were first published, they still have a freshness of insight and a depth of theological truth that challenges those who discover them—either again or for the first time. In the late nineties World Literature Ministries of the CRC released a Russian version of the *Institutes*. Jeffrey Busscher, a mission worker in Russia, says this about the impact of these new volumes on the Russian people:

> Through the Institutes *people are being challenged in their Christian walk to dig into the Bible, to read and pray and seek God and a clearer understanding of him—leading to a clearer understanding of what their role is in exercising their gifts in the body of Christ as well as in reforming society at large. We have little comprehension in Russia of how God would use Christians to impact their society and address justice issues. Thanks to the appearance of the* Institutes *and the subsequent groundswell, these issues are being addressed and will be by the church.*

WLM has also received enthusiastic endorsement of the *Institutes* from the Russian people. Pavel Simakov writes:

> [The Institutes] *is probably the best book I have ever read. And I know that I am not alone in my opinion. Many people have asked to read my copy of the book. There are only 20,000 copies available in all of Russia—a drop in the sea. So sadly, it's possible that this brilliant book will stay unknown for many people. Even libraries cannot promise to get a copy for those who ask for one. The Russian people are a reading people; even on a business trip they will pick up a book. For our people—especially those like me who study religion—this book is simply a grant from heaven.*

—Ed.

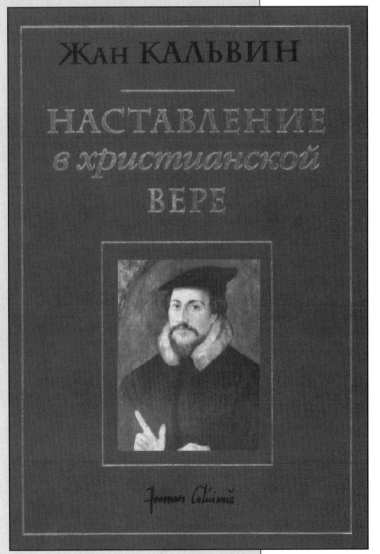

ing to our tastes today than it once did. We noted earlier how many churches are abandoning use of the word *Reformed;* our use of the name John Calvin is suffering a similar fate. The reason is simple: fewer and fewer people recognize who the man was or what he stood for. He is part of a North American denomination's ancient European past.

A quick refresher. Why did some CRC ancestors so committedly root their sense of identity in the name of John Calvin? What was so magical about his style? Was he charismatic? A TV preacher? Who was this guy?

Explaining Calvin, telling his story, reviewing his *Institutes,* then writing the history of his followers (who include, of course, the American Puritans of Plymouth and Massachusetts Bay) would take years. Many people have dedicated their life to that task, and not because Calvin was so charismatic, so popular, or so dear. Let's put it this way—it's almost impossible to overestimate the power of John Calvin, not only in Europe but even more so, perhaps, in North America, certainly in the U.S. In economics, in art, in politics— one cannot do an analysis of American culture without noting the effect of the Puritans, who were Calvinists.

It was the Puritans who created one of the first viable colonies of Europeans in North America. Where others failed, they succeeded; and many historians will begin an explanation of their success in New England by citing a comprehensive and cohesive theological vision. Among other truths, that vision made claims that these individuals were the elect, the people of God, and hence pilgrims on a journey to

righteousness. The nature of that faith and its peculiar forms gave the New England pilgrims and Puritans an intense and immense commitment that other settlements seemed to lack. No other early colonial event featured a group of people united by a vision of this life and the next, a vision that had at its core the belief that government and this life itself was redeemable—was meant, in its essence, to bring praise to the Creator and Sustainer of the universe, God Almighty.

Of the three major Reformation groups—the followers of Zwingli, the followers of Luther, and those known as Anabaptists—the Calvinists descend (if they can be said to descend at all) from Zwingli, whose view of Scripture, you might remember, was more exact and encompassing than that of Luther. Zwingli argued that the Bible was an important guide for more than simply understanding the nature of salvation, that it could help us evaluate and structure church life in a variety of ways.

So did John Calvin. His *Institutes of the Christian Religion* went beyond Luther in that it began not with justification by faith, that most famous of all Reformation doctrines, but instead with the knowledge of God. Calvin wanted very badly to create a comprehensive system of doctrine and knowledge that would not, because he could not, separate religion or faith from life itself. The Heidelberg Catechism's first question and answer is deeply important here. "My only comfort in life and death is that I belong to my faithful Savior Jesus Christ." That comfort in being elect or chosen by God's immutable decrees of salvation was at the core of a Calvinist worldview. Calvin and his followers believed that the God who loved them was seated in majesty above all our human silliness. He was God, and he loved them. That's where life with God began.

Calvin did not side with those mystics of his day who would have insisted that humans need to seek and find a kind of union with God. Rather he believed that it was God himself who reestablished the bond with fallen humanity. To Calvin, and according to the Westminster Catechism, the goal of human beings—the reason for our existence—is to glorify God and enjoy him forever. Calvin felt that service to God was far more our concern than personal salvation, since God had already determined who would be saved.

Where today there is some reluctance among us to associate too closely with the broader evangelical efforts to "save souls," whether that be in the form of Billy Graham-type crusades or Promise Keepers rallies, that reluctance in part stems from a historical base in Calvin's own beliefs about God Almighty. Calvin believed deeply that such commendable work is secondary because its ends are already God-determined. Instead of emphasizing the need for us to accept salvation itself, Calvin emphasized service—that is, living out of the salvation God has given us and being a Christian in every walk of life.

Calvin's view of our salvation is built on his view that God chooses us for salvation, on our election (by God, not us) to life eternal. Calvin understood that that doctrine could be frightful, and that it could be misused—and it can. Where people blindly take their election for granted, the doctrine is abused. Where it is used, simply, to condemn others, it is abused. That the doctrine has been misapplied and only half understood during the history of Calvinism and the CRC goes without saying.

But really, how do we know about ourselves? Really, how does anyone know for sure that they are saved?

Calvin insisted on three criteria as a means by which the elect can assure themselves that they are chosen: a profession of the true faith, the maintenance of an upright life, and attendance upon the sacrament of the Lord's Supper. When these three outward characteristic behaviors were in place, said Calvin, one could assume a believer to be one of the elect.

Sociologically such obvious outward markings created a kind of community, which is something Luther's followers could not so easily create. Luther maintained that the elect could *not* be so easily or definitely identified, that they were known only to God. Calvin, on this score, was closer to Zwingli, who had also maintained that a proper profession of faith was essential to distinguishing God's chosen. Like the Anabaptists, Calvin felt a purity of life was also immediate and important. But to the tests Zwingli and the Anabaptists brought to assessing the Christian life, Calvin added something new—a deep regard for the sacrament of the Lord's Supper.

That view was built on a belief about Holy Communion that fell somewhere between Luther's and Zwingli's. Calvin believed that Christ was really present in the sacrament, not in the bread and the wine, but through the Spirit's presence in the hearts of believers. Such theological distinctions may seem tedious to us today, but that view enabled Calvin to stay somewhat united with historic Christianity in its reverent attitude toward Holy Communion, while still breaking from Roman Catholic sacramentalism.

Via a profession of faith, a godly life, and attention to the Lord's Supper—because these three criteria were all publicly visible—Calvin visualized a community of the elect that was capable of becoming a holy commonwealth, a Christian society and culture, a culture for which God had great plans. Enter the word *kingdom.* The society of the elect had a calling, the establishment of the kingdom of God, said Calvin.

Calvin didn't assume that this new kingdom was something accomplishable in his lifetime, nor did he assume that humans themselves would soon recreate paradise;

he wasn't as comfortable with apocalyptic thinking as was Luther, or, for that matter, the Anabaptists. The last judgment, from Calvin's perspective, wasn't necessarily going to come up on next year's calendar.

This lack of a sense of the immediacy of the end of the world is important in Calvin's theology and can be said to provide the basis for a social gospel meant to redeem the fabric of society itself. Calvin was not a stargazer. Unlike many others, he didn't listen daily for the last trumpet. His concern was more fully aimed at the world that God had created, the world he loved so much that he sent his only Son. That's why Calvinists spent considerably more time thinking about a Christian society than did the Lutherans or the Anabaptists.

The Reformation Wall, Geneva, Switzerland.

It was that arrangement of ideas that the English Calvinists carried with them to New England. What they were interested in was the idea of a Holy Commonwealth, a Christian society that all the world would see as a "city on a hill," as Governor John Winthrop claimed, using scriptural language. Some historians claim the English Puritans fully expected their New World adventure to be little more than an errand, a laboratory experiment meant to fashion and build a uniquely Christian society, which would then become the blueprint for remaking Christian Europe.

It's important to note too that Calvinism—more than Lutheranism, for example—has been both credited for and discredited by its association with economic capitalism. Calvinism, with its emphasis on a godly life in the muddle of this world, undoubtedly blessed its adherents with an earnestness in their callings in life—not simply an earnestness in their personal walk with God. Business enterprise was certainly not to be shunned, but visualized as a way in which believers could find their mission, their calling, in life. Calvinism's stress on living righteous lives also made the crass accumulation of profits unseemly, but that doesn't mean that all of those who consider themselves Calvinists find making money hand over fist reprehensible—or sinful, for that matter. After all, when Cotton Mather wrote the history of the New England colonies several generations after their inception, he maintained that "piety produced prosperity, and the child devoured the mother." One of the sad lessons of life—no matter whether one's profession is shaped by the Lutheran, Roman Catholic, Anabaptist, or Calvinist

history—is that there are those who say they believe and don't—or don't practice it.

Why all of this Calvinist history? Why go on and on about something nearly five hundred years old when it seemingly has so little to do with the age of megachurches and Microsoft?

Because sometimes, even often, our differences are rooted in historical circumstances. History never exactly repeats itself, but it does move in strangely familiar fashions—what comes up, must go down, as we say. Fashion changes—wide ties shrink to pencil thin, then fatten once again. The pendulum swings. Wars break out, peace comes at last—and war breaks out once more. There are echoes of our past in the communications of our present.

For instance, the word *kingdom* likely brings to mind different ideas in CRC heads than it does to Southern Baptists. Some CRC members feel discomforting prickles when teary-eyed individuals stand up in front of others and talk about their close relationship with Jesus Christ. Is that simply because they're cold fish? Their being emotionally hesitant may be part of the reason for their reaction, but the history of the CRC, rooted as it is in Calvinism, undoubtedly affects us, just as our ethnic, geographical, and familial heritages shape the way we confront behavior around us. Calvin didn't stress personal salvation or our "coming to Jesus." He likely would have been uncomfortable with that kind of language.

It is important to note, once again, that where contemporary evangelical Christians praise the CRC and its tradition, they do so largely because the CRC has contributed to the evangelical cause in ways that can be said to find their source in Calvinistic thinking. For instance, in a recent article in *Christianity Today,* Philip Yancey claims to admire the CRC because of the way it "advocates 'bringing every thought captive' under the mind of Christ." Our "tiny" denomination, he says, "has had an enormous influence on science, philosophy, and the arts." There are other contributors to that "enormous influence," but certainly John Calvin's integrated, philosophical, and this-worldly approach to faith and life is the historical base for what Yancey notices and commends.

CALVIN IN GENEVA

John Calvin was a quiet, sensitive man who said little about his inner life. While Calvin's beliefs gained significant adherents throughout Europe, his own life was hardly settled. When William Farel persuaded him to stay in Geneva, Farel's intent was to create a truly Christian city. In 1537 all Genevans were asked to swear a loyalty oath to a Protestant statement of belief. Such unanimity is always difficult, of course, and many Genevans resented Calvin and Farel and their views.

The city council itself opposed the two preachers and expelled them a year later. Calvin wound up in Strassburg, where he'd intended to go two years earlier. He became a pastor to a congregation of French Reformed refugees. While in Strassburg, he came under the influence of Martin Bucer, a remarkably gifted theologian and statesman who honed Calvin's still-rough edges as a pastor and political organizer. Calvin also met and married Idelette de Bure, the frail widow of an Anabaptist. Idelette's powerful piety and Calvin's equally intense devotion to her taught the Reformer a warmth no university lesson had ever conveyed to him.

Having watched the city turn to chaos in the absence of Farel and Calvin, the Geneva council invited both preachers back in 1541. Although Farel went back immediately, Calvin claimed he'd "prefer a hundred other deaths to that cross." Once again, however, Farel talked him out of Strassburg and into Geneva.

Although the town council had accepted Calvin's revisions of the city laws—a job he undertook in an effort, once again, to create a uniquely Christian community—peace was hardly at hand. What Calvin attempted to do—not unlike what took place in the American Puritan theocracy—was bring every citizen under the moral teachings of the church. Thus, church law and civil law became one and the same.

From the vantage point of the twenty-first century, it's not difficult to predict the problems that can occur when the church creates

> ## *Calvin's Geneva*
>
>
>
> Many historians have asserted that the people of Geneva were subjected to a "moral reign of terror." Undoubtedly by our standards Christian discipline at times degenerated into pettiness, foolishness, and even cruelty....
>
> The consistory met weekly to deal with domestic quarrels, fornication, rebellion against parents, drunkenness, superstition, ignorance of doctrine, and like offenses. To give examples, a woman of seventy-two was disciplined for becoming engaged to a man of twenty-five; a barber was censured for tonsuring a priest; a man was reprimanded for making a noise during a sermon; another man was forced to make public confession for naming his dog "Calvin."
>
> —*To All Generations: A Study of Church History*
> by Frank Roberts (Grand Rapids, MI: CRC Publications, 1981).

Calvin's deathbed.

civil law. We have, after all, similar situations throughout the Middle East today.

But when members of the CRC today speak about a "world-and-life-view," such talk has roots in the theology and world-view of John Calvin, a man who spent much of his life attempting to build a more visible "city of God" in Europe. Certainly the phrase is not singularly Calvin's; but its intent—to convey a strong and vibrant commitment to *this* life, not simply the life to come—is a legacy of Calvin's unique branch of Reformation ideology. We have been, since the beginning of the CRC on this continent, part of the theological heritage of John Calvin. Whether we remain such is yet to be determined.

In his final two decades at Geneva, Calvin put a stamp on Reformed thought that has not been erased since. He preached a gospel of grace in which the sovereign God of all history—with not the slightest tinge of human aid—rescues a world that has plummeted toward hell since the fall of humanity. That was the gospel he brought to his congregations, a gospel of value not only to those who inhabited the pews, but to human culture itself. To Calvin, one's profession of faith deeply affected how one looked at politics, at art, at life itself. From his insistence on just wages for the working class in Geneva, to his installation of a sewer system that improved living conditions, to his steep anger at a rich man who laid oppressive interest rates on the backs of the poor—John Calvin issued the call that has echoed in Reformed churches for centuries: "Honor the Lord in every area of life."

CHAPTER 3

The Bloody Reformation: The Netherlands

I t may come as a surprise to some, but the CRC was deeply multicultural long before it was officially organized in North America. After all, no single individual is so crucial to its history as John Calvin, a French theologian who preached at a Swiss church but deeply affected generations of Dutch Christians, who then brought variations on his theology to the United States and Canada.

How did Calvin come to have such a profound influence in the Netherlands? Some say it's simply a matter of climate. Calvin's theology prospers in the cold, blustery climates of northern Europe and America, where weather seems, as often as not, an enemy. The austere doctrinal system some define as Calvinism simply will never do as well in Tahiti or South Florida. There's something about cold and wind and the untethered forces of nature, some say, that makes living quite demanding. Calvinism outfits folks with a sense of calling that's equal to the demands of the rugged task of life itself in places like Scotland and northern Europe.

That's a cute argument, but there's much more to it, of course. What we know is that from the late sixteenth century to the 1940s, the Netherlands was so influenced by the moral character of John Calvin's theology that the mind of the entire nation seemed to function in a way that could be described as Calvinistic. Because the history of the CRC is so predominantly Dutch, we need to understand the history of the Netherlands to get a sense of Calvin's influence.

In 1522, Luther's German New Testament was translated into Dutch, introducing the Scriptures to the people. At that time, the Netherlands was a very loosely associated group of provinces that most frequently operated independently from each other. Instead of acting as a unified country, these provinces were the "nether" (or low) lands—emphasis on the plural.

Luther's New Testament, influential as it was, never really created a significant following for the German Reformer among Dutch provinces. Zwingli's influence was also minimal, perhaps because of his participation in the bloody civil war in Switzerland.

Calvin's reputation and strength began by way of the French-speaking ("Walloon") churches in the southern provinces today considered Belgium. In 1536, Calvin published his Geneva Catechism; within months it was being used in those Walloon congregations of French-speaking and Reformed believers. Over the following half century, Calvinism seeped northward,

Typical dyke road
seen in Dutch
polders.

province by province, carried by refugees fleeing bloody persecution throughout Europe.

When Charles V became king of Spain, he was also Duke of Burgundy, so he assumed control of territory that later became part of the Netherlands. What he didn't inherit, he soon conquered, moving patiently from Friesland (1523), all the way to Gelders (1543). But the Spanish empire was large, and Charles was busy, so his half-sister Mary, widowed queen of Hungary, was given charge over the entire region. Beginning with her announcement in 1525 that Luther's name was not to be mentioned aloud in these provinces, she decreed that loyalty to the pope would be universal and warned all Protestants that they would regret their heretical brand of the Christian faith. For twenty-five years the persecution intensified, reaching the boiling point in 1551, when nearly all the worshipers at a Protestant service in Ghent were ripped from their prayers and exe-

Protestant iconoclasts destroying statuary in Roman cathedrals, August 22, 1566.

cuted. Before the horror at Ghent, provincial nobles had been consenting if not cooperative parties in the persecution; but after that massacre, no one, from the most powerful ruler to the lowliest citizen, could look past the blood in the streets. An appeal was sent to Charles, asking that he rein in his sister—which he did. The argument, incredibly, was essentially economic—shopkeepers found themselves without needed customers.

In 1555, Charles' son Philip II took power when his father abdicated; but as his father before him had done, Philip gave control of Dutch territory to a sister, Margaret of Parma. Under Margaret's hand the cruelties mounted once more. Protestant persecution rose until several provincial nobles once again appealed for moderation, fearing that half their population would be exterminated. In response, Margaret graciously decreed that Protestant clergymen and political leaders would continue to have their goods confiscated, but instead of being burned, these heretics would simply be hanged.

Margaret's unique brand of mercy was not yet strained, however. She further agreed that if such Protestants repented of their apostate ways, she would end the confiscation of their goods and, quite graciously, substitute beheading for hanging.

One of Margaret's victims, Guido de Brès, demands a special note. De Brès, a Walloon, fell to Protestant persecution during Margaret's rule. De Brès was author of the Belgic Confession, one of the central confessional documents of the CRC throughout its history.

As bloody and awful as persecution may be, history shows that when it occurs, it often creates effects that are opposite from those it is designed to carry out. And so it was in the Netherlands. During this era of horrendous suffering in the still-forming Dutch territories, the peculiar gospel voice of the Reformation found sympathetic ears during the many funerals the inquisition caused. A group of nobles—one of them Lutheran, one Roman Catholic, and another a Calvinist— began once more to openly oppose the persecution. They called themselves "the Beggars," a name that became affixed to their revolutionary movement. The Beggars' activities created a symbol—a beggar's sack—that began to appear everywhere among the recalcitrant as evidence of both widespread dissent and the futility of the monarchy's goals.

Philip II (1527-1598), Spanish monarch who attempted to quell the spread of Protestantism in Europe, and the Netherlands especially. His policy led to the Eighty Years' War, 1568-1650.

The Beggars mounted a fierce opposition to Margaret, but when the most radical of them ransacked churches and burned a cathedral to the ground, she responded by inaugurating the bloodiest hour of the persecution. At the urging of the pope, Philip sent Ferdinand Alvarez de Toledo, the "Duke of Alva," into the lowlands, along with sixteen thousand veteran soldiers. What Alva's army wrought, his "Council of Turmoils," was so ingeniously cruel that even Margaret was moved to resign.

By 1570, the blood of Dutch Protestants pooled in every footprint left by Alva and his vicious army. In that year, as if God were adding a curse of his own, floods covered major portions of the Netherlands, and after the floods came the plague. Then Alva imposed new taxes and put the very survival of the Dutch populace in question.

In 1573, Alva's troops— exhausted by their own bestial efforts at persecution— were defeated by a people's force led by William, Prince of Orange, a man known also as William the Silent. Ironically, William had once been a favorite of Charles II, and when the king had abdicated from his throne, he rested his weight on the arm of the man who would soon become the sworn enemy of the crown.

William of Orange was born into a Protestant home but was Roman Catholic at the time he took up the cause of revolu-

Alva's Bloody March

The gallows, the wheel, stakes, trees along the highways, were laden with carcasses or limbs of those who had been hanged, beheaded, or roasted; so that the air which God made for the respiration of the living, was now become the common grave or habitation of the dead. Every day produced fresh objects of pity and of mourning, and the noise of the bloody passing-bell was continually heard, which by the martyrdom of this man's cousin, and the other's brother or friend, rang dismal peals in the hearts of the survivors.

—T. M. Lindsay, *History of the Reformation* (NY: Charles Scribner's Sons).

tion. The battles he faced with Spain and the Roman Catholic Church prompted him to convert to Lutheranism, and then, in 1573, to profess the Reformed faith.

Throughout his campaigns William was poorly supplied with arms and supplies, but when he was told he should appeal for help to a foreign potentate, he replied, "We have the greatest of all potentates, the Lord of Hosts." William of Orange is something of a Dutch George Washington—a patriot, military hero, revolutionary, and father of his country.

Spain finally recognized the independence of the Dutch territories in 1648, but already in the late 1570s, the countryside of the northern provinces especially were essentially freed from Spanish control.

William of Orange became the leader of the United Provinces, the northern tier of provinces in the Low Countries, a new independent republic characterized by something relatively unheard of at the time—freedom of worship to all. The Union of Utrecht (1579) offered freedom of worship to Catholics, Lutherans, Calvinists, and even Mennonites, and thus began the peculiarly Dutch tradition of religious and ethnic toleration that, long before the rise of Hitler, enabled Jews from all over Europe to emigrate to the Netherlands and avoid persecution and death in their home countries.

THE SYNOD OF DORT

For twenty years I have been teaching at an institution endowed with a name totally foreign to the vast majority of North Americans. That institution's name is Dordt College. Every five years or so, some student comes up with what he or she

believes to be a brand-new idea whose time has come: rename the college. Since no one knows what a *Dordt* is, the students say, why not call the place something more contemporary, something more pronounceable, at least something that can't be so mercilessly mocked. In 1970 *The Bananer*, a parody of *The Banner*, called Dordt "Warp College"; but students for nearly all of its half-century history have been "dorks" or "warts." Not so very appealing.

Fifty years ago a significant number of individuals, those most set on creating a college out here at the eastern edge of the Great Plains, decided that the appropriate name for this institution should be what it is today—Dordt. The intent wasn't to confound anyone or to create a great question for some eventual CRC version of *Trivial Pursuit*. These founders wanted to celebrate a name that had meaning to them, even if, a half century later, that word has little meaning to their great-grandchildren.

In some ways, the name Dordt College is itself emblematic of the difficulties resulting from the process of assimilation into American culture and its effects on all kinds of immigrant peoples—which is, in a way, the major theme of the story of the Christian Reformed Church in North America. A shared history, similar customs, prevalent religious orientation, even a way of eating potatoes become, for the time immediately following immigration, the strongest means by which any people—Dutch or Mexican or Italian or Korean—distinguish themselves and thereby find their identity in North America's polyglot culture. Often the immigrants themselves set certain ethnic behaviors in stone when they arrive, creating an interesting phenomenon. An immigrant people, when contrasted years later to the folks from their culture of origin (those who stayed in the old country) always look like quaint leftovers from another time, relics, even fossils—people who are neither really Dutch anymore, nor American. CRC folk who pride themselves on their Dutch heritage are really chasing a phantom. The wooden-shoe images marketed during "Tulip Times" throughout North America are often as peculiar to contemporary Amsterdamers as they are to Americans without a drop of Dutch blood.

But in the push and pull of everyday life, identity is no cheap commodity. We like to be grouped, for instance, as professionals (those who play violin), as devotees of certain sports (Green Bay Packer fans), as regionalists (Midwesterners or folks from the Pacific Northwest). But we also like to forge our identity on more than a set of organizational memberships or a shared profession. We need only to remember French-speaking Canada to realize that ethnicity is often important in our determination of who we are.

And what is ethnicity? That's another million-dollar question. It's tulips and Wilhelmina peppermints, to be sure, but it's also much, much more. Ethnicity is a complex arrangement of customs, manners, and an orientation toward life.

In North America, maintaining an identity in a world fraught with cultures of all sizes and shapes has prompted people to examine and commit themselves to old ways. An argument could be made, for instance, that some of the early Dutch immigrants' fervor about keeping the Sabbath day holy, while outwardly grounded in theological reasons, was at least in part created by the need for some behavior to mark them as separate, to give them identity. Here, as elsewhere, ethnicity and faith worked together in a complex way to create and maintain a sense of who a people wanted to be. Some still argue that the real motivation for Christian schools was to keep Dutch Calvinist kids away from the world.

When that august group who founded Dordt college got together to create a name for a new Iowa college, the name they came up with was more meaningful to them as inheritors of a Dutch Reformed tradition than it was to anyone else on the landscape. Today, as a result of the CRC's continued process of Americanization, the meaning of the name seems almost lost.

Dordt College, Sioux Center, Iowa, founded in 1955.

So why was the word *Dordt* important at all? Most members of the CRC will likely recognize that it's a name affixed to another of the three forms of unity found at the back of the *Psalter Hymnal*—the Canons of Dort (even though the spellings are slightly different). Like Guido de Brès's Belgic Confession and the Heidelberg Catechism, the Canons of Dort are meant to steer the ship, to give direction to our understanding of what the Bible means. It's an old standard, and just because it's in the *Psalter* doesn't mean anyone ever reads it, of course. It's there nonetheless, and it's there because of the "Great Synod" of Dort, a defining hour in a developing Reformed church and mind.

Because Alva's march to rid the lowlands of pagan Protestantism began in the southern provinces where the French-speaking Walloon churches were stoutly Calvinistic, a wave of Walloon refugees fled north in front of the sweep of the bloody inquisition. But it wasn't the French speakers alone who were carrying the banner of Calvin's own unique Protestantism. The persecution of Protestants throughout Europe created refugees everywhere, and often enough those refugees

Jacob Arminius (1560-1609), pastor in Amsterdam who taught that the doctrine of divine election depended on God's knowing beforehand just who would accept the gospel. Arminius has been improperly designated as the founder of all free-will theology (i.e., Arminianism).

picked up something of the new and democratic urgings of Reformation thought. Clearly, when they returned home, they weren't the same folks who'd left. In 1571, even before Alva's defeat, enough Calvinists were inhabiting the northern provinces to hold a synod, a central meeting at a city named Dort. Forty years later, on November 13, 1618, the assembly known as "The Great Synod" was called to order in the same city.

Although twenty-eight representatives from foreign churches attended the Synod of Dort, most of the delegates and all of the officers were Dutch. They included eighteen representatives from Dutch provincial governments, thirty-eight ministers, twenty-one elders, and five theological professors.

Missing from the cast of characters in the Dort drama was the one man whose views most clearly shaped the synod's difficult agenda: Jacob Arminius. During the 1580s a Protestant writer, Dirck Volkerts Coornhert, had launched attacks against Calvin's view of predestination by arguing that God does not decree a person's salvation; he claimed that his reading of the Bible indicated that human beings also have a hand in the process. What he argued was that we are not simply passive recipients of God's love, but active participants. Arminius—who was a student of Calvin's Genevan successor, Beza, before becoming a preacher in Amsterdam—was asked to silence Coornhert with a good strong dose of Calvin's definition of predestination. But when Arminius read the case Coornhert had created, he was the one who did the changing. In 1603, with Coornhert's views in his briefcase, his heart, and his mind, Jacob Arminius took a chair in theology at the University of Leiden, where he taught until his death in 1609.

Other professors at Leiden feared the new views of Coornhert and Arminius, not only because those views represented a significant departure from what they considered to be Calvin's sense of election, but also because those views—new and exciting as they were—became very popular on campus. Before Arminius arrived at the Leiden campus, one Francis Gomarus, a staunch Calvinist professor already teach-

Meeting of the National Synod of Dordrecht (1618-1619), copied from the original painting located at the city hall of the city of Dordrecht.

ing there, did everything possible to prevent Arminius from taking the chair he ultimately was granted. Gomarus succeeded for some time in stalling the appointment, but finally couldn't prevent it. In 1612, weary of the popularity Arminius's ideas found among the students, Professor Gomarus resigned.

This footnote to our history merits a little closer look because in the resignation of Francis Gomarus two issues surface, issues that seem especially compelling since they resonate with more contemporary events in the CRC. The first has to do with the nature of the dispute—that is, its theological substance. Was Gomarus picking at straws here? Was his theological dispute with Arminius so esoteric, so arcane, that it wasn't worth his time and energy? Today, some would claim it was, arguing that no theological fight is worth waging when the unity of Christ's body is at stake. There is, after all, no question about the faith of Arminius. The man was no atheist. He was a strong believer in the saving work of Jesus Christ. Clearly, Gomarus's departure in a huff seems, four hundred years later, to be the kind of nit-picking unworthy of Christians commanded to be peacemakers.

Gomarus felt very strongly that something important was at risk here, something crucial to the nature of the faith he'd affirmed. One of the distinguishing pillars of Calvinist theology was and is election, as we've seen earlier. Because we are elect, Calvin suggested, we need not spend all our waking hours pondering our personal salvation. Because God has chosen us by his eternal decree, he wants our service in this world. We do God's will best by carrying his cause into every battle of life. But more on that in a moment.

Gomarus's behavior in disagreeing with Arminius and those who followed him is sadly reminiscent of the way Christians disagree in our day as well. If you're like me, you can feel for Gomarus, a man convinced that the "new age" teacher created a tidal flow of ideas that threatened the heart of the gospel—in his case, God's sovereignty. Think of him, from his office window, watching Arminius and his faithful following of students. Imagine Gomarus getting frustrated with himself for his inability to accept contrary opinions. Think of him looking up at the sky and seeing it fall.

How do we deal with significant and even fundamental differences within the body of Christ? How wide is the tent? How broad is the definition we use to identify

ourselves? At what point do we, like Gomarus—whether progressive or conservative—simply take leave of our chairs and walk away? Should we ever?

These are difficult questions, questions that Calvin and Luther, Zwingli and Menno Simons all faced. How can we be civil and loving when the nature of our disagreements goes to the very heart of what we believe?

We shouldn't think of the conflict created by Jacob Arminius as something merely personal—between himself and Francis Gomarus—because the controversy was much broader. Two parties formed: the Remonstrants (who were pro-Arminius) and the Counter-Remonstrants (who were pro-Gomarus). By 1614, Gomarus's Counter-Remonstrants were talking of separation from what had become the Remonstrant majority in the Dutch church; by 1616, they were doing it—in Rotterdam and elsewhere. In the face of constant bickering, the people themselves became restless, and the issue turned political, as such theoretical disputes most often do. Our own personalities outfit substantial issues in human flesh. The civil leaders of four provinces finally decided to convene a synod and settle the theological dispute between Calvinists and the disciples of Jacob Arminius.

It may be difficult for us to understand exactly how the relationship operated, but we need to remember that at this time church and state in the Netherlands, as elsewhere in Europe, were really in a kind of marriage. The civil authorities—government officials—who convened the synod laid down specific rules for its deliberations. The theologians were not simply to debate the issues, but to judge right and wrong. Furthermore, the magistrates ordered that all judgments should be made by way of scriptural grounds. Specifically kept out of the decisions were the Belgic Confession of Guido de Brès and the Heidelberg Catechism, both of which were decidedly Calvinistic.

From early on in the deliberations, the outcome of the synod became evident. The Arminian Remonstrants were going to lose—and lose big. In fact, two months into the assembly—on January 14, 1619—the Remonstrants were evicted from the meetings after protesting the authority of the synod too vigorously. From that point on, all judgments upon the Remonstrants themselves were made exclusively on the basis of what Arminius and Coornhert had published.

On April 23, 1619, the "Great Synod" adopted the "Five Heads," the third of the doctrinal standards adopted by the Christian Reformed Church. Nine respected delegates, six from Dutch provinces and one each from England, Germany, and Geneva, prepared these canons. On April 24, the synod began deposing Arminian professors and preachers, so that when the meetings finally ended, about two hundred Remonstrants found themselves out of a job.

When synod adjourned on May 29, the Canons had taken their place beside the Heidelberg Catechism and the Belgic Confession. A new church order adopted at that synod insisted that all persons in any teaching capacity in the church had to subscribe to these three standards—does that sound at all familiar?

But there was more to the Synod of Dort than a new church order, the necessity of subscription to confessional documents, and the deposition of the Remonstrants. That synod also declared that the singing of hymns (except those found in the New Testament) was forbidden—from that point on it would be psalm-singing or no singing at all in the Dutch churches. In addition, instruction in the catechism was mandated and made simpler by the provision of two versions of *Compendium of the Christian Religion,* a title, by the way, still used for CRC catechism instruction as recently as the 1960s. And, after dismissing all foreign delegates on May 13, the synod, influenced by governmental delegates in attendance, gave Dutch civil authorities increased power over the church—a move that has more significance as our story moves forward.

THE LEGACY OF THE GREAT SYNOD

So what? Who but a few egghead historians might ever call Dort the "Great Synod"? For most of us, I'm sure, the Canons of Dort are an obscure document tucked in the back of the *Psalter Hymnal.* The vast majority of members of the CRC would likely have some trouble summarizing this confession's contents or explaining its historical relevance to our time. We live in an age when theology and doctrine—our knowledge of God—is seemingly not significant. I'm sure most members of the CRC would say a "personal relationship with Jesus Christ" is far more important than a deeply considered understanding of God and this world, even though the very core of our historical theological heritage suggests that such individualism is less important than a life of service.

Yet, we are inheritors of all this history. Some would say it's baggage that can and should be dumped. Others might say that this history is at the very core of our identity. Whatever its place in the contemporary world of the CRC, its influence on our history is undeniable.

As we noted earlier, Dort outlawed certain types of music. As former *Banner* editor Andrew Kuyvenhoven once quipped to me, "When the Lord kicked the devil out of heaven, he fell into the choir loft." Music—its tempo, its style, and its lyrics—can generate controversy (pardon the

This controversial issue of *The Banner* provoked heated debate about the ethnicity of the CRC.

understatement). In the congregation where I worship, nothing is more controversial today than what and how we sing together. Several members are energetically entertaining the possibility of beginning a new fellowship whose character would be determined largely on the basis of the manner by which they sing. The Great Synod's deliberations over music both reflected and created a significant suspicion of hymns. Some things, it seems, don't change.

But there's so much more here. Look at the legacy of the Great Synod: a church order at once congregational and yet presbyterian; a church order so solidified that some, even today, maintain that the CRC looks to its order as if it were revelation; a system of local church administration by the elders, officebearers pledged to uphold the three doctrinal standards (Belgic Confession, Heidelberg Catechism, Canons of Dort), all of which were set into place with the Great Synod; catechism preaching once each Sunday (Do we still do that? Do people expect it?); an official church visit to every member family each year (for years this practice was called *huisbezoek,* long after the disappearance of the Dutch language from the CRC; there was, after all, no English or American evangelical equivalent practice).

All these practices are part of the package we inherited from Dort. They were carried to America with Scholte, Van Raalte, and thousands of other Dutch Calvinist immigrants. What's more, some historians claim that the original English pilgrims, William Bradford's Plymouth Colony, were deeply influenced by Dort, since his people, the Brownists, were in the

Netherlands at the time of the synod, after having escaped religious persecution in England and before coming to the New World. To us, it may not be the Great Synod, but there is no doubt that the Synod of Dort plays a major role in our denominational history.

But what of the central controversy of the synod—the rift between those who believed in a strict view of predestination versus those who argued for a measure of human will in the process? Is the Remonstrant conflict simply an interesting theological skirmish that illustrates how we believers seem more interested in cutting perfect theological figure-eights than in doing the Lord's work?

In a *Banner* editorial, John Suk gently criticizes a speaker at the 1996 Youth Unlimited Convention because "his revivalistic sermons included more of an Arminian than a Calvinist perspective on salvation." He goes on to assert that God has certainly blessed the efforts of the speaker, just as he has blessed the efforts of the Mennonites, and the Roman Catholics, and the tent-preachers of American revivalism.

But then he offers a warning. "What I fear now," he says, "is that on the last lap of our Americanization we'll thoughtlessly cash in our Reformed confessional heritage for the mistaken notion that we need no creed but Christ. . . . If we drift down that path, we'll become a church that favors Arminian preaching, and a church in which people measure one another's orthodoxy by the parachurch groups they support rather than by the confessions they believe in."

Is the Great Synod really out of sight and out of mind? It's obvious that John Suk,

who, when compared to his predecessors at the editorial helm of *The Banner* seems quite young, believes Dort isn't simply a name we stumble on only after blowing dust away from our theological history. He finds the distinctions battled over at Dort to be very much worthy of our continued study and vigilance.

Maybe there is another question here—not how many members of the Christian Reformed Church of North America would take his position, but how many care? That's what I wonder sometimes.

And that brings me back to where we started: should Dordt College continue to wrench eyebrows with its incredibly obscure name?

You call it.

THE LURE OF REASON

The Great Synod of 1618-1619 was the last national synod convened in the Netherlands for two centuries. During those two hundred years new ideas altered the way people in the Netherlands and throughout the West looked at life and faith. For the most part, those ideas fit beneath the handy designation "The Enlightenment."

What is suggested by the phrase is simple: humanity was "enlightened." The principle vehicle for our enlightenment was a belief in human reason—often as opposed to divine revelation. Instead of believing in a divine source for inspiration and truth, humankind turned its focus on itself and the world. Throughout the West and in North America, people believed that reason was king, that real truth was discoverable and verifiable in the here and now, not in some supernatural guidebook like the Bible or the Koran or in some individual's grand vision of what was, is, or might be. Steady thinking, hearty logic, and plain old common sense were perfectly capable of leading humanity into a future of progress and, well, "enlightenment." A well-tuned brain is, by the standards of the Age of Reason, "the light of the world."

The doors of the church are not impenetrable to the changes in the culture within which it lives and breathes. During the Enlightenment, philosophy and theology became increasingly more difficult to distinguish. Theology seemed to be more a matter of logical constructs which, when perfectly designed and pieced together, were thought wonderfully persuasive—on the basis of reason, of course. In the Dutch Reformed tradition, the fusion of rational philosophy and confessional theology took the form of what is called *Scholasticism*, a word constructed upon a medieval portrait of the scholar as someone who spends most of his or her time paging through old books in the basement crannies of some ancient library.

Even though Scholasticism is often associated with the deep theological study of monks in the Middle Ages, after the Reformation a new and more worldly-wise form of this intellectualism appeared in the Netherlands. A Scholastic is someone who takes great joy in building intellectual towers out of theoretic propositions, one doctrine placed gingerly atop another. Depending on your preference, I suppose, what results is either an Eiffel Tower or a house of cards.

When taken into the classroom (as it was in Dutch universities after Dort), Scholasti-

cism resulted in endless discussions of theological speculation, discussions in which each truth was stretched to its rational end. Taken into the pulpit (as it was across the Netherlands by the late 1700s), Scholasticism called for thoughtful listeners to admit, "Yes, I agree," to an often intricate and multilayered theological design. Agreement was, for all practical purposes, intellectual. But whenever the preaching of the Word of God becomes so abstract as to be coldly rational, it rarely evokes anguished confession of either sin or belief. When Christianity is little more than an assent to certain theological truths, the Holy Spirit's work is perfunctorily dismissed—even banished—from the sanctuary.

One of my favorite Stanley Wiersma (written under the pen name Sietze Buning) poems is titled "Obedience." It tells the story of a rural Iowa family who awaken on the Lord's Day to a foreboding sky thick with roiling blue-gray clouds. Their grain is ripe for the harvest, but their obedience to the Lord puts them in the wagon and on the way to church, even though hail seems imminent. As the skies promised, the storm hits. Every farm family hears the hail's hooves pound the roof of their church. Each parishioner knows the crops are being pummeled as the people worship the Lord. Even though the preacher appears to understand the trauma, when he opens the Word he holds forth on five reasons for infant baptism, a theme that seems startlingly irrelevant to the sounds of destruction outside. His commitment to doctrine at a time when the traumatized believers huddled beneath the steeple obviously needing something

Stanley Wiersma (Sietze Buning)

For a small denomination, the CRC has produced an amazing number of gifted writers. Their evaluations of the "nest" in which they were nurtured run the gamut from clinical detachment, dishonest distortion, deliberate caricature, conspicuous silence, honest objectivity, to grateful appreciation. One of these writers, Stanley Wiersma, better known as Sietze Buning, captures the foibles and eccentricities of his Calvinistic upbringing with great affection and sensitivity. He

notes warts and blemishes with a candor suffused with compassion.

In his all-too-brief life, Sietze authored two books of poetry, *Style and Class* and *Purpaleanie,* in which he looked at his heritage with a benevolent sympathy. His poems point beyond the legalism, small-mindedness, and traditionalism to something worth cherishing. He writes about little Middleburg, Iowa, and the church of his youth with bemused affection. He describes a father so careful to observe the minute rules of Sabbath-keeping that he will not harvest a crop imminently threatened by a devastating storm. The crop is lost, but the Holy Sabbath is affirmed.

This same father, in a touching gesture of solidarity with the animal world, rejoices in giving the horses a day off from their labors. They may frolic in the fields on Sunday and receive a double ration of oats to mark the day. Sunday, in Sietze's fond reminiscences, is not a day of torpor and indolence but a holy day that becomes a holiday.

Stanley Wiersma (1930-1986), poet and Calvin College English professor who wrote voluminously about the religious perception of Dutch Reformed immigrants—especially in Iowa.

Sietze embraced with enthusiasm the world-and-life view of the founders of the church he loved. An enthusiastic and much-loved professor at Calvin College, he made his mark upon the lives of countless students. His friends remember with bittersweet pain his gifts as a storyteller.

Stanley Wiersma died after a brief illness in Amsterdam in 1986. The stilling of this golden voice is a loss still keenly felt in the church and the school he loved. —WDB

more pastoral seems a good example of a commitment to Scholasticism. What Scholasticism does, finally, is promote form over content.

Historians of Dutch Calvinism trace the rise of Scholasticism to Gijsbertus Voetius, who began teaching theology at Utrecht in 1636 after being one of the youngest delegates at the Synod of Dort. But our tendency to stereotype movements and individuals within the history of the church in order to tell the story often leads us to miss the human richness and complexity evident in most every individual we meet.

Gijsbertus Voetius (1589-1676), leading theologian at the University of Utrecht and founding father of Dutch pietism.

by all measures, a conservative, his ideas ran counter to the prevailing intellectual movements all around him. He thought it crucial to assess critically the way Christians should live, thoughtfully and reverently, before the face of God. The Christian life was more than an abstraction to Voetius.

His most famous lecture, "Piety Joined to Science," discusses in typical Scholastic detail the relationship between piety—what he would have defined as the way a believer should live—and the attitudes he recognized in the Enlightenment forces all around him. His vision was born, as most of our innovations are, from a peculiar blend of what he believed and what he saw confronting him and the rest of God's people in the world.

Many of his most challenging debates were over issues arising from activities the CRC has, in the past, called "worldly amusements." The specific issues may differ—he warned against dance, ballet, comedy, and dice—but the nature of the warning is similar. Christians are too busy practicing godliness, Voetius claimed, to be throwing away time on such useless forms of recreation. He was, in his own way and in his own time, trying to be obedient.

Think that's strange? Last weekend, my family and I spent an evening at a movie theater, a welcome break after the end of a long semester. We saw—all of us—the latest James Bond movie. When I left, I felt dirty—not because of scintillating sexuality or the blasphemous sense that technology is the answer to all our problems, but because the whole movie seemed to me to be so worthless. I could have been doing better things. We paid over thirty dollars

Take this man Voetius, for example, someone who can be used as a benchmark for the Scholasticism so rampant in the throes of the Enlightenment. Voetius was not simply a cold theoretician. He was a talented architect of intellectual and theological inquiry, but he didn't spend his late nights counting the angels capable of fancy footwork on some minute point of doctrine. He was a believer who worked tirelessly to keep the faith in a time when forces in the broader culture offered new and inviting paths. Even though he was,

for five tickets, an insubstantial sum you might say. But when I came out of that theater, I had the deep abiding sense that it was thirty dollars shot to Hollywood. I have something of Voetius in me too.

Perhaps no one understood the contributions of Voetius better than Abraham Kuyper, a man whose name will appear later and much more frequently in the story of the CRC. Kuyper's interest in Voetius and his ideas led to a lengthy study that became his own doctoral dissertation. People who want to understand Kuyper, some would say, need to understand Voetius, the Scholastic—and the believer.

Voetius's attempts at obedience to the will of God bring us back to Stanley Wiersma's poem. The dominie goes on and on about infant baptism in the middle of the catastrophic hailstorm outside, but when Sietze's parents leave, they are refreshed by simply having been there, at church, in the presence, I'm sure they would have said, of God Almighty. Here's what Sietze says:

> Later at dinner Dad said,
> "God was testing us. I'm glad we
>   went."
> "Those psalms never gave me such
>   a lift as this morning,"
> Mother said, "I wouldn't have
>   missed it."

But Wiersma's reflections on the ravaging hailstorm range farther than the simple piety of Mother and Dad, and move us closer to a definition that changes in every age, and yet, paradoxically, remains the same. From the vantage point of the time of his reminiscence, Sietze says that his father's not getting in the grain that Sunday morning and, as a result, suffering the near total loss of the crop because of his parents' strict Sabbatarianism seems a cold and unpitying form of righteousness. And yet, he remembers the incident fondly. There's more to it, he says.

> Fathers often fail to pass on to sons
> their harvest customs
> for harvesting grain or real estate or
>   anything.
> No matter, so long as fathers pass on
>   to sons
> another more important pattern
> defined as absolutely as muddlers
>   like us can manage:
> obedience.

> —Excerpts from "Obedience,"
> *Purpaleanie and Other Permutations* by
> Sietze Buning (Orange City: The
> Middleburg Press, 1978).

CHAPTER 4

The Prince and the Pulpit

The church is the bride of Christ. Her members are citizens of his kingdom. But just as Christ's kingdom has never been the only kingdom in which Christians have lived, so also he is not the only king before whom they have had to kneel. The biography of Christ's bride is a chronicle of sometimes flirtatious, often adulterous, occasionally abusive relationships with other, more human kings.

That Christians should have political allegiances and obligations is inescapable. Look at the differences between U.S. and Canadian members of the CRC. Canadians sometimes refer sarcastically to *The Banner*'s classifieds as the western Michigan want ads. Ties to nationality and provinciality, ties to geographic regions and even towns within a county are strong and, in certain situations, tenacious. That affiliations to church and nation should occasionally jostle with each other or even go to war is not hard to understand; they quite regularly and naturally vie for our attention and loyalty.

"Render unto Caesar that which is Caesar's" has been our yardstick for two thousand years, but we've been consistently uncertain how to apply that truth, basically because application isn't as easy as the rule of thumb Christ offered makes it

sound. Even the Enlightenment principle of separation of church and state doesn't make the distinctions perfectly clear. While such a principle may separate the two institutions (removing the *organization* of the church from the *government* of the state), the separation never leads to a complete breakdown of the relationship. It can't. The same woman goes to communion on Sunday and to the polls on Tuesday (if she's from the States, Tuesday is voting day). It's one thing to call for the separation of two institutions; but to divide loyalties, to balance allegiances, to live as citizens of two kingdoms at one time—that's something else.

"Church and state" stories make the evening news quite regularly, of course—from government aid to parochial education to the outright ban on school prayer to the legality of nativity scenes on the front lawns of court houses. Should creationism be taught in public schools? Is opposition to abortion really a matter of faith—and

> ### First Amendment, U.S. Constitution
>
> ❦
>
> Congress shall make no law respecting an establishment of religion or prohibiting the free exercise thereof.

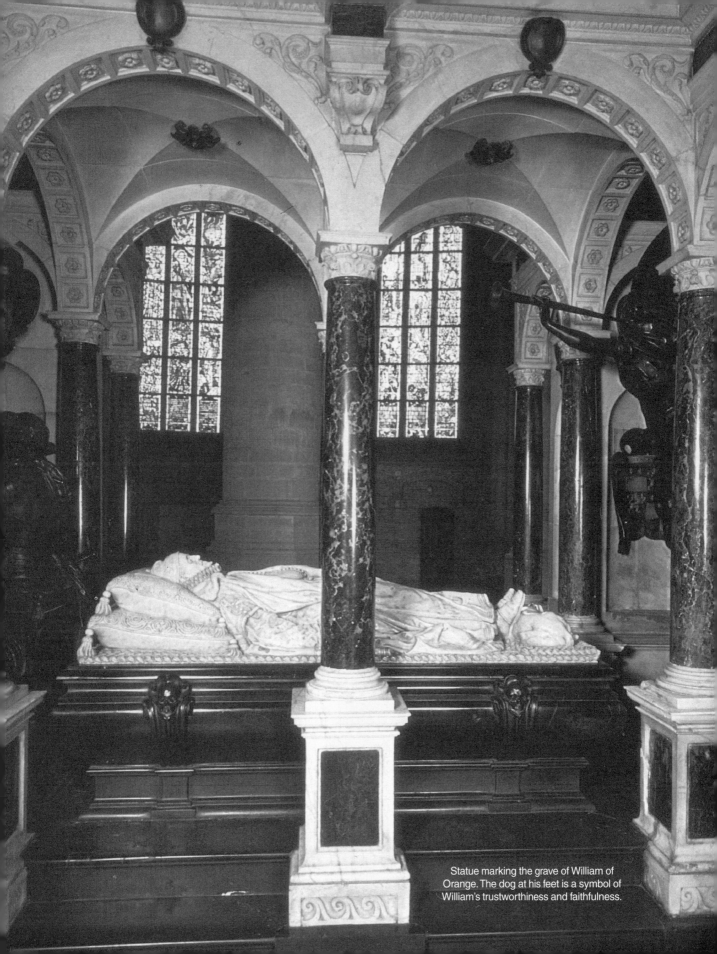

Statue marking the grave of William of Orange. The dog at his feet is a symbol of William's trustworthiness and faithfulness.

In the U.S. prayer was banned from public school classrooms in 1962.

(or premier, or president): "Thus saith the Lord," and when should the preacher say "As you wish, your majesty"?

THE HOUSE OF ORANGE

When the Reverend J. Bogerman, President of the Synod of Dort, adjourned that assembly on May 29, 1619, he had done the work of both the church *and* the state. His synod had been convened by order of civil authorities. Ground rules for deliberations were issued from the throne, not the pulpit. During the final month of its work, the synod hammered out guidelines for future church-state relationships. In the church order adopted at Dort, secular provincial leaders were given veto power over the calling and ordination of pastors and given representation in consistories and provincial and national synods. To our eyes, the marriage between church and state back then was a strange union, even though it was fairly ordinary practice throughout Europe at the time.

While modern North Americans may regard *any* governmental infringement on church affairs as too much, that was not the view of the seventeenth-century Dutch princes. They felt that Dort's orders deliberately skimmed over the power they had coming. The States General, which governed the united provinces as well as most of the provincial states themselves, refused to approve Dort's church order because it failed to give Caesar what was rightfully his—or so they believed.

Such refusals made little difference at first, since the churches used the new church order anyway. But what the churches, by law, could not do was convene another national synod. That call

therefore something that the state cannot regulate? These are tough questions, and they stay with us precisely because they are not easily answered.

The dialogue between the pulpit and the throne provides the backdrop for the drama we're about to witness in this chapter of the story of the CRC. It's primarily the story of one more synod, one which, like Dort, shaped the history of the Christian Reformed Church in North America, even though it was convened on another continent forty years before the denomination itself began. Running through the story is a hauntingly familiar question: when must the preacher say to the prince

could come only from the palace. Dutch princes, disgruntled at the crumbs they felt they'd received from the table at Dort, refused, out of hand, to convene another national synod. For two hundred years they refused, and that refusal figured strategically in the events that followed, events crucial to the history of the CRCNA.

In 1650 a "Great Convention for the Consideration of Union, Religion, and War" made the Reformed religion of Dort "the official religion of the union." As historian D. H. Kromminga noted, "It was not strictly speaking a state church, but its religion was the religion of the state"—that is, the structure of belief officially associated with the state itself.

William of Orange (1533-1584), founding father of the Netherlands Union of Utrecht, 1580, and dominant hero of the Eighty Years' War (1568-1650). Assassinated by an agent of Spain's Philip II in 1584.

Such a situation was not unique, of course. After a fashion, Italy is still a Roman Catholic nation and much of Scandinavia is officially Lutheran, even though describing just exactly what that means is not easy. Today, calling a particular religion the state religion may be no more significant than calling the meadowlark the Iowa state bird.

Nonetheless, it is interesting that Lutherans, Roman Catholics, and Calvinists all had moments in their histories when they were made the religion of the country by government mandate and were thereby somehow tethered to national politics and government. The significant exception to that rule in European history are the Anabaptists, who have an old and worthy tradition of opposition to politics and any kind of national culture. Think of the Amish as the most visible example of that tradition, or the Mennonite ardent tradition of pacifism. Anabaptists have never officially held power the way that Lutherans, Calvinists, and Roman Catholics did; furthermore, they have a long history of suffering at the bloody hands of fellow believers of those very traditions, believers who so efficiently occupied the seat of power.

That oppositional history makes our understanding each other somewhat difficult even today, even though the sinful Calvinist persecution of the Anabaptists is so far behind us that it is long ago forgotten. It is simply very difficult for many Calvinists, Lutherans, and Roman Catholics, for example, to understand the passionate extent of Mennonite pacifism. Dutch Calvinists would likely find pacifist silence in the face of Nazi oppression unimaginable. But then, it's not easy for those committed to pacifism in the Anabaptist tradition to understand how good, believing Christians in World War II could carpet-bomb most of Europe.

We have different histories. Calvinists have fought wars; in fact, we've started them. Calvinists, Lutherans, and Roman Catholics have been part of state militias for centuries. Those who create the state, after all, take upon themselves the responsibility for holding it together when both internal and external forces work to bring it down. In contrast, those in the Anabaptist tradition have, through almost five centuries, grown and flourished in opposition both to war and to state politics in general. Such separate histories carry great weight in the way each of us see and evaluate the culture around us. We are undoubtedly much less distrustful of politics, government, and civic law than those in the Anabaptist tradition. We may also be far less distrustful of "the world."

The official sanction given to the Reformed Church in the Netherlands in 1650 created worldwide prestige for that church and gave it significant political muscle in the Netherlands, attributes that continued for more than two centuries. Slowly but surely, the united provinces became economically powerful and rapidly expanded their colonial empire, taking with them the official state religion. A thirty-sixth article was added to the Belgic Confession requiring that "magistrates should have the gospel preached everywhere," a ruling that made Christian missions a state obligation.

So as Dutch colonies were planted from the East Indies to the shores of New York and the tip of Africa, the Dutch Reformed Church was transplanted into hundreds of thousands of acres and types of fresh new soil. Regrettably, the East India Company and other Dutch firms frequently hired weak-kneed and ill-prepared "missionaries" merely to fulfill the letter of Dutch law, then placed them aboard ships with the sincere desire that they would forget their calling once they put their foot down on new land. Commercial interests dominated. Nonetheless, these missionary efforts were

sometimes gloriously successful, despite mercenary greed.

In terms of faith and purity, the Dutch church paid a steep price for political prestige. During this time, the influence of the state on the church was devastating. The absence of national synods virtually guaranteed the erosion of orthodoxy. As the decades rolled by, major theological questions were left unanswered. Unless an argument could be settled locally, it would not be settled at all. Where a heretical preacher became a prince's favorite, he could spout wacky ideas every seventh day with smug disdain for church discipline. Provincial synods could take action, but civil authorities regularly intervened by providing shelter and salary for deposed clerics. Provincial synods could effect national change only by proposing carefully worded decisions, mailing such proposals to other provincial synods, and adopting concurrent resolutions. But then as now, synods were prone to modify every resolution. Thus, while the Reformed faith was "the religion of the state," the state's policies were cutting that religion from its historical and confessional moorings.

Throughout these two centuries, orthodox Calvinists struggled to keep the faith in a time when the government's focus was to keep the peace at all cost. Theology was far less important to the state, after all, than the common good. Ecclesiastical skirmishes were specifically outlawed—and with good reason: they'd already taken an enormous toll in a bloody series of wars throughout Europe in the seventeenth century.

By 1750, Dutch civil authorities were enforcing a "tolerance" that made room for all kinds of theological propositions. When two preachers, Holtius and Comrie, argued that such tolerance was dismantling orthodoxy, the government banned their book, *The Examination of the Concept of Toleration.* The state, in much of the eighteenth century, was largely intolerant of all views but tolerance.

The church, like society itself and each of us individually, has propensities and urges. Some of its members, by virtue of their own individual experiences and history as well as their predilections, are more conservative. Conservatives like to sit in the same pew week after week. On their free nights, they'd much rather stay at home than leave the hearth. Their idea of a great vacation is returning to the same cottage they've always visited the third week of June. Conservatism stakes out its theological positions and won't be moved. We need our conservatives to help us keep good track of what's been crucial to a definition of faith throughout the ages.

Other believers are, by virtue of their own experience and predilection, more liberal or progressive. Going to the same cottage every summer would seem irritating and stultifying; they'd much rather go places they've never been before. Progressives are uncomfortable with the status quo because they've always got their eyes elsewhere. Having to stay at home makes the four walls around them seem like a prison; they get edgy around boundaries of any kind and only hesitantly set them up for themselves. We need our progressives to keep us from navel-gazing.

Progressives show us new paths; conservatives keep the weeds down on the old ones. Progressives long to experience new ways; they love to expand their horizons. Conservatives honor the old ways with unending devotion. We need our conservatives to keep us at home and our progressives to get us out of the house. We need both.

Some eras require progress and liberalization; the old forms need to be stretched and even broken, the old wine poured into new skins. In those times trailblazers like Calvin and the Reformers are essential to radical change and new vision. However, in times of radical flux all around, the church can be dizzied if it doesn't have its feet solidly planted on the ground.

By the late 1700s, the corrosive effects of the Enlightenment could be seen everywhere in the Netherlands, both in civil society and in the church. Rationalism was the order of the day in both pulpit and classroom. No longer did people assume truth to be some supernatural revelation of your, mine, or the other guy's deity. Instead, truth was that which could be understood, thought through, reasonably determined. This God business is okay for morality, Enlightenment folks would argue, but look at the trouble it's given us—a whole century of bloody warfare. Most of the thoughtful leaders in Western culture told themselves it was time to stop and rethink this whole business of religion. There'd been enough fighting.

The religion of the day was Deism, a theology based on what is, well, reasonable. The American scientist/patriot Ben Franklin surveyed the variety of religions in the world, drew them up in a chart on his mind, then determined what was true and good about all of them by just plain thinking about it. What he came up with was a fairly simple list of doctrines:

- That there is one God who made all things.
- That he governs the world by his providence.
- That he ought to be worshiped by adoration, prayer, and thanksgiving.
- That the most acceptable service of God is doing good to man.
- That the soul is immortal.
- And that God will certainly reward virtue and punish vice either here or hereafter.

Franklin, who claims in his *Autobiography* that he never attended church after his boyhood, held on to more elements of historic Christianity than did Thomas Paine, an American and world revolutionary whose writing likely did more to spark the American Revolution than any other single tract. Paine defined this rationalistic faith with a pamphlet titled "The Age of Reason." In it he offered his personal creed: "I believe in one God, and no more; and I hope for happiness beyond this life," he wrote. Then he offered his second point: "I believe in the equality of man, and I believe that religious duties consist in doing justice, loving mercy, and endeavoring to make our fellow-creatures happy." That's it.

Benjamin Franklin (1706-1790).

It makes sense, right? In the confusion and bloody madness surrounding ecclesiastical warfare throughout Europe, Paine thought it right that one should simply winnow out from all religions what's verifiably best—choosing that, of course, on the basis of what makes sense. What the world needed, Franklin and Paine would argue, was a functional religion, one that promoted peace and not more bloody discord.

"Every national church or religion has established itself by pretending some special mission from God, communicated to certain individuals," Paine wrote. "The Jews have their Moses; the Christians their Jesus Christ; . . . the Turks their Mahomet; as if the way to God was not open to every man alike." Some disagreed with Paine's point of view, of course. One hundred and fifty years later, President Teddy Roosevelt called Paine a "filthy little atheist."

But Paine's formulary for Deism gained thousands of devoted subscribers, especially among society's movers and shakers. Although it had no churches, no synods, and no bishops, Deism was the creed of intellectuals throughout the Western world. This new religion didn't deny God so much as put God in his place, a place designated for him by Deists themselves.

What we need to understand about the story of the CRC is that in some quarters in the Netherlands, Deism was thought to be perfectly compatible with the Reformed faith. Where the Reformation's basic confessions were remembered, Scholasticism was smothering the warmth of faith under layers of cold, intellectual arguments. The confessions became fossils, mummy-like

Large house and barn in Groningen—typical of wealthy-class "*dikke boeren*."

symbols of dead orthodoxy. To many, the confessions were, at best, museum pieces. To others, the confessions were to the mind and the spirit what the stocks on the village square were to petty thieves. To still others, those confessions didn't even exist.

By 1780, revolution was brewing in the Netherlands, as it was all over Europe and, of course, in the colonies of North America. In the Netherlands, the middle and lower classes had carried the brunt of economic hardships for decades. With growing hostility, they blamed their woes on the prince, William V of the House of Orange, and the city fathers who supported him. "Patriots" (those most inclined toward revolution) accused political leaders of callous disregard for the common folk and leveled attacks on leading Reformed clergy, who guarded their self-interest by keeping up their cozy relationship with William. Convinced that violence was the only language the government understood, the Patriots used force to take control—first of villages, then of larger towns, and eventually of cities (most notably Utrecht).

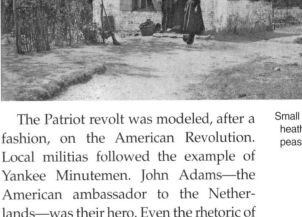

Small house on the heath—typical of peasant families.

The Patriot revolt was modeled, after a fashion, on the American Revolution. Local militias followed the example of Yankee Minutemen. John Adams—the American ambassador to the Netherlands—was their hero. Even the rhetoric of revolution came from America; Dutch patriots armed themselves with American pamphlets (Thomas Paine's, in fact) to fire broadsides at the House of Orange.

Since the early 1600s, when it championed Calvinism against Arminianism, the House of Orange had been politically aligned with Christian orthodoxy. Never mind that the government had enforced toleration; every member of the House of

Orange was Reformed. As a result, the Reformed church maintained a privileged position in the land. But the Patriots, who demanded individual rights and civil democracy, were not happy with a privileged religion or a privileged ruling class. Thus, the sides were created—to the right, the House of Orange, representing orthodoxy; and to the left, the Patriots, insisting on open toleration for any system of faith.

In 1787, William V called for Prussian help, got it, and crushed the rebellion. Patriots who survived fled by droves to France, where they urged French intervention in the Netherlands. In 1795, the stepson of the French Revolution, Napoleon Bonaparte, marched north into Dutch territory. Those Patriots who had fled eight years earlier followed in his wake; those in hiding emerged to salute his arrival. In a matter of months, the Netherlands belonged to Napoleon, and the House of Orange was hiding out in England.

Everywhere in Europe the church had been married to the throne, but now the thrones were crumbling—and with them the alliances between church and state. We might be tempted to say, "Those who live by the state, die by the state," and in a way, it's true. However, God's church abides the foibles of its own members, whether those foibles are perpetuated by government leaders or parish preachers, whether they're princes or peons. In the Netherlands, with Napoleon's blessing, the Patriots held a National Convention of the Netherlands which, on July 18, 1796, decreed separation of church and state on the basis of these well-known principles: liberty, equality, and fraternity.

In the eighteen years following Napoleon's takeover, the Netherlands became the Batavian Republic, which did not last; then the Kingdom of Holland (ruled by Napoleon's brother Louis), which did not last; and finally a part of the Empire of France, which likewise did not last. By 1813 Napoleon was alive but not well. In the long reach of his empire, he'd overextended himself and was steadily losing control of his territories. On March 30, 1814, Prince William of Orange returned from England and seized power once more. He mounted the Dutch throne as William the First, King of Holland. For two uncertain years, William maneuvered carefully to stay afloat in a tense situation, but by 1815, when Napoleon went down in the mud at Waterloo, William's position was secure.

During the nearly two decades of French rule, the status of the Reformed churches in the Netherlands had changed drastically. The government took control of church properties, then sold them to pay for the ever-ballooning expense of Napoleon's war efforts. Ownership and authority in schools were transferred from church to state. Dutch preachers, accustomed to government-paid salaries, found themselves subject to the people's good graces, their salaries a matter of what they could gain by the contributions of their congregations. So even those preachers most swayed by rationalism—most liberal, in other words—welcomed the return of William with open arms. Among the clergy, the old divisions were quickly erased by the extremity of their position and the brokenness throughout society in general. With the return of a king from the House of Orange, at least there was hope.

William I had left the Netherlands when he was twenty-three years old. He returned eighteen years later with a political philosophy molded and shaped by his English exile. He'd studied the established Anglican Church and noted how the British throne had used it. And he'd enjoyed regular contact with the King of Prussia (his cousin), who was uniting that country by enforcing a union between the Lutheran and Reformed factions. William was no fool. He had picked up good political sense in England, as well as a direction for his people.

The Netherlands to which he returned was a babel of religious and political opinion and bickering provinces. The challenge to a monarch was obvious: unify the nation. True to his family legacy, William I was House-of-Orange Reformed. True to his political instincts, William decided to control the nation by controlling the church. He set out to make for himself a Reformed state church, an institution in which the pulpit took instructions from the throne.

THE SYNOD OF 1816

The story of the 1816 Synod is not particularly complex. There were no competing factions, no steamed oratory, no dramatic expulsions. On January 7, 1816, a new church order was summarily announced to the people of the Netherlands. Their ecclesiastical structure had become a department of the state.

There were whimpers of protest but no thundering speeches denouncing the move. And by the time the consequences of the new order were clear, the radical reorganization was permanent.

Provincial assemblies were the only significant church meetings the people remembered; there had been, after all, no national synod for two hundred years. With a single turn of the king's wrist, those same provincial assemblies were abolished in favor of a new national assembly that would meet annually and exercise immediate control over all French- and English-speaking congregations. Dutch-language churches would continue their tradition of classis meetings, but the classis itself as a unit of ecclesiastical rule was stripped of power and became little more than a teatime for preachers. In the place of classis, the king created a classical board and, in lieu of provincial synods, a provincial board.

Most important, *all* members of *all* boards were appointed by the king, and *all* delegates to national synods came only from those boards he designed and chose. As an insurance policy—to protect rambunctious and wealthy laymen from challenging the power of the throne—the king reduced non-ministerial membership to one layperson on each board. By removing laity, he could assure loyalty—clergy, after all, were again receiving salary from the king and were therefore securely in his pocket.

The church order of Dort had specified psalm singing and nothing but psalm singing for Dutch churches (with the exception of a few other texts from Scripture, the law, and the creed). The new 1816 church order *required* that each worship service include one or more songs from a collection titled *Evangelical Hymns*.

The credit for this innovation must not be given entirely to William. *Evangelical Hymns* had been assembled as early as 1805 and introduced, with provincial synod approval, by 1807. But William marched the church's use of these hymns two steps further—by including this explicit directive, the 1816 assembly took on the church order of Dort, an order still held dear by some churches and many individuals.

Besides a new organization and new songs, the 1816 Synod gave confessional loyalty a whole new definition. The Synod of Dort had both followed and instituted a Form of Subscription (also called a Formula of Assent) with which all church officers declared their allegiance to the church's confessional standards. That form, like the one still used in the Christian Reformed Church today, confessed adherence to the standards *because* (in Latin, *quia*) these standards are faithful to the Word of God. The 1816 regulation made the language of the subscription formula ambiguous by substituting the Latin word *quatenus* (meaning "in as much as" or "in so far as" or "to the extent that") for *quia.* Therefore, in using the new form, preachers and teachers pledged allegiance to the Reformed confessions only "to the extent that" these confessions agreed with Scripture. This looks innocuous enough, but read "major change."

One doesn't need to be a linguist to understand the shift. According to an 1898 description by the Reverend Henry Vander Werp:

> *This ambiguity in the text of the Formula of Assent allowed minis-ters to preach their private opinions of the truth, instead of the truth as expressed in the standards of the church; and ere long the sheep of Christ's flock were tossed to and fro, and carried about with every wind of doctrine by the sleight of men and cunning craftiness. A single new word created a shift in meaning which made one's attention to doctrine* relative, *subject to personal preference.*

The new subscription form mandated one other substantial change. References to the Canons of Dort were simply deleted, obviously because that confession was a scourge to both the new rationalists and old Arminians. William's purpose was to make the Dutch church as inclusive as possible and thereby avoid unsavory doctrinal and ecclesiastical conflict.

Despite these significant edits, the new forms sailed through the 1816 Synod with little conflict. After all, the House of Orange was popular, the Netherlands felt the joy of independence once again, and, lest we forget, the preachers were remunerated by the state. Two hundred years had passed since Dort, and the Enlightenment had most certainly shaped the concept of church government. People were weary of war. Peace looked promising. They looked forward to some semblance of order in both church and state.

What's more, the reorganization plan was itself a masterpiece of political precision. It deftly cut out the critics, who, had they desired to protest, would have nowhere to take what William might have called their carping. The king had wrapped the church in the folds of his royal robe, and the result was pervasive silence surrounding a few muffled groans.

REVIVAL

While William was remodeling his church into a department of state, an evangelical movement was fanning out across the continent. At first glance the revivals look like isolated, spontaneous explosions—one in Scotland, one in France, a few others in Switzerland, Germany, and the Netherlands. They were, however, neither spontaneous nor disconnected. Some common history was shared by uncommon characters, whose traffic through Geneva tied them inseparably.

Already in 1737, the German Count Nicolaus von Zinzendorf had founded a "society of brothers" committed to a communal lifestyle that emphasized piety, renewal, and evangelism. The headquarters

---

George Whitefield

George Whitefield was an outstanding preacher during the Revival. His first sermon in his native town of Gloucester was of such fervor that someone complained to his bishop that he had driven fifteen people mad. The famous actor David Garrick once said: "I would give a hundred guineas if I could say 'Oh' like Mr. Whitefield." Whitefield is generally thought of as a fervent persuader, who left others to build churches out of his converts. Certainly his letters to Wesley, and his entrusting the care of his English societies to Harris in 1749, underline his lack of interest in the administrative task of raising and caring for infant churches. But he founded the English Calvinistic Methodist Connexion, whose first conference met in 1743. . . . These churches, mainly in the south and west of England, kept up a separate existence until they were absorbed into Congregationalism in the nineteen century.

George Whitefield (1714-1770), leading evangelist of the Great Awakening in the United States of America (1720-1770). Worked with the Wesley brothers in England, but was most famous for his seven evangelistic tours of the American colonies.

Whitefield centered his theology on the old English Puritan themes of original sin, justification by faith and regeneration. Sometimes he was militantly Calvinist, but he preached with a rare passion for souls. "Calvinistic Methodist" was indeed a term with real meaning when applied to him.

His preaching style was dynamic and compelling; he spoke with fervor, yet in a style plain, unadorned, and often colloquial. His physical bearing commanded attention and the range of his voice was astonishing. Anglican pulpits were often barred to him: his open-air services were often interrupted, and he was a favorite target for anti-Methodist propaganda.

—*Eerdmans' Handbook to the History of Christianity*
(Grand Rapids, MI: Wm. B. Eerdmans) pp. 440-1.

Barbara von Kruedener

Barbara Juliana von Kruedener (1764-1824) was a Russian-born pietist. Unfaithful to her husband, a Russian minister of state, she formed an attachment with a young French officer, which was described in her idealized autobiographical novel, *Valerie.* A few months later (1804) during a sojourn at Riga, she experienced a sudden conversion, after which she held pietistic conventicles throughout Wurttemberg. As a confidante of Czar Alexander I she was regarded by some as the prime mover of the Holy Alliance with Prussia and Austria. Alexander, however, contended that he had conceived the treaty while at Vienna in 1815. Further conventicles sprang up in 1816-1818 in northern Switzerland and southern Germany. She died during a visit to the Crimea.

—*The New International Dictionary of the Christian Church,* p. 572.

for this society was Oberlausitz, Germany, where, among a great many others, evangelist B. von Kruedener—a woman preacher who sparked revivals across Germany and into Switzerland—picked up many of her key ideas.

In 1799, Robert Haldane, a Scottish lay evangelist with a sparkling evangelical message, founded the first "free church" in Scotland. It was a congregation free from government support, free to preach the historic (Reformed) faith, and free with the gospel message of repentance.

Inseparable from this movement is the American Great Awakening of 1740, a time when, according to Ben Franklin's *Autobiography,* "It seemed as if all the World were growing Religious; so that one could not walk thro' the Town in an Evening without Hearing Psalms sung in different Families of every Street." Perhaps the leading figure in the American Great Awakening was an Oxford graduate and Calvinist preacher who conducted evangelistic campaigns in the U.S. as well as in his native British Isles. What Whitefield was to the American Great Awakening, Robert Haldane became to the European revival of the early 1800s.

By 1810, revivals had spread all over, but most of their trails led back to Geneva, Switzerland, where a sizable group of students, pastors, and professors had formed an evangelical society. This group received a steady stream of visitors from the "society of brothers" founded by von Zinzendorf. Madame von Kruedener paid a call and left a deep impression as well.

When Robert Haldane took his revival campaign to John Calvin's Geneva, he drew the Academy students away from lectures by Enlightenment professors and into membership in the evangelical society. A young preacher named César Malan was so impressed by Haldane that he led his congregation out of the Swiss state church to found a "free church" according to Haldane's blueprint.

But first, Malan led a evangelical crusade into the Netherlands, where the Dutch poet and historian Willem Bilderdijk was gripped deeply by his message. Bilderdijk was an ardent "Orangist" who blamed the decay of both church and state on the ideas of the Enlightenment. Occasionally, with respect to national affairs especially, Bilderdijk could sound like the Reverend Jerry Falwell, the American fundamentalist and former leader of the Moral Majority. Both have argued that a nation will achieve greatness when its leaders return to the religious principles that made that nation great. Bilderdijk's appeal was directly to Dort, of course. He longed for a Dutch monarch who would again raise Dort's flag of orthodoxy. It's easy to imagine his glee at the 1813 return of the monarch—*and* his disgust at William's 1816 Synod.

Bilderdijk was brilliant, eccentric, and outspokenly orthodox. When his fervent conservatism cost him a chair at the University of Leiden, he moved to the edge of the campus and set up an unofficial "night school" in his parlor, rather than seek another academic position elsewhere. Soon enough he attracted a small circle of disciples, including two precocious Jewish converts: Isaac da Costa, a gifted writer, and Abraham Capadose, his cousin, a medical doctor of Portuguese descent. These three—Bilderdijk, da Costa, and Capadose—became leaders in a movement known as the *Reveil* (literally, a "wake-up call," like the bugled reveille that rouses solders from their sleep).

The *Reveil* significantly affected two movements crucial to an understanding of the birth of the Christian Reformed Church—the *Afscheiding,* an 1834 secession from the Dutch state church; and the *Doleantie,* another secession fifty years later.

The reason is clear: Bilderdijk, da Costa, and Capadose were no bantam-weight intellectuals. They attracted a remarkable crowd and a dedicated following in Leiden because they were smart, urbane aristocrats, sophisticated, worldly-wise, financially secure, and polished. And while that description may make some of us wince, what they carried with most fervency was the conviction that the Dutch church had departed from a "simple gospel." The hollowness of their own experience with Enlightenment thought prompted them to try to restore orthodoxy to the church around them, and to do so by way of creating interest within the student body. Through their intense and provocative late-night discussions, *Reveil* leaders inspired young people with orthodox theology and a spirit of piety the likes of which no rationalist could comprehend, even if he wanted to.

By 1830, the *Reveil* had spawned an active student organization on the University of Leiden campus, where it was dubbed the Scholte Club after its leader, Hendrik Pieter Scholte, later to become the

Willem Bilderdijk (1756-1831), Dutch poet, monarchist, and proponent of religious reform prior to the Afscheiding (Secession) of 1834. Hero of Henry P. Scholte and the Scholte Club members.

founding father of the Dutch-American colony at Pella, Iowa. Anthony Brummelkamp, Gezelle Meerburg, Simon Van Velzen, Louis Vaehler—all held membership in the Scholte Club, all were influenced by *Reveil* leaders, and all ultimately participated in the 1834 secession from William's state church. The youngest member, and the last to graduate from Leiden, was Albertus C. Van Raalte, the father of Holland, Michigan.

Both the *Reveil* and its offshoot, the Scholte Club, campaigned vigorously for reformation in the state church. But after 1830, the campaigns took different directions, and the two streams did not merge again until sixty years later. Above all else, Bilderdijk, da Costa, and Capadose were aristocrats, irrevocably committed to the House of Orange. Though they were galled by the 1816 Synod, they retained the conviction that a pure state church gov-

Tombstones and historical plaque in the Holland, Michigan, Pilgrim Home cemetery, marking the graves of the Rev. A. C. Van Raalte, his wife, and other family members.

erned by a glorious nobility was the best hope for church renewal. They were urban and urbane men who lived and died near the seat of Dutch power, and they prayed daily for the king.

The influence these three men had over their students, however, was limited to the years those students were attending the university. The club itself faded as its membership graduated. The strongest leaders, Scholte and Brummelkamp, moved into rural provinces, where they were ordained into the ministry.

In the country villages the king himself, son of the famed House of Orange, was adored as the hope of orthodoxy. But among the common people at least, the advisors who flocked around the throne—political appointees, cabinet ministers, civil officers, all those who finally make up any government—became the objects of escalating scorn. For too long governmental power had been siphoned out of rural territories and into the cities. A new, appointed nobility was growing disgustingly paunchy while it fed at the public trough in Amsterdam—or at least, so it appeared to countryside critics. Citizens in villages like Ulrum, far removed from urban power centers, held the government bureaucrats in the same regard that residents of the U.S. hold for much of what goes on "inside the beltway" in Washington, D.C., or Canadians hold for what happens in Ottawa. Only the king stood above the daily, withering criticism. Since the Dutch Reformed church had been married to the unpopular government at the 1816 Synod, the church organization suffered every blow aimed at the bureaucracy.

So in 1834, when the Reverend Hendrik de Cock led his Ulrum congregation out of the state church, the Scholte Club veterans were among the first and best prepared to follow. They remained true to the *Reveil* in piety, but only in piety. In politics they moved away from Bilderdijk and his city friends. Though they kept an abiding deference for the king himself—witness the name "Orange City," given to northwest Iowa's first Dutch hamlet by immigrants who were hardly among the Dutch upper class—the Scholte Club's graduates parted ways with their Leiden mentors by supporting and then leading a secession out of William's remodeled state church.

For the better part of two centuries the questions that emerged from the changes at the 1816 Synod have been repeated among one descendent fellowship of the Dutch Reformed churches, one that became the Christian Reformed Church. These often-asked but seldom fully answered questions have come, after a fashion, to define our denomination. The docket from William's 1816 assembly reads like an agenda from any of a dozen of recent CRC synods: What music is appropriate for church worship? What is the limit of the church's authority? How shall we insure the confessional purity of the church, especially among its leadership?

From the 1857 founding to the twenty-first-century future, the history of the CRC has been defined, in part, by questions such as those. From time to time they've been answered, only to emerge again. Perhaps we continue to ask them because they are, like all wonderful questions, not answered simply.

CHAPTER 5

The Mind of Piety

The first time I ever met a real Dutch person I was eighteen years old, selling permit stickers to campers at John Michael Kohler State Park on the western shores of Lake Michigan. I don't remember the man's name, but I remember his accent, his long blonde hair, his thick brogue, and something, at least, of his address—somewhere, the Netherlands.

I was conscious of the fact that I was Dutch-American, my nameplate pinned proudly to my chest. I pointed to it. "My name is Schaap," I said. "I'm Dutch myself, although my family's been here for generations."

He looked up at me strangely.

"There's quite a large group of Dutch people living right around here," I told him, assuming that he'd find that interesting.

But his eyes narrowed. "You're 'de kind who can't ride bikes on Sunday," he said, rolling his r's. "'Ve got rid of all of 'dose."

When he walked away, somewhat arrogantly as I remember, I had no choice but to conclude that he was right. I was one of those.

Piety is faith made flesh. It's the everyday practice of our commitment to God. No one can be a believer without showing that faith in some distinctly visible ways, because deeply felt faith deeply affects human behavior—yours and mine. Piety—the thankful response of the believer to grace itself—is not so much required of the believer as it is perfectly natural. When we come to know God intimately, our response to our Creator, a response that comes genuinely from the soul, is the expression of our faith, our piety. It is our song, our witness, our love, our sense of righteousness.

But when it wears a public face, as it has to, it can be stifling to some and silly to others. Among human beings at least, the perfect is often the enemy of the good. The Dutch national I met that day didn't know we were Christians by our love—rather, he knew we were strange by our Sabbatarianism.

Some historians claim that the coming demise of the Puritan theocracy was evident already in 1630, when the Massachusetts Bay Colony made church attendance mandatory. Undoubtedly such legislation was an attempt to create greater piety among the populace; but when *not* going to church results in a hot afternoon in the stocks, what should be a natural, voluntary, and joyful response to our salvation isn't at all natural or voluntary or joyful. It's forced. Forcing people to be faithful argues, quite convincingly, that they're not.

Exterior of the Zwolle cathedral. Although originally Roman Catholic, all of the cathedrals in the Netherlands became Reformed Church property during the Eighty Years' War.

At some Christian colleges, chapel attendance is mandatory—for good reason. Chapel exercises can bring the believer closer to God, can deepen and strengthen faith. Going regularly can build a commitment to a pattern of devotion and worship. It builds piety.

At other Christian colleges, like the one where I teach, chapel attendance is volun-

The Blessing
by Jean Baptiste
Chardin
(1699-1779).

tary. But there's something messy about voluntary chapel attendance, certainly from a public relations standpoint. While hundreds of kids are in chapel, singing and praying and worshiping God, outside the auditorium hundreds more are milling around doing nothing. It doesn't *look* good. And it's not. I wince when I hear students arrogantly claim to be graduating without once having been to chapel.

But then I've spoken in mandatory chapels where hundreds of students read newspapers, sleep, or munch taco chips in chorus. Mandatory chapels are full of people, but often empty of attention. No one

can *require* piety, because when it is required it's not piety at all.

And yet we try. We make attending chapel mandatory, we "force" our kids to pray at meals, and on some Sunday mornings, if the truth be told, some of us push ourselves to church. Most of us who've been raised in the CRC keep some kind of Sabbath code, even if it bears only faint resemblance to the exotic rules our grandparents lived by.

Piety, saddled as it is with our human and therefore fallen response to God, is a sticky wicket, as they say. If we don't prompt our kids to do the "things of faith," then maybe they'll never do them. On the other hand, when we push people to do something for righteousness' sake—whether it's attending *two* Sunday services, sending their kids to a Christian school, attending Promise Keepers, raising their hands to the Lord when they sing praise to God, or attending chapel—we risk the danger of making righteousness public performance. Faith as show. At that moment, lots of people, some of them Christians, look for the exit signs.

What makes all of us wince is in-your-face righteousness. The Pharisees were the quintessential pietists—they had righteousness down to a science. Jesus Christ called them a generation of vipers with good reason: for them, piety had become a code, a matter of the "right" behavior, a system that was not only inhuman but downright heresy. You don't have to hang around Christians very long before you come to understand that the line between piety and hypocrisy is sometimes paper thin, because piety is most meaningful and virtuous when it is the private response of a single thankful heart and mind.

It is much more hazardous than it is difficult for us to outline the paths of righteousness in human terms. How I live out my faith—how I practice my piety—may be nowhere near your way of living out your faith in the world. What's more, when I enforce my standards of piety on others—whether it's praying before and after every meal or participating in a service project or speaking in tongues—I can create a nest of hooks.

So while piety is essential, it's also dangerous. While it grows bountifully from our commitment to Jesus Christ, it makes a stumbling block the size of a Colorado boulder. "For many Christians piety is like cod-liver oil," says Calvin Seminary Professor John Bolt. "They can swallow small doses of it from time to time, but too much of it makes them gag."

The whole phenomenon is made more difficult by the fact that as human beings we want everyone to share in the sources of our deepest joy. We go white-water rafting, get thrilled to the bone, and want all of our friends to share that same experience. That reaction is even more true of our experiences of faith. We are wonderfully blessed by Marriage Encounter or Cursillo, and we think nobody else's life is really complete unless they receive the very same blessing we did. The path we take to God becomes so precious that we want badly to prescribe that same path for everybody else. It's a perfectly human, and fallible, reaction. And, of course, it quite simply negates God's own plans for each of us as individuals.

So what can be said about piety? It's personal, and it's essential. In fact, we can't help being pious. It's the pattern of behavior by which we live out our faith.

But the practice of piety is a tangle we'll never fully resolve in our own human flesh. It's something we do, something we have to do; but when we do it, it's full of traps. Such is life, post-Eden.

That Dutch national wasn't completely wrong, much as I hate to admit it. The single attribute he used to characterize the Dutch Reformed people who'd left the Netherlands in the nineteenth century was created by their deep and visible sense of piety. Piety has molded the shape of the Christian Reformed Church—and it still does. Piety makes many CRC folks pray before eating a cup of soup in the kitchen or a rack of ribs in a restaurant. Piety created a mealtime regimen of family devotions that eventually wore out the leather covers of many a Bible. Piety brings the family around the piano to sing. A child's piety says, "Now I lay me . . . " On some perfect Sunday mornings, it's the practice of our piety that brings us, somewhat grudgingly, to church, only to say when we leave that it really was good for us to have been there.

The roots of Reformed piety go back at least as far as John Calvin, whose "Golden Booklet" was a treasury of devotions. In the seventeenth century, Gijsbertus Voetius—who we've already spoken of as the foremost Scholastic in the Netherlands—championed piety in the church. Abraham Kuyper, another important character in the story of the CRC, was a voluminous writer of meditations, meditations loved by thousands.

The roots of the CRC are found in Geneva and Dort, but the peculiar shape of its more prominent forms of piety probably emerged from a movement that flowered across the Netherlands in the early 1800s.

CONVENTICLES: HOTHOUSES OF PIETY

Since our first parents' crashing fall and their post-haste exile from God's garden, we have all been dragged into their wake. We're held down by our sin, walled out of God's flowering grace. On our own, our cause is hopeless. We can be brought back to the garden of God's love only if God himself carries us back, the way a parent carries a child to the curb of a busy street. That's precisely what God has done in Christ Jesus. For centuries this story is the gospel's plot: our sin and God's grace; our messing up and Christ's blood cleaning up after; our dropping the ball and God carrying us nonetheless to the goal.

The gospel most familiar to Dutch Reformed congregations in the early 1800s, a gospel heavily influenced by the Enlightenment, took a bit of a different tack. The message was "onward and upward." The University of Groningen trained young preachers in a theology of human potential. Instead of discussing slimy old sin and human filth, instead of remedying our sad state with grace so brilliant as to be blinding, the lesson taught was one of human dignity—I'm okay, you're okay. Think positively. Pull your life together and dream dreams, see visions. You can do it. Human potential.

Such doctrines satisfy and even energize those whose self-image slums around in darkness. Lots of human beings—Christians and non-Christians alike—need to raise their chins. But when such moral lessons teach that getting on top of the blues is a matter only of self-will, a matter of looking into the mirror and seeing something good and nice and lovely, then the gospel of our sin and Christ's redemption is vividly short-circuited.

To Enlightenment minds, Christ wasn't necessarily outside the process; he might even have played a role. Look what Jesus did, after all—he was despised and rejected of men, a man of sorrows. Yet he took upon himself the burden of our sin and achieved a victory that marked him with greatness throughout the centuries. Enlightenment preachers liked to make the point that Christ can be a model. A Savior? Well, after a fashion. But we find real joy when we learn to love ourselves.

By the late 1820s this brand of Christianity, built on confidence in the resilient human spirit, had infected parishes across the Dutch countryside. The old confessions and their piety were absent from seminary curriculums and not to be heard from pulpits. Preachers stirred their congregations with eloquent calls to be decent, to be nice; they used the Bible as a sourcebook for morals, a godly Aesop's fables. Virtue was the end, really, of religion. In form and style, worship was largely unchanged— the same liturgy chugged along as if what it carried didn't differ substantially from the old cargo. What had been dropped along the way, however, was the message of sin and, therefore, the message of grace.

We might note in passing that even America's favorite roly-poly patriot, Benjamin Franklin, a man who stopped going to church when he was but a kid, still held the virtuous life in very high regard. He was, in other words, big into morality. Once, in a fit of moral energy, he drew out a list of the major character flaws people carried—intemperance, anger, laziness, and so on—then tried, unsuccessfully, to rid himself of those in a concentrated attempt to make himself "good." Morality, to this icon of the American Enlightenment, really *was* religion. So what was happening in the Netherlands at that time was not at all isolated from what was happening in other parts of the world.

But in the shadows of those Dutch churches where dominies held forth on the dignity of the human character, lesser folks—people of lower social standing— were gathering in farmhouses for worship of a whole different species. In those homes and barns, Christians recovered the warmth of the gospel, something they felt was missing entirely from their churches. House churches (or *conventicles*, as they are known), furnished with the old doctrines from Heidelberg and Dort, sheltered a piety that was a stranger to what many of

Home of Jan Peters Van Tongeren, used for worship during persecution of the seceders (1834-40). Once located in the hamlet of Van Tongeren, the house has been demolished.

them called the "Groninger preaching" of the Enlightenment.

The conventicle tradition was not new in the Netherlands in the early nineteenth century. For nearly three centuries conventicles had provided places of worship in which Dutch lay preachers flourished and developed. But in the early 1800s the conventicle took on new importance in communities. Where before it had existed alongside the organized church—sponsoring midweek prayer meetings, for example, or Bible studies—now conventicles, especially in the northern areas of the Netherlands, began to usurp the place of the organized church.

By 1830 the worship in most conventicles was fairly well-defined. Psalm singing, Scripture reading, and prayer dominated. In addition, the meetings featured regular readings from the confessions and the "old fathers" (John Calvin was first among the patriarchs). Less sturdy and rather unReformed or unCalvinistic views and practices occasionally crept in, stressing a piety that bor-

Not Worthy

The deep introspection fostered by the conventicles had its darker side. Its effects are still evident in many conservative churches in the Reformed tradition on both sides of the Atlantic.

For members of these churches, the emphasis on not only *knowing* but also *experiencing* our sinfulness and unworthiness before a righteous God raises real doubts that God will actually save them. These Christians often wrestle so much with the conviction of their own sinfulness that it overshadows their assurance that they are redeemed children of God.

This brand of piety can lead to a real hesitation to partake at the Lord's table. In a number of conservative Reformed churches that grew out of the conventicles, Lord's Supper attendance is very low. Even confessing members in these churches are so convinced of their unworthiness to participate that they rarely do. Some have been known to rise to accept the invitation, walk partway down the aisle, then shake their heads, and dejectedly return to the pew. That's how threatened they are by Paul's words that unworthy attendance will result in condemnation. Even on their deathbeds some of them, when asked if they knew they were going to be with Jesus, could only say, "I hope so . . . if he'll have me."   —Ed.

Farm interior used for house worship (conventicle) gatherings as an alternative to mainline patterns of worship in the Netherlands.

dered, in some cases, on an unhealthy fascination with one's own salvation.

The conventicles, part of the CRC's own history, were an interesting phenomenon. Piety they had in spades. Among their favorite works were volumes of devotional literature that were already two hundred years old by the early nineteenth century. What that material offered them was what they weren't getting from their organized church—deeply personal and introspective forays into their souls, adventures in salvation.

The kind of faith that grew from these conventicles is somewhat difficult to describe but quite relevant to our time, with all the hoopla attending our approach to the year 2000. What came to characterize the people in this conventicle tradition was their fascination with devotional literature that went so deep into the nature of spirituality that the literature itself appears to have been more important to them than the Bible. At best, this meditational literature offered self-examination and spiritual renewal; at worst, it locked good human beings into a world so small that all they could make out was the drama of their own salvation, their own personal pilgrimage. What is possible in such intense study of one's own relationship to God—such minute examination of an individual's sin and salvation—is a kind of idolatry all its own, an intense preoccupation with matters particularly and powerfully personal. In a way, believers taken too deeply with the state of their own souls can't see the forest for the trees.

Twenty years ago a movement called "Key 73" grew out of American Evangelicalism. Its focus and purpose was twofold: to bring the gospel to those who didn't know the good news and to revive the church throughout North America.

During 1973 the CRC, as well as the Reformed Church in America and many, many other denominations, established and carried out their own programs to meet the aims of Key 73. In many individual churches, small groups were formed (then a new phenomenon Christians borrowed from group therapy). Members of those groups were given study material, then urged to speak candidly to each other, from the heart, maybe for the first time.

At the time I lived next door to a medical doctor, an Iranian Jew who has lived peacefully for several decades in a town that once was populated almost exclusively by Dutch Americans. He's learned to appreciate members of the CRC, as well as members of other faith communities, even though he doesn't consider himself a Christian. He told me that often small groups, like those encouraged by Key 73, became intensely personal and confessional, sometimes prompting individuals to confess sins long buried in their pasts, sins that might well have involved other members of the congregation. Although he wasn't part of any of the groups, he heard much about them from his patients. That year, he said, he had more business than he'd ever had before—on small group nights people would open up their hearts, examine themselves publicly, and then go home, completely unable to sleep. He claims he never

treated more psychosomatic illnesses than he did in 1973. Tension, fear, guilt—all found expression in phantom aches and pains.

What the story illustrates is the conventicle tradition in its extreme. Knowing the state of our sin is essential to knowing our salvation. But an overly intense examination of ourselves and our hearts can become traumatic. What's more, the process itself can become a drug. When the conventicles moved into that kind of dangerous territory, their intense examinations would become all they ever wanted from faith—they became the very purpose of Christianity. Like Cotton Mather, the American Puritan who in self-loathing for the state of his soul would spend all day on

Evangelism Thrust

Evangelism Thrust was planned and promoted by the Board of Home Missions as the CRC's approach to the broadly-based evangelical program called Key 73. It was developed under the leadership of Rev. Marvin "Mike" Baarman, executive secretary of the board, and Rev. Wesley Smedes, its minister of evangelism.

During the fifties and sixties the CRC did extensive church planting, greatly increasing the number of congregations in the denomination. Evangelism Thrust was designed to increase that number even more by making each congregation an evangelizing unit. The program was field-tested over a wide area in 1972 and carried out in 1973.

While it failed to impart a method of evangelism that could stand the test of time, Evangelism Thrust helped to create a mission mind in the congregations, a mind that has endured through a wide variety of evangelistic strategies. In the decades that followed, mission leadership borrowed methods of evangelism from evangelical circles rather than trying again to create a distinctively Reformed method of evangelism. Campus Crusade's Four Spiritual Laws; James Kennedy's Evangelism Explosion; the Schuller Institute; Bill Hybels' seeker service have all been extensively promoted. —TEH

his face in his study, that intensity offered an escape from life and could become almost an end in itself.

On the other hand, when the examination of the soul was measured, and when it offered the joy of the old gospel's basic rhythm of human corruption and divine redemption, such examination created healthy piety, a strong practice of belief. Children born into conventicle families were nursed on piety drawn from the Heidelberg Catechism, a piety not characterized as "having Jesus in my heart," but "belonging, in life and in death, to my faithful Savior." That piety is founded on the belief that we are his more fully than he is ours. Both the Belgic Confession and the Canons of Dort show an uncompromising divine grace set against the backdrop of human depravity. Shaped by these confessions, conventicle faith—and the piety with which it was expressed—became a call not to ethics but to repentance, not simply to become good productive citizens but to become truly and certainly converted. These too were the people that Dutch man camping in Wisconsin was talking about— my people, those who couldn't ride bicycles on Sunday.

It doesn't take a genius to understand why the Dutch conventicles became centers of discontent after the 1816 Synod, a synod that had deftly set aside the Dort church order and moved authority from local congregations to urban centers. While preachers who'd gone hungry during the revolutionary period appreciated paychecks now guaranteed by William's state church, many pious farmers, shopkeepers, and homemakers got nothing at all from the new arrangement but a sense of real

loss. Power had been vacuumed to the urban centers of the church, and the common people's chances to reform the church were reduced from slim to none.

After 1816, conventicle leaders increasingly valued the Dort church order. It is ironic that groups meeting *outside* the church were concerned about preserving rules by which to live *inside* the church, but the phenomenon also demonstrates that most conventicle leaders expected the church one day to be reformed, making the conventicle unnecessary. For the time being, however, through their allegiance to Dort, the conventicles nourished both opposition to the state church and an affection for a tradition that is more peculiarly Reformed.

Many evangelical traditions have their own sheaf of hymns, and new ones are continually being created. At churches all over North America this Sunday some musician will stand up and strum a guitar or hit a piano and try to teach a congregation something freshly minted from his or her imagination. Today it's impossible to keep up with the explosion of music with a contemporary sound. But the songs that rang from Dutch farmhouse conventicles were neither new nor contemporary; they were the psalms, from beginning to end. Perhaps one of the reasons we have trouble naming the church hymnbook anything but the *Psalter Hymnal* is some ancestral urge to keep music drawn from the biblical poetry that has, for centuries, been the foundation of our worship.

We need to remember too that William's synod had mandated that *De Evangelische Gezangen* ("The Evangelical Hymns") be used in public worship. In response, as Albertus Pieters has recalled, some worshipers simply refused to sing along.

The Battle Over Hymns

Over a century later and half a world away, echoes of this original battle over psalms and hymns still reverberated in surprising places.

In the 1980s, thirty years after the last massive influx of Dutch immigrants into the CRC, the CRCs in Edmonton, Alberta, had become sufficiently Anglicized to retain only one combined Sunday afternoon Dutch service for all twelve of their congregations. One pastor tells of an elderly widower who would invariably sit on the front pew and loudly belt out the psalms. But when a hymn was announced, no matter how biblical and inspiring, he'd look daggers at the pastor, keep his lips tightly sealed, and steadfastly refuse to join in for the duration of the song.

One Sunday, as he was about to shake the pastor's hand on the way out of church, he was tapped on the shoulder by another elderly Dutch immigrant, who asked him why he did not sing along with such animated, inspiring hymn-singing. Turning to meet his questioner, the elderly gent raised his voice loudly enough so that no one could fail to hear: "A solidly Reformed worshiper does *not* sing hymns in church!"

"Well," responded his questioner meekly, "I'm sure glad *I'm* not a solidly Reformed worshiper!"

—Ed.

Historians claimed that sometimes when hymns were announced from the pulpit, the protestors would put on their caps to indicate that they were not joining in the worship for the duration. Some would march out and remain outside until the hymn was finished. Then again, some wouldn't return at all, only to become more fervent psalm-singers in nearby conventicles. (And you think your church has problems!)

One of the advantages of singing the psalms is that they offer the Bible's own piety. There's a distinct confessional difference between David's "As the hart pants for running waters, so longs my soul, O God, for thee," and a TV evangelist singing, "I just want you like mad, Jesus." "My God, my God—why hast thou forsaken me?" is a lament unparalleled by anything in the world of Christian contemporary music. But there is a matter of taste here, and today any judgment about matters like music is largely assumed to be chauvinistic, the judgment of one culture over another. What that means practically, of course, is that to some, a particularly strong contemporary hymn may be as meaningful as Psalm 23, and therefore as fitting for congregational worship.

But the psalms have always been a favorite among Reformed people of all ethnic backgrounds, perhaps in part because of their covenantal character, their emphasis on *us*, God's people—not *me* and my relationship to Jesus. For generations, they've been a better fit in Reformed fellowships than most gospel hymns. But let's not be blind to the truth here: the conventicles treasured the psalms for political purposes as well as for the purity of their piety; singing David's songs clearly separated them from changes in worship and theology all around them—changes that they grew to dislike with an ever-increasing passion. They considered the psalms peculiarly *biblical, covenantal,* and, well, *Dutch.* It's not at all blasphemous to assume that sometimes they sang the psalms with a sneer, missing the point completely.

The wound inflicted most deeply by the 1816 Synod was the change in the Form of Subscription. The vow once intended to preserve unambiguous orthodoxy had been made ambiguous. The change of one word had allowed room for intellectual wiggling and, to many, encouraged a bland, lukewarm faith. When William dismantled the vow of orthodoxy, conventicle leaders concluded that in the Netherlands, as Gordon Spykman later observed, "Reformed Christianity was practically dead." By insisting that the vow written at Dordrecht was the only insurance for trustworthy leadership, the conventicles again stood apart from the state church, showing a piety that was peculiarly *orthodox.*

Conventicles dotted the Dutch landscape in the rural areas by the 1830s, fostering a remarkable and lasting piety, sometimes a dangerous piety that separated its members from life itself. At the same time, the conventicles became increasingly contrary to the state church, hothouses of dissent where the seeds of secession were easily planted and nurtured to maturity. "The decay of the Dutch church provided the occasion, the revival produced the spark," John Kromminga once noted. "But many hearts had been long prepared to respond—to respond negatively to the decay and positively to the revival." (*In the Mirror: An Appraisal of the Christian Reformed Church*, p. 14.)

That response came in 1834, the year of *de Afscheiding,* the separation.

AFSCHEIDING

It was not only in conventicles that the Dutch state church ran into resistance. Even William's court preacher, the Reverend D. Molenaar, fueled the dissent. He had been incensed first when the National Synod celebrated the three-hundredth anniversary of the Reformation (in 1817) but refused to commemorate the Synod of Dort's two-hundredth birthday (1819). Eventually Molenaar published a blast at the state church titled *Address to All My Reformed Fellow Believers.* This 1827 work was, as D. H. Kromminga describes it, practically "a program for the Secession."

But Molenaar was unique among the clergy, and even he published his celebrated *Address* anonymously. Most religious movements are begun by leaders who attract a following, but that was not the case for the *Afscheiding.* Here a widespread movement among the laity was finally discovered by the few clergy who were themselves intellectually curious, occasionally gifted, and consistently revival-minded. The movement was well on its way before the clergy got on board. That phenomenon is neatly illustrated in Herbert Brinks's telling of the story of Jetse Bottinga and the secession movement in the northern Dutch province of Groningen.

> *Jetse Bottinga was a traveling book salesman who wandered from Leeuwarden in Friesland to the towns*

and villages of Groningen and northern Drenthe. Until 1820 he had been a butcher in Leeuwarden, but thereafter his residence changed often, and he became a well-known figure, trudging the narrow roads of the northern province.

The news he was able to bring from neighboring villages made Jetse a welcome visitor in towns such as Ulrum; he also packed an inventory of devotional literature that many pious townspeople read to supplement the liberal preaching they heard from the pulpit. When asked, Jetse himself conducted religious exercises in the living rooms of his clients. Although well known, Jetse was but one of many lay leaders who led devotional exercises outside the regular worship services of the Reformed Church in the Netherlands.

The function of the lay preacher was well established throughout the Netherlands (since it had received official sanction in 1571). Traditionally, the conventicles met for midweek exercises, but during Jetse Bottinga's active years (1820-1850), many of his followers had discontinued regular attendance at their churches because they found the preaching too liberal. Instead, they met in each other's homes on Sunday, where they sang Psalms, prayed, and read Wilhelmus A. Brakel, Jacobus Koelman, and a short version of John Calvin's Institutes.

Thus, in 1829, when Hendrik de Cock became the minister of the Reformed Church in Ulrum, he discovered a pious circle of parishioners, some of whom neglected his services to meet privately with Jetse Bottinga or with other lay leaders in the village. Within a short time de Cock became acquainted with one of Bottinga's followers who, seeking catechetical instruction, visited the parsonage regularly. Expressing a conviction he had gained from the "old authors," this parishioner said, "If I must contribute one sigh to my own salvation, I am eternally lost."

Such expressions of total dependence on God's grace surprised de Cock, for his own training had completely neglected the traditional doctrines of the Reformed Church in the Netherlands, and when his church

Interior of Ulrum Reformed Church— the church served by Hendrik de Cock (1829-1834), the founding father of the 1834 Afscheiding (Secession). The first dramatic events of this religious confrontation occurred in this building.

members introduced him to such confessional statements as the Belgic Confession and Canons of Dort, the young preacher read them for the first time. His instruction at the University of Groningen had emphasized a completely different brand of theology.

Hendrik de Cock
(1801-1842).

Brinks goes on to describe how de Cock's preaching style changed from lectures on an ethical Christianity to urgent messages of human sin and divine grace. Then:

By 1833 the little church in Ulrum became the focus of controversy because de Cock's preaching attracted parishioners from neighboring towns and provinces. They came from the wooded district of Friesland, from Drenthe, and across the German border in East Frisia. On some occasions as many as seventy wagons lined the streets of Ulrum.

As news of this phenomenon spread, several of de Cock's colleagues visited Ulrum to witness the matter, and one of these, after hearing de Cock preach, wrote to warn him of his dangerous behavior. He declared that de Cock had become a rabble-rouser, leading "a tribe of uneducated folk who possessed little more intelligence than the cattle they tended." De Cock replied that he would be glad to compare his "ignorant" congregation with that of his accuser, for "you," he wrote, "have difficulty conducting two services on a Sunday. During the second service

you preach to nearly empty benches. Here the Lord gives the people the desire to fill the church both morning and evening. . . . You conduct catechism two or three times per week with poor attendance. Here catechism is well-attended five and even six times each week."

The crowds massing to hear de Cock's sermons required a larger church building. But when funds had been collected to that purpose, officers of the state church refused to approve building expansion and called the plans "building revolution" instead. De Cock responded by preaching in neighboring pulpits as well as his own, thus going to the audience that had been prohibited by space from coming to him.

Within forty-eight months of de Cock's radical turn, two pastors, L. Meijer Brouwer of Uithuizen and Benthem Reddingius of Assen, published separate tracts with a single theme: de Cock and his preaching are downright dangerous.

Hendrik de Cock was not amused. Neither was he bashful. Brouwer and Reddingius shortly found themselves featured as title characters in de Cock's *Two Wolves in the Sheepfold of Christ.* That booklet cost de Cock a two-year suspension from office, beginning in 1833. At first he was suspended with salary. But when he wrote the preface to a little volume titled *The Evangelical Hymns Tested, Weighed, and Found Wanting,* de Cock's salary was also withdrawn.

In a series of decisions made on October 13 and 14, 1834—after more than a year of wrangling over discipline with the Provincial Board and National Synod—de Cock and his Ulrum consistory decided to break from the state church. A century later Henry Beets distilled the grounds for secession, as given by de Cock and his consistory, into five simple points:

1. A falling away from the pure doctrine of the Reformed Church, as expressed in its own standards.
2. A hierarchical form of church government and arbitrary regulations.
3. The introduction of unsound hymns.
4. A new and dubious-sounding form of subscription.
5. Unfaithfulness of preachers regarding their ordination vows.

Whatever else might be said of these grounds, none would have constituted a new worry in any conventicle discussion. These were complaints discovered by de Cock, not invented or created out of thin air.

Evolving as it did out of the conventicles, the *Afscheiding* was no monumental movement at its beginning. But it was tenacious, and it wasn't about to be thwarted. Those who withdrew from the state church in 1834 were convinced to the bone that theirs was the pure church, the true church; furthermore, they knew in their souls that it was not they but the state church that had seceded from the Reformed faith. They believed, as Henry Vander Werp later explained, that since 1816 "heretics of all descriptions had found a refuge in the state church, and there they found themselves well nigh as safe as the unclean beasts in Noah's ark." That the Ulrum congregation believed it was the faithful remnant and William's state church was the real seceder is clear from the letter that followed de Cock's document of secession.

If recipients are willing, as Christians, as true Protestants, as Re-

Second Service Attendance

There is nothing new under the sun. That's evident when we compare Sunday observance and the lack of attendance at the second service today with the situation at the time of the Protestant Reformation.

Then, as now, churches struggled to maintain a distinct and clear Reformed position. Synodical decisions tried to carefully pick a path between the Scylla of profaning the Sabbath and the Charibdis of Jewish legalism. The second service was not nearly as faithfully attended as various synods wished. In fact, some preachers had to be coerced into conducting a second service at all.

In 1574, the Synod of Dort called on the government to "prohibit selling, buying, drinking, working and walking during divine services." If the local magistrates refused to comply with this reasonable request, an appeal was to be made to the prince (Acts, art. 47). The same synod declared in the following article (48) that the government should excommunicate those who continued these practices.

The Synod of Middelburg (1581) also requested the magistrates to prevent the profaning of the Sabbath, but the Great Synod of Dort (1618-1619) went a step further. It requested that stern billboards ("*strenge plakkaten*") should be erected in public places, strongly forbidding any desecration of the Lord's Day not only by daily work, but especially through activities that kept people from attending the second service: *spelen, zuiperijen en welgerijen* (gaming, boozing, and sensual indulgence). Interestingly enough, this is the first reference we find that specifically mentions a second service.

Whether the second service was poorly attended because it was a Catechism service is a moot point. There were a number of reasons that came into play. We read of *slap pickeyt ende naliaticheyt* (spinelessness and neglect) on the part of both preachers and their potential audience. Preachers were lax in encouraging people to come to the second service, and the people evidently much preferred *spelen, zuiperijen en landarbeid* (gaming, boozing, and working the land).

—Ed.

formed men, to join in the consistory's rejection of all teachings, laws, and ordinances which conflict with God's Word and the Forms of Unity which agree with that Word, then we are immediately ready for reunion. But if this does not come to pass, we shall continue together with our pastor and teacher on the old foundations, God's Word and the Forms of Unity.

When Hendrik de Cock awoke on the morning of October 15, 1834, he was the first and the only pastor in the Seceder Church. That he knew. What he certainly would have never foreseen is that almost one hundred and sixty-plus years later someone like myself in a basement room of a house on the plains of Iowa would be writing about him in a way meant to explain and understand a whole denomination of North American folks who grew as a fellowship out of the break he and his parishioners created. But it did. And here we are—you and I.

It must have been terrifying, in a way, for him to make that decision. Existentialist philosophers like to talk about the terrifying joy of freedom. While finding one's freedom by breaking away from a long-established organization—in this case, a church, ordained by God Almighty—may well seem the only possible remedy to an impossible situation, it must have been arduous to part company with so many people, some of whom undoubtedly were friends and colleagues. Equally difficult was seeing a path into a future without the comforts of traditional time and space. Exhilarating in its daring, passionate in its convictions, promising in its potential, the

Afscheiding, like any church split, had to be accompanied by monumental emotions, emotions that wouldn't fade from the collective memory of a people who'd risked everything to follow their convicted sense of God's truth.

Since 1517, the church of Christ has been regularly divided and redivided. Always there exists among the fellowship a reforming group—not necessarily doctrinal enthusiasts, but people who bear witness to their conviction that the communion of which they are a part needs badly to return to something more pure. In every age there are "puritans." What some theologians call the "visible" church is a tangled and broken assembly—and then some.

From the Reformation on, individuals and groups have left the church or been put out of it, and, once outside, created a church of their own. Today, Lutherans come in a variety of packages, as do Baptists. Calvinists range from those Presbyterians who have little sense of their histories and see doctrinal differences as nothing more than human constructs, to bodies of Reformed believers so closed they barely trust each other. Talk about liturgy among many Roman Catholics today, and in a minute you can pick a fight. When believers are convinced that the church of which they are a part is tainted beyond reform, they walk. To avoid the charge of schism, secessionists must be convinced that what they are leaving is no longer, in fact, the body of Christ. That takes confidence—and sometimes ego. It takes convictions so honed and sharpened they can cut almost anything.

Descendants of the *Afscheiding,* as we are, have a heritage of breaking away. In the thinly populated county where I live, full of Dutch-Americans, many of them children of the *Afscheiding,* there's a little town—no more than three hundred people. In that town is a small Reformed Church (RCA) and, now, a new church, a church that left the CRC. The public school is long gone, a victim of consolidation. But there are still two schools—one of them, the Protestant Reformed school, graduated about a half dozen students; the other, a Christian school, attended by the kids from the newly formed "Alliance" church as well as what remains of the old CR church, graduated just a few more. On the long gravel roads outside of town—and even in the village—there are folks who've worshiped at the Netherlands Reformed Church in a nearby town for years and years and today send their children to the Netherlands Reformed School in a nearby town.

All of those fellowships stand by what we call "The Form of Subscription." All of them baptize children, offer communion, preach the Word (twice!) every Sabbath, and bring their praise to God. Among the members there are few, I'm sure, who don't pray or don't consider themselves children of their heavenly Father. Most North Americans have no way of comprehending the thin differences that separate the people of that tiny town; to any sighted outsider, the men all wear feed caps, attend church faithfully, and generally appear burly and strong. They all look alike, as do their wives—and their kids.

The purifying impulse in all of our fellowships must always be weighed against the destruction such attention to detail creates, not only in families but in overall Christian witness. Our heritage of seces-sion has at least two dangers. The first is that our senses become dulled to the evil of schism, making us insensitive to spasms in Christ's earthly body when men and women rip it apart at will. In the end, such insensitivity justifies not secession but schism, and does so on the thinnest of grounds: "I'm not getting my way, so I'm out of here."

The other danger is that descendants may one day begin to celebrate secessions like birthdays and wedding anniversaries. Secessions must surely be remembered, but not with candles and cakes. Breaks in the body of Christ need to make us remember our brokenness; we need to feel a corporate sense of shame at the condition of the fallen church, and we need to feel it with an urgency that prompts us to seek to restore what has been broken. Families have been broken and scarred for generations by broken churches.

Orthodoxy is a wonderful thing to hold and to cherish. It requires a level of vigilance that many aren't capable of maintaining. But it can be an incredibly destructive weapon when it's taken from the arsenal of our own human sin. Love without truth is silliness, really; but truth without love is murder.

The *Afscheiding* legacy contains a deep piety and a powerful drive for purity, a determination to hold fast to the miraculous truth of the gospel. For its tenacity in pursuit of righteousness, we may well, and should, give thanks. But we should not forget the cost of brokenness. That cost is still being paid.

CHAPTER 6

The Crisis of Youth

What is unique about the *Afscheiding* of 1834 is that the secession was so small and so unplanned. Often, especially in the history of American church secessions, when congregations break from the larger fellowship, they move to a fledgling organization that's diligently planned, if not already in place and running. In other words, they know where they're going.

Contemporary seceders from the CRC can take some measure of pride in being traditional in that regard, for even though the first congregational departure occurred years ago, at the time of this writing there is only the beginning of a sturdy alliance, a collective system. Those we've lost in the past several years departed into something of a vacuum, a place where there was no clear future, just as Hendrik de Cock did when he pulled his Ulrum congregation out of the state church. They knew very well what they'd left behind, but they too had only the foggiest notion of where they were going.

Whether one assesses that phenomenon as convicted bravery or perilous blindness, or whether one simply chalks up such lack of foresight utterly to deep faith in the hand of God, depends, I suppose, on how you read the politics of the event. I have no doubt that some state church folks snickered at the belligerence of a few green and rugged farmers. I wince a little myself. And at least one nineteenth-century CRC spokesman, in a typically old-fashioned manner, cited the absence of planning as proof of divine providence: "This was the Lord's doing; it is marvelous in our eyes."

The Ulrum consistory acted without official documents. Some neighboring congregations promised sympathetic support, but the seceders had no precedents to appeal to, no models of local churches who had survived secession from the state church (and we need to remember that it was a *state* church they were leaving, which, in some ways, ups the odds of their eventual demise). They had what they judged to be "just cause" for secession—that's for sure—and underlying that just cause, of course, the double-fisted confidence that God himself had willed their withdrawal. That's no mean commodity. That same admirable megaconviction created the first successful English colony in the New World.

So it's not difficult to see why a nineteenth-century CRC commentator could so easily describe Ulrum's departure as God's choice in the matter. If church growth theorists today were to chart the explosive

Kampen, home of the
Theological School that
trained many pastors of
the CRC.

expansion of the movement created by the *Afscheiding*, they'd have to conclude that the seceders were doing something right. Chances are, church-growth people would immediately create seminars and how-to documents by the ream. But we're not talking about megachurches here; we're talking about the early nineteenth century and small movements among what Abraham Kuyper used to call the "little people."

Even though significant growth did occur in the Secession Church, the seceders' path was hardly smooth as silk in those early years. The independence of spirit that characterizes those who are fierce enough to break from the church (and sometimes family and friends), an independence bolstered by the unshakable conviction of righteousness, is a character trait that doesn't always make for selfless teamwork. Not all martyrs die for good causes, but whether they depart for good reasons or bad, they share one characteristic: indomitable convictions. They're not pragmatic, not compromisers, not peacemakers. They know where they stand, and they shall not be moved.

First, the government attempted to smother the secessionists under layers of legal and economic sanctions. But instead of dampening their enthusiasm, this persecution only made the seceders stronger and more determined. Then internal bickering started up within the fledgling movement—bickering that emerged when what might seem to us trifling differences were aired, and, more significantly perhaps, when regional leaders jockeyed for control of the movement.

Along came a potato blight, which prompted many a European (including the Dutch) to consider leaving the old country and starting over in North America. Think of it—leaving, lock, stock, and barrel, for America! From the angle of those people committed to staying, watching people emigrate one hundred and fifty years ago was not that much different from watching people die. Old friends were, in both cases, gone. One didn't pick up a cheap fare on KLM to visit Opa and Oma. Departing meant saying goodbye, period. So in the secessionist movement, the upheaval caused by the prospect of emigration was consequential.

All told, the period after secession was, as Henry Beets later called it, "the crisis of youth."

GROWTH OF THE SECESSION

On Tuesday, October 14, 1834, de Cock's consistory notified state church authorities that his congregation was leaving the fellowship.

That came as no surprise. Despite his two-year suspension, de Cock had maintained an intimate relationship with his congregation, and earlier skirmishes with neighboring preachers had made him notorious. Even the king, responding to de Cock's appeal for regal intervention, had taken time to send him a sharp rebuke. That trouble was reaching the boiling point in the Ulrum congregation was no surprise to anyone attuned to what had been going on for some time.

It's likely that de Cock himself was not surprised when several constables were waiting for him at the Ulrum church the following Sunday morning. They stationed themselves at the base of the pulpit, under orders to block de Cock's entrance.

The leaders of the state church intended to make their point visibly: the dominie could end his suspension by secession and claim this motley band of malcontents as "his church" if he so desired, but the space behind the pulpit was going to be clearly marked out as government territory.

De Cock had no interest in trespassing. Flanked by the constables, he turned to the congregation that had assembled that morning, then mounted a pew and proceeded to deliver an enthusiastic sermon on Ephesians 2: "For it is by grace you have been saved, through faith—and this not from yourselves, it is a gift of God—not by works, so that no one can boast." The text was both familiar and a favorite of the conventicles, a gallant call to piety in the secession's first ruggedly public hour of testing.

When de Cock returned that afternoon, the government moved a step further and locked the church building by nailing the doors shut. Undeterred, the preacher marched to the parsonage barn next door, invited his congregation to join the cattle, and offered them what those present remembered as a moving sermon on a not-at-all-unexpected topic: the first and second questions of the Heidelberg Catechism.

But the state church was not about to go down without a fight. Six decades later Henry Vander Werp told the story of the following Sunday.

> *No less than 150 soldiers were present to prevent de Cock from preaching in his church, and after that almost every religious meeting of these and kindred minds was rendered impossible by the higher authorities and the irksome offi-ciousness of the king's servants. On the 31st of October de Cock was sentenced to pay a fine of 120 guilders . . . and [to serve] three months imprisonment for his having preached in a pew! De Cock appealed to a higher court, but on November 28, the first decision was confirmed and de Cock at once imprisoned.*

Frouwe de Cock is credited with influencing her husband to question the liberal teaching of his seminary training.

By the time the jailhouse door slammed shut behind him, de Cock had been joined in secession by the ex-leader of the "Scholte Club." Hendrik Pieter Scholte had left his *Reveil* mentor, Bilderdijk, at Leiden, to become pastor of a state church in Genderen, Noord Brabant in the southern Netherlands. The Friday before de Cock seceded, Scholte had traveled north to preach and administer baptism in the Ulrum congregation. Given their pastor's suspension, the Ulrum church was dependent on visiting preachers for the sacraments; given their pious tradition, they would have their children baptized only by someone they approved of. Scholte met their doctrinal criteria.

What exactly happened on that Friday isn't recorded anywhere, but whatever Scholte said was enough to make local officials take forceful steps to keep him out of the pulpit on the following Sunday. What is known is what Scholte *did* on that Sunday—he chose the highest point on the Ulrum churchyard, turned to those faithful who had assembled, and held forth anyway. This is what Vander Werp records:

He was, on the 29th of October, without any investigation on the part of the government or the church, first temporarily suspended from office with right of salary; eight days later, November 7, he was suspended with loss of salary; and three days after this, November 10, he was removed from the ministry, and his congregation tendered their "Declaration of Secession" to the church and its king.

Scholte too was out. Nonetheless, as the calendar counted down the last days of 1834, the *Afscheiding* could not have been described as a mass movement. Two churches, one north and one south, headed by two suspended preachers and populated by parishioners who were, at most, working class, uneducated folk, were its sum total. But in the two years that followed, the folks who left became a force to be reckoned with. More than two hundred congregations joined the ranks of the secession in the next twenty-four months. Mainly its clerical leadership came from one-time members of the Scholte Club, its lay membership from the conventicles that had long been smoldering in a kind of discontent with the way things operated in the state church.

Practically the entire Scholte Club enlisted for service in the secession. Besides Scholte himself, G. F. Gezelle Meerburg, Louis Vaehler, Anthony Brummelkamp, Simon Van Velzen, and Albertus C. Van Raalte all traded in their *Reveil* loyalty to the king's church for leading roles in the *Afscheiding* revolt.

The stories of three of these secessionist preachers, Brummelkamp, Van Velzen, and Van Raalte, are fascinating. They were brothers-in-law, all having married De Moen sisters, a family long active in conventicle circles. But each of these men came to the movement at separate times and by separate routes.

Original theologians of the Kampen Theological School (left to right): Simon Van Velzen (1809-1896), Anthony Brummelkamp (1811-1888), Helenius de Cock (1824-1894), Tamme F. DeHaan (1791-1868). Between 1857-1880 all the leading pastors of the CRC were trained by these men in either tutorial or classroom settings.

Anthony Brummelkamp was ordained after his graduation from Leiden, but his ordination did not mean he agreed with the state church on the issues brewing around the country. He refused to baptize children of nonprofessing members and wouldn't allow hymns to be sung in his church. When his classical board questioned him concerning his objections to hymns, his answer was judged "insulting to those who had collected the hymns." For that insult, he was deposed. On October 7, 1835, he became a preacher in the secessionist church.

The hymns also brought disharmony to the life of his brother-in-law Simon Van Velzen. When his classical board demanded a pledge of obedience to the requirement that hymns be sung, Van Velzen, in a rather clever play on the state church's revised Form of Subscription, offered the officials obedience "in so far as" or "to the extent that" (in Latin, *quatenus)* the church order conformed to the confessions. His response was not enthusiastically received. On December 9, 1835, Van Velzen was suspended and joined his brother-in-law Brummelkamp in the growing ranks of the *Afscheiding* clergy.

Albertus Van Raalte was not yet a brother-in-law when he applied for ordination in the state church. In a series of official interviews in 1835, he proved he was sound in both mind and character; but he wouldn't pledge fidelity to the 1816 church order and was therefore judged unfit to serve in the king's pulpit. On March 2, 1836, at the first synod convened by the Seceder Church, Van Raalte was approved for ordination. The following week he joined Brummelkamp and Van Velzen by

confession and family, taking Christina Johanna De Moen as his bride.

What the Scholte Club provided for *Afscheiding* leadership, the conventicle tradition provided for *Afscheiding* membership. In many settings the conventicles themselves simply became congregations. When civil authorities used a law to prohibit groups of more than twenty persons from meeting, large conventicles of forty or sixty simply became two or three secession churches of no more than twenty members. These preexisting conventicles had much to do with the phenomenal growth of the secession churches. Because its members were largely drawn from these conventicles, the *Afscheiding* was not so much the beginning of a revival among the Dutch Reformed people as it was the result of fires long smoldering.

DISCRIMINATION AND DIVISIONS

Those very conventicles had, for years, been staging areas for assaults on the "Groninger school" of theology and preaching. The gospel of Groningen had been molded by modern theories of human potential to become an encouraging gospel, a means by which to reassure a more affluent society of their own faith. It was preached by refined clergy with manicured nails, ruffled shirts, and impeccable manners, men who considered boorish behavior the deadliest of mortal sins. Their manner and spirit are quite obviously evident in the title of their favorite magazine, *Truth in Love: A Theological Journal for Cultured Christians.*

That those genteel folks would consider the tougher, less cultured seceders nothing but troublemakers (*rustverstoorders)* is obvious. From the Groninger perspective, the revolt wasn't merely theological, it was also social—maybe even more significantly social than theological. After all, this homey religion of sin and grace preached by a man like de Cock and his raucous farm buddies had broad appeal among classes of people who were, well, less than shining examples of Dutch society in its grand tradition. Many of those louts already felt themselves outside the bounds of good Dutch life, disenfranchised by the 1816 Synod and its church order. As James Bratt observes,

> *Where the secession took hold, there were significant correlations between social status and ecclesiastical direction. The "big farmers," the local aristocracy, the "progressive" and "enlightened" elements of society ridiculed the movement; the hired hands, the poorer farmers, and the small tradesmen (but not the destitute) composed almost its entire membership. . . . official provincial reports for 1836 described seceder membership as having "for the most part . . . from the lowest ranks," "uncultured," "the least significant," "no man of name" among them.*

> —*Dutch Calvinists in North America* (Grand Rapids, MI: Wm. B. Eerdmans, 1984) p. 6.

Just exactly how the government envisioned these people was likely conditioned, in part, by the plague of revolts that had swept out of Europe's lower ranks. Because of that recent history of rebellion and warfare, Dutch political leaders found it difficult to trust any organization composed of people from the lower classes, those not truly "cultured." To our ears, one hundred and fifty years and a continent away, the description of de Cock as "the most dangerous man in society" seems titanically overblown, as does the characterization of Scholte as "a maniac."

But while the *Afscheiding* pastors put their names in history books, history was made just as securely by the common people, who, Bratt says, were "treated with the utmost contempt, as the pariahs of the community." From 1834 to 1840, seceders were subjected to discrimination that was sometimes systematic, sometimes erratic, but always ugly. Local authorities invoked articles 291-294 of the Napoleonic penal code, a leftover law that was handy for police action. As D. H. Kromminga noted, "The fact that those rules forbade unauthorized gatherings of more than twenty persons with a view to prevent political disturbances only" didn't hamper their use of the old law in the least. Quite regularly they carried out all manner of harassment on what were primarily religious gatherings. If more than twenty seceders worshiped at a time, one of them became eligible for fines and imprisonment—and sentences were only rarely suspended. Jobs controlled or influenced by the state were denied to seceders. Their children were denied education. Dutch troops, ostensibly sent into *Afscheiding* territory to "maintain peace and tranquility," were quartered in secessionist homes at the expense of the seceders themselves. In a nation that prided itself upon enlightened religious tolerance, those opposing Enlightenment notions found precious little of it themselves.

In 1840 King William I abdicated and William II mounted the throne, bringing with him a policy of more leniency toward seceders. Even then, however, isolated conventicles and Seceder Church congregations continued to be harassed. But from beginning to end, the persecutions were aimed only at the seceders. Bilderdijk, da Costa, and others in the *Reveil* circle, also longtime critics of the state church, went about their business as usual; they were, after all, guilty of neither secession nor lack of culture. It is difficult, from this distance, to argue convincingly that the persecution carried out against the *Afscheiding* was solely religious. What happened was, in addition, something akin to class warfare.

Even in the face of this kind of persecution, with a powerful enemy looming over its midst and assaulting them regularly, provincial leaders of the secessionist movement found team play with each other almost impossible. In the north, where the secession began, de Cock was the recognized authority. After Simon Van Velzen's wife died, Van Velzen joined de Cock at Ulrum. Together they formed what we might call "the northern party," a union ferociously committed to Dort, both in church order and in theology. To them, what was of highest importance was doctrinal orthodoxy, their chief concern that the church become "a purified replica of the national church" working under "the authority of the denomination's general synod." By definition, the northern party were puritans, committed to purifying the church, showing the state church where it

had gone wrong and what it should have been all along.

Brummelkamp, Meerburg, and Van Raalte were inclined to preach the experi-

---

Who's "In" and Who's "Out"?

Throughout history the church has struggled to distinguish those who belong to the true church from those who belong to the false church. Undoubtedly that important but difficult challenge has spurred the development of creeds and confessions. But where to draw the line?

Clearly, someone who steadfastly denies the earliest confession "Jesus is Lord" can be planted firmly in "the cabal of Satan." But what about those who confess that Jesus is Lord but who deny the doctrine of the Trinity or of predestination—or who refuse to have their children baptized? Where do we place *them*? How about people who continue to attend churches that ordain women to church office?

This difficulty of discerning the true church from the false church continued to plague the secessionist movement as well. Herbert Brinks recounts ("Another Look at 1857: The Birth of the CRC," *Origins*, Vol. IV, No. 1) how in 1839 Van Velzen installed as his copastor for the Province of Friesland a certain R. W. Duin, a preacher who had run into trouble in Germany for his secessionist views. However, Duin soon ran afoul of the movement for a number of reasons. Brinks mentions a key one:

> Duin argued that all churches which preached the doctrine of salvation by grace were true churches, but he alone defended that position; the other pastors and nearly all the officeholders asserted that true churches maintained confessions which were compatible with the three forms of unity. . . .

Today, more than ever, no-creed-but-Christ evangelicals and Christian Reformed believers embrace each other as sisters and brothers in Christ . . . while these same CRC members are squarely assigned a place in the false church by their counterparts in other Reformed denominations, churches that still steadfastly subscribe to the same three forms of unity that their CRC counterparts subscribe to—the very same ones that got Duin into so much hot water.　　　　　　—Ed.

ential side of salvation more than the doctrines of election and reprobation. In matters of church order they tipped toward local authority. They may also have had a more conciliatory approach toward local congregations of the state church. Known as "the Geldersche party," because they ministered in the central province of Gelderland, this trio and its followers sided with the northern party of de Cock when conflict broke out with Scholte, beginning in 1837.

Hendrik Scholte was the prominent voice in the territory to the south. Unquestionably, he was the most independent leader in the movement. While the *Afscheiding* drew its formidable strength from rural territories, Scholte culled his followers from the cities of Amsterdam and Utrecht. In preaching he focused heavily on the imminent return of Christ, a decidedly millenarian approach. In church order, he assigned autonomy to the local church and regarded the general synod as an interesting source of advice, but nothing more. In doctrine, he may have been orthodox, but he definitely promoted, among his followers, the most stringent tests for righteousness. Of all the secessionists, Scholte's expectations for piety among his people were the most strict and the least tolerant.

Less than three years after de Cock's withdrawal, these three parties went to war themselves over doctrine and church order. By the 1840s, when Van Raalte moved his center of operations to Holland, Michigan, and Scholte removed practically his entire following to Pella, Iowa, the triumph of the de Cock party, who had already been winning most of the battles, was assured. But before emigration, mutual suspicion and charges and counter-charges of heresy polluted an ecclesiastical atmosphere shared by groups who, oddly enough, had so much in common and so obvious an enemy. Since leaders in each party also constituted the faculty of their own region's seminary, each faction molded its own brand of preacher

The title page from one of Hendrik de Cock's most notable writings.

VERDEDIGING

VAN DE

WARE GEREFORMEERDE LEER

EN VAN DE

WARE GEREFORMEERDEN,

bestreden en ten toon gesteld

DOOR TWEE ZOOGENAAMDE

GEREFORMEERDE LEERAARS,

OF DE

SCHAAPSKOOI VAN CHRISTUS

aangetast door TWEE WOLVEN en verdedigd

DOOR

H. DE COCK,

GEREFORMEERD LEERAAR TE *ULRUM.*

PHILIPP. 3 : 2. Ziet op de honden, ziet op de kwade arbeiders, ziet op de versnijding.

JOHANNES. Geliefden gelooft niet eenen iegelijken geest, maar beproeft de geesten, of zij uit God zijn : want vele valsche profeten zijn uitgegaan in de wereld.

2 COR. 4 : 3, 4, 5. Indien ook ons Evangelium bedekt is, zoo is het bedekt in de gene die verloren gaan, in dewelke de God dezer eeuwe de zinnen verblind heeft, enz.

TE GRONINGEN, BIJ

J. H. BOLT, 1833.

and shaped those individuals with its own form of theology, thereby perpetuating for generations what might have been a short-lived conflict.

The most sizeable defection from the *Afscheiding* movement occurred with the founding of the *Kruiskerken* ("Churches Under the Cross") by L. Smit in 1840. Smit and his followers lodged various objections, first against the state church, from which they withdrew, but then against the Seceder Church, with whom they temporarily had affiliated. Herbert Brinks has observed that the *Kruiskerken* movement arose from lay leaders who once headed conventicles but were summarily displaced by *Afscheiding* clergy. Undoubtedly the lay leaders having to play second fiddle helps explain their discontent—as well as their eventual departure to the American colonies founded by Scholte and Van Raalte.

CLOSING OLD WOUNDS

Although the sons of the *Reveil* became the fathers of the *Afscheiding*, and although both reform movements were marked by piety and committed to orthodoxy, the icy distrust between the two movements never really thawed. Bilderdijk and his followers were more cultured and more tightly bound to the institutions of their time; they believed that secession from the state church was evil; de Cock and Bilderdijk's Scholte Club students thought leaving the church very much necessary. The leaders of the *Reveil* felt panicked at the prospect of religious rebellion cut loose among the unlettered rural rabble, and to the end maintained that William's state church could be cleaned up and set on a

course towards more orthodox goals. With no less conviction, the finest minds of the secession saw the state church as utterly hopeless, driven to persecution of orthodoxy by heresy that was both endemic and systematic. Not until the *Doleantie*—a third reform movement most closely identified with Abraham Kuyper—arose in the 1880s could those separate but kindred theological movements finally unite.

What did much to ease tensions, however, was the wholesale departure of Scholte, Van Raalte, and their many followers to North America in 1846. Their leaving created a new division—one of geography; but it also served to transplant both the conventicle-secessionist traditions, as well as the territorial rivalries, from Europe's lowlands to the American frontier.

A footnote here. The *Reveil* phenomenon, so significant in the story of the Christian Reformed Church, has its own twentieth-century descendent. Howard Evan Runner grew up in a conservative Pennsylvania town and attended a conservative Presbyterian church. He graduated from Wheaton College, a conservative, evangelical college, in 1936. From 1941 to 1943 he was a member of the Society of Fellows at Harvard University, though he eventually received his doctorate (in philosophy) from the Free University of Amsterdam.

In 1951 Runner was named to the faculty of Calvin College in Grand Rapids, Michigan. There, over three decades of teaching, he earned a reputation as an avowed "Dooyeweerdian," a fan of the Dutch philosopher Herman Dooyeweerd, a man who sought passionately to bring a cohesive philosophical structure to Christian thought. Strangely enough, Runner, a man of conservative American evangelical stock, came to be considered a peculiar Dutch radical because his beliefs were, to the minds of many more traditional students, quite extreme.

Runner was convinced that North American society needed to be thoroughly remade along lines that followed from Dooyeweerd's Christian philosophical system.

Runner was possessed by a consuming urge to reform and created a significant following on the campus at Calvin College. However, he was never able to command much recognition in the denomination as a whole or in the society he wanted so badly to reform. Runner created and maintained his own *Reveil*; the Scholte Club's twentieth-century descendent became a student organization Runner inaugurated during his long teaching career at Calvin.

"He organized the Groen van Prinsterer Society—popularly known as the Groen Club—at Calvin in 1953," recalled Henry Zylstra. "Formally, it was simply a student club. Substantively, it was Runner's instrument for molding students into a new consciousness of

Herman Dooyeweerd (1894-1977), developer with D. H. T. Vollenhoven (1892-1978) of the philosophy of the Law Idea (*Wetsidee*) that was widely influential among post-World War II immigrants. Dooyeweerd's major proponent in the U.S.A., Evan Runner, taught philosophy at Calvin College from 1951 to 1981.

their task in American and Canadian society." In the end, although his efforts had some life-changing effects on certain students, those efforts "did not contribute to a reformation, not even within the limits of the Christian Reformed Church, whose average member does not know who H. Evan Runner is," lamented Zylstra. At Calvin, the Groen Club quietly faded away in 1970.

And if the name H. Evan Runner is not known widely within the Christian Reformed Church today, at least in the U.S., the identity of this "Groen" is an even greater mystery, even if he was undoubtedly a good choice to be patron saint for Runner's student club.

Guillaume Groen van Prinsterer, born in 1801, was a Dutch royal archivist. In 1830, while working in Brussels, he heard a powerful sermon by Jean Henri Merle d'Aubigne, a member of the German evangelistic society at the crossroads of the European revival of the time. Groen van Prinsterer went home a thoroughly changed man. He was soon spending evenings in the company of Bilderdijk. By the 1840s he had become a leading *Reveil* spokesman, and by the time of his death in 1876, he had become an ardent defender of orthodoxy, someone who had profoundly influenced a man who would someday be prime minister, Abraham Kuyper.

Though Groen van Prinsterer never joined the secessionists, his sympathies were with an orthodoxy as pure as theirs. As someone who had himself come to the gospel through an evangelical campaign, his concern was that Scholasticism had frozen Reformed thinking, leaving the confessions brittle and useless. He feared the gulf that was appearing between doctrine as an intellectual pursuit and piety as religious behavior, between the minds and hearts of too many believers.

Groen van Prinsterer wrote and taught a revival theology that was less broken by separate movements, less prone to keep Christian thought (like that defended by the northern party of de Cock) separate from emphasis on piety (like that practiced by the likes of Brummelkamp and Van Raalte). Groen van Prinsterer brought all the energy of sincere and convicted Christian piety outward into society—a different direction than that chosen by

Afscheiding pietists, many of whom were most dynamically driven by an inward and evangelical piety. He captured emotion and feelings into a reform movement that had its source in doctrine but took aim at life and culture.

What's more, he didn't practice his own piety from some safe haven far from the madding crowd. Groen van Prinsterer's piety was busy; it led him to the center of his nation while the storms of war and crises swept in. His was a day-to-day faith; it put callouses on his hands as well as his knees. Van Prinsterer forged a link between the American preacher Van Raalte and the Dutch Prime Minister Kuyper that

The Christian Heritage Party

A Christian political party along the lines called for by Van Prinsterer and Kuyper has been formed in Canada. The Christian Heritage Party was founded in Hamilton, Ontario, in November 1987 and is presently based in Welland, Ontario. It ran sixty-three candidates in the 1988 federal election. In the 1993 and 1997 federal elections, that number dropped to fifty-nine and fifty-three candidates respectively. The party is presently headed by Ron Gray.

While it has hardly taken the country by storm, the CHP has been able to participate in the political process in a way that places Christian biblical principles in the forefront. Its platform is based on biblical ethics, a conservative view of the role of government, family values, and the sanctity of life.

The official name of the CHP comes from its call for Canadians to return to their Christian roots. It makes the arguable assertion that Canada's heritage was decidely Christian in the past, and that somehow the slide into secularism and relativism must be reversed.

While the CHP has made some inroads in the Reformed community in Canada, it has not received the active support of the majority of CRC members. The CHP has not been able to galvanize the CRC community into believing that the positions it has taken on issues like poverty, justice, aboriginal rights, or the economy actually reflect solid biblical thinking. The jury is still out on whether the CHP will present the kind of political witness that CRC members will actually come out to support.

The nonpartisan approach taken by Citizens for Public Justice represents another option that also has a loyal but limited following in the Canadian CRC, as does the Association for Public Justice in the U.S. But neither of these groups has made much headway in gaining widespread CRC support either. While in principle CRC members may have adopted the worldview of Kuyper and Van Prinsterer, in practice they are as apathetic to a specifically Christian witness in the public arena as the average North American.   —Ed.

would otherwise have been missing. As Gordon Spykman put it,

> *Van Raalte could say, and it needed saying, "It will go hard with the man who fails to take refuge in Jesus Christ." But ongoing reformation called for a Kuyper, who, later in the nineteenth century, would open up the meaning of that confession with his proclamation, "There is not a single square inch of the whole universe of which Christ does not say, 'This is mine.'"*

—*Pioneer Preacher: Albertus Christian Van Raalte* (Grand Rapids, MI: Heritage Hall Publications, 1976) pp. 70-71.

G. Groen van Prinsterer (1801-1876), aristocratic proponent of church reform but not a seceder. He organized a Christian political movement that prefigured the successes of Abraham Kuyper.

From Toronto to Sioux Center to San Diego, all across North America, there are pockets of Christian Reformed people who still revere the name of G. Groen van Prinsterer a century after his passing. Where that view is still aired, it often comes packaged with a discussion about politics and Christian witness—about the necessity of creating a Christian political party.

Groen van Prinsterer's most ardent followers are convinced that the reformation of Canadian and American society will come not through the politics or theories of Jerry Falwell or Pat Robertson, the positive thinking of Robert Schuller (himself a grandchild of the *Afscheiding)*, the revivalism of Billy Graham, or the family practice empire of James Dobson. To this slowly dying minority, Groen van Prinsterer's successful marriage of deep piety and directed social action represents the very best efforts both to know God in the soul and carry God's Word dynamically into the world God loved so much he gave his Son to save it. They look for a significantly different positioning of the Christian witness in society and, in particular, politics.

But Groen van Prinsterer, who in his later years was known as "the general without an army," is losing his admirers today as well. Falwell, Schuller, Graham, and Dobson are all household names in both Christian and non-Christian circles. The vast majority of CRC members undoubtedly recognize those names and know something about what they are up to; many give generously to support the efforts of their various ministries. At the same time, Groen van Prinsterer is little more than a fading memory. Today most CRC members would take one look at the seemingly unpronounceable name of Groen van Prinsterer and simply wince, the way people do at the really tough questions.

But we are getting ahead of ourselves. We have, after all, America itself to consider.

CHAPTER 7

The Dream of Immigration

To some—especially the poor and disenfranchised—immigration promises miracles. It offers the promise of starting the whole business of life over again with the prospect of better fortunes—an idea most of us find appealing at some point in our lives. Immigration promises that almost all of life's stains— the stigma of a lesser social class, the curse of hopeless poverty or discrimination, even our old sins and sorry reputations— can be washed away in one radical relocation.

Even today, millions seek that promised miracle by leaving the Midwest, say, for the Sun Belt. Many try to start over, and many succeed. They begin a new life by leaving what's troublesome behind them and starting over somewhere new, somewhere else. But others who try fail to make the fresh new start they were anticipating, and some of those rue the day they ever left.

At a neighborhood picnic several years ago, I watched a fight break out between two seventy-year-old women, both of whom had left the Netherlands for America before the Second World War. One of them, a short, almost cherub-like woman, rife with smiles, told me that her family's immigration to America was the best thing that had ever happened to her.

Poor, often hungry, with no hopes of advancement in the Netherlands, her father had chosen the dream and decided to take the risk of a new, rich land, a new opportunity to make his fortune by the sweat of his brow and the work of his hands. Simply stated, in moving his family to America, he wanted more—and he got it. A half a century later, his daughter, now retired, looked at her own wonderful brick house, her scrapbooks of pictures of a large and happy family of her own, and she pronounced her parents' decision of many years ago very, very good.

But another voice demurred. Another immigrant woman, a woman with thick, dark eyebrows who lived up the block in a small frame house, had a different story. Her husband had died when he was young, leaving her alone with a severely handicapped son. She heard the first woman's joy in the glories of immigration, and she begged to differ in a tone so acrimonious it was almost a sneer. Immigration, she said, was the worst thing that had ever happened to her. If she were back in the Netherlands, she said, her son would be far better cared for, because in the old country people paid attention to exceptional people. In America, she said, everybody's just after their own big, fat piece of the pie. Nobody cares for those who aren't

106

able to pull themselves up by their boot-straps. She would have given anything, she said, never to have come.

The cherub-like woman smiled, went back for more coffee, and found a new conversation somewhere else. The woman who lived in the frame house sat at the same picnic table all night, speaking only to those few who'd wander over to talk.

The two women were immigrants with two different stories.

What Canada and the United States have offered to millions of dreamers through the last few centuries is the same valuable commodity, no matter what their ethnic or racial background. Whether they're Mexican or Costa Rican, Korean or Chinese, Sudanese or Egyptian, newcomers are all looking to find something in Canada or the United States they think they can't get in their countries of origin—opportunity. If they succeed in immigrating to one of these two countries, what almost always characterizes their behavior is hard, hard work.

Dutch immigrants of the late nineteenth century, some of whom had never seen a plow before they left Ellis Island for South Dakota, thought a chunk of American prairie guaranteed a level of economic success they could only dream of in Zeeland or Gelderland. Farming a century ago was nothing like farming today; it required strain and sweat, but nothing of the technological know-how and industrial-sized machinery it does today. Back then farming was, for the most part, menial labor. And menial labor is what immigrants of all sizes and shapes and colors nearly always do. Why? Because those are the jobs that are open to them. More established, more cultured, more refined folks don't want to do menial labor. So immigrants pick up garbage, slaughter cattle, clean motel rooms, run convenience stores in the most dangerous neighborhoods—because even bad jobs here pay tons more than they could have earned "back home." Even today, immigrants follow economic dreams; they're looking for prosperity via a long, hard road of opportunity that still seems to them a rainbow.

My wife tutors a young Hispanic woman named Mimi, one of hundreds of Spanish-speaking immigrants moving into northwest Iowa. By day, she works at a meat-packing plant. Her first job after coming to northwest Iowa was to reach into the skulls of dead hogs and remove the brains, a job she did at a wage considerably less than ten dollars an hour. Today, she's moved up at the plant; even though she can't weigh a hundred pounds and isn't more than five feet tall, she herds hogs with an electric prod. At night, she has a part-time job at a grocery store. She loves her language lessons, but sometimes she just can't make it—she's too busy working. Not all Anglo northwest Iowans are excited about the sizeable influx of Hispanics in the area, but few locals would work as hard as Mimi does at the jobs she willingly takes on. She thinks she's doing well.

In the nineteenth century, the economic dreams of millions of European immigrants were embellished by familiar biblical imagery that made the immigration even more appealing. Hendrik Pieter Scholte was one of those millions, even though he was hardly one of the poor and huddling masses. When he adjusted his wire-rimmed glasses and spread the map

of America across his desktop in the Netherlands, Scholte, like other immigrant leaders, heard God offering his covenant people another land of promise as rich as Canaan, the land once held out before Abraham. Scholte's motives in leaving the Netherlands were not simply economic advancement. He was, after all, hardly a pauper himself. He wanted the promised land.

Scholte, like the other most prominent leader of Dutch immigration in the mid-nineteenth century, Albertus C. Van Raalte, was educated, refined, and cultured. While Scholte's people looked to America for economic opportunities, Scholte saw it as a place to build a new Christian community. From day one, his enterprise had as its objective the establishment of a society of Christians. Not unlike the pilgrims of William Bradford's Plymouth colony more than two hundred years earlier, Scholte's followers had in mind a peaceful Christian community, a "Pella," a place of refuge as well as a center of economic opportunity. They came as optimists; some might even call Scholte and Van Raalte "utopians." They wanted to put persecution and poverty behind them, swap what they had in the old country for an opportunity at something new and glorious—a shot at freedom and prosperity, but even more importantly the chance at a new society of good Christian people.

That I'm sitting here today typing all of this on an expensive personal computer; that I spent many years getting a good education; that this week my wife and I will spend a week at a beautiful cabin in Tennessee owned by an immigrant Hollander who's become prosperous; that I work at an institution of higher education descended in great part from the dreams of those immigrants; that we own great bikes, good cars, and a fine house; that we have money in the bank—all of these things are part of the success story that is so mythically American. Scholte and Van Raalte and their thousands of followers, like millions of their era and others—and like my wife's friend Mimi today—came to North America for opportunity, and they got it. Most of their descendants, economically at least, have good lives, much better than those immigrant great-great grandparents could ever have imagined.

Europe's tired and poor were not at a loss when it came to optimism, but success was never instantaneous. The American frontier was no theme park, and while there were people to help the newly immigrated, "making it" was dependent almost totally on desire, industry, perseverance, good health, and good fortune. Immigration's grandest dreams are never immediately realized. "Having it all" may look like something achievable with a good, sturdy, five-year plan, but success never comes easily—and never did. Mimi spends hours and hours herding hogs. All that glistens isn't gold. In 1847, it didn't take long before the shining optimism of Dutch immigrants recently planted in the deeply wooded Michigan lakeshore and on the wild and fertile Iowa prairie was sorely and pervasively tested.

FLEEING THE WRATH OF GOD

Secession from the state church in the Netherlands was an act of treason. No matter how loudly preachers bellowed at the evils of the "Groninger school," the fact remained that seceders had, by their very separation, cursed the House of Orange. From a loyalist angle, the king had asked for nothing more than obedience, but these rude clods had thumbed their ignorant noses at the throne. What they'd done in breaking away was not only in very poor taste, it was downright illegal.

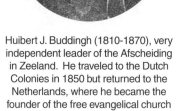

Huibert J. Buddingh (1810-1870), very independent leader of the Afscheiding in Zeeland. He traveled to the Dutch Colonies in 1850 but returned to the Netherlands, where he became the founder of the free evangelical church movement.

Before 1840, seceders were regularly abused, harassed, threatened, fired, jailed, and fined. H. J. Buddingh, a leading secessionist preacher, visited local jails more often than local pulpits. He didn't join the seceders until April 1838. But he soon became the secession record-holder in the "most fines levied" category, amassing penalties of over 40,000 guilders—which is, by present rate of exchange, over a half-million dollars.

Frankly, many early secessionists were ferociously independent souls who had, even before the persecution, earned solid reputations as malcontents. That characterization neither detracts from the quality of their piety nor justifies the discrimination they suffered, but it does encourage speculation that in the end persecution created an effect entirely opposite from what it intended. Instead of breaking their resolve, it strengthened it, and thereby insured longevity for the secessionist movement. The discrimination and persecution the secessionists suffered created a powerful motivation for solidarity among a clan of otherwise rugged individualists. They found some unity in being outcasts. Their already stout faith was only strengthened by the behavior of those who led them off to jail and told them they were faithless. They saw themselves as martyrs like the early Christians. In a world hostile to their beliefs, they became, eventually, immigrants—children of the Lord on a pilgrim's journey to a new land.

Were the seceders the only residents of the Netherlands faithful to God's Word? Of course not. Entirely faithful people stayed in the state church—real believers, strong Christians. But the tyrannical persecution the dissenters suffered helped them believe with great certainty that they were undoubtedly God's people.

That seceders suffered both political and religious persecution is a fact that cannot be denied. But politics and religion were only two factors in the decision to immigrate. Mainly of working class and farming families, the seceders were hurt badly by a soggy and depressed Dutch economy in the 1840s, a period when wages nose-dived and taxes rose painfully. The percentage of the population needing public aid rose from 13 percent in 1840 to 27 percent a decade later. Poverty roamed the countryside, malnutrition was everywhere, and there seemed to be little public charity could do to alleviate the attendant grief and sadness.

Although farm families had food to eat and something left over to sell at the beginning of those hard times, in 1842 Russian food supplies flooded Dutch markets, driving down prices for home-grown produce and sending farmhands into unemployment lines and tenant farmers into bankruptcy. Times got worse.

Then, in 1845, a potato blight scorched farmland like a roaring prairie fire throughout most of Europe. The resulting loss of income made distressed and despairing agriculture workers all across Europe see leaving the old country once and for all as the only legitimate alternative to a future that seemed to offer only years and years of more suffering. Thousands of Irish left for America.

Technically, the blight was nothing but *phytophthora infestans*, a lowly little fungus routinely treated today. But in 1845 Dutch farmers knew neither the name of the horror nor its cure. As they stood at the edges of their fields watching lush, green plants wither and blacken, all they knew was that it destroyed their livelihood. By September of that year the government reported that of 79,477 planted *bunders* (a *bunder* is an area of about two-and-a-half acres), 65,516 had shriveled up and died.

The effect was devastating. During the previous economic collapse, diets had changed as the nutritious potato had replaced beef and pork and even wheat-based breads. The potato, after all, was cheaper. But the devastating blight ended the reign of the potato; the adopted staple disappeared. As the winter of 1845 set in, philanthropist Otto G. Heldring visited rural provinces and reported that what he witnessed was nothing less than famine. The whole economic structure was in ruins. No one was working. The poor were surviving—barely—on cauliflower or turnips. But many—whole families—were without food altogether. He reported that "as many as 400 beggars came to his door during the three days preceding Christmas," and then he offered this striking example of poverty: "One father, head of a family of nine . . . earned no more than sixteen Dutch cents a day."

The next year offered little relief for weary bodies and spirits, only a pathetic replay of 1845. The deep and personal piety of the conventicles had always maintained that God's hand was somehow evident in the affairs of our lives—ruling, guiding, blessing, and cursing. People knew that God's hand was there; God had to have something to do with the suffering all around them. To many, the blight, the depression, the hated foreign goods lining market shelves, and the incredibly severe winters were abundant evidence that God had withdrawn his blessing from a nation many had been reared to look upon as God's country—the Netherlands. The nation no longer belonged to the Lord.

The House of Orange had become a house of ill-repute, its occupants no longer defenders of the truth but prostitutes to the Enlightenment. To the seceders, it seemed remarkably evident that they alone were the remnant orthodox—a fact made certain by their persecution. Infidels were waging war upon them with the very blessing of the crown, infidels who, years ago, had been godly people.

The handwriting was on the wall. Glory had departed from the homeland.

Divine justice was descending on the nation in vengeance for the entire catalog of its sins.

Many hungry Dutch farmers stood on the banks of canals watching German immigrants pass by on their journey to a land of milk and honey. Each passing month new letters arrived from a few Dutch settlers who'd cashed in everything for the opportunity to emigrate to America. The Groningen relatives of Klaas Janszoon Beukma, for example, watched their potatoes rot at the very same time they were being fed a steady diet of letters from his Lafayette, Indiana, homestead. Beukma praised his prolific farm and the strong market prices for his crops. He told his starving relatives that he owned "two horses and two colts, two milch cows with calves, and seven hogs." In one letter, he trumpeted his joy: "Here I have found what I was looking for—bread and freedom, now I have no worry about the future of my children."

Dockside in Rotterdam.

Imagine reading those words in the turmoil of persecution and the throes of economic devastation. Imagine reading that optimism in the face of your own despair. Imagine looking down at rotting crops, ill health, starving kids, and a bleak future. Imagine hearing your own relative sing so gloriously, while what you see and hear all around you is political and religious heresy as the reigning dogma. Just imagine reading Beukma's joyous American epistle and *not* wanting to forsake the horror for something that sounded like paradise. Immigration seemed an answer to prayer.

SCHOLTE STAKES OUT IOWA

Mrs. Semira A. Phillips stood on her front porch and watched Hendrik Pieter Scholte's immigrant flock traipse past her Oskaloosa, Iowa, home. It was the week of August 15, 1847. Heat, cold, wind, storms—weather comes in spades on the Great Plains, and powerful rainstorms had drenched the prairie on Monday. Today, the storm clouds were nowhere in sight. Today the sun was baking the heavy prairie grasses dry.

Mrs. Phillips claims that few of her friends had even seen a Hollander before that great trek of folks went west past her home.

> When they came along the road in various kinds of wagons drawn by various kinds of teams, we gazed in wonder at their quaint and unfamiliar appearance. Their dress was strange to us. Women were perched upon high piles of queer-looking chests and boxes and trunks, many of them wearing caps, but no bonnets. Some of the men, and women, too, wore wooden shoes, which was entirely new to us. . . . Some stabled their teams with us, some camped out in the lane or barnyard. But whether they had their meals in the house or by a campfire, or simply took a lunch in their hands and sat on the wagon tongue to eat it, not one of them failed to bow their heads and give thanks.

> —*Netherlanders in America* (Grand Rapids, MI: Wm. B. Eerdmans, Co., 1955, 1989) p. 176.

Scholte's hundreds were on their way to establish Pella, their dream "city of refuge," named for a place early Christians fled to to avoid persecution in Jerusalem.

Hendrik P. Scholte himself must have seemed a curious pioneer, no match for Daniel Boone, Davy Crockett, or any of a dozen other American buckskinned heroes. Scholte was a preacher, highly educated, cultured, and sophisticated. He once had dreams of becoming an artist with brush and canvas, even studied art for some time as a young man. He'd been raised in the home of a middle-class Amsterdam businessman who had died when Hendrik was a boy. When his mother and brother both died several years later, leaving the family business without leadership, Hendrik gave up his art studies to return home and take up the enterprise.

In 1827, however, after only two years at the helm, Scholte sold the factory he'd been running and enrolled in the University of

H. P. Scholte (1805-1868).

Leiden. By 1829 he'd changed his course of study from art to theology, and soon he'd become both leader and namesake of the "Scholte Club," a group of students who spent their days studying on campus and their nights in Bilderdijk's nearby apartment, the place that became the headquarters of the *Reveil*.

After graduating and then contributing to the Ulrum secession in the north and leading his own in the south, Scholte's career in the Seceder Church tailed off. His commitment to congregational autonomy and his marked lack of enthusiasm for Dort's church order and confession put him on a collision course with the northern party of de Cock and Van Velzen. By 1840 already, the collision had occurred; de Cock's vision of things had won the day, and Scholte was summarily dismissed from the Seceder Church.

Even though the animosity that prompted his ouster was so intense that it afterward carried across the ocean to Dutch immigrant communities in America, the immediate consequence of his eviction from the group was quite negligible. Although a majority of people in congregations throughout his region sided with him (in some cases, splitting churches), Scholte continued his pastoral duties as he'd begun them.

In 1832, the year he'd left Leiden, Scholte had married Sara Maria Brandt, but she died twelve years later, leaving him with their three young daughters. Sometime later Scholte married Mareah Krantz, a

Mareah Scholte (1821-1892), at seventy years of age.

vivacious twenty-four-year-old, a gifted painter herself, a talented musician, and a spritely conversationalist who could charm parsonage guests in several languages (including English). Even late in life she was described as beautiful and "fun loving." She was, by temperament and experience, perhaps, accustomed to having her way; some might call her spoiled. As Henry Lucas suggests, she certainly was "not the stuff from which successful Iowa pioneers were made." By some accounts, when her husband announced his intent to emigrate to America, she sputtered profusely. Once settled on the rich but featureless Iowa prairies, she took to calling herself "a stranger in a strange land." But if she brought to America a self-indulgent tendency to pout, Mareah also won great sympathy, for her life was by no means easy: she buried seven of her nine children before they reached adulthood.

Initially Scholte had opposed the idea of emigration with strong theological arguments. God had placed people in the nations where he meant them to be, he reasoned. Only when God's people were absolutely prevented from obeying the Lord—when they were kept from making a livelihood, raising their families faithfully, and engaging in worship—could they truly justify leaving the homes where the Lord God had placed them. But as secessionist woes mounted and glorious descriptions of America became commonplace, Scholte was elected president of the "Netherlands Association for Emigration to the United States of America," which he had helped to found.

When several seceder families in Scholte's region announced plans to emigrate together, Scholte commissioned their leader, Hendrik Barendregt, to serve as *voortrekker* ("scout") for a larger party to be led by Scholte himself. Barendregt's group of eight families and five single men arrived in New Orleans on November 19, 1846; one month later Barendregt sent a glowing report from St. Louis. Tell "brother H." in Rotterdam, he wrote to Scholte, "that as a baker in St. Louis he can more readily live as a gentleman than as a burgher in Rotterdam."

In mid-1846 Scholte began his own preparations for emigration. He sold his house and the church building for five thousand guilders—enough to pay passage for the poorer members of his congregation. Though he'd once hoped to leave in October of that year—a plan that fell apart when Mareah fell ill after the death of her first child, a three-day-old son—the additional months he was forced to stay in the Netherlands gave him time for meticulous planning. By the time he was ready to go, four three-masted ships were chartered to carry nearly nine hundred of Scholte's followers to America.

On April 2, 1847, the *Catherine Jackson* departed Rotterdam for the New World. Ten weeks later it arrived in the Baltimore, Maryland, harbor, followed soon by the *Nagasaki,* the *Maasstroom,* and the *Pieter Floris.* Always the aristocrat, Scholte booked passage for his own family (including Mareah's sister Hubertina) on a steamship, the *Sarah Sands,* thus reducing

six weeks on the high seas to a thirteen-day ride in a comfortable cabin.

After docking in Boston and committing his family to the tender mercies of a "Mr. Norton, in Connecticut," Scholte began his search for land. He went first to Albany, New York, to meet with Rev. Isaac Wyckoff, a Dutch Reformed preacher who had befriended Van Raalte a few months earlier. From Wyckoff, Scholte gleaned firsthand information on Van Raalte's Michigan colony. Even before leaving the

---

A Report from Barendregt

The passage was certainly full of novelty and excitement; I had never imagined that such a huge ship could be tossed about by the waves in such a frightening manner. Many times I could not walk so much as four or five feet without using two hands to prevent myself from falling. This has strengthened me remarkably. Of the whole 180 passengers probably but 10 were not seasick, and I was fortunate enough to be among them. On one occasion a huge wave crashed through the hatch; I was soaking wet and my wife, who was already in bed, was thoroughly drenched. Although I held up well throughout the trip, at that moment I thought we would be drowned. But the Lord does all things for our good. We didn't experience anything of special note: eight women gave birth during the voyage without help from a doctor or nurse. Of these newborn, two died along with two other children and an old woman. Thus five died. When we came to New Orleans, we sailed up the Mississippi by steamboat the St. Louis.

Imagine, the distance between New Orleans and St. Louis is 500 miles, a trip which took nine days, all the while traveling amid the forest. At this point the river is about as wide as the kil in your neighborhood. They cannot use sailing ships here because the current is always strong, and they can't pull the ships with ropes and horses because the banks are covered with trees. . . .

—*Write Back Soon: Letters from Immigrants in America* by Herbert J. Brinks (Grand Rapids, MI: CRC Publications, 1986).

Netherlands, Scholte had been leaning toward "the western frontier," especially Iowa, where he assumed the lowland topography and good soils would look rich and familiar and manageable to his people.

But on January 30, Van Raalte had written his brother-in-law Anthony Brummelkamp to say that Scholte should give up on Iowa and take up residence with his group in western Michigan.

Scholte was not impressed. He claimed that the native American tribes in western Michigan were too untrustworthy, that the place was too far north geographically, and that its lack of roads and bridges made it inaccessible. The Iowa land, he thought, wouldn't have to be painstakingly deforested like the Michigan lakeshore country. He was convinced that his followers wanted "meadows, cattle, and farm lands as soon as possible, and that they would not relish taking up the axe in place of the spade and becoming dealers of wood."

Hendrik Barendregt, an immigrant, reported, "I had never imagined that such a huge ship could be tossed about in the waves in such a frightening manner."

So instead of turning his attention toward western Michigan, Scholte visited officials in Washington, D.C., from whom he secured maps of available government lands, and then contracted for transportation to St. Louis. From May 22 (when the *Catherine Jackson* made port) to June 12 (when the *Pieter Floris* finally arrived), he stayed in Baltimore, greeting each load of immigrants and dispatching them by way of trains, canal barges, and Mississippi steamboats to St. Louis. On July 6 he joined them there. After finding housing for his family and others, he took four men with him upriver to Keokuk, Iowa, and from there fifty-five miles northwest to Fairfield, home of the United States land office for the Iowa territory.

In Fairfield, the Reverend Moses J. Post, a Baptist missionary who'd canvassed the whole Iowa prairie, urged Scholte to consider Marion County, a fertile stretch of earth between the Skunk and Des Moines rivers. There, if he could convince settlers already holding claims to sell their properties, Scholte could plot his own "city of refuge." With Post as their guide, Scholte's party headed west until they stood on "the rise of land which in a few weeks was to be named Pella." Less than a week later, Scholte had negotiated the purchase of everything in sight, eighteen thousand acres of land, including cabins, crops, and cattle. Settlers from whom deeds were purchased were given one month to vacate, and word went back to St. Louis: "We have land."

FROM "STRAWTOWN" TO "GARDEN CITY"

It was autumn before all of Scholte's immigrants arrived in Pella. The evening

A view of Pella in 1848 and (below) what the city looks like today.

Iowa air was already carrying the chill of early winter, so Scholte had a log cabin built for his family. Mareah detested the place and wondered aloud about whether the "great white house" her husband had promised her in the new land was just so much fiction. Other families lacked even a cabin's luxury. They carved square holes in the earth, building walls of sod and roofing their dirty huts with a layer of sticks covered by a mat of prairie grass. From a distance these dugout homes looked like a village of straw huts, giving Pella its first nickname: *Strooijen Stad* or simply *Stroostad*, "Strawtown."

Henry Beets reports that Scholte's colony was battered, especially by bad weather, during its first two years. A substantial number of Pella's first settlers also ran out of funds by summer, 1849. But two factors came to the village's rescue. The California gold rush in 1849 filled Iowa highways with "gold fever," creating tons of dreamers willing to pay high prices, in cash, for the Hollanders' produce. In addition, two hundred and fifty newly arrived immigrants, who moved into town during July 1849, brought an infusion of hope and resources.

Jan Berkhout, one of the 1849 immigrants, published a pamphlet detailing his wretched journey to Pella and his disillusionment with what he found there, putting a damper, for a time, on immigration; only two dozen showed up in the next three years. But in 1854 nearly six hundred new citizens arrived from the Netherlands, helping fill out a spacious village of large lots. Those handsome lots, when festooned with colorful gardens created by the Dutch love for flowers, changed the way most everyone looked at the settlement. What neighboring Americans had once derided as "Strawtown" became "Garden City."

But things didn't work out so smoothly for the settlement's leader. Because of his determined leadership and the vigor with which he pursued it,

Scholte paid a price in personal reputation. He was accused of both mistakes and mismanagement, charges made easier because Scholte had purchased all eighteen thousand original acres in his own name and kept no adequate records thereafter. Henry Lucas is probably right in saying that the fires of criticism were fanned by "Scholte's multifarious commercial dealings." His wide-ranging commercial interests, in one sense, perhaps, a requirement for anyone playing leader of the colony, were undoubtedly dangerous to a man whose basic vocation was a preacher of the Word.

But by the time he and his hundreds were safely rooted in Iowa soil, Scholte was far more than preacher to the many who'd followed his dream. He was the land agent, of course, the main real estate broker in town. But he was the banker too, and an agent for the New York Life Insurance Company. In his spare time he was the publisher of the *Pella Gazette*, a notary public (the only one), and an attorney. In fact, despite his ministerial calling, he once served as counsel in a divorce case.

Scholte maintained a regal carriage around town and always had a strong and dominating personality. Perhaps, in those early days, he was guilty of nothing more than attempting to insure the viability of the all-encompassing vision he had for his community—he wanted nothing less than to make a financially and culturally secure settlement on a fairly nondescript chunk of prairie ground. But there's good reason to believe that all the trouble that followed Scholte wasn't simply the result of petty jealousies and whining troublemakers. Had they known him, Scholte's own Iowa descendants today would likely scratch their heads and chortle a bit, then say, "That Scholte—he was a character, all right," because he certainly was.

Although he maintained contact with Van Raalte's Michigan colony, Scholte never joined either what is today the Reformed Church in America or the Christian Reformed Church. Having skirmished with secessionist leaders in the Netherlands over his own separatist notions, he avoided all the old-country clashes immigrants lugged along to America, and picked up instead other crusades and political allies in the New World. So Scholte, who was among the foremost

Letter from G. H. Meyer (Pella)

I am pleased that you have asked me to report concerning our colony because some people look down upon it. But they entirely misrepresent Pella. Some people who moved back to St. Louis have made themselves unworthy of Pella, and now, to justify having left, they do nothing but belittle and slander our beloved servant of Jesus Christ, Rev. H. P. Scholte.

Now, friend, I will respond to your question. Carpenters have a lot of work here, and they earn a dollar per day. Brickmasons earn that same wage, but they have less work as there are not many bricks here yet. There is not much work for painters because we have as yet too few nice houses. Work is beginning to improve for tailors, and it is also good for shoemakers. Laborers earn fifty cents per day working from 7 a.m. to 6 p.m.—and work of all sorts is becoming more available. At first there was not much work here, and even farmers had too little. One reason for that is that there is less wood to be cut here than in other colonies. But even though the prairies and farmlands are without forest, the countryside is beautiful. The roads are good enough for transportation, but we have not yet harvested a crop to use them.

—*Write Back Soon: Letters from Immigrants in America* by Herbert J. Brinks (Grand Rapids, MI: CRC Publications, 1986).

This sod house is typical of the original dwellings occupied by settlers in South and North Dakota.

of the seceders, is our ancestor only in that his old-world ties commingle with our own—the CRCNA is descended directly from the seceders.

There are those among us today who would say that not only was Scholte a visionary when it came to establishing a colony in the New World, he was also visionary when it came to ecclesiastical affairs. Despite his old-world history and his secessionist credentials, once Scholte came to America, he became almost quintessentially American, not only as an entrepreneur and political leader among American political parties, but even in matters of doctrine and belief.

For the most part, Scholte jettisoned the word *Reformed* from his vocabulary, wanting no part of it—theologically or culturally. As William Kennedy has pointed out, Scholte's own confessional stance anticipated what we might call the very core of contemporary American evangelicalism. He was, for instance, a premillennialist, asserting that Christ would come a second time before the thousand years of his millennial rule, a position that made him pessimistic about the nature of the times he was in. He believed deeply and argued passionately for the American concept of separation of church and state. He disliked denominations and would likely have been happy repeating an often-heard quip of some Christians today—"No creed but Christ." He remained deeply pietistic, deeply concerned about his own individual spirituality. What's more, he maintained that every Christian required some notable spiritual experience in order to consider him or herself part of the body of Christ. Sound familiar?

In all things, Scholte wanted his people to be Americans, to follow his path (he is reputed to have published the first anti-slavery book west of the Mississippi not that long after coming to America). He wanted the residents of his city of refuge to move smoothly into the new culture rather than remain cloistered within the fortress walls of ethnic and religious seclusion.

These theological and cultural positions hardly served to endear him to those who had followed him to America or those who continued to emigrate. In the mid-1850s the individual churches of Pella were severely divided into five factions, each of which had their own view of their visionary leader.

In September of 1856, Van Raalte himself was called to Pella to advise the faithful amid doctrinal rancor that had grown increasingly difficult. His visit resulted in the organization of the Protestant Reformed Church of Pella, a congregation known today as the First Reformed Church.

But difficulties continued in the Pella area, even though those who once had disagreed had been so duly joined together. Not altogether uncharacteristically, the brothers and sisters of the new fellowship were not of one mind. The issues so divisive in Michigan—and in the Netherlands—had a similar effect on the Iowa prairie.

In April of 1865, some members of the church that had split from Scholte addressed a letter to the Grand Rapids Classis of what was then known as the

After several modifications, the original H. P. Scholte house still stands in Pella, Iowa, and is open to the public as a museum.

True Dutch Reformed Church. The request was simple: send someone to preach for members of a group who, not unlike those dissenters in Michigan, were not dissatisfied in the newly established Reformed Church.

On August 2, 1866, the Rev. D. J. Van der Werp, sent from Michigan, met with a group of men who would become the charter members of First Christian Reformed Church, Pella. A document was drawn up and signed by forty-two people, then sent to the consistory of First Reformed. Freely translated in an early historical booklet of First Pella CRC, the document reads as follows:

> *We, the undersigned, hereby declare that we withdraw from the ecclesiastical fellowship of the Dutch Reformed Church and choose from now on not to be members of that denomination any longer.*
>
> *We have returned in doctrine, discipline, and worship to the stand of the Reformed Church in the Netherlands and have affiliated ourselves with the True Dutch Reformed Church or* De Ware Hollandsche Gereformeerde Kerk.
>
> *Pella, August 2, 1866*

Thus, First Christian Reformed Church of Pella wrestled its way into the world.

So Scholte lost his leadership position in the church he had successfully guided through immigration. Only seven years after his arrival on the prairie, he was suspended from his own church for what some considered shadowy business dealings. In his final years, he became even more convinced of his premillennialist views and his strong opposition to the institutional church. To say he never admired the CRC would be an understatement. In 1868, in his own magazine Scholte had this to say of the new denomination:

> *We cannot conclude any different than that denomination which deceives itself and others with the title* ware gereformeerde kerk *is the wickedest district in the contemporary Babylon, with its choking atmosphere destroying the spiritual life and hindering spiritual maturity in grace . . . a lantern without light and a temple without God.*

Hendrik P. Scholte died in that very year, 1868, a sad and almost tragic figure, estranged from the colony he had worked tirelessly to establish, a member of a denomination no larger than his own parish, a place in which he had only occasionally delivered sermons.

In Search of the Dream

During the 1830s and '40s harbors from Boston to Savannah were stuffed with boatloads of European immigrants sailing into "the American dream." They poured off gangplanks, many of them carrying visions of glorious bounty for themselves and their children. The nation's population doubled, and much of the increase could be seen in the territory where Scholte went hunting for land: the population of the Mississippi Valley rose from four to ten million in those years, but only a small number of them were Dutch.

Aside from a few notable leaders like Scholte, the Dutch Reformed immigrants to the United States in the mid-nineteenth century were those who had the least to lose by immigrating—and most to gain by starting over in the new country. Many in the Netherlands were more than happy to see them go. After all, what did these rude swains really contribute to Dutch society? There were no cultural or political leaders among them, no artists, no great theologians, no CEOs of major corporations. If there were any immigrants at all from urban areas like Amsterdam, they were, at best, day-laborers. Most who left the Netherlands were, to the Dutch who stayed behind, boors, farmhands, an assorted crew of local yokels. To more urbane Hollanders, they were little more than trash. Their chance to affect the course of American culture notably seemed slim at best.

Out of hundreds of thousands of immigrants marching westward, cutting a trail into the frontier with a dozen languages, the sum total of Dutch immigrants in 1846 was 979. In 1847, the year Scholte's party arrived, a grand total of 2,631 Hollanders entered America. In most areas of the new country, their number was so small that they were simply mistaken for and then generally mixed with German immigrants.

One tragic story must be retold. In November 1847, over two hundred Dutch immigrants were within sight of their North American destination, Sheboygan, Wisconsin, aboard their passenger ship, *Phoenix*. In the middle of the night before their arrival something happened—to this day exactly what is unknown—to ignite the ship. Soon enough, the whole vessel was engulfed in flames. It was late November, and the water of Lake Michigan was icy. In a matter of minutes any human being would die of hypothermia in its cold clutches. That night on the *Phoenix* a number estimated at two hundred died; very few survived.

Strangely enough, this tragedy, the greatest loss of life on the Great Lakes in the nineteenth century, is barely remembered today. Why not? Perhaps because Dutch immigrants were barely noticeable in the swarming masses of Europeans who came to this country at that very time. But there may be another reason so few know of or remember this tragedy, a reason that is, in itself, instructive today. The fact is, no one will ever know exactly how many Dutch folks died on that ship that night in November 1847; and the reason is, at least in part, that few Americans really cared. These people were, after all, immigrants—not really Americans. They talked "funny"; they had strange ways. Their values seemed odd and eccentric. They weren't like real Americans. They were only immigrants.

To be an immigrant is to be a minority in a world that belongs to someone else. It is ironic that roots in the old world become more, not less, important for many who immigrate. But then, it's easy to lose a sense of identity in a majority culture so dominating that it wipes out your very language. When there is nothing familiar around us—when buying a loaf of bread is a harrowing experience—then the smell of your own kitchen or the memory of your backyard in the old country is itself a refuge. In a strange land, we base our identity most easily on what we remember from a place we once called home. We already know we are not Catholic, but we begin to understand that we aren't

Norwegian either—not interested in Vikings or *lutefisk*. We're more serious about what we don't do on Sunday than the rest of the Americans around us, so we continue to invest in Sabbatarianism, not only because it's something our confession mandates, but also because it gives us a sense of who we are and what we are about in the middle of a culture that's sometimes downright scary. We hold fast to remnant pieces of the past—the way we eat potatoes, what it is we sing on Sunday, a certain kind of ritual at weddings.

Even though Mareah Scholte called herself "a stranger in a strange land," and it was Hendrik Scholte who vehemently preached the necessity of divorce from an ethnic culture his own disciples had trouble leaving behind, it was the father of Pella, Iowa, who penned the words now neatly typed and posted in a china cabinet that lines the west wall of the living room in his Pella home. Almost one hundred years after his death, one can still feel immigrant lonesomeness in his words, the need to touch something that brings back childhood memories, to hear midnight announced in the darkness by the same tolling clock that marked the house in another place and time:

> Now, all of us have treasures of one sort or another for which we have a weakness, so to speak. Being here, and having brought these things with us, we will feel less strange in these new surroundings; and in the meantime it gives us a chance to get used to the new manners and customs more easily if we are surrounded by the old familiar things we hold dear.

Even in Mareah's mansion, the place he built for his wife in his new Pella, a place insulated against the howling prairie winds, someone like Hendrik P. Scholte still needed the reassurance that life itself had not begun in this strange new world.

If we've never been able to incinerate the wooden shoes, our reluctance is at least somewhat understandable.

CHAPTER 8

A Tulip in the Wilderness

Because no two individuals dominated nineteenth-century Dutch-American life like H. P. Scholte and A. C. Van Raalte, no two characters are as central to our own early history, the history of those who would become the Christian Reformed Church. Both men were seceders from the state church in the Netherlands, devoutly committed to their God and the Christian faith. Both were educated as preachers and led their respective churches, and both possessed the strong leadership characteristics required by immigration. Both functioned as magistrates, businessmen, and financial advisors as well as pastors in their local communities.

Yet, as Robert Swierenga says, "These two immigrant leaders were destined to clash." Although both were born with "steel in their bones," Swierenga claims their personalities and religious temperaments differed so much that it was difficult for the two men to keep cordial personal relations. For the sake of both the men and their followers, it was likely advantageous that they established and governed colonies five hundred miles apart.

They'd been unlike since birth. Scholte was born into the home of a Lutheran industrialist and raised in the city amid pleasant wealth and high culture. Van Raalte was one of seventeen children raised in the home of a preacher who was well-established in the state church of the Netherlands. Scholte grew up listening to dinner conversations about wage demands and industrial competition; Van Raalte could never forget the deep piety of his father's prayers for a troubled church.

Scholte was an *Afscheiding* enthusiast. He helped start the secession movement in the northern provinces and founded it himself in the south. Van Raalte joined the secession reluctantly; he retained great respect for his father as a preacher and as a human being and was certainly not as committed as Scholte to blasting away at the heresy of the church both of them eventually left. Van Raalte wanted to be ordained in his father's church but was refused by church authorities after his graduation from Leiden. Although he was a member (the youngest) of the Scholte Club at the university, the secession church was really Van Raalte's second choice.

Scholte was as much a loose cannon as Van Raalte was a peacemaker. Scholte avoided the Synod of Dort as if it had no meaning for the modern Netherlands. As a result he more than occasionally brawled with de Cock's northern party, who held to the old church order tenaciously. Coming

Early Holland, Michigan, prior to the introduction of the automobile.

down right between de Cock and Scholte—both theologically and geographically, Albertus Van Raalte and his brother-in-law Anthony Brummelkamp, wherever possible, chose for compromise instead of conflict.

When it came to immigration, Scholte was no pie-in-the-sky dreamer. He had thoroughly analyzed the economic aspects of the undertaking. He took nearly one thousand followers along to the Iowa prairie, where he handed them eighteen thousand acres of the very finest farmland in the state and region. When they arrived, some of that land had already been planted. Scholte came to America with a vision of economic and political prosperity. He became, in every sense, an American. He attended political conventions and made immediate peace with Iowa's Baptists. Even his choice of the name Pella, taken from Christian history rather than Dutch geography, reveals his aggressive desire to become American. Half the streets in his first township map were given American names—Columbus, Washington, Franklin, Liberty, Union, Independence.

While Scholte came to America to be American, Van Raalte had altogether different motives. He called his colony Holland, or New Holland. Van Raalte's dreams ran much closer to the dreams of the American Puritans of two hundred years earlier. He wanted a uniquely prosperous yet pious Christian community in western Michigan, a pure American colony unstained by national sins, isolated by the very strength of its godliness, and safely enclosed within itself. He wanted a community of Dutch saints, an imported

Holland village shimmering on the American landscape, echoing each evening with strains of Dutch psalms. He wanted nothing less than a Christian city on the shores of Black Lake, a witness to a world in need of God and his Son, Jesus Christ. He wanted political life to witness to the love of his Lord.

With one hundred pious and ill-equipped seceders, Van Raalte tackled the Michigan wilderness. He could well have joined Scholte; in fact, Scholte was confident that his younger protege would do just that—head for St. Louis with his group and eventually establish, with him, a significant colony in Iowa.

But Van Raalte eventually steered his little group to the western shores of Lake Michigan.

THE MOVE TO MICHIGAN

Sometime in 1845, Rev. Albertus Christiaan Van Raalte must have measured the difference between the starvation that characterized life in the Netherlands and the bounty reportedly available to all in America and determined that a few thousand miles to the New World seemed a small price to pay for apparent opportunity. He decided to emigrate.

But as weighty as these economic factors were, Van Raalte's decision to leave home, family, and friends was not motivated primarily by a desire to escape starvation in the Netherlands. Even though he longed for a place where seceder children would have enough to eat, the strongest arguments he made to consider leaving the Netherlands were based on his faith, not on the economic state of affairs. What he wanted more than anything was a colony in which the children of the *Afscheiding* would receive a Christian education.

Both motivations were there, of course, which accounts for the fact that today many people with Dutch roots, when studying the immigration records for their own ancestors, find two motivations noted—economic and religious.

By early 1846, both Brummelkamp and Van Raalte were busily promoting emigration among the seceders. Scholte was still debating the pros and cons when the brothers-in-law

Albertus C. Van Raalte (1811-1876).

organized an emigration society and drafted a constitution ("Rules for the Society of Christians for the Holland Emigration to the United States of North America"). Their constitution suggests Van Raalte's image of an unmolested colony, a place so remote and so isolated that its leaders "could prevent the intrusion of strangers who might be detrimental to the society," a society of saints.

In May of 1846, Van Raalte's emigration society paid passage for two impoverished farm families from his Arnhem congregation. Without society aid, a few more individuals left Arnhem on June 4 and settled near Milwaukee, Wisconsin, by late July. As the summer wore on and the potato fields surrounding Arnhem blackened, letters began coming back from America. Families who'd left Arnhem destitute were now in the New World—what's more, they were delighted to be there.

In June, Van Raalte and Brummelkamp published *Aan de Geloovigen in de Vereenigde Staten van Noord-Amerika* ("To the Faithful in the United States of America"), an unabashed appeal to the Reformed people in America for assistance to Dutch immigrants leaving the pathetic conditions in the Netherlands for the glorious opportunities promised by a new life in a New World. According to this pamphlet, immigrants sponsored by Van Raalte's society would seek nothing more than "one of those uninhabited regions in America" where starvation could be prevented. "Our people" wanted just such a place, he said, because they wanted to "enjoy the privilege of seeing their little ones educated in Christian schools."

A month later Brummelkamp and Van Raalte collaborated again, this time to produce what quickly became the most convincing argument in favor of emigration to America: *Landverhuizing, of Waarom Bevorderen wij de Volksverhuizing en wel naar Noord-Amerika en niet naar Java* ("Emigration, or Why Do We Advocate Emigration to North America and Not to Java?"). In the very first year of its publication, this pamphlet went through three printings.

By August, Brummelkamp had decided to stay in the Netherlands, but Van Raalte was on his way. On Sunday evening, September 20, he delivered a parting sermon to his Arnhem congregation—part of which was staying with Brummelkamp, part of which would be leaving with him on a steamer that next Tuesday morning, bound for the port of Rotterdam. On Thursday evening they set sail for America under the canvas of the three-masted

Southerner. Van Raalte, who was thirty-five at the time, and his wife Christina Johanna, who was thirty-two, were accompanied by their five children (ages nine, seven, five, two, and five months), as well as their servant Tennegje Lasker, who was forty. They were assigned passage in the ship's cabin; the names of 102 steerage passengers were included in Captain Tully Crosby's log (one of these passengers returned to port before the ship departed).

Albertus Christiaan Van Raalte with his wife Christina (De Moen) Van Raalte.

While the *Southerner* made its way through sometimes stormy seas, two ministers in what is now the Reformed Church in America were waiting to meet Van Raalte's party. Thomas De Witt, pastor of the Collegiate Church in New York City, had just returned from the Netherlands, where he'd met Scholte, read Van Raalte and Brummelkamp's tracts, and promised substantial aid to seceder immigrants once they docked in New York City.

Reverend Isaac N. Wyckoff of Albany, New York, had met the immigrant party that left Van Raalte's church on June 4 and later settled in Wisconsin. Wyckoff, who spoke and wrote Dutch fluently, had been powerfully impressed by the piety of these people. He'd helped organize the "Protestant Evangelical Holland Emigrant Society" in Albany and, while Van Raalte suffered seasickness in the mid-Atlantic, he'd published an English translation of the appeal "To the Faithful in the United States" in the October 15 *Christian Intelligencer.*

On November 17, the *Southerner* sailed into the New York City harbor. Within hours, Thomas De Witt was shaking Albertus Van Raalte's hand. The following day, hoping to make the western frontier before winter set in, Van Raalte's band headed up the Hudson River to Albany. There, Isaac Wyckoff welcomed them with extraordinary warmth—and with copies of Van Raalte's appeal, now printed in English. Thus, during his first week in America, Van Raalte had been embraced by two Dutch-speaking preachers of the Reformed Church in America, a kindness he would not soon forget.

Christian Education

In spite of its small size, the CRC has played a major role in significant Christian ministries in North America.

Although long known for its initiative and encouragement of Christian day schools, the CRC was not alone in the field. Roman Catholics, Missouri Synod Lutherans, and Seventh Day Adventists are also committed to Christian education for their children.

However, it can truly be said that the Christian schools founded by Christian Reformed parents, in harmony with the Reformed world-and-life view, have often served as a model leading to the organization of thousands of schools dedicated to Christian teaching by other evangelical churches in North America.

What's unique about these schools is that they are nonparochial. That means that they are not tied to churches. They are operated by independent boards elected by parents, in line with the Reformed Kuyperian understanding that education is primarily a *parental* responsibility. While the CRC church order clearly requires congregations to foster and promote the development of these schools, their administration and governance falls outside of the appropriate sphere of responsibility and competence of the institutional church.   —WDB

From Albany, still hurrying to beat the inevitable snows, Van Raalte's party moved west to Rochester and then on to Buffalo. About thirty members of his group found jobs in Buffalo and elected to stay the winter there. Van Raalte himself was still uncertain about a final destination. He was inclined to join the earlier group who'd settled in Wisconsin, near Alto. On November 27, he and the remaining two-thirds of his party boarded the *Great Western*, a steamer that had been trapped in Buffalo's harbor by bad weather. On board the steamer, heading west through the Great Lakes, Van Raalte wrote to Brummelkamp, describing his hopes for a Wisconsin colony and his fear that winter would block their travel in Detroit.

The captain of the *Great Western* promised winter employment for anyone willing to work in the Eber B. Ward's shipyard in St. Clair, a small town north of Detroit. Several families accepted this proposal and moved to St. Clair, where most of them stayed at an old warehouse throughout their first winter in America. With one group in Buffalo and another in St. Clair, Van Raalte had fewer than fifty souls to keep warm and fed when ice finally sealed the shipping lanes at Detroit.

Now frozen into Michigan, Van Raalte decided to investigate that territory before moving on to Wisconsin in the spring. Led by a Native American guide and John R. Kellogg, an Allegan County judge living in Kalamazoo, Van Raalte swung through central and southwestern Michigan in the days following Christmas of that year. It was probably December 31 when the scouting party (with Van Raalte still struggling to master snowshoes) arrived at Rev. George N. Smith's mission outpost on the south edge of Black Lake, along the shoreline of Lake

Michigan. It was the Dutch preacher and the American judge who, on New Year's Day in 1847, stood in two feet of snow along the Indian trail stretching northwestward toward Black Lake and determined the exact site of the Dutch settlement that would be known, simply, as Holland.

Van Raalte returned to Detroit, then tramped back and forth across western Michigan, thoroughly covering the triangle marked by Grand Rapids, Muskegon, and Holland, and picking up soil samples that convinced him the land was rich. Even today, some historians question the

Typical of the first homes built by settlers in the late 1840s.

sources for his soil samples, as well as his competence for making that judgment; it's very doubtful he saw through Michigan's heavy snows what his loyal followers encountered when, come spring, they brought their families through the thaw from Buffalo, St. Clair, and Detroit. What they discovered rather quickly was that "the village of Holland was then, excepting [one] sandy hill . . . a low-lying, sandy, and somewhat swampy bit of land."

But Van Raalte had been persuaded that the shores of Black Lake would cradle a healthy colony. Railroads were already being built into Michigan, and the Great Lakes carried ships three seasons each year. Massive forests would provide wood for homes and barns and fuel, as well as plank roads. There was ample water, obviously. People considered the woods to be healthful country, while the prairies, like Iowa (or so it was claimed), were dangerous, spewing disease for several years after the rich earth had been turned up by the plow for the first time. For seven thousand dollars, Van Raalte bought three thousand acres from a Mr. C. Palmer and his wife, who, by Van Raalte's account, lived in New York. With a combination of his own funds and some borrowed capital, he added another thousand acres of government land. He spent all he had and then some to insure the future of his dream: an insulated colony of true believers.

By March 17, forty-three of Van Raalte's immigrant troops had followed him through the dense Michigan forest and were cutting trees for cabins. One of those wielding an axe was Van Raalte himself. Scholte's wife Mareah might have demanded a mansion on the prairie, but Christina Van Raalte was evidently content to move into the "plain board shanty" her husband had ready when she and the children, with their servant, Tennegje, arrived in the bright sunshine of May.

SURVIVAL

Egbert Fredericks was one of the first in Van Raalte's party to see Black Lake in the spring of 1847. Judging from his reports, he

Pillar Church, Holland, Michigan

It was Winston Churchill who said, "First we shape our buildings, and then our buildings shape us." The majestically simple Pillar Church in Holland, Michigan, reflects well this insightful view.

Erected in 1856, just nine years after the first ax felled the first tree in the thick forest surrounding Lake Macatawa, Pillar Church—which can rightfully be called the "mother church" of the entire western branch of the Reformed Church in America and the Christian Reformed Church—has withstood storm and stress, both in nature and in the church.

In the early years the church was known as the First Reformed Church of Holland. Inside its walls, its first pastor, Rev. A. C. Van Raalte, preached with vigor and evangelical tenderness for more than eleven years.

After Van Raalte's death in 1876, the congregation was polarized on the question of freemasonry. When the Reformed Church in America decided to permit local option for members of the Masonic Lodge, the majority of the First Reformed members voted to leave the RCA in 1883 to become an independent congregation.

Pillar Christian Reformed Church, Holland, Michigan—the mother church of the western Reformed community. Van Raalte was its first pastor.

However, in 1884 the congregation made an astounding and, for the city of Holland, shocking decision. They decided to join with the secessionist CRC. That decision to hand over a significant historical site was, of course, traumatic for those who remained loyal to the RCA. So for many years, Pillar Church, known for much of its history as Ninth Street Christian Reformed Church, stood as a symbol of division and separation in Holland.

Today, however, the relationship between the two Reformed denominations is congenial. Each year thousands of tourists visit the church, which has an excellent historical collection of the pioneer days in the colony. A large plaque in the sanctuary reminds visitors of A. C. Van Raalte, pastor and founder of both city and church.

—WDB

was in awe of both Van Raalte and his taste in New World real estate:

> *We viewed with astonishment the mighty giant trees which perhaps were two centuries old, some of them a hundred feet tall and six feet in diameter, all growing on a rolling terrain of various kinds of soil; and the dense underbrush cut up by streams and creeks fed by springs and bubbling waters, a desert wild, fit only as a home for the timid creatures of the forest. Nevertheless, this was the place, declared Dominie Van Raalte, where a city and a number of villages should rise, where an extensive Dutch colony should be planted, where we and our children would enjoy an untrammeled existence, serve our God freely and without restraint, and thank Him for His gracious kindness. We plain folk from the province of Drenthe, of course, did not have such exalted ideals, but nevertheless we believed in a good deal of what he kept before our eyes, and so courageously went to our labors with frequent prayer to God.*

> —*Netherlanders in America* by Henry Lucas (Grand Rapids, MI: Wm. B. Eerdmans, 1935, 1989) p. 89.

Behind Fredericks's mention of courage and prayer lies a story of considerable grief, however. By the close of 1847, and in the days the followed, the colonists learned the brutal difference between Van Raalte's dream in the Netherlands and the reality of the frontier. The immigrants who'd entrusted their lives to him had been chosen not on the grounds of useful employment in the American wilderness, but on the basis of financial need and piety. These were no coonskin-capped wilderness men, but people who'd never picked up a knife, hunted deer, faced a bear, slapped mosquitoes, or experienced anything close to a Michigan winter. They had no idea of how to fell a tree without dropping it on themselves. None of them had ever built a log cabin or planted a garden under the shade of what must have seemed like a million trees. Not one of them, back in the Netherlands, could have imagined the deep shadows of acres and acres of forest land.

Although their relations with Native Americans remained peaceful, the Hollanders were a constant frustration to the Indians. For generations the indigenous people had made maple syrup in the forest, annually leaving behind the tools and troughs used in the process. Van Raalte's immigrants, assuming the wood troughs had been deserted, used them to feed their pigs. The Native Americans concluded that the Dutch folks were thieves. What's more, they claimed, the Hollanders were by nature so filthy that it was impossible to live anywhere near them.

But from the Native American point of view, the gravest offense of the immigrant community was the way the Dutch carried out their property designs; land that had never had anything other than a spiritual owner before was suddenly drawn and quartered into plots, fenced into portions these new and strange inhabitants somehow claimed to be their own. The Native Americans assumed that the only way to deal with such an odd sort was to move out—which is exactly what they did, resettling in northern Michigan near what is today Traverse City.

When the winter snows of 1847 melted, the warm spring sunshine brought more than pleasantness. It roused mosquitoes across the swamps north of the village, armies of them, each combatant equipped with malevolent weaponry. By June, sickness blanketed every makeshift bed in Van Raalte's colony. On June 20, when a new group of immigrants landed on the shores of Black Lake (to found what became the village of Graafschap), Van Raalte, sick with fever, greeted them.

Disease decimated the colony throughout that first summer—as well as the next. Log huts made of uncured timber held more water than they kept out. Lean-to structures covered with hemlock branches were better homes for toads and all kinds of vermin than for the immigrant newcomers who shivered beneath them. There was never enough food. The immigrants' clothing was all wrong for the climate, both summer and winter. And, as the Indians had complained, the hygiene practiced in the colony was hardly, well, characteristically Dutch.

From June 1847 through August 1848, a deadly combination of malarial infection, dysentery, scarlet fever, smallpox, and other viruses brought activity in the new colony to a standstill. On August 22, 1848, Hendrik Van Eyck arrived in Holland to find "sick people in every home, sometimes as many as five or six in one house. Evil fevers reigned everywhere, people looked like shadows returned to earth." Fathers, too weak to build coffins, buried their children with their own hands. The

> ### Letter from Immigrant A. De Weerd
>
>
>
> The church is well attended here on Sunday, and it is blessed with the true proclamation of the gospel as provided by our Pastor, A. C. Van Raalte. Yes, brother and sister, the earnestness with which he preaches is beyond description, and the way in which the Lord equips him is wonderful. I never heard him preach that way in the Netherlands.
>
> —*Write Back Soon: Letters from Immigrants in America* by Herbert J. Brinks (Grand Rapids, MI: CRC Publications, 1986) p. 3.

area around the original settlement was, and still is, filled with unmarked graves.

Later, Van Raalte remembered those first months as a "heartbreaking and discouraging time." As their leader, he suffered for his people; but he suffered himself as well. "Never," he wrote, "had I been so near collapse as in those crowded log houses, in which each family had to manage to live in a few square feet of space. I saw how all sorts of family activities—housekeeping, being sick, dying, and care for the dead—had to be discharged." Henry Beets reports that exactly half of a company of twenty-two Frisians who'd come in 1847 were gone by the next year. On one occasion, Beets relates, Van Raalte broke into sobs during public prayer. "O Lord, must we all die?" he asked.

When a Dutch physician visited the colony on his way to Scholte's Pella, he was of no substantial help. After all, the maladies he encountered were completely unfamiliar to him, there was no medicine anywhere in the colony, and no one had any money to pay for medicines that might have been purchased elsewhere. To find money with which to build an orphanage for children whose parents had died in those early years, Van Raalte had to collect and sell all the remaining jewelry the immigrants had taken with them.

It is impossible for people today—in three-story Victorian homes or lakeside estates or even in small post-war bungalows—to imagine such degradation. Death was rampant. Grief was monumental. Despair must have lurked in every shadow of the great forest land.

But the immigrant story doesn't end in influenza. Even today, there is a pattern to the immigrant experience in North America: those who come sacrifice for those who follow. The opportunities the New World presents are only occasionally immediate; more often, making it is a matter of a obtaining a future blessing for one's children. A third and still youthful generation of today's Dutch Canadians can hear myriad stories about how hard it was in those early years.

Today the triangle of western Michigan land Van Raalte hiked over that first winter, looking for the right place, is booming. Even by North American standards, the region is affluent. Those unmarked graves lie like forgotten memories beneath manicured lawns and perfectly landscaped gardens. People spray so mosquitoes stay away from screened-in porches. Today, churches are air-conditioned, and this year it's likely that few preachers will cry publicly. We've come a long way.

But we've also left something behind. That jewelry, the last bit of excess those original settlers gave up, was offered in a good cause. It allowed the construction of a "small, frame, two-story building." But that orphanage, so dearly paid for, soon went out of business because every last orphan was adopted by a family from the colony. Every single one. Every abandoned child found a home.

UNION WITH AMERICANS

Between the exacting jobs of burying the dead and governing the settlement of survivors in those first years, Van Raalte the colonist remained Van Raalte the preacher. His people, who'd come basically for religious reasons, needed shepherding by the Word as well as deed. A colony had to be built, but so did a new church in a new land.

On April 23, 1848, Van Raalte met in the newly-formed community of Zeeland with consistories of the colony's four recognized churches to establish an official classis. Represented were the congregations in Holland (Van Raalte with his consistory) and three nearby villages: Zeeland (Rev. Cornelius Van der Meulen and consistory), Vriesland (founded the previous June by Rev. Maarten Ypma, now present with consistory), and Graafschap (which had no pastor and sent a lay delegation). That first classis meeting dealt with two discipline cases concerning the permissibility of marriage, and adopted as its rules the entire church order of Dort, thus cementing the New World to its Old World *Afscheiding* tradition.

Classis met once again on September 27, 1848, to consider an invitation to join with the "Dutch Church," or the "Dutch Reformed Church" (today, the Reformed

Church in America), which had asked the classis to attend their synodical assemblies. With illness still wracking the colony, however, the new classis decided to decline the offer on grounds of "the pressure of local business and the difficulties connected with a new settlement."

Thus, the marriage between Van Raalte's "Classis Holland" and the Reformed Church in America was postponed but not cancelled. The following spring, when the Rev. Isaac Wyckoff of Albany visited the colony, the romance flourished and union was assured. For Wyckoff, the visit was an opportunity to see the fruits of his labors among the immigrants he'd supported since their arrival in New York. For Van Raalte the visit offered a chance to ask a powerful American ally to help rescue a young colony whose very life was threatened by disease and suffering.

According to the report submitted by Wyckoff, there were, by the time of his arrival, seven congregations and four clergymen in the new colony. Christian education was their dominant concern. Holland and Zeeland, the two largest villages, had already established schools, despite waves of crises sweeping over the settlement. But the churches could barely support themselves or their

Graafschap CRC today and a re-creation of its first building.

pastors, let alone teachers for their schools. What funds they'd had with them were exhausted by the purchase of land.

On June 4, 1849, Wyckoff met with representatives of the colony's churches. Later on, when the matter of church union was much more disruptive in the colony, those who wanted to reject affiliation with the Dutch Reformed Church argued that this meeting was not an official gathering of the classis—which it wasn't. Furthermore, they claimed that congregations in the colony never ratified the conclusions of this meeting—which they didn't. Official or not, however, the meeting between Wyckoff and representatives of the local churches dealt with the question of union, and the Albany preacher went home thinking that Van Raalte's "Holland Classis" had asked to become part of the already existing American denomination.

In a revealing—and, ultimately, historically important—paragraph of his report, Wyckoff describes the colonists' only reluctance concerning the possibility of union. He also describes how he put their fears to rest:

> At the classical meeting, it was soon made known that the brethren were a little afraid of entering into ecclesiastical connection with us, although they believe in the union of brethren and sigh for Christian sympathy and association. They have felt to the quick the galling chains of ecclesiastical domination, and have seen with sorrow how strict organization according to human rules leads to formality on the one hand and to opposition of tender conscience on the other, that

> they hardly know what to say. I protested of course that it was the farthest from our thoughts to bring them to bondage to men, or to exercise an ecclesiastical tyranny over them. And I stated that they would be most perfectly free at any time they found an ecclesiastical connection opposed to their religious prosperity and enjoyment to bid us a fraternal adieu and be by themselves again.

—*Netherlanders in America* by Henry Lucas (Grand Rapids, MI: Wm. B. Eerdmans, 1955, 1989) p. 509.

Based on Wyckoff's report, his denomination's next synod (1850) approved the admission of Classis Holland alongside its existing Classis Michigan, recognizing the unique Dutch character of the immigrant colony. Classis Holland sent "as our representative . . . A. C. Van Raalte, pastor and minister in the church of God, instructing him in our name to give and to ask for all necessary information which may facilitate the desired union."

By the time Van Raalte returned from the synod in Schenectady (and visited the Wisconsin settlement), the union was a reality. On October 30, 1850, he gave a reassuring report to the next meeting of Classis Holland, describing the generous welcome he'd received. Expenses for his trip had been paid, evidently at Wyckoff's urging, by "the churches in the East," and the pioneer preacher brought back to his classis a load of books and educational materials. Standing on the floor of classis, holding that material aloft, Van Raalte undoubtedly told his own colony's constituents how useful all of this bounty would be, not only to himself but also to the children, for whom the entire enterprise of immigration had been made in the first place.

There were early skeptics in the colony, especially among the lay preachers, who warned that any link between the new colony and the Dutch Reformed Church was an unnatural and impossible union. But Van Raalte would never have left the Netherlands had he been given to heeding the advice of skeptics. He wanted the merger, he pursued it, and he achieved it. It may have been the first tangible evidence he'd had since leaving Arnhem that his colony had a place and a future beyond the broadly scattered graves marking places where hopeful immigrants had fallen after only a year or two in the land of opportunity.

Like Hendrik Scholte, his Iowa colleague, Van Raalte paid a price for his leadership role. Gordon Spykman offers this summary:

> To his admirers Van Raalte was a vigorous leader, a gifted preacher, a veritable "modern Moses," a scholar whose competence was duly recognized in 1860 by an honorary doctorate from Rutgers University. To his critics he was the landlord of the colony, dictator of the local church, political boss of the town, and pope of the classis.
>
> —*Pioneer Preacher: Albertus Christiaan Van Raalte* by Gordon Spykman (Grand Rapids, MI: Heritage Hall Publications, 1976) pp. 19-20.

Christian Reformed historians have been both admirers and critics of Van Raalte. In the *Afscheiding* and on the basis of his immigration leadership, Van Raalte is, no doubt, a hero. But to some, his merger with the Reformed Church in America makes him less hero than goat.

Some CRC historians have chided Van Raalte. The irenic Roelof Kuiper, for example, admitted in 1879 that "no mortal is wise at all times. Dr. Van Raalte, too, committed errors. Maybe he was in too much of a hurry at times, and relied too much on human aid (*Voice from America* [Grand Rapids: Wm. B. Eerdmans, 1970] p. 82)." Others, like Henry Beets, have robustly blasted away at Van Raalte and his merger:

> Indeed, of such a loose mode of procedure, and such a haste in forming an ecclesiastical union we have not found a parallel anywhere in Church History. In our days people would speak of "railroading it through." We repeat: it seems incredible the way our sensible pioneers rushed the matter. Did they not know: haste makes waste?
>
> —*The Christian Reformed Church in North America* by Henry Beets (Grand Rapids, MI: Eastern Ave. Bookstore, 1923) p. 43.

And yet, can it really be surprising that Van Raalte sought union—and found it—with the American Dutch in the East? After all, the man loved his father, who never seceded. He was summarily barred from the ministry in the state church on the basis of his associations with secessionists. He was, by nature, a peacemaker, not an individualist. Chances are, he avoided Scholte because he recognized the man had idiosyncrasies that would eventually bring dissension between them. Most historians are confident the two couldn't have made a team. What's more, his colony was devastated; death knocked on most every door. His people, aided by Indians and Americans, were only slowly learning the ways of life in the American frontier. And Wyckoff had been there to greet them on their first steps from the boat. He'd translated the appeal Van Raalte himself had penned to American churches. The American churches offered blessed relief.

So is it really surprising that he gratefully and even joyfully accepted their hand, full as it was of love and mercy? Maybe Scholte would have walked away. But Van Raalte?—no.

The union that followed was something of a mixed marriage, an odd match of immigrant frontier Hollander with red-white-and-blue American. From the moment the two fellowships took their questionable vows, what resulted was an uncomfortable relationship, even though

personal relations between Van Raalte and Wyckoff remained warm and friendly. Before the union, Van Raalte had campaigned for solidarity with the Dutch Reformed Church. Afterward, he had all he could do to fight for the life of his agreement. He laid himself and his leadership on the line to put some three thousand Hollanders (a few less than a thousand communicant members by 1849), very few of whom could speak English, onto the membership rolls of a denomination a thousand miles away with a two-hundred-year history in the New World.

When Van Raalte compared his frontier outpost with the sturdy American institution of the Dutch Reformed Church, there likely appeared no choice. What Wyckoff offered was union with a fellowship that included men like the Honorable Theodore Frelinghuysen, United States

Historic home of Rev. A. C. Van Raalte, founder of Holland, Michigan. The parsonage had twenty-one rooms and was built around Van Raalte's much smaller home on Fairbanks Ave. A showpiece in the city, it contained a beautiful cherrywood staircase and solid cherrywood planking. It was here that Van Raalte died in 1876, just short of thirty years after his arrival in the area.

Senator (1829-1835), chancellor at the University of New York, and 1844 vice-presidential nominee on the ticket headed by Henry Clay.

On the other hand, it's almost impossible to assume that Van Raalte did not harbor some misgivings about the commitment he made. He was, after all, a seceder; he himself had suffered at the hands of a bureaucratic institution capable of incredible arrogance toward people who were cut from the same cloth as the many he'd led to western Michigan. He knew very well that the typical Dutch Reformed Church member from the banks of the Hudson River had very little in common with his Black Lake woodchoppers. They hadn't, after all, experienced the horrors of the 1836 Synod, hadn't chartered a theological path back toward Dort, hadn't faced blighted potato fields and the nasty jibes of state church neighbors. The two groups were, in a word, different.

At the very core of Van Raalte's dilemma, however, lies a question that the CRC has faced ever since—how will we survive in this land?

That was, of course, the question faced by both immigrant giants. Scholte, who may well have been an American in spirit and theology even before he left the Netherlands, chose instant involvement. In theological terms, he left most of the fractious disputes back in the Netherlands, choosing instead, in founding Pella, to personalize his faith into something he'd stowed in his heart and soul, a faith he'd created in rather classic American fashion. Like a real frontiersman, he was afraid of nothing, strode into long-established American political camps as if they'd been

awaiting his arrival, and aspired to be the mover and shaker he was. In the process, he often left his followers behind, scratching their heads and growing more and more embittered.

Van Raalte, right from the onset, had a wholly different agenda. He wanted to keep his people together in a sanctified brotherhood. His vision was more utopian, finally, and much more reminiscent of the Puritan experience in the early seventeenth century. He was interested in a Christian community and Christian education. Perhaps his most controversial act was uniting with an already established American church. But the Dutch Reformed Church was, after all, a church that at least knew the language of the Synod of Dort, even if it wasn't enthusiastic about all of its tenets. There can be little doubt that among Van Raalte's most deeply felt motives in this union was the very existence of this Christian community he'd been working so hard to establish.

The outlines of this whole discussion—the differences between Van Raalte and Scholte and their various paths in the earliest years of their colonies—begins to form a new question created by a new world. Most comprehensively stated, the question was—and is—the question of Americanization. The Dutch immigrants of the mid-nineteenth century, like those who came to Canada and the U. S. following World War II—and like those of every ethnic and racial background who make the radical move to a new country—faced never-ending questions created by the overwhelming power of American culture to reshape people's minds and hearts. Americanization is the process by which people lose what they were or refashion it to become something new, something American. Something is gained when a people melt into American culture; but inevitably something is lost too.

James Bratt, in his *Dutch Calvinism in Modern America*, explores the history of Dutch Reformed people using the complexities of the process of Americanization to illumine some of our most heated controversies. Whether or not Van Raalte ever considered his decision in light of that process, his colony's membership in the Dutch Reformed Church was most decidedly a step out of provinciality, however meager, and into something larger and definably more American—as many of his detractors were and still are willing to point out. The union with what would become the Reformed Church in America was surely more than a move to Americanize, but it was at least that, as well.

Let's shift this matter forward a century and a half. Twenty years ago in Phoenix, Arizona, individual members of local CRC churches skirmished just a bit about whether to participate in a Billy Graham Crusade coming to the city. The issues were rarely defined clearly, but some expressed a reluctance to participate in the whole "revival" tradition. Others couldn't begin to understand why. They simply assumed that anyone not participating would be denying the efficacy of grace—"Why, Billy Graham's Crusade would be wonderful. After all, thousands would be converted."

1966 Billy Graham Crusade.

I was a graduate student at the time, maybe not all that zealous. I didn't sign up to be a counselor, nor participate in any of the pre-crusade meetings or prayer sessions as other church members did. I was busy, but so were others who attended everything, I'm sure. But I went to the crusade, and I appreciated Graham's preaching, in addition to experiencing the joy of being one of many thousands assembled in the stadium. And the music—there's something about hearing George Beverly Shea sing "How Great Thou Art" that's unforgettable.

But once the altar call began, I felt strange. I watched other people from my church move immediately toward the aisles and begin to make their way down to the front. I knew what they were doing—

they were preparing, on cue, to take their places as counselors. But when I saw those aisles filled so quickly with prayer counselors, I felt this horrible sense of being manipulated—the gentle chords of "Just As I Am" playing in the background as Graham himself pointed at hundreds of folks already coming forward and begged sinners to join the throng.

From the compulsion I felt at that moment, I recognized, perhaps cynically, that something more than a true response to God was going on all around me. The harmony created by music, Graham's own voice, and the hundreds already going forward compelled participation by creating an emotional vitality so strong it was palpable. I wasn't brought to the front of the stadium that night. I realized that the

prayer counselors would have tons of people to deal with already, so I didn't leave my seat. But it felt strange *not* to go forward. The movement around me, heavy-laden with emotion, the masses of humanity streaming down to the podium, pressed me hard to get to the front like thousands of others.

I'm fully aware of the blessing Billy Graham's ministry has had on individuals around the world, bringing many to the gospel. And I'm also not blind to the fact that Graham himself has been an icon Christian in the culture at large for decades. Wonderful things happen at such revivals. But that night I felt that I understood something of the "psychology of the group." And please don't take this wrong, because I'm not drawing a parallel, but that night I also understood more clearly how good, strong German Christians, believers every one, could fall for an orator like Hitler and orchestration such as his henchmen created at Nazi mass rallies.

Billy Graham is a saint; Hitler is the most universally recognized sinner of the twentieth century. I'm not, in any way, making a comparison of individuals, only of strategies. Being there at the Graham crusade—in spite of my own conviction that many people may have been saved that night—made me uneasy, not because of anything Graham said, but because his methodology seemed to me to be emotionally manipulative.

Why?

Was my reluctance a throwback to my tradition of theology—the Calvinist view that personal salvation is sometimes overplayed at the expense of building the Kingdom? Or was it simply the stern and forbidding nature some feel characterizes doctrinal Calvinism?

Or was it an ethnic characteristic? An effect of my icy northern European roots in a people who don't touch much, don't really like to share their inner selves? A people who are somehow naturally skeptical of emotional highs?

Or, as a graduate student, was my reason overwhelming my heart, fending off the Holy Spirit's urgings? Was I incapable of allowing for the miracle of God's grace?

Was my hesitation borne from something of all of those factors? Was my reaction created by a sense that this was simply not my religious tradition? Why couldn't I be joyously overwhelmed, like so many, by the spectacle of thousands pouring down the steps toward the podium? Was it my sin?

Whatever combination of any or all of the above created my unease, what is obvious is that revivalism itself was something questionable to me, something not completely trustworthy. As a tradition in Evangelicalism, it is, undoubtedly, something more "American" than my CRC-draped sensibilities were accustomed to.

There are, after all, some theological differences. On the basis of a strong belief in God's sovereignty and his immutable decrees, Calvinists of most ethnic varieties have, for better or for worse, long felt uncomfortable around talk of "personal relationships to Christ." What's more, the Synod of Dort forged its confession in the burning embers of Arminius and his followers, people who wanted very much to assert human will—a personal decision—in the process of salvation. The most defining element of crusade events is exactly the opposite—the emotional and intellectual path such worship takes goes directly to that kind of momentous decision, a commitment and a public testimony of a personal choice for Christ. If Graham *only* preached, after all, he wouldn't pack stadiums.

Maybe I wasn't being a good American Christian. Tons of CRC folks would gasp at my reluctance to participate. "Why shouldn't we do revivals?" they'd say. "It's just our tradition that makes us stick-in-the-muds—that's all it is, our frumpy tradition."

Right here—as the CRC struggles through its first baby steps in the New World—it's not a bad time to begin to outline one of the major questions faced by the Christian Reformed Church *in* North America throughout its history, a theme we will return to again and again and again: when are we simply traditional, too Dutch, too fortress-like, too exclusive? At what point is our hesitancy to involve ourselves in the matters of the culture around us simply a result of our heavy wooden shoes?

From the first months of their American ventures, Scholte and Van Raalte must have understood that aside from malaria or heatstroke on the prairie or cutting a settlement out of the forest land, one of the most difficult obstacles the seceders would face would be nothing more than the simple question of how exactly they should mingle with the world around them—not only as Christians, but as Calvinist Christians. Specifically, what would they have to give up in the process of becoming Americans? What would be worth the price?

The theoretical stump they stumbled on in the New World's terrain is not simply a clunky old obstacle we can haul away in a pickup truck. It stays there in the story of the CRC. We see it again and again. And, even today, I'm sure it has not entirely disappeared.

But we'll see.

CHAPTER 9

Birth of the Christian Reformed Church

Being a deacon had never been Teunis Keppel's childhood dream. He was an adventurer, not a church man. An eligible bachelor, he'd signed on with Hendrik Barendregt's scouting party for Scholte's American emigration plans. Once in the New World, he'd been infected with an insatiable itch to see what was over the next hill or around the next bend.

On Christmas Day in 1846, Keppel had fallen in love with St. Louis, then a brawling immigrant town on the western frontier. Three months later he was in Michigan, helping Van Raalte plan his first sawmill. A scant ninety days later he stood beside Scholte on the Iowa prairie, surveying the place soon to be known as Pella.

But while passing again through Van Raalte's colony a few years later, Teunis Keppel put down sufficient roots to be named a deacon in the pioneer preacher's church. Because he was a deacon, he was in a consistory meeting one hot summer evening, August 22, 1853.

The Reverend Albertus C. Van Raalte filled the consistory president's chair, leading the church council just as he led most every council in which he took part. It was not only his chair, it was also his consistory, his church, and his colony. He was older than he was when the colony first took shape in the woods of western Michigan, probably wiser too—not simply the innocent pilgrim who'd mounted snowshoes and stumbled along the shore of Black Lake five years before. The wilderness had toughened him—deprivation and death had likely made him less susceptible to visions of grandeur. He had bad memories to deal with now—the loss of friends, too many funerals, the death of children, public tears. He probably looked at Teunis Keppel across the room and wondered who this man really was—this man making a report that didn't sit well with Preacher Van Raalte.

Difficult days never brought down a man like Keppel; if life became too confining or constricting, he simply lit out to the territories. In fact, the local paper would report the following October that Keppel, along with two of his friends, had left Michigan for the gold fields of California; and they weren't going as missionaries. Keppel was an adventurer who left on a search for his pot of gold when he saw rainbows out west, or anywhere for that matter.

Van Raalte lacked the opportunity and motivation to take off at a moment's notice. From the beginning, this colony had been his project—and the Lord's. Others could gallivant; Van Raalte had to stay put and

Noordeloos, Michigan, ca. 1900. This village, along with Graafschap, Polkton, and the city of Grand Rapids, supported a founding congregation of the CRC.

endure the grim meetings of his consistory, meetings that weren't picnics and were often full of personal criticism.

Two days after that hot August meeting, Van Raalte sat at his desk reviewing Article 4 of the clerk's minutes:

> *Deacon Keppel had learned from Plaggemars that the church member Hoffman, a farmer, already during more than a year spreads slander about our minister, that his reverence for the sake of money has brought our congregation to become an impure church.*

Teunis Keppel (1823-1896).

That irritating charge was nothing new to Van Raalte. He'd heard it before, the complaint that he had engineered the union between his classis and the Dutch Reformed Church (the Reformed Church in America) for purely personal reasons—financial reasons at that. After all, people said, Van Raalte's trips were paid for, weren't they? His salary and pet projects were subsidized. He received grants to distribute to other preachers. According to some people, the handwriting was on the wall: Van Raalte had sold out or bought off—or both.

When he'd first proposed the union, resistance had come only from distant and outlying areas of the colony. But since 1850, when the merger was finally approved, opposition to his leadership and the marriage he'd created had grown noisier and meaner and closer. What began with insinuation—"Who knows for sure what Van Raalte's getting out of this one?"—grew into accusations that were finally aired at the April 1853 classis meeting by the preacher from the Drenthe church: "We were sold to the [Reformed Church in America] by Rev. Van Raalte for a good purse of money," he claimed.

Van Raalte understood that most emotional charges would disappear with time and cooler temperatures. He had been confident that the opposition to union with the Reformed Church in the East would fade after a few turns of the calendar. But that's not what was happening. What had begun as a little local grumbling had grown into dissension that apparently wouldn't be silenced by a year or two of time. The criticism, like a cancer, was proving to be beyond easy treatment. What had happened on August 22, at a meeting of his own consistory, made Van Raalte uncomfortably aware that those whining voices had spread discontent to the very doors of his own congregation.

NEW VILLAGES, OLD LOYALTIES

Once, while still in Arnhem, Van Raalte had drawn a map of the ideal colony. He had pictured a wheel of villages planted around a hub, a central town that would be the headquarters for affairs of church and state. The actual geography of Van Raalte's colony didn't look much like that blueprint because the topography made such straight lines impossible. Van Raalte had put his people down on the shores of Lake Michigan, not in the middle of Wisconsin or Iowa.

Black Lake gave Holland its northern border. Looking across the lake, colonists peered into heavy swamps and marshes, home to blueberries, bears, and mosquitoes—especially mosquitoes. To the east and south, beyond stands of pine and hemlock, skyscraping oaks towered over maples until both gave way to grassland islands which, when tilled and broadened, promised rich farmland. It was here that the newer settlers plotted out villages once they'd passed through Van Raalte's lakeshore town.

Through the woods south of Holland, seventy citizens of German Bentheim—a county (in their dialect, a *Graafschap)* nestled against the Dutch border—planted a village six months after Van Raalte founded Holland. The pioneers of Graafschap had a German tradition of conventicle worship and secession parallelling that of Van Raalte's own. In fact, the Bentheim Secession of 1838 was, in part, precipitated by Van Raalte's own sermons delivered in that region on Christmas Day 1837 and New Year's Day 1838. He had also helped draft Bentheim's articles of secession before escaping back to the Netherlands, German constables at his heels.

Graafschap's infancy was like Holland's. Its founders' first homes were shelters cut from boughs of evergreen trees. Graafschap's first few settlers had learned the same lessons everyone else in the colony had: while the trees protected them from wind, they kept out little rain and no mosquitoes. For the first year of their existence, Graafschapers made the four-mile trek to Van Raalte's worship services each Sunday, but the early leadership of the colony itself was undertaken by those lay

preachers who'd headed conventicles back in Germany. In 1848, Graafschap's colonists constructed a log church, and those same lay preachers returned to the pulpit. Ties to Van Raalte and his colony were loosened.

The following year a group of seceders led by the Rev. Seine Bolks left the Dutch province of Overijsel and headed for Michigan. Bolks had been a Van Raalte disciple in the Netherlands. After studying for the ministry at Van Raalte's "seminary," Bolks followed his mentor's direction, first in the fights the seceders waged with the state church, and then, two years after Van Raalte, in emigration.

When word arrived that Bolks and twenty families from his Dutch congregation were coming to the colony, Graafschap quickly called him to be their pastor. Whether Van Raalte planted that notion in Graafschap's consistory is not known. He might have hoped for such a turn of events—but it didn't work out. When Bolks saw the "improvised parsonage" that the Graafschapers intended for him and his family, he headed off to found a new village southeast of Holland, a village he named—as one might expect—Overisel.

A few miles east and slightly north of Holland, Jan Rabbers settled the village of Groningen in 1847. Unlike Graafschap and Overisel, both of them farming communities, Rabbers intended Groningen to become a center of trade and commerce. During the early years—as Rabbers created his sawmill and other business ventures, and while Van Raalte struggled to find places for new immigrants to bury their dead and settle church disputes—it appeared that Groningen rather than

Holland would become the leading village in the settlement. But over the years a combination of factors conspired against Groningen, and the new community eventually faded.

Farther east, the villages of Drenthe and Vriesland were settled. Drenthe was founded by Jan Hulst, a farmer from that province, who was joined by a large batch of farmers from his home territory during mid-June 1847. Meanwhile, Vriesland, a village just north of Drenthe, was begun by a colony of Frisians led to America by their pastor, Rev. Maarten Ypma. Though Ypma had been trained by de Cock, not Van Raalte, he was "an unassuming person, poor, willing to suffer with his followers." He had little stomach for church fights and splits, and no desire to oppose Van Raalte in any particulars.

Month after month boatloads of immigrants docked at Black Lake, paid courtesy calls on Van Raalte, and moved to the outer edges of his settlement. Thus, the borders of the colony constantly expanded away from Van Raalte's center of power, Hol-

Typical nineteenth-century Drenthe farm in the Netherlands.

land, and his control of the populace grew increasingly thin. Unlike Scholte, who'd brought nearly a thousand loyal followers to Pella, Van Raalte had struggled into Holland with a mere hundred. Later arrivals weren't necessarily opposed to him as a person, preacher, or civic leader, but neither were they devotedly committed to him. It wasn't Van Raalte who dominated Graafschap, after all, but lay leaders who lived in the village, had led the immigration movement, and stood in the newly constructed pulpit of its log church. The roar of Jan Rabbers's mill could easily drown out the voice of Albertus Van Raalte in Groningen. And in Overisel and Vriesland, Seine Bolks and Maarten Ypma were themselves the "pioneer preachers" who commanded a loyal following.

By 1850 Van Raalte's settlement had all the internal cohesion of a tossed salad. It was, in fact, a collection of mini-states, each with its own name, character, history, leadership, and loyalties. What came over to the new country in provincial pieces appeared to be destined to remain in just that shape, each name convenient and appropriate. The institution with the best chance for really unifying the whole group was the church. To the extent that Van Raalte could dominate his colony's church (that is, Classis Holland), he could dominate the colony.

Two distinct forces in the church worked tirelessly against him, however. First, the conventicle heritage provided stubborn resistance to every attempt at centralized leadership and church union. Steeped in a long and powerful tradition of very local worship and gathering, the conventicle spirit lived on in the new country in the

Bird's-eye view of Drenthe, Michigan, ca. 1908.

hearts and souls of those who'd grown up within its fierce independence. In villages like Graafschap and Groningen, this powerful tradition made Van Raalte's attempts at unification seem impotent. Time and again he had to employ all of his eloquence to quiet the troubled minds of believers in those places.

The other snake in Van Raalte's New World garden was the venomous legacy of Old World theological divisions among the seceders. The Dutch fight that ultimately split the American colony was the question of being unequally yoked—specifically, what level of cooperation could or should be maintained with the orthodox believers who had remained within the state church after the secession. Today, we might translate that same question into something more familiar—"Just exactly how big is our tent?"

Brummelkamp and Van Raalte had strenuously argued that the secession

church should work cooperatively with sympathizers in the state church. But the rougher and tougher northern clan, led in this fight by Van Velzen, demanded an absolute break—no looking back, no cooperation on any venture, no union for any goal whatsoever. Nothing but a strictly independent course of action, with stress on developing the Reformed character, would satisfy Van Velzen's demands. Some secessionists very much enjoyed drawing lines in the sand on Lake Michigan shores, just as they had in the Netherlands.

Once enough trees had been felled, enough cabins built, the colonists had time to look around and think and remember. They finally had time to unpack old ecclesiastical skirmishes, baggage carried along weightlessly on steamers and flatboats. That baggage, their own history of battling, cost nothing at all to transport all the way from Europe—but it likely had more effect on life in the colony than all of the Old World goods packed diligently away in strong, well-belted storage chests.

A TALE OF TWO VILLAGES

Between the 1850 marriage of Classis Holland to the Reformed Church in America and the 1857 birth of the Christian Reformed Church, loyalty to the merger became, in large part, a test of loyalty to Rev. Albertus C. Van Raalte. Compare, for exam-ple, the history of two of the colony's villages: Zeeland and Noordeloos.

Zeeland had been cut into the wilderness five miles northeast of Holland in the heat of the 1847 summer. More than four hundred and fifty Zeelanders had left the old country to found this village named for their home province, even though not all of them arrived and stayed in Michigan. Two laymen, Jannes Van De Luyster and Jan Steketee, each brought one shipload of immigrants, while a third group was led by Rev. Cornelius Van Der Meulen. Van Der Meulen had studied with Hendrik Scholte but back in the Netherlands had actually been more closely associated with Van Raalte.

Van Der Meulen's group had a difficult trip over—disease crippled them and scoundrels nearly wiped them out. Once in the New World, his Zeelanders suffered every hardship Van Raalte's colony had suffered, so much so that a strong bond formed between the two groups. Likewise

Rev. Koene Van Den Bosch (1818-1897), founder of the Noordeloos congregation and the only ordained pastor in the CRC from 1857 to 1863.

with their leaders. Van Der Meulen became and remained deeply loyal to Van Raalte through whatever difficult moments arose in the crucial issues both colonists faced.

When Classis Holland met in Van Der Meulen's Zeeland sanctuary on April 8, 1857, the agenda included the possibility of a secession from the newly formed alliance with the Reformed Church in America. No one from the host pastor's congregation pulled out. The chain of loyalty was strong: Zeeland was linked to Van Der Meulen, Van Der Meulen was loyal to Van Raalte, and Van Raalte be-lieved in the union of Classis Holland with the churches in the East.

Noordeloos, on the other hand, was a hotbed of seces-sion. The area had been a collection of farms holding down clay fields north of Holland since 1848. For a decade, new immigrants settled the region until in 1856 villagers voted to form a congregation and call their own preacher, thus leaving the fold of Zeeland's Van Der Meulen. Rev. Koenraad (Koene) Van Den Bosch brought to the colony his family, twenty-nine fol-lowers, and the name Noordeloos for the settlement, the name of the village he'd left in South Holland.

Back in the Netherlands, Van Den Bosch had been a student of Wotter Kok, a zeal-ous defender of dominies de Cock and Van Velzen. While Van Raalte and Brummel-kamp had preached moderation toward "the faithful" in the state church, Van Den Bosch had been schooled in a more radical segregation: to him, the pure *Afscheiding* church was to avoid, at all costs, any corrupting influences of the Dutch Reformed Church *(Hervormde Kerk).* Van Raalte's moderation was not met with sympathy, nor was he a hero in the lectures delivered manfully by Rev. W. Kok.

In 1857, as talk of secession rolled across the colony, Van Der Meulen's Zeeland congregation still recalled the early days—plagues, Van Raalte's courageous leadership through the long list of misfortunes and sadness, charity shown by De Witt and Wyckoff, and the new colony's need for guidance and aid from some already established institutions. But Van Den Bosch's Noordeloos congregation heard only second-hand reports of "the old days." What they found in North America was a community already on its feet.

Rev. Cornelius Van Der Meulen (1800-1876), founding pastor of Zeeland, Michigan. Last church served was in Grand Rapids, 1861-1873.

Since they hadn't arrived until 1856, they saw no need for the marriage of Classis Holland and the Reformed Church in America, and, with the old country's animosities deeply set within them, they refused to give their blessing to the union.

Van Den Bosch himself couldn't shake the troublesome image he carried of Van Raalte, an image he'd picked up from his mentor, Wotter Kok. He couldn't forget that the Van Raalte in Holland was the same man who, Kok maintained, had proposed actual cooperation with the church that had persecuted the seceders in the Netherlands. Less than a year in the pulpit of a church built from Michigan trees, and Van Den Bosch was already explaining to the saints at Noordeloos that the evils of

the apostate *Hervormde Kerk* in the Netherlands were not at all unlike those sins now committed by the Reformed Church in America. They were one and the same, those two groups, he said—the only difference being nationality. What Kok and Van Velzen had charged against the church in the Netherlands could just as accurately be charged against this denomination in the East. There was heresy everywhere, and Van Raalte, true to his old moderate ways, didn't have an undying commitment to doctrinal orthodoxy. What he'd loved both before immigration and after was nothing more than mergers and unions.

On March 14, 1857, Koene Van Den Bosch acted. "By this I notify you," he wrote to Classis Holland, "that I can hold no ecclesiastical communion with you, for the reason that I can not hold all of you who have joined the [Reformed Church in America] to be the true church of Jesus Christ."

When Classis Holland received Van Den Bosch's letter on April 8, 1857, the first man to his feet, the first speaker lamenting Van Den Bosch's "unsubstantiated accusations," justifying the 1850 union, and defending the character and reputation of Albertus C. Van Raalte was the Rev. Cornelius Van Der Meulen of Zeeland.

YEARS OF EROSION

Some accounts of the very beginnings of the Christian Reformed Church imply that church life in Van Raalte's colony was sweetly serene until, without warning, all tranquility was shattered by a storm of protest that came thundering through the settlement in the spring of 1857, leaving carnage in its wake. Occasionally, Koene Van Den Bosch is singled out as the brigadier general of dissenting troops. Some like to suggest that the 1857 secession from Van Raalte's decade-old union with the Reformed Church in America was in actuality the fruit of suspicion planted by a lone elder from Grand Rapids, a man named Gijsbert Haan.

But what happened to lead to the events surrounding the birth of the Christian Reformed Church in North America was less a single phenomenon than a process. Years of bickering, most all of it lugged along in old personality clashes and theological rifts from the Netherlands, ate away at unity and cohesion in the new colonies in western Michigan. And when the break finally occurred, the numbers were hardly staggering. When the smoke cleared after the 1857 break and the tally of those who left Van Raalte's union was taken, two hundred and fifty members—about 10 percent of Classis Holland's total membership—had departed to found the newly formed Christian Reformed Church, the denomination whose story, lest we forget, I've been telling.

Mr. and Mrs. Gijsbert Haan (ca. 1860). Haan was a leading elder and proponent of secession in 1857. For a time (six months) he convinced his pastor, H. G. Klijn, to join the secession, but Klijn returned to the RCA that same year.

Already in 1851 Albertus Van Raalte had spotted trouble on the horizon. At an April 30 meeting, Jan Rabbers and another Groningen elder had asked classis to bless a separate congregation for their village. Previous to their request, they had worshiped in Zeeland with Van Der Meulen. Van Raalte protested vehemently, outraged by what he recognized as geographic factionalism, which he assumed would likely encourage more theological factionalism.

> *The starting point [for the founding of these little churches] is generally a certain discontent, or a certain passion for independence, to secure greater self-government; so that presently any one who is dissatisfied will . . . feel free to gather about him some who live at a distance, in a remote corner of the congregation, and to organize them into a new church.*

Van Raalte, a strong leader, was no clairvoyant, but then, it required no mystic power to foresee what was going to happen as more and more splintering congregations were encouraged by their church fathers. The proliferation of these little churches, he warned, would be the death of union within the classis. "The churches will be split up and weakened," he predicted, "with the result that all interests which require unity that they may be rightly promoted, will be enervated and neglected." Van Raalte could see it coming. Unless he could control the churches, he could not maintain control over the settlement. A litter of small, scattered churches could never be supervised, nurtured, and influenced.

By the 1851 fall classis meeting on October 14, Van Raalte was defending the classis against charges brought forward by an elder then serving the Vriesland church, Gijsbert Haan. Haan was no lion roaring through the colony. He was, to Van Raalte, more like a bothersome mosquito. It is very clear from the record that Van Raalte, aggravated and annoyed, took frequent slaps at elder Haan, with little success. Nonetheless, Haan's buzzing didn't cease. "To labor under incessant disapproval causes nerveless hands and indifference," Van Raalte complained in the classical minutes. If the carping critics didn't learn some manners, "soon the nefarious system of the Independents will get the upper hand to such a degree that each congregation will keep itself to itself." Van Raalte was angry. He had his hands full.

Gijsbert Haan was neither the chief irritant nor Van Raalte's only source of irritation. Earlier in the fall a good portion of Graafschap's congregation had seceded with lay preacher J. R. Schepers. Schepers's group then asked Classis Holland to "install" him as their preacher, even though, as far as classis was concerned, Schepers had never been ordained. Their request for Schepers's installation was denied, the secession was roundly condemned, and classis went on to other matters.

But, like many a hairline crack, factionalism continued to spread across the face of the colony. A few months later, in a February 18, 1852, letter signed by Schepers and addressed to Classis Holland, the seceded preacher asked that he and his congregation be taken in by classis. Only there was one hitch to the request:

"We make no promise to unite with the Albany denomination," a reference, of course, to Classis Holland's merger with the Reformed Church in America. Classis declined Schepers's offer, of course, but only twenty-four months after Van Raalte had finally secured his merger with the "Albany denomination," his own classis had suffered its first secession—and the merger itself was named as part of the grounds for their leaving.

By 1853 the Reformed Church in America was the object of increased suspicion among Van Raalte's critics. The spring classis meeting of April 27 was punctuated by accusations that the RCA was "not being faithful in doctrine and discipline." To quiet fears, some delegates suggested sending a delegation to the next synod to investigate. Van Raalte and others protested. A synodical delegation should be fraternal, they argued, not a witch hunt. Classis then decided to send a fraternal delegation of one—Albertus C. Van Raalte.

But before Van Raalte left town for synod, he had another secession on his hands, this one led by the pastor at Drenthe, Rev. Roelof Smit, who, like Koene Van Den Bosch, had been Wotter Kok's student in the Netherlands. Smit had arrived in the colony in 1851 and, according to one report, hadn't finished "a fortnight in Michigan when he already slandered Van Raalte." Union with the RCA was Drenthe's major ground for secession from Classis Holland. According to Van Raalte's own account, a meeting had been held in Drenthe, and "brethren from Holland, Zeeland, Vriesland, Overisel, and Grand Haven" had attended. Those who'd convened the meeting claimed "that there

were now reasons enough to take counsel with one another to secede from the Classis of Holland." Their grounds were simple: Classis "had joined itself to [the Reformed Church in America], and . . . many voices in the church had expressed themselves in favor of that thing." In a special meeting of classis held May 25, 1853, Smit was deposed on eight grounds. Classis sent him a letter explaining to him that he was "deplorably incompetent," in addition to being a troublemaker. But no matter what Smit's failing might have been, still another secession was taking place, this one also on the grounds of Classis Holland's union with the American Reformed churches in the East.

From 1853 to 1855, with some exceptions, relative peace took over in the classis. Van Raalte attended annual General Synods, returning to classis each year to reassure everyone that the Reformed Church in America was sound on matters of Reformed doctrine.

Rev. Hendrik G. Klijn, who had recently arrived from a parish in Wisconsin, even proposed a kind of ecclesiastical peace treaty between the churches of Classis Holland and the seceding churches of Schepers and Smit. Everyone agreed that it was better "to bear with many follies than to permit so numerous a portion of the church to be torn away, and a chasm of bitterness and estrangement to be made permanent." However, no one knew just how to proceed with peacemaking, and the idea died on the floor of classis.

Then, during the summer of 1855, new fighting broke out. Calls for reunification were forgotten as bitter charges were exchanged at the fall meeting of Classis

Holland. Grand Rapids (formerly of the Vriesland church) elder Gijsbert Haan and Zeeland's Rev. Van Der Meulen argued over the question of just exactly how Reformed churches in the East were supervising the Lord's Supper. Haan had lived in the East for two years, learned the English language, and had always been a keen student of Scripture—and a secessionist in the Netherlands. His criticisms were not simply of the Old World; he'd listened to sermons in New York and New Jersey and found them wanting. He told people in his Grand Rapids church, and throughout western Michigan, that preachers from American churches rarely preached sound doctrine. He felt many members of Eastern congregations were sorely lacking in piety and found too many—including some pastors—holding memberships in Masonic lodges. He reported that in the East itself, some had already broken away from the mother church for its laxity.

There were several complaints about a pamphlet titled "Call to the Unconverted," written way back in the seventeenth century by the Puritan divine Richard Baxter, but subsequently republished, even translated into Dutch, and distributed in the mid-nineteenth century by the American Tract Society. Some preachers passed along the tract, while others thought it woefully universalist in its argument—that is, it assumed a doctrine that suggested that every last human being could be saved. Such an idea was, of course, heretical. But there was more heat at that classis. The mood was not lightened in the least when delegates read an apparently anonymous letter containing "the vilest and most malicious slander against Rev. Van Raalte."

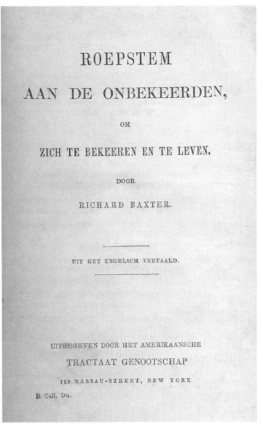

ROEPSTEM

AAN DE ONBEKEERDEN,

OM

ZICH TE BEKEEREN EN TE LEVEN.

DOOR

RICHARD BAXTER.

UIT HET ENGELSCH VERTAALD.

UITGEGEVEN DOOR HET AMERIKAANSCHE
TRACTAAT GENOOTSCHAP
150 NASSAU-STREET, NEW YORK
B. Call, Du.

This Dutch translation of Richard Baxter's pamphlet "Call to the Unconverted" was distributed in Van Raalte's colony during the 1850s. Many considered the booklet to be Arminian and blamed Van Raalte for allowing the book's distribution.

In October, 1856, Koene Van Den Bosch, who'd picked up his eye for heresy at the feet of Wotter Kok and a penchant for fiery oratory from his own sharply discriminating character, chaired the classis meeting. Graafschap brought its latest round of protests: that the RCA used hymns in worship, a charge weighted with a great deal of history among the colonists. From the chair, Van Den Bosch listened closely to Van Raalte's defense of his Eastern friends: "Reformed churches in all countries at all times have had hymns and still have them," Van Raalte claimed. Besides, he added, hymns sung in the Reformed churches "are not to be compared to those of the Netherlands," which he claimed were "frequently mutilated" and "forced" upon the churches. Van Den Bosch's affection for Van Raalte was thin long before this classis; Van Raalte's defense did little to change his assessment.

But nothing made the Noordeloos leader more upset than Classis Holland's refusal to discipline those churches in the colony who'd admitted none other than the Rev. H. P. Scholte, founder of Pella, to their pulpits. Scholte had vacationed in Holland during the summer of 1856, and during his stay had preached in several churches. The minutes of classis calmly report that Van Den Bosch had studied under W. Kok, that W. Kok was a defender of *Afscheiding* founder de Cock, and that de Cock had convened a synod that had tossed H. P. Scholte out of the secessionist church fifteen long years ago. It was that simple.

Now, here in the Michigan wilderness, Van Den Bosch, who'd begun to think of Scholte as a heretic more than a decade before, was forced to listen to Van Raalte, himself no great friend of the Iowa maverick, defend the man. To Van Den Bosch, Van Raalte must have seemed a wishy-washy accommodator, a man whose commitment to truth could be severely compromised when he saw political or even economic advantage. Van Raalte's love for God was obvious, but his love for peace and tranquility seemed to be greater. To Van Den Bosch, the great leader of the Holland community seemed mealy-mouthed, spineless, and unprincipled. Finally, when Van Raalte and friends opened their pulpits to Scholte and then defended their actions, Van Den Bosch felt that the difficult decision to leave or stay had been made for him. Almost nothing could have more quickly convinced the preacher from Noordeloos that this church, like the state church of the Netherlands, had cut itself away from its own moorings.

In December of 1856, at a special meeting of Classis Holland, one of the final items of business was the decision to appoint Rev. Koene Van Den Bosch to preach the sermon when classis would gather the following April. That decision was the last decision Classis Holland would ever make about Koene Van Den Bosch.

On April 8, 1857, Classis Holland and its titular head, Albertus C. Van Raalte, acknowledged the loss of four congregations in western Michigan. Van Raalte himself called their departure a "schism," while the classical records generally refer to their leaving as a secession. Christian Reformed historians like Henry Beets speak of "notices of withdrawal" and "the return of 1857."

Two elders and a deacon representing the tiny congregation in Polkton signed an April 1 letter of secession. They told classis they were leaving because "your denomination fraternizes with those who are in opposition to the doctrine of our fathers, and this is very well known to you, if you are honest."

Van Den Bosch's sizzling note from Noordeloos was in sharp contrast to Rev. Hendrik G. Klijn's more charitable letter from the Grand Rapids church, a congregation that also seceded. Klijn began with "cordial thanks for the love and honor" he'd experienced in Classis Holland and then begged his fellow "ministers of the gospel" to be "ministers of the secession," willing to do in 1857 America what their fathers had accomplished in 1834 Holland. Klijn obviously didn't want to secede from Classis Holland; he wanted Classis Holland to secede with him and the others from the Reformed Church in America. What he did, however, is leave the fellowship.

Half the charter members of the Christian Reformed Church came from the Graafschap congregation, the only church that submitted a list of grounds by which to justify the 1857 secession. The first three grounds were variations on one theme: the Reformed Church in America had deserted the church order adopted by the Synod of Dort.

First, "The collection of eight hundred hymns, introduced contrary to church order." Hymns that the RCA had grown to love over the centuries evoked memories, of course, of "Evangelical Hymns" that the *Afscheiding* had silenced in the Netherlands.

Second, "Inviting [men of] all religious views to the Lord's Supper, excepting Roman Catholics." The immigrants believed in a closely guarded communion table; for two years, reports reaching the colony claimed that the "Albany church"

Secession or Schism?

The history of the Christian church, from its early days till the present, is saturated with division and strife.

The Protestant Reformation of 1517, although surely necessary, turned out to be a mixed blessing. It spawned multitudes of separated churches, to the embarrassment of all who take Jesus' prayer seriously: " . . . that all of them may be one, Father, . . . so that the world may believe that you have sent me" (John 17:21). Even more embarrassing is the fact that the church is still being divided when no great truths are at stake.

We have nuanced the problem by designating different kinds of division. When true believers are persecuted by autocratic religious powers, we rejoice in their staying together and preserving the church. We have a different problem when true believers find themselves in a church that has clearly deserted the gospel, but they themselves are in no danger. There we have left open the option of staying to continue the battle for truth or seceding to preserve an organization that can rightly be identified as part of the true church. The Secession of 1834 in the Netherlands would appear to pass muster in view of the fact that the church had seriously degenerated, and the faithful were being persecuted for not acquiescing in the status quo.

However, not every secession is so clearly legitimate. The Secession of 1857 that formed the CRC out of the Dutch Reformed Church is more difficult to justify today. Perhaps instead of even trying to justify it, we need to understand it in the light of the tragic experiences of many of the CRC's early members while in the Netherlands. These immigrants were afraid of any alliance that might rob them of their hard-earned religious freedom.

However, there was a strain of separatism in the Secession of 1857 that was schismatic in the sense that it was willful and had no appreciation of the need for unity. That spirit has continued to find a place in the bosom of the CRC. It showed all along in our quickness to bless any and all separatism working in the mainline churches. Through the years many spiritual and ecclesiastical misfits were taken into the ministry of the CRC with the appeal that they could no longer live in the "liberal" church of their origins. Rarely were their stories checked out. We "rejoiced" in having registered a plus in the ongoing battle for "purity." Too often we lived to regret it.

Today that same spirit is rending the fellowship and life of the CRC. It seems that the chickens have come home to roost.

—TEH

was allowing not only an "open" communion—that is, unguarded—but a *wide-open* communion.

Third, "Neglecting to preach the catechism regularly, [to hold] catechetical classes, and [to do] house visitation." It's uncertain how broadly true this charge was. It is true that, in some of the Reformed Church in America congregations, American revivalism had hit the pulpit and Sunday schools had found the classroom.

Allegations Against the RCA in the 1857 Secession of the CRC

1. Did not sufficiently honor the 1834 secession (Afscheiding).

2. Excessively tolerant definition of the true church.
   a. Cooperated with unorthodox churches in printing educational materials.
   b. Practiced partly open invitation to the Lord's Supper.

3. Mild Calvinism.
   a. Did not subscribe to the "rejection of errors" which accompanies the Canons of Dort.
   b. Invited H.P. Scholte to preach in the Zeeland church.
   c. Distributed the somewhat Arminian booklet "Call to the Unconverted" by Richard Baxter.

4. General disregard for church rules.
   a. Encouraged hymn singing (800 hymns).
   b. Irregular catechism preaching.
   c. Irregular family visitation.
   d. Terms of officeholders not properly regulated.

—*Classis Holland Minutes 1848-1858* (Grand Rapids Printing Co., 1943) pp. 48, 224, 235-251; and H. Beets, *De Chr. Geref. Kerk* (Grand Rapids Printing Co., 1918) pp. 64-99.

But nothing so gnawed at the immigrants as the American view of the *Afscheiding*. The Reformed Church in America had left the Dutch state church amicably almost a century earlier (1771-1772). Since then, old roots had withered. Establishing the *Afscheiding* in opposition to Enlightenment preaching and the other ills of the state church, meant next to nothing to Americans. There had been no charges of heresy thrown by the RCA against its mother church, no secession from it, no persecution by it. For the most part, they'd been untouched by the conflict and were, at best, oblivious to its effects upon the new immigrant church way out there in frontier Michigan.

But members of the churches in Noordeloos and Graafschap and Grand Rapids remembered that suffering all too well. Children were told glorious tales of *Afscheiding* heroism. The seceders had suffered ostracism, physical abuse, and all kinds of indignities for their view of truth—God's Truth. They were martyrs, after all, and their immediate descendants, even though they now lived in America, were not about to forget the travail and the glory of persecution.

Of all grounds for secession submitted by the Graafschap church, none is more telling than this:

> *What grieves our hearts most in all of this is that there are members among you who regard our secession in the Netherlands as not strictly necessary or [think that] it was untimely.*

The Eastern church appeared to have little sympathy for the consequential trials of the immigrants' immediate past. They didn't know or understand, and their negligence—even worse, their paternalism—served only to aggravate old wounds. Nothing healed. Although there was no blood shed, the body of Christ was split once again.

The 1857 secessionists might have been willing to forgive some evangelical hymns, close their eyes to open communion, tolerate some flexibility in preaching and teaching. But there was no chance that they would accept the notion, tacitly or openly suggested, that the *Afscheiding* was a mistake. There was too much history there.

"We are obliged to give you notice of our present ecclesiastical standpoint," the Graafschap church told Classis Holland, "namely, separating ourselves from your denomination, together with all Protestant denominations with which we thoughtlessly became connected upon our arrival in America." This passage is rife with the staunch commitment of an individual people, a solid group of like-minded Dutch secessionists, who simply would not be unequally yoked to some adulterous American partner.

Then, remembering Rev. Wyckoff's original pledge, the Graafschap church reminded Van Raalte and his compatriots that the Albany preacher "gives us the liberty to walk in this ecclesiastical path."

Koene Van Den Bosch's leadership of the Graafschap break on April 8, 1857, is the American birthday of what has become the Christian Reformed Church in North America. It is our own birthday.

At this point, not to mention the significant departure of thousands of members of the Christian Reformed Church in its last two decades would be to avoid what is painfully obvious. While the number of CRC members who have left for more progressive fellowships, added to those who have departed for worship styles more expressive and evangelical, would undoubtedly amount to a significant number itself, no single break from the Christian Reformed Church in North America in the last thirty years has been as traumatic as the leave-taking of those thousands who came to believe that the CRCNA was bending the knee to the idols of our time.

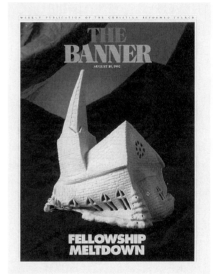

Their immediate reasons for leaving—women in ecclesiastical office, a flirtation with evolutionary theory, waffling on homosexuality—differ from those who left the Reformed Church in America in 1857, the state church in 1834, or the Roman Catholic Church during the Reformation. But there are parallels, as most conservatives would quickly, and even defensively, point out. For behind the shadows of changes that they believe foreshadow doom to CRC fellowship lies what they assume to be a view of Scripture altogether too anxious to accommodate itself to our time.

There are, undoubtedly, cultural reasons, not just theological reasons, for disputes between fellow believers—differences in taste and living patterns by which we structure our lives. But looming more dangerously in the minds of those who've left or are still threatening to leave is a perception not too different from perceptions

Van Den Bosch and the 1857 seceders held—that something good, pure, and righteous is being lost in the church. Those thousands who have left revere what they consider to be theological flawlessness, and in their quest for purity, they are willing to break fellowships, even though some of them understand regretfully the cost.

Their departure changes the body, of course. Once an entire flank is gone, those who remain behind need to locate a new point of balance. The Reformation, after all, created a counter-Reformation within the Roman Catholic Church. Members who once relied on others to pull hand brakes on some controversial issues now find themselves in the difficult position of having to say no themselves. To old-fashioned moderates who've now become conservatives, it was easier somehow when others said no. On the other hand, some CRC members simply say good riddance to all of those who have departed—no matter what direction they've taken on leaving. But where that happens, there is little love, little respect, little toleration, no matter what side one takes in the wars still being waged in the CRC.

If our history tells us anything—at least our early history—it is that we are a fiercely independent group of believers. In Peter De Vries's *Blood of the Lamb,* an old man, proud of the history of dissent in his denomination, says simply, "You can't split bad wood." Arrogance drips from that assessment as blood might from an axe. Let's face it, there's a good deal of glory in standing fast, Luther-like. But for those of us left behind to pick up the pieces, such an attitude smells much like the first of the seven deadly sins—pride.

Our legacy is battle-scarred in the name of righteous truth. We come to our fisticuffs today quite honestly, since apples don't fall far from the tree. Ethnic humor is deeply politically incorrect, but it's fair to say that most of us can laugh when people say that three Hollanders gathered together means there must be at least two churches. That's our character and our history. Some think the whole works should be summarily forgotten—don't even tell the story, they might say.

Does our history of warfare or a propensity for battle somehow excuse our breaking up God's church? Certainly not. Does our inability to get along with each other reflect poorly on the body of Christ, a fellowship supposedly characterized by love, "the greatest of these"? Of course it does. Does our constant warfare keep others from worshiping with us? Undoubtedly. Does it distract us from being God's hands in this world? Yes, it does.

So why do we do it? Why are we constantly beating each other up, walking out of fellowships, berating each other for whatever supposed error comes most quickly to our minds? Why can't we all get along?

Sin, of course. Our own confessions announce the validity of that answer. When confronted by choices, our human nature, Adam's own legacy, urges the wrong alternative—even when we think the wrong one is the right one. We're capable of real beastliness, even though we're created in the image of our Maker. There may be some out there who won't agree with this assessment, but I believe all of us, at some time or another, would rather walk away than try to love those with whom we most vehemently disagree.

Love is the answer all right, but it seems impossible—never as easy as the prescription itself. That's why the commandment to do it occupies the position it does in Scripture—"the greatest of these." Followers of Christ are admonished to love, not because it's nice or sweet or sentimental. It isn't. It's tough, really tough. Living in community, bearing each other's burdens, forgiving each other's beastliness—as well as our own—taxes every bit of our commitment to a living God. "They'll Know We Are Christians by Our Love," that old sixties standard, is a whole lot easier to sing cross-legged on the floor of the youth room than it is to practice with real live people who get incredibly annoying.

And the thousands who've left? Add to that the families your church has lost in the last ten years to other churches down the block with better youth programs, more entertainment, a more exciting way of worshiping God, or more charismatic pastors. Why stop there? Keep adding to the column—put up the number who left so they could raise their hands in worship or do what they very well pleased on Sunday. That's not all—throw in people who left not because of some bellyache about the church, but because they had a falling-out within their own families. Add the adulterers who found coming back to the church they'd worshiped in far too difficult and simply immigrated to a new church world. Throw in the young couples who wanted more kids in church school, or the singles who wanted a fellowship with others like themselves.

What links the motivations in all of these situations is a desire to find something better, a wish to migrate somewhere to a place that seems, at least at first glance, more accommodating and loving—and well might be. Not long ago, I left a CRC congregation myself. It wasn't pleasant, and I wouldn't wish what happened to precipitate that departure on anyone. It will stay with me as long as I live as failure—mine. But what finally led my wife and me out of the fellowship was the overwhelming sense that we were beyond the reaches of love in that church—that love *we* could generate for others, or others could generate for us. We left because we could not see a future in a place where we could not love or be loved. We broke away because maintaining and building community—loving other human beings over time and in spite of their and our own human sin—is so incredibly difficult.

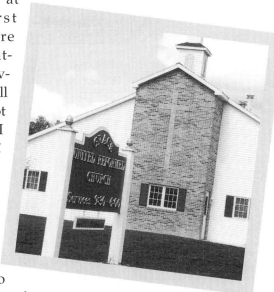

Grace United Reformed Church, Caledonia, Michigan.

Our rifts, our secessions, our breaking away arise from the heart of our very human character, regardless of ethnic background or theological creed. We create animosity quite naturally from the darkness of our hearts.

Does that mean that the Christian Reformed Church in North America should erase its past and seek immediate reconciliation with the Reformed Church in America? Or should we go even farther back—does it mean we should seek a union with the Roman Catholic Church? After all, we all believe there are good Christians, good believers in that fellowship. Shouldn't we simply go back to the source of our rambunctious battling natures and start all over? Wouldn't the Pope be thrilled!

Rev. Leonard Verduin used to tell me that all truth is elliptical—it has two foci—not simply a single center, like a circle. I'm no philosopher, but I do know that much of the chaos of our lives can at least be understood by Verduin's simple diagram. For while love is the antidote to warfare, truth is the antidote to falsehood. What we seek to balance, in all of our bickering, is those two important elements of life: love and truth. I am convinced that someday ministers who seek truth alone will be punished for the fact that their adamant prescriptions created irreparable damage among

CRC and RCA

The CRC secession out of the Reformed Church in America in 1857 was a painful experience for both communions. It led to much unhelpful competition between the two denominations throughout the first hundred years of the CRC's life, with rival congregations in nearly every town and country community.

Eventually, because the proximity of the congregations made it impossible to ignore each other, a kind of ecumenical relationship developed between these churches. This bond was given formal recognition through a "correspondence" relationship between the interchurch committees of the two denominations.

Early in the 1970s the two committees determined to work seriously on bringing the two churches into closer fellowship. That had been nigh to impossible as long as the CRC recognized only one category of fellowship, a "sister church" relationship, which meant that the two would be one if not for geographical separation. Geographical separation was not the problem in this case. When the CRC established the new category of "churches in ecclesiastical fellowship" in 1974, the way was opened for a more promising relationship.

The synod of the CRC voted to accept the RCA as a church in ecclesiastical fellowship early in June 1976. The very next week, the secretary of the interchurch relations committee addressed the General Synod of the RCA, which had just voted to accept the invitation of the CRC to enter that relationship. He pointed out that the decision just taken marked the end of the secession of 1857, and that the two churches were essentially reunited. The synod rose to sing the doxology.

But that formal reunion could not completely erase the brokenness of over one hundred years. The difficulties of getting beyond formalities in ecumenicity are impressively formidable. Today the CRC and the RCA, although not one, are very good friends and are not engaged in throwing stones and hurling accusations at each other.

That's fortunate, for the intermarriage of our members in most communities is such that we would be insulting our relatives! Unity can be promoted in more ways than one.   —TEH

people who once loved each other—families, brothers and sisters in Christ. We *must* love.

But we must also seek truth, God's truth. And there is falsehood around, lots of it. Most obviously, falsehood lies in adoration of any God other than the I AM. We worship ourselves when we care about me first. We worship money when we seek it at the expense of devotion to God or love of our families. We worship culture when we bring adoration to the arts—to fine music or literature. We worship America or Canada when we come to believe that these are somehow God's chosen nations. We're capable of all kinds of idolatry, and only a nose for truth and an ear for righteousness, only the mind of Christ can help us find our way.

Following a path of righteousness means sorting, discriminating. There are things we don't do. There are places we don't go. We find it difficult to retain long-term friendships with those who don't discriminate as we do. We try—not without failure—to live a life that is different from those who don't hold faith as dearly as we do. We try—and we fail—to put God foremost in our lives. We try—often with mixed results—to establish a way of life that recognizes, in all aspects, that our God reigns. We seek truth too—just as we seek to love.

Sometimes, sad to say, those two noteworthy and treasured goals move us in separate paths. Our quest for truth builds walls where they may be unnecessary; our quest to love destroys walls but makes us vulnerable to attack and influence from all sides.

Too often, those who place love above all else do so thoughtlessly and to their peril. Too often, those who pursue truth do so without a smidgeon of love. Love without truth is meaningless sentimentality; truth without love is coldly inhuman. Between those two, we live and die, saved by grace alone, striving to maintain some balance.

The answer to the dilemma posed by the necessity of both love and truth is plainly on view in the Scriptures, in the love chapter, 1 Corinthians 13, a passage whose last line I've already quoted twice. Paul admonishes us with these words: "Love is patient, love is kind. It does not envy, it does not boast, it is not proud." Let those who seek to build their own kingdoms of faith remember those words. "It is not rude, it not self-seeking, it is not easily angered, it keeps no records of wrongs." Tough stuff.

But there's more. "Love does not delight in evil." Someone somewhere is going to have to help us understand what evil is—Movies? Slot machines? Adultery? Card-playing? Destruction of the rain forests or humpback whales? Late-term abortion? Lack of concern for the poor? Homosexuality? Homophobia? Racism? Sexism? Feminism? Evolution?

"Love," says Paul, "rejoices in the truth."

Lord, help us learn both to know the truth and to love each other.

CHAPTER 10

Twenty Years an Orphan

The Rev. Robert Schuller has gained a significant national presence in the United States by preaching a gospel of positive thinking, a creed he certainly didn't inherit from his Dutch Reformed roots, but instead borrowed and fashioned from an American preacher of great renown—and his own RCA mentor—Dr. Norman Vincent Peale. Throughout his many years of ministry, Schuller has championed a gospel of self-assertion, of determination and idealism so quintessentially American that, given his gifts of personal charm and grace, his popularity isn't much of a mystery.

At some times in our lives we could all use a stiff shot of the elixir Schuller offers weekly on his television show. It's not particularly difficult for anyone to find him or herself inundated by life's sorrows and tragedies. Getting older can, by itself, be depressing (says someone turning fifty this year). Despite all our money, our materialistic culture seems adept at creating a whiny unhappiness that often expresses itself in a kind of childish melancholy—too often many of us feel like a kid three days after Christmas, lots of toys and very little joy. We're richer than almost everybody in the world, but as a culture we require weekly treatments on the therapist's couch. Because there's so much emotional sadness in this fabulously wealthy culture of ours, Schuller's pithy little sayings, his television gospel of positive thinking, come as a welcome antidote to our blues. When he tells us to pull up our chin, sometimes that's exactly what we need to hear and do.

Schuller's gospel empire doesn't need my accolades nor should it be much annoyed by my criticism; but let me say— off the record, please—that I'm not one of his staunchest supporters. Sometimes in his ministrations of sweetness and joy, the gospel is radically trivialized to a commodity no more hearty than a smily face. I know that the Lord God Almighty uses all varieties of voices and witnesses, and I'm sure he's used Schuller magnificently, but don't believe for a minute that I'm a big fan.

That a sweet-talker like Schuller came from a Dutch Reformed tradition that had its roots in the secessionist movement in the Netherlands is even somehow understandable. Once he grew old enough to assess the lay of the land around him, he recognized a basic kind of unhappiness in people, even good people. My own opinion is that his particular brand of positive thinking grew out of his own background in a culture that has often generated very little respect for itself.

Former
Cramersburg,
Saskatchewan,
CRC in transit (after
it was sold), 1923.

Let me generalize here for a moment; you don't have to agree. I believe that the Christian Reformed Church culture has had a very low self-image for a long time. Like Garrison Keillor's Minnesota Lutherans, we're rather shocked when someone from outside the tribe actually likes us. We win a convert, and almost immediately we give him or her a podium. At synods, brand-new converts to Reformed doctrine gather delegates' attention immediately; older and often wiser family members draw little more than yawns when they step behind the mike. Maybe it's another case of familiarity breeding contempt, but I've seen this happen more than once.

An example. People who were present at the Rev. Stephen Schlissel's initial appearance at synod will never forget the way he stunned the delegates with a fasci-nating story about his own childhood fas-cination at his family's Passover practices. Delegates were nonplussed. Here was someone—an "outsider," a convert from the Jewish faith—delivering a mesmeriz-ing speech about a tradition foreign to most delegates, advising them on how they should rethink baptism and profes-sion of faith. Other voices were also in favor of looking anew at the practice of children at the Lord's Supper, but it was Schlissel's speech that carried the day. He played a major role in bringing the issue of children at the Lord's table to the top of the denominational agenda.

Today he and his unique group of believers in New York City are no longer part of the Christian Reformed Church. They left—and he did, leading them—bit-terly, after opposing the denomination's stance on a variety of issues, after years of rancor and vitriolic discontent. For one synodical moment, the newcomer Steve Schlissel, a convert from Judaism, looked, to many delegates, refreshingly capable of taking leadership in a denomination he dumped on just a few years later.

We sometimes invest deeply in new-comers like Schlissel, in part because we don't always trust ourselves or each other. Ralph Waldo Emerson's "Self-Reliance" is not one of our three forms of unity, nor is it printed in the back of the *Psalter*. But even if the essay does contain flat-out heresy, maybe it ought to be required reading.

Why don't we have a good self-image? Some might say, I'm sure, that lack of self-reliance grows like a Russian thistle from our old-time commitment to the doctrine of total depravity. Others might add that we don't trust ourselves because we've

A Sudden Reversal

Soon after Stephen Schlissel was admitted to the ministry of the CRC, he began leveling serious criticism at the denomina-tion, claiming that the CRC was not faithful to the trust commit-ted to her. Schlissel publicly charged that some of the profes-sors at Calvin Seminary were "whores." His criticism drew wide attention.

Schlissel spoke at large rallies sponsored by the Concerned Members organization in which he censured the church and the seminary. He was a charismatic and powerful orator, and his speeches were enthusiastically applauded. Attempts by the seminary to meet with him in an honest and forthright manner were fruitless. He granted that at times he used some excessive language but took refuge in his Jewish culture. After promising to take a different approach, he quickly reverted to the same accusations and style of attack.

Eventually the churches in Classis Hudson took disciplinary action that ended in his deposition.   —TEH

always been little more than one big extended family; like brothers and sisters we know each other too well to give each other much credit. Whatever the reason, my feeling is that we're basically reticent about ourselves and others; more than that, we're convinced that we're just a little bit odd. And maybe we are.

You may disagree with what we are today, but when we take a look at what we were in those first decades of our existence in North America, we have reason to be more than a little unsure of ourselves. Any close look back at our first struggling years as a denomination is bound to raise some eyebrows. By all estimations we were, it seems, a strange and unbecoming group.

When the group who left Van Raalte's union with the Reformed Church in America met together in those early years, funerals generally occupied their attention. The very first denominational fight concerned the legitimacy of having a corpse in the church building. Some said dead bodies desecrated God's house. Then, when a widow adorned her husband's rude casket with a spray of flowers, she was found guilty of "worldliness," a weighty charge back then, but wielded with impunity, it seems, over a wide array of behaviors we've come to practice today without as much as a blush. In those early years, for instance, when Christian Reformed gravediggers covered excavated sand with fresh-cut sod, they were blasted for their "wicked hiding of death's horror." Okay.

In one congregation elders prompted a brawl by starting the process of church discipline against those who purchased fire insurance; the elders claimed buyers lacked confidence in God's eternal plan for his

elect. Another group nearly split over the question, "May elders read sermons from the pulpit or only from a reading desk?" In another discussion, some claimed that the wearing of a mustache—presumably by men—was sinful. And in one community a young man caught whistling was hauled

A Poor Stick in the Pulpit

One minister was a self-admitted "poor stick" in the pulpit. With a rueful grimace, he would confess that in the area of sermon delivery, he was bereft of all gifts.

He learned this lesson soon after he graduated from seminary and received his first call. During the period of consideration, he was requested to demonstrate his gifts in the pulpit to a hushed and expectant congregation. At the end of the service, he was approached by an elderly lady, who candidly told her fellow Frisian, *"Jo moatte us berop mar oannimme: wy krije dochs net in goeie."* ("You'd better take our call. We won't get a good one anyway.")

—WDB

before his consistory on the charges that he'd been heard "calling the devil," a piece of superstition likely borrowed from some American source, since it was without precedent in the Dutch Reformed tradition.

For the first decade of its existence, the Christian Reformed Church was a Dutch baby, an orphan, trying to figure out who it was in a still strange environment that often seemed rife with the gleaming attractions of Vanity Fair. We were very weak and, for the most part, leaderless. We were entirely capable at any moment of going up in flames we set ourselves with endless internal bickering.

Most of the official documents from those earliest days are lost. No one can pinpoint the birth date of the denomination itself. Henry Beets claims that the seceding congregations organized a classis meeting in April of 1857, while John Kromminga and others name October 7 as the date of the first classical meeting and "the actual origin of the Christian Reformed Church in America."

Though the specifics are lost, we do know the major events from those first years. Before the 1857 summer had cooled into September, Rev. Hendrik G. Klijn, pastor of the Grand Rapids church, had left the

Map of Dutch settlements in West Michigan ca.1880.

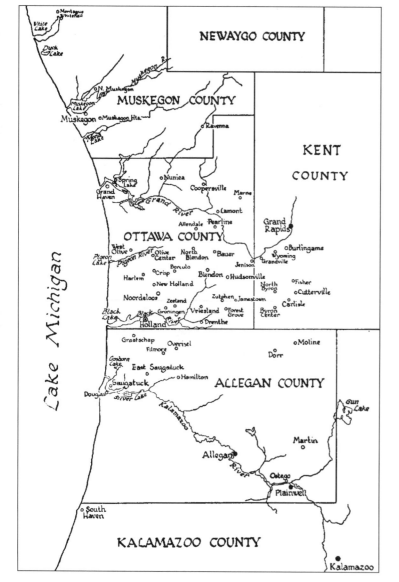

fold to return to the Van Raalte group. So had the Polkton congregation, one of the four original seceding churches. But a group from Grand Haven and another from Vriesland decided to send delegates to the October 7 meeting.

It would be wonderful to point to that meeting as a great defining moment in the history of the Christian Reformed Church. It would uplifting if we could quote from a litany of inspired speeches proclaiming God's goodness, or his divine rule over all of life, or the renewed mission of bringing the gospel in bright and shiny packages to the unchurched. It would be edifying if there were, on the record, some expansive vision for this new fledgling fellowship of believers. But that October meeting is remarkably void of the materials needed for grandiose myth-making. Delegates included a single clergyman and a dozen lay leaders, most of whom had lugged along their own list of often conflicting views. They represented no more than two hundred fifty people, immigrants all of them, the whole assembly well-insulated from American culture by a language they didn't understand and divided from each other by infrequently traversed miles of thickly-wooded Michigan wilderness.

What bound them was their deeply held commitment to do the Lord's will, a near reverence for the tradition of the Synod of Dort, and a profound antagonism to an "unholy alliance" with the Reformed Church in America. The history of the Christian Reformed Church in those first years is, according to Henry Zwaanstra, a series of "internal conflicts and unfruitful controversies." Infighting threatened the life of already weak congregations. Classis meetings were riddled with lists of charges and countercharges of heresy as long as your arm. The founders of the CRC hammered away at each other in one petty dispute after another, while around them the United States plunged into the economic depression of 1857 and began the march into a long and bloody Civil War. By 1863, Zwaanstra claims, the future of the church was so bleak that "discontinuing the denomination was seriously considered."

For more than a century, the seceders' initial decision to pull out of Van Raalte's union with the Reformed Church in America has been debated—specifically, whether the grounds for leaving were substantial enough to warrant the break with a fellowship that had provided leadership and promised a place in the sun of the New World. Just exactly how anyone assesses the break will undoubtedly be affected not only by his or her view of the issues offered by the seceders but also of the relative importance of defining what is right by specific theological (and cultural) views. Certainly accommodation and compromise with a larger community offered its own kinds of rewards—and righteousness. But so did orthodoxy. Oddly enough, truth and love, back then as now, often go to war.

Assessing our own early history is difficult and controversial. The struggle between breaking away and staying with the union is reflected by the fact that even today discussions concerning a merger with the RCA have a way of resurfacing every few years. No single aspect of that controversial decision reveals our own continuing struggle with that issue as clearly as the judgment different historians have made on a man whose name has appeared earlier in the story, Gijsbert Haan, an immigrant with a special knack for irritating Van Raalte himself.

Haan was a rug weaver born in Hilversum, the Netherlands, in 1801. After landing in America forty-some years later, he lived for a time in Albany and Troy, New York, before making his way west to the new colony and settling in Vriesland, just a few miles from Holland, in the fall of 1849. When Haan came to the Michigan colony, his report of the conditions in the Reformed Church back East were miserably sour, and his views on the ministry of Rev. Isaac Wyckoff were particularly stinging—so much so that when Van Raalte and Wyckoff negotiated the 1850 union, Haan became incensed. Three years later, after he'd moved to Grand Rapids and been elected elder in the church there, he began badgering Van Raalte about the union at every classis meeting he attended. By 1857, Haan was one of those who convinced the Grand Rapids congregation to pull out of the RCA.

All of those who have investigated this portion of the history of the colony in western Michigan agree on Haan's physical presence: he was tall, lean, and handsome. But after that assessment, there's no consensus at all. RCA historians recall him as a nagging malcontent, an ill-formed rascal, a whining critic. CRC writers, on the other hand, have routinely described Haan as a thoroughly dedicated, theologically sensitive, altogether honorable man.

Consider, for example, this portrait drawn by John Hagar, an RCA historian:

> *No matter how we try, it seems impossible to produce any positive historic evidence that would warrant classifying [Gijsbert] Haan as an*

expert witness in the field of Reformed faith and practice. All the efforts of Christian Reformed apologists to make an expert out of Haan seem to fall short of the mark. . . .

At this point it is instructive to remind ourselves what . . . Haan was not. [Gijsbert] Haan was not a stable personality. This is evident from his erratic behavior in the matter of his church affiliations and loyalties. Between the years 1835 and 1874 he made not fewer than six changes in church membership. First he was in the Hervormde Kerk in the Netherlands, and then he was out of it. Next he was in the Christian Seceder Church in the Netherlands, and then he was out of it. Then he was in the Reformed Dutch Church in America, and behold, he was out of it. Next he was in the Christian Reformed Church in America, and then he was out of it. Now he is back in the Reformed Church in America; and—no surprise—he is out again. Finally, he is back in the American Christian Reformed Church, where he remained a scant five years. With the exception of one change from the Christian Seceder Church in the Netherlands to the Reformed Church in America, every change was made under duress and strife and ill-will and secession. Such a record does not bespeak stability of character or constancy of purpose.

—"Gijsbert Haan: A Study in Alienation," *Reformed Journal,* November 1969.

Now read, in contrast, this sketch by CRC historian D. H. Kromminga:

> [Gijsbert Haan] had his training as an elder under the leadership of Van Velzen and was qualified to form an independent estimate of the situation, and his judgments evinced such a clear grasp of fundamental principles as secured for his word great influence among the settlers. . . .
>
> He had had contact with Reformed leaders and churches in the East and related his observations to anxious inquirers in the colony. . . . [He] clearly forecast all the disastrous results [of merger with the RCA]. Haan evidently had a remarkably correct picture of the leveling influence of American interdenominational fellowship.

—*The Christian Reformed Tradition* by D. H. Kromminga (Grand Rapids, MI: Wm. B. Eerdmans, 1943) p. 108.

Saint or sinner? Like all of us, a little of both. One hundred and fifty years later, how we pitch his role has much to do with our assessment of the results of his adventurous campaigning. It's an exchange that is finally slated to die, however, as the specific motivations for the break between the CRC and the RCA recede ever further into our collective pasts. What's more, different perspectives on Gijsbert Haan are constructed on the assumption that he was single-handedly responsible for the creation of the Christian Reformed Church. He wasn't. He was very much present and accounted for, all right—he left his tracks all over what meager records remain. But his was only one voice; there were more. Still, it's likely that no one irritated Van Raalte more than Gijsbert Haan. It was Van Raalte himself who penned the minutes of the classis meetings, and the minutes call Haan mean.

But the secession that created the Christian Reformed Church in North America was neither unprecedented nor a surprise. It was not just the work of one man, Gijsbert Haan, but the culmination of a general tilt toward withdrawal. From the date of the merger with the RCA, Van Raalte had felt pressure created by antagonism to that decision. Part of the Graafschap church pulled away; then two-thirds of the Drenthe congregation seceded. Both groups made the

merger itself the main ground for their secession. Gijsbert Haan was not involved in either of those assemblies.

Haan was typical of other immigrants landing on the shores of Black Lake during the 1850s. Those *Afscheiding* leaders from the northern provinces of the Netherlands had been, from the very beginnings of the secessionist movement in the old country, a shade or two more cranky both in their criticisms of the state church and their planned courses of action. Long ago in the Netherlands, some of them had considered Van Raalte, the adoring son of a *Hervormde* preacher, too liberal. Without wasting time after their

Synod 1888 met at Spring Street CRC in Grand Rapids, Michigan.

Main Street,
Zeeland, Michigan,
ca. 1900.

Egyptians." Van Den Bosch, along with the smattering of immigrants who with him founded the Christian Reformed Church, was committed to the intellectual platform of the northern *Afscheiding* party. It's altogether feasible that Gijsbert Haan, when taunting Van Raalte in classis meetings, may have delighted in playing to that audience. But he certainly didn't create it, nor was he alone.

The key issue was not Gijsbert Haan's personality but Van Raalte's merger. Although his intention was probably kindness, Isaac Wyckoff, according to Kromminga, had gone "beyond his mandate in offering terms of union to the colonists at the meeting of June 4, 1849." Both the Particular and General synods were stunned by Wyckoff's move, but they both finally approved the offer after the fact.

What's more, Wyckoff's pledge that if the merger didn't work out, the immigrants could "bid us a fraternal adieu and be by themselves again" proved even knottier. Kromminga says that Wyckoff's offer wasn't warranted by any historical precedent in Reformed polity. Furthermore, nothing about the offer was ever put plainly and forthrightly on the public record in either of the two bodies. "It is hard to see in this offer anything but an attempt on the part of Wyckoff," Kromminga says, "to overcome the hesitation of the colonists by a bit of salesmanship which he never expected to be used in later disputes."

But that escape clause was used, and used frequently. The provision Wyckoff had given for allowing for withdrawal from the union was proof in the eyes of CRC founders that the merger had never been more than a trusting nod, not even a

arrival in America, immigrants from these northern provinces, rightly or wrongly, drew a parallel between the Dutch *Hervormde Kerk* and her daughter church in the New World. If the 1834 secession in the Netherlands was justified—and no one would doubt that—then an 1857 secession in America was equally righteous.

Even though, as we've said before, Haan offered his opinions based upon his own experiences in the American church, others didn't need any American experience to come to the same conclusion. Koene Van Den Bosch, for example, had been in America only a few months and had acquired no firsthand information about the churches in the East when he proclaimed Van Raalte's merger, according to Robert Swierenga, "a welcoming of the Assyrian and begging bread of the

solid handshake. After all, the clause making the arrangement provisional was never formally adopted. Therefore, the 1857 withdrawal was, formally at least, a secession—not merely, as Beets liked to call it, a "return" to a previous status. At the same time, those who seceded could justifiably argue, as they did, that Wyckoff had pledged to them the right to dissolve the union unilaterally whenever it seemed necessary. For instance, R. T. Kuiper, writing in *A Voice from America About America* in 1879, claimed that many had interpreted the character of the merger as *provisional,* "for otherwise they would not have joined."

For more than twenty years after the 1857 break, both denominations made the writing of tracts condemning each other into something of a pastime, if not an obsession. Two RCA writers created *Voices from the Holland Reformed Church,* which, in the CRC view of R. T. Kuiper, used "tact, ingenuity, and cleverness" to caricature the 1857 withdrawal as the result of nothing more than "local troubles and personal feuds." An 1869 tract from the CRC side carried a title so weighty that it seems on its own to be a monograph:

> *An Exposition Based on Official Sources of the Actual Conditions of the Reformed Protestant (Dutch) Church in America [i.e., the RCA] and a Defense of the Basis of the Return of the True Dutch Reformed Church in America [i.e., the CRC] to the Old Standpoint Forsaken in 1849.*

Rev. Peter Hoekenga (1876-1927), preaching for Helping Hand Rescue Mission in Chicago about 1914.

Gijsbert Haan himself penned a shrill *Stem Eens Belasterden* ("Voice of One Slandered") in 1871, and the Rev. F. Hulst defended the CRC position in an 1874 *Zamenspraak* ("Dialogue").

What little energy the fledgling church had in those early years was consumed by the effort to justify its own existence. Those actions are neither unusual nor surprising—breakaway churches like the CRC, no matter what they've departed from or become on their own, always carry with them one defining feature—they are always cocksure of what they are *not*. The task of building up a body that defines itself primarily on negatives is no easy task. Sharing a common enemy can be solidifying for a time, but once the crisis has passed, a new defining principle is required.

A quick story. Not many years ago, the Protestant Reformed denomination (a group that has its own time in the story of the CRC) held its annual young people's convention at Dordt College. At the time, a student I knew was dating a boy from that denomination, and she was doing custodial work at the college. After a large group session at the college chapel, this student of mine found dozens of one-page handouts explaining in vivid detail how Protestant Reformed kids should evangelize their Christian Reformed friends.

She cried. She bawled, in fact.

It may be difficult for us to believe that a group from such a similar doctrinal tradition would spend the time of hundreds of young people going over a sheet full of pointers on how to bring CRC kids to Christ. But they did. I saw the sheet myself. Apart from whatever theological or sociological grounds Protestant Reformed peo-

ple might offer to explain their actions, what's true of the Protestant Reformed was and may still be true of the CRC as well: breakaway fellowships tend to define themselves primarily on the basis of *what they're not*. Many of us know that in some isolated denominational hamlets a specifically CRC identity has long been maintained primarily by contrast with the RCA. By God's grace, that era is finally ending. But for years, many of us recognized ourselves more fully by what we weren't—RCA—than what we were.

The glory of secession is always perceived to be the retention of purity and the intention of righteousness; but in the history of denominational strife in the Reformed fellowship, as well as many others, breaking has never meant an escape from sin—or its pernicious effects.

Years after those first decades of CRC existence, John Kromminga, who lauded Gijsbert Haan, allowed that early CRC leaders had probably "overemphasized the importance" of RCA evils. At the same time, he wanted it noted that "Van Raalte and his followers consistently minimized the dangers and errors [in the RCA] and sometimes ignored them completely."

On both counts Kromminga was probably right. Few knowledgeable members of the Reformed Church in America today would deny that to this day significant theological differences remain between that denomination's Eastern and Western bodies. Old Gijsbert Haan may have been illtempered, but he was not completely wrong.

Let's just say that there are skeletons in the closets of both houses.

AN INFANCY WITHOUT GROWTH

Henry Beets, in his 1923 history of the Christian Reformed Church, labeled the stretch between 1857 and 1880 the "Period of Struggling Early Life," a good banner to drape over some very troublesome years.

Part of the struggle had to do with status and money. Well-heeled immigrants who'd arrived early and built comfortable homes and lives in the wilderness weren't all that interested in the rigorous hellfire preaching of Koene Van Den Bosch, so the community's established leaders stayed away from the Christian Reformed Church. Membership there simply cost too much. By severing relationships with Van Raalte and the RCA, Henry Lucas says the newborn CRC lost all access to funds that still flowed from the East. Made up mainly of farmers and recently transplanted immigrants, the new denomination was literally dirt poor—and manifestly uncool.

Constant friction wore down unity and resolve. Each attack on the Reformed Church in America prompted a return blast. And the CRC's own unending internal bickering, as constant as breath itself, left as many casualties as external strife.

Much of the struggle had to do with size. The Christian Reformed Church was tiny, minute. For years it didn't grow an inch. Less than 10 percent of the settlers had joined the new denomination— about one hundred and fifty families in all. That may be a good-sized congregation today, but even then, as a denomination, it was minuscule. Some of its members, grown tired and worn by all the fighting, simply walked back to the fellowship of the RCA. The Grand Haven church went back to its Dutch roots and became something of an American conventicle, a house church. Attempts to plant new congregations in Wisconsin didn't meet with much success at all.

So although the CRC eventually attracted a stream of immigrants to its rolls, in the 1850s and '60s that immigrant stream was barely a trickle. By church growth standards, the entire denomination seemed dead in the water.

One of the reasons for the slow growth was that fewer immigrants were arriving during those years because economic conditions were improving in Europe. The potato blight had passed, and discrimination against secessionists had ceased. There simply was no cause to immigrate.

Also, the U.S. economy had collapsed the year the Christian Reformed Church was founded. Railroads and other industries had overextended their holdings, especially in real estate, and the only means by which they could recoup capital was to dump what they had. But there were no buyers. The result was economic depression.

As reports of the American financial crisis were carried to the shores of the Netherlands, would-be immigrants changed their minds and stayed put. In 1857, 1,775 Dutch immigrants walked down the gangplanks from foreign ships and onto American soil; in 1858, only 185 arrived. Since economic conditions improved in the U.S. only when war between the States broke out—and few immigrants could be lured by the prospect of a brutal Civil War—the number of Dutch immigrants arriving annually reached eight hundred again only after the war ended in 1865.

Hardship stories were also communicated to the Netherlands. Reports from the American colonies were no longer of a land flowing with milk and honey. The romance was fading. Turning soil and felling trees—the hard work of establishing community on the frontier—isn't work for folks with soft hands.

The tragedy of the *Phoenix*, a propeller-driven steamboat on Lake Michigan, was enough to make prospective immigrants reconsider leaving their homes. Nearly a decade later, another tragedy occurred, making travel even less appealing. On September 1, 1856, the *Ocean Home*, carrying eighty-eight Dutch immigrants, collided with an English ship at sea. According to Henry Lucas, the crew, evidently confused and panicky, "failed to remove a heavy object that had fallen across the stairway," leaving seventy-eight of the immigrants pinned below deck as the ship slipped under the waves.

But even without the tragedies, travel to the New World was a gruesome prospect. Dutch families read descriptions of ocean passages like that of Jelle Pelmulder, who'd sailed the *South Carolina* in 1855 and recorded this note cited by Henry Lucas:

> *The berths were arranged along the sides of the vessel in two tiers, one above the other. They were so low that a person could scarcely sit up in them. The bedding rested on unplaned wooden boards. The passage between the tiers of berths was piled with boxes containing goods, tools, and other articles. The air in the steerage quarters was fetid, combining the smell of tar with the odor of men, women, and children crowded into an inadequately ventilated space. . . . In the cook's galley was a cast-iron stove with eight places for pots. This stove was the sole means of preparing the food for the 286 passengers and the crew. . . . During and after storms, with the attendant seasickness, conditions in the stench-filled steerage were horrible. Disease spread among the passengers.*

> —*Netherlanders in America* by Henry Lucas (Grand Rapids, MI: Wm. B. Eerdmans, 1955, 1989) pp. 480-481.

With ads such as this, few prospective immigrants ran madly after tickets for an ocean voyage.

Dutch preachers proved even harder to attract than Dutch farmers. For years the Christian Reformed Church tried to coax clergy to give up a pulpit in the Secession Church in the Netherlands for a new ministry in Michigan or Iowa. But for all their offers, few Dutch dominies showed up. Emigration, after all, wasn't for everyone—certainly not for those who'd accumulated any kind of nest egg in the old country. From the fall of 1857, when Grand Rapids preacher Rev. Hendrik G. Klijn left the fledgling fellowship of the CRC to return to the RCA, until 1863, the entire ministerial force of the CRC numbered one—Koene Van Den Bosch, a pious man of very little education, willing to exist in utter poverty, given to holding very stout positions and, according to

Henry Beets, a man with a "violent temper."

Van Den Bosch was eventually joined by a colleague, Rev. W. H. Van Leeuwen, who became pastor for the Grand Rapids church in 1863. But in the infancy of the CRC, it was the zealous, if uneven, ministry of elders in the various congregations that propped up the fellowship.

The congregations that deserted Van Raalte intended to reunite with the Secession Church in the Netherlands; they said as much in their 1857 letters to classis. But when Van Den Bosch and Klijn asked their Dutch mother church for bread, they got a stone. Many members of the denomination were devastated when their petition was denied. But the mother church simply couldn't be sure of what it was supporting thousands of miles away. Reports were, after all, sketchy and conflicting.

Three years later Van Den Bosch sent an emotional appeal, begging recognition for the new American denomination. The Dutch Synod of 1860 once again refused his plea. In 1866 Van Raalte himself was the RCA fraternal delegate to the Dutch Secession Church; his reports, as can well be imagined, did nothing to polish the image of the Christian Reformed Church in America. When in 1872 the CRC eventually sent its own official delegation to a Dutch synod, the Christian Reformed representatives were seated, according to Beets, "only after considerable debate and with the expressed declaration of

Wilhelmus H. Van Leeuwen (1807-1882), pastor of the first CRC in Grand Rapids, 1863-1867, who trained at least one student for the ministry. When he came to Michigan in 1863, his only cohort was Koene Van Den Bosch until Douwe Van der Werp arrived in 1864.

synod that it refused to judge" the merits of the 1857 secession.

For Dutch preachers, it was not merely the miserable passage aboard stinking ships that discouraged relocation in America. It was also a deep suspicion that the CRC was an ill-gotten child in search of legitimacy.

Those few early decades were hardly wonderful for the CRC. Since contacts with the American world around the church itself would have been unheard of and there were no immigrants to add to its rolls, growth was minimal at best. The church lacked educated clergy to give it any guidance, and its own role model—the Secession Church in the Netherlands—refused aid. The CRC in those first years was an orphan, barely alive in the American wilderness.

GROWING UP AND SPREADING OUT

John Kromminga once wrote that "It was no race of intellectual giants which founded the church in the wilderness." Although his characterization may seem cruel or insensitive, and although real wisdom is not necessarily conferred by the completion of a graduate degree, Kromminga's analysis is likely not far afield. But our appraisal both of the people who left Van Raalte's union and the individuals who led that departure has to recognize that these were folks who were very much accustomed to finding their own way. For a generation or more in the Netherlands, many of them had grown up with a conventicle background of fierce independence from authority. In the conventicle tradition, intellectual prowess and/or a fancy diploma were no more coveted than badminton skills. What was important was

The first meeting place of CRC students training for the ministry was this Graafschap, Michigan, parsonage.

(Center) Douwe Van der Werp (1811-1876), pastor of the Graafschap CRC (1864-1872), was also the seminary instructor and held classes in the Graafschap parsonage.

piety and an uncompromising devotion to God.

If they are to be successful, however, all movements such as the gathering of believers who comprised the Christian Reformed Church in its earliest years, require more than fervor; they also require wise leadership. The first individual brought into the fellowship who offered not only real gifts of leadership but also a magnanimous character was Rev. D. J. Van der Werp.

Van der Werp was gracious and bright, a gifted writer and a fine teacher. From his pastorate in Graafschap, to which he was called in 1864, Van der Werp produced the first issue of the denomination's long-running magazine, *De Wachter,* on February 14, 1868; he was convinced that, if it were to

survive, the CRC needed a unifying voice. Not long after, he was elected denominational stated clerk, an office he held for the next seven years and would have stayed in longer had not cancer taken him to the glory he'd anticipated all of his life.

Van der Werp and the other ministers in the fledgling fellowship were more than simply the spiritual leaders in the community. Most CRC preachers today want to be called "Pastor," as in "Pastor Ed" or "Pastor Dan," perhaps because *Reverend,* with its implications of saintliness, costs a bit too much. One can't be *Reverend,* after all, and win the young people's pie-eating contest. But *Dominie,* which sounds fearfully much like *domination,* is even more expensive, especially in a time when preachers think of themselves as servants.

But many of those early preachers were, in fact, capable of dominating. When they ruled with an iron fist, or when their petulance was on display for all the world, they could be royal pains; but when they were gracious, caring, and wise—why then, they were gracious, caring, and wise. They were leaders not only because they opined themselves as leaders, but also because their followers looked to them as such. It's quite likely that leadership meant, back then, a much stiffer clerical collar than it does today. Apparently, that's what preachers and lay folks both wanted and expected.

By 1868, Van der Werp's parsonage at Graafschap was not only the family home, it was also something of a seminary. The dominie understood that this young church required trained clergy. But

De Wachter (The Watchman)

At the end of 1985 the venerable Dutch language publication *De Wachter* appeared for the last time in its 118-year journalistic life span.

In the early years of its history, *De Wachter* served as a vigorous and polemic defender of the CRC. With elan and enthusiasm it entered into the fray against institutions and individuals who dared to challenge the denomination's right to exist. In the closing decades of the nineteenth century these battles were waged in blunt and increasingly archaic Dutch.

But there was also another side to this periodical. Meditations, sermons, devotional articles, poetry, and information about the struggling but steadily growing denomination captured the attention of the reader.

In generations gone by, in prairie villages, in lonely farm outposts, and on Main Street America, the mail carrier's appearance with *De Wachter* was greeted with fervent anticipation. Weddings, anniversaries, obituaries, and, of course, *beroepen* (calls) were carefully monitored. From Paterson, New Jersey, to Houston, British Columbia, *De Wachter* functioned as a molder and unifier of the church.

In the twentieth century, *De Wachter* maintained contact with the "old country" and kept alive the legacy and tradition so precious to those who had left their native land. Particularly after World War II, the periodical served as a bridge to help the thousands of immigrants coming to the United States and Canada become better acquainted with their new denomination.

After the turbulent sixties, *De Wachter* subscriptions declined dramatically. The CRC became less mono-ethnic and embraced multiculturalism. A Dutch language periodical, no matter how progressive and Reformed in orientation, became less and less viable. The death knell came when synod more or less reluctantly authorized its demise in 1985.

De Wachter's editors, listed here, have served the church and its Lord with distinction. Each spoke prophetically to his time. Especially in later years, *De Wachter* breathed an ecumenical and progressive spirit while carefully maintaining faithfulness to our Reformed heritage. Historians in generations to come will read its yellowing pages with respect.

The last issue of the CRC weekly *De Wachter* includes this photo containing mastheads of nearly all the Dutch-language publications that once served the immigrant community from coast to coast.

Rev. D. J. Van der Werp, 1868-1875	*Prof. B. K. Kuiper, 1918-1922*
Rev. G. E. Boer, 1875-1878	*Rev. H. Keegstra, 1922-1948*
Rev. G. Hemkes, 1878-1884	*Rev. E. Van Halsema, 1948-1964*
Rev. L. J. Hulst, 1884-1888	*Rev. W. Haverkamp, 1964-1983*
Rev. G. E. Boer, 1885-1894	*Dr. S. Woudstra, 1983-1985*
Rev. A. Keizer, 1894-1918	

—WDB

he didn't stop there. By the time the flow of immigrants picked up again after the Civil War, jammed on board between farmers and tradesman and their expectant families were Dutch preachers he'd persuaded to serve the new American denomination.

When Van der Werp became too ill to keep teaching, the church decided to start a full-fledged American seminary. Rev. G. E. Boer was relieved of his parish duties in Grand Rapids to become the faculty of the Theological School of the Christian Reformed Church. On

Gerrit E. Boer (1832-1904), first professor of Grand Rapids Theological School, 1876-1904.

March 15, 1876, he delivered a convocation address entitled "The Training of Future Ministers of the Gospel." The following morning, according to John Timmerman in his book *Promises to Keep,* Boer began teaching his seven students in a regimen that included Dutch, Latin, Greek, Hebrew, General History, Dutch History, Geography, Psychology, Logic, and Rhetoric. Timmerman adds, "Since this apparently consumed but a fraction of his energy, he also taught Dogmatics, Hermeneutics, Exegesis, Isagogics, Church History, Symbolism, and Practical Theology."

Boer was an interesting man and a good fit for the early Christian Reformed Church. Like the people he served, his roots were rural and provincial; he wasn't highly cultured or sophisticated. He'd started his own theological education when he was thirty. John Kromminga describes Boer this way: "pietistic in temperament . . . homiletic in preaching . . . kind, fatherly, reverent, but without pre-

tensions to scholarship." He taught future preachers, not future scholars.

By the late 1870s, the crisis of leadership in the CRC was past. Almost single-handedly, Van der Werp and his recruits had filled the gap for a crucial decade.

Along the immigrant route from the Atlantic to the Midwestern colonies, Christian Reformed groups began to organize—first in Paterson, New Jersey; and then in Monsey, West Sayville, and Rochester, New York. Often, the pews in Rochester—just like those in Cleveland, Ohio, and Lafayette, Indiana—were filled mainly with immigrants who stopped only long enough to take temporary jobs and then moved again, westward.

By the time the CRC was fifteen years old, congregations were organized or organizing in Oostburg, Wisconsin; Roseland and South Holland, Illinois (areas then called "Low" and "High Prairie"); and just a bit to the north and west in Ridott ("German Valley"), Illinois. But when most Dutch immigrants were cleared to leave Castle Garden, they had one of the major colonies in mind—western Michigan or central Iowa.

In Holland, Michigan, the big news of 1857 was not another secession from Van Raalte's church. What troubled immigrants most was the fact that the shallow channel dug by early colonists to connect Black Lake and Lake Michigan had filled with sand. The channel was the colony's economic lifeline. Without it there were no ships. Without ships there was no commerce.

While the CRC organized its classical affairs in the fall of that year, Holland's civic leaders were appealing to the State of Michigan for help that had been promised—or at least hinted at being promised—a decade earlier. "Ten years ago we began to knock at your doors," read the petition to Congress, according to Henry Lucas in *Netherlanders in America*. "Since that time we have been constantly engaged in a life-and-death struggle in the wilderness and on a desolate shore, tantalized with an insufficient beginning of our harbor work, and cruelly kept in suspense."

By July 1, 1858, the suspense had been lifted, a new channel had been dug, and the steamboat *Huron* was right there on Black Lake, its run linking Chicago, Illinois, and the immigrant colony at Holland, Michigan. Though the *Huron* was undoubtedly a step up from the dusty rattling of a stagecoach, the major advantage of the new channel was not a traveler's luxury but the colony's economy. From that time on, Holland's mills and factories and stores flourished. All the products generated from west Michigan's ample forest resources—cordwood, bark, logs, lumber, shingles, and staves—were shipped out, and the colony once again began to grow, spreading slowly up toward Grand Haven, Spring Lake, and Muskegon, as well as eastward toward the already expanding city of Grand Rapids.

A young and now nameless woman was the first Dutch immigrant to Grand Rapids, where stands today's "headquarters" of the Christian Reformed Church. She'd come in 1847 to look for her fiancé, who'd immigrated, then pleaded with her to join him in the New World. Unfortunately, he wrote from Grand Rapids, Wisconsin (now Wisconsin Rapids), not Grand Rapids, Michigan. With the help of Van Raalte, who came to interpret for her, officials were able to get word to her fiancé, and he came to bring her to the other side of the lake.

Soon after this incident, other immigrants found their way to the rapidly growing city of Grand Rapids. When poverty decimated Van Raalte's colony in the late 1840s, young women moved to Grand Rapids to earn their living as housekeepers, and young men found jobs in the city's factories. Some married and stayed.

When crops failed in the colony, especially in 1851, more families packed up and headed for Grand Rapids. In 1853, a batch of immigrants, frustrated because of failing commerce in Holland, moved to Grand Rapids, intending to return as soon as the harbor at Black Lake was opened. But by the time the harbor was made, they'd put down roots in the city on the Grand River.

Meanwhile, the new residents were joined by a group of disillusioned immigrants who had followed a Rev. Buddingh to Ravenna, north of Grand Rapids. When, Lucas says, the somewhat unpredictable Buddingh gave up on what he saw as insufferable conditions—little to eat except turnips and shanties hardly fit for human life—his followers left Ravenna and moved to Grand Rapids.

By the 1860s Grand Rapids was building a reputation for manufacturing fine furniture from local hardwoods, and with each passing year, more of the hands molding American tables and chairs were those of Dutch immigrants settling in the "City on the Grand." Many of those hands belonged to folks who came into the Christian Reformed Church. Whole neighborhoods were created, many of them with their own churches.

Meanwhile the church also continued to grow in Iowa. Scholte's "Strawtown" was earning a new nickname, *"Moeder Pella,"* the mother of colonies. The rich, black earth of Marion County seemed a dream to Dutch immigrant farmers, its lure irresistible. But the law of supply and demand took force after the Civil War, and the price of the Iowa ground increased as the population rose. Soon men like Henry Hospers, founder of Pella's *Weekblad,* the local newspaper, and later village mayor, became convinced that another colony was needed to support the increased population of new land seekers making the trip from the Netherlands.

According to Henry Lucas's account of the establishment of the northwest Iowa colony, in March, 1869, Hendrik J. Van der Waa, J. Pelmulder, and several others met in Henry Hospers's office to plan a new colony. After considering sites in Kansas, Texas, and Oregon, a committee was commissioned to look at northwest Iowa. On April 26, the committee climbed aboard a covered wagon behind Van der Waa's newly acquired team of mules and headed across the prairie for Sioux City.

When they arrived on May 10, a kindly land agent gave them the information they were looking for. Less than two weeks later, Lucas says, they were back in Pella describing land so beautiful that, in typical recruitment hype, "it surpassed anything in Marion County." Immediately they drummed up membership in a new associ-

ation for colonization *(kolonisatie vereeniging)* whose ranks rocketed to eighty-two people in no more than an hour, all of whom had signed up for part of the 17,920 acres the leaders claimed available for new settlers.

By the spring of 1870, final sites had been selected on the rich prairie north of Sioux City—in Sioux and Lyon counties—where thousands of acres of cheap government and railroad land were still available. Lucas claims the Pella send-off was enthusiastic: friends and relatives lined the streets to wish God's blessing on those second-generation colonists who were heading north and west. After prayers, the wagon train—with Van der Waa and his mules in the lead—pulled away from the town square to the accompaniment of psalms and hymns.

During the first summer in Sioux County, most settlers built earthen dugouts, which provided shelter during the first year. They dug holes about five feet deep on the south or east side of a hill, thereby avoiding overpowering prairie winds, and roofed the hole in the ground with poles covered in sod, making the whole place a kind of "Strawtown North." But within a year the village of Orange City boasted several homes, a blacksmith, a shoemaker, a hotel keeper, and even a barber who, in fine American tradition, doubled as a pharmacist—hence the ever-present red and white barber pole outside the office. Other settlers, who'd followed another immigrant path across America, left Wisconsin and arrived in northwest Iowa to establish the town of Sioux Center, a town a few miles farther north and west of Orange City.

Charlie Dyke, Sioux County's earliest historian, recounts an amazing story of Jacob Koster, who set down his land claim at a spot that is today Sioux Center's Central Park. Busy with the work of turning virgin soil, Koster and his family had little time for entertainment or recreation. But one day Koster decided to locate the source of a column of smoke he'd seen to the south, an indication that someone, probably someone white, had settled somewhere close. In search of that homestead, he and his family walked over the sloping prairie hills in grass that sometimes grew taller than they were. Eventually, they came upon a cabin, which, they assumed, meant that the inhabitants were white settlers and not Native Americans.

Somewhat afraid of walking in on strangers, and self-conscious about their meager skills with the English language, the Kosters hesitated visiting their first Sioux County neighbors until a woman appeared from the door of the sod house. Amazingly, providentially, Koster recognized the woman immediately as someone he'd known from his boyhood days in the Netherlands. There, in the middle of the wide expanse of prairie, two immigrant Dutch folk, childhood friends, met once again.

The process of creating a society out of wilderness—whether that wilderness was forest or prairie—always required enormous physical strength, as well as the patience to endure those earliest days of deprivation. The prairie can be immensely hostile—the winters beastly cold, the summers beastly hot. And always there is wind. In 1873 Rocky Mountain locusts stripped the wheat and oat fields just before harvest. A year later, just as the settlers emerged from Sunday worship, they heard a roar that sounded much like thunder, even though there were no clouds in the sky; the locusts were paying another call.

But by 1875 abundant harvests brought hope, even though it was tested again by the return of the locusts in '76 and '77, furious rain storms in '78, and a combination of drought, storms, and insects in '79. Despite it all, the colonists hung on, and by 1880, when lush crops and balmy summer weather finally settled in for a season, their future in northwest Iowa was ensured.

Throughout this period of colonial expansion, the Christian Reformed Church was being pushed along by the wave of colonists leaving western Michigan and central Iowa, the strongholds of Van Raalte and Scholte. By 1868, Illinois had sufficient number of churches to establish its own classis. In 1877, Classis Iowa emerged. Classis Hudson was added in 1878. The CRC, like the Dutch immigrants it served, was growing up and spreading out over a land mass so wide and broad that most of its own members, accustomed as they were to the tight confines of a tiny North Sea country, still couldn't grasp the expanse.

But one shouldn't be deceived about the Christian Reformed Church in the year 1880. Despite its growth from several dozen families and individuals in the Lake Michigan woods, it was still tiny—all but invisible in the massive expanse of a New World already teeming with thousands upon thousands of other immigrant peoples from throughout Europe. The Dutch weren't the only inclusive people after all—witness the names of towns and cities across the Midwest: New Prague, New Ulm, New Glarus, New London, New Berlin, as well as New Holland.

A century-and-a-half later, such clannishness seems almost self-righteous—a mind-set that built fortresses undeniably comforting to be in but impossible to enter from without, the only requisite password the correct ethnic surname. What we need to remember is that these people were hardly Americans. Today, the Christian Reformed Church in North America numbers among its parishes Spanish, Korean, and Lao congregations, more recent immigrant fellowships, who, like the denomination's own founders, find the American melting pot a bit less foreboding if they can anchor themselves to an identity forged more particularly in the "old country."

Walls function in two ways—they keep some in and others out. When the primary function is motivated by bigotry or a refusal to acknowledge the dignity of other human beings, then a community is defining itself by hate or fear—and not by love.

But here as elsewhere, the balance between conflicting goals—both of them good—is not easy to maintain. On the one hand, it cannot be wrong for African Americans to maintain a unique African-American culture. Nor is it wrong for Korean churches to want to hold on to some identity in a culture that threatens their own. Maintaining some ties with the past is necessary. We are, in part, what we've come from. But in this North American polyglot mix, to stay entirely apart is to miss the richness that diversity—and ultimately growth itself—offers. Throughout the years, Canada has been most divisively racked by the problem of Quebec separatism, specifically the desire on the part of its French-speaking people

1904 funeral of Professor Gerrit E. Boer. The hearse is passing in front of the Grand Rapids Theological School, located then on the northwest corner of Franklin and Madison streets. The school was renamed Calvin Theological Seminary in 1916.

to stay homogenous. What many Canadians ask themselves is at what point are French-Canadians Canadians first, and French-speakers second?

And then there is, of course, the matter of the Great Commission, which makes ethnic exclusiveness impossible for believers taking a hand in the saving work of Jesus Christ. The mission impulse in all of us stems from Christ's own admonishment to move out, to go into all the world and tell the good news. A believing fellowship that doesn't tell the story of the Lord God of heaven and earth is sinfully hiding it under a bushel or burying it in the ground. It's a whole lot easier to preach to the choir than it is to the streets.

But the process of immigration itself—not to mention the enterprise of creating communities where there had been nothing but an endless expanse of prairie or virgin forest—kept Dutch-Americans together, just as it kept those tired and hungry masses who'd left Ireland or Norway, and just as, today, it keeps together those with roots in Southeast Asia or Central America. Simple survival, after all, was not guaranteed. They had to build a community.

In 1857 there had been only one classis and four wavering congregations in the Christian Reformed Church. By 1880, there were four classes and thirty-nine churches. Of those thirty-nine, only nineteen had pastors. Most were tiny—just a few families. Lucas quotes sources which said that in 1880, the entire Classis Hudson reported only 271 families; Illinois was still smaller—only 175. Meanwhile, Classis Iowa totaled, in its seven churches, only 140 families.

Although some congregations in the older settlements had adequate facilities in the thirty-five or so years that had passed since immigration, conditions on the prairie especially were truly spartan. According to Henry Lucas, an 1873 guest preacher in Orange City considered the sanctuary there "the most unattractive building in which I have ever delivered a sermon."

> *Imagine a small rectangular frame structure, perhaps ten meters long and five wide, with a stove and benches around it. That is the school. Behind this structure they built a shed, like the cross piece of the letter T. A few boards nailed to some supports serve as benches. . . . That shed built on to the school constitutes the church building. On week days a partition divides the rooms, but on Sunday, for services, they take down the boards and windows of the upper part—and the church is ready for the meeting.*
>
> —*Netherlanders in America* by Henry Lucas (Grand Rapids, MI: Wm. B. Eerdmans, 1955, 1989) pp. 344-345.

The church in the wilderness had been an orphan for twenty years. It had survived, but was remarkably thin and weak. The mother church in the Netherlands wouldn't own its American child. The future looked better than the past, but the CRC in 1880 was hardly robust. It required nutrition, lots of it, in many forms.

CHAPTER 11

The New(er) Calvinism of the Late Nineteenth Century

As a kid, I was not a reader; I was a jock. I'm not sure that the two are mutually exclusive, but I do know that when I was growing up, I gave very little time or respect to anything other than baseball, basketball, football, or whatever other athletic competition was current. Small-town America, where I was born and reared and where I still live, makes an idol of athletic achievement. Every last small town on rural "blue highways," those state roads angling off the interstates, has mounted its own hall of fame on a billboard at the village limits— its list of state championship teams. Judging by the size and placement of those signs, who won championships and when is a bigger deal than the list of veterans who fell in Vietnam, Europe, or the South Pacific.

Perhaps it was athletics that kept me from reading; but then, if I hadn't played third base on the sandlots of Oostburg, Wisconsin, I may well have found some other reason to avoid libraries. The fact is, I didn't read much. I do remember liking those old orange biographies in the Christian school library, as well as a couple of contemporary novels that brought my adolescent senses shimmeringly close to what my own ethos told me was sin. But if I thought about writing and Christianity at all when I was a kid, I simply concluded that when Christians wrote stories, they wrote the ones I could borrow from the church library. For me, a boy born and reared in the middle decades of the twentieth century, Christian fiction meant *The Sugar Creek Gang.*

Perhaps some church libraries still make room on their shelves for *The Sugar Creek Gang* series, but I doubt those novels made it through the last several decades. They were likely a phenomenon that grew out of the crusades in evangelical America, a movement conceived by people like Dwight L. Moody and characterized by deep piety and evangelistic fervor. The purpose of the books was obvious: to bring adolescent boys to Jesus.

The plot was always the same: the gang of boys (Tom Sawyer and Huck Finn types, except exceedingly more tepid) would get into trouble, then work their way out of their difficulties by coming somehow to understand better what Jesus Christ both offered and required. The stories always ended sweetly—always. The bad kid always found his way to Jesus in some stirring climax.

My trouble was, I wasn't stirred. An adolescent boy myself, I found the stories sappy and silly. The boys in the books were

Along with the baggage of late-nineteenth
and early-twentieth century immigrants came a new
"brand" of Calvinism.

nothing at all like the boys I hung around with. And the way they resolved their problems in no way resembled the way we solved things on the sandlot. Either *we* weren't Christians, or the Sugar Creek Gang was out to lunch. I chose to believe the latter—and not because I was so sure that my own behavior, or that of my friends, was perfectly sanctified. I simply understood that the world of the Sugar

Creek Gang was more Christian cartoon than real.

I can point to a few quickly passing moments in my high school career when I thought writing was something interesting to do and even acknowledged that God had given me some strengths in writing. But for the most part I had no idea, no guess at all, that someday I'd be sitting here typing out page after page of stories,

Leonard Verduin

At 101 years old, Leonard Verduin is the oldest minister in the CRC, the nestor of its clergy. Verduin's long life span covers most of the history of the denomination.

As we approach a new millennium, the renaissance man has just about disappeared from the world cultural scene. There are only a few left—and Leonard Verduin is among them.

Born in March 1897 in South Holland, Illinois, Verduin was the son of the first child baptized in the Christian Reformed denomination. Verduin served only one regular congregation—Corsica, South Dakota. He made his greatest contribution at the University Chapel in Ann Arbor, Michigan, where he served as chaplain for more than twenty years.

Leonard Verduin combined great learning, profound insights, and spontaneous wit in his preaching. His pulpit style was relaxed and informal. He disdained theatrics, but made use of hyperbole and humor to drive home his point. Students, now gray and elderly, fondly recall the mischievous twinkle in his eye as he wrestled with a seemingly heretical but ultimately totally orthodox solution to a scriptural problem. Famous as well was his pithy summary: "All truth is elliptical."

Frequently Verduin and his late wife, Hattie, served in *loco parentis* for scores of homesick students, many of whom were being confronted with a challenge to their faith in the secular surroundings of the University of Michigan.

Verduin became a respected authority on the Mennonites and Anabaptist groups. His obvious sympathy for them comes to fullest expression in his excellent volume entitled *Stepchildren of the Reformation*. At 101, Verduin completed the manuscript of his latest book, *Where We Went Wrong*.

Verduin's successor at the University Chapel, Don Postema, who served as student pastor at Ann Arbor for thirty-four years, pays this tribute to him: "Verduin had a reputation as a man of many skills, a scholar, a writer, and a passionate preacher. People at the chapel and university acknowledged him as one who integrated the intellectual integrity of the Reformed faith with the demands of university life and thought. His motto was, 'The Old Faith for the Modern Man.' The old truth packaged in the idiom of the times . . . a remarkable man of God."　　—WDB

Leonard Verduin.

novels, and devotionals—and loving it. The only pattern I knew for Christian writing—bringing the act of creating a story together with the Christian faith—was the style and substance offered to me in *The Sugar Creek Gang* novels. And I knew that kind of writing wasn't for me.

In that sense, my college education was liberating. It taught me that being a Christian writer did not necessarily mean creating a new generation of *Sugar Creek Gang* novels. I began to understand, long before I'd ever heard of the well-known Reformed Dutch theologian Herman Bavinck, what the man meant when he said that Christianity requires two conversions—one to Christ, and another back to the world. And today I know this: preaching and storytelling are two altogether different tasks. That's not to say that storytelling or fiction writing doesn't have a moral message; it always does. But whether or not a story is truly successful is much more dependent on how it works than what it says.

In that way, writing is no different from, say, laying cement. If a Christian mason wanted to witness to the Lord's saving grace in all that he did, and if he determined therefore that he would only fashion crosses in cement, eventually the poor guy wouldn't have many customers. If he wanted to be the best mason he could be, he'd have to know every last thing there is to know about laying concrete and erecting block walls. He'd have to ensure that his driveways would be flat and smooth, that they'd hold their set for decades. He'd have to know the very best mix. In short, he'd be far better off studying masonry than preaching. That's also true for bas-

soon players, garbage collectors, stand-up comedians, and Zamboni drivers.

Which introduces a dilemma: where does our commitment really belong—to the Lord or to the world? The answer is not as easy as it might appear, and it's made more difficult by the Bible's differing uses of the word *world*. Many biblical passages warn us that the world is an evil place: "I will punish the world for its evil, the wicked for its sins" (Isa. 13:11) or, in a slightly different spin, "What good will it be for a man if he gains the whole world, yet forfeits his soul?" (Matt. 16:26). The apostle Paul, his pointer finger waving, offers this clear warning: "Do not deceive yourselves. If any one of you thinks he is wise by the standards of this age, he should become a 'fool' so that he may become wise. For the wisdom of this world is foolishness in God's sight" (1 Cor. 3:18-19).

And yet perhaps the single most recognized Bible verse says this: "For God so loved the world that he gave his one and only Son, that whosoever believes in him shall not perish but have eternal life" (John 3:16). The psalmist, speaking for the Lord of heaven and earth, says, "The world is mine, and all that is in it" (50:12). And Christ tells us that we "are the light of the world" (Matt. 5:14).

What is the Christian's role in this world? How do we see the culture around us? In which of the events and behaviors of "the world" should we happily participate? Perhaps the question really is this: What should we stay away from? Wonderful Christians do stay out of the mainstream—the Amish, for example, or any of a dozen Roman Catholic orders who fortress themselves in cloisters. Some evangelical Christians turn their radios to James Dobson only, watch only Gospel films, read only Christian books, send their children to Christian schools, and consider Christian political action only that which is prompted by such issues as abortion and pornography.

To be "in the world, but not of it" requires some subtle positioning. The question of loving God or the world is poorly phrased as an either/or statement. For once again, the truth seems to have two foci; the statement is not either/or but both/and. To love God is to love God's world—not at the expense of loving God, but *because* we love him.

Few Christian traditions offer believers such a firm foundation for living in the world and examining culture as the Reformed faith. There. I've said it. From my point of view at least, that feature of our confessional heritage is our undeniable strength. Dealing with culture itself is something we in the Reformed tradition have done very well by insisting that the task of a Christian is *not only* to be close to God (it is that), *but also* to create Christian community, to work for the kingdom of Christ. I thank God for that heritage, for a tradition of faith that still gives me the means by which to know my salvation *and* the world in which I live.

We are at that point in the history of the Christian Reformed Church when the issue of "the world" and its place in our view of things comes to the fore. That issue does not emerge from the heat and smoke of denominational battles at the turn of the nineteenth century, because that period of our history may well have been one of the most calm and settled we've ever gone

through. Even though as a denomination we had already staked a forty-year claim in North American soil by the turn of the twentieth century, in order to understand our own history we need to go back to the Netherlands, once again, to fill out a profile of a church still changing from within.

ABRAHAM KUYPER

No single figure—not even the good Rev. Scholte and his compatriot Van Raalte combined—has been so central to shaping the mind of the Christian Reformed Church as Prime Minister Abraham Kuyper, a Dutch preacher, statesman, and journalist who only made it to North America once. To understand the history, the theology, and the tradition of the Christian Reformed Church, we need to look very closely at the man who, perhaps more definitively and effectively than any other individual in the history of Dutch Calvinism, affirmed the lordship of Jesus Christ over all of life.

Kuyper not only theorized on the role of the Christian in society; he also practiced what he preached. Several times he was elected to the Dutch Parliament, and he assumed the office of Prime Minister from 1901-1905, a period during which the Dutch government faced the difficult challenges of a national railroad strike, the war between Japan and Russia, and helping to resolve the South African Boer War.

Kuyper was a voluminous writer of political treatises and theological studies, but he was no ivory-tower philosopher or theologian. In addition to his more "academic" work, he served as editor and columnist for a daily Christian newspaper and its weekly religious supplement. Many

Abraham Kuyper (1837-1920), preacher, journalist, statesman.

Christians heard that columnist's voice as clearly as the voice he used as a statesman.

Kuyper always appreciated the ordinary people, especially ordinary people of faith, people he called *de kleine luyden* (literally, "the little people"). Perhaps as a result, the strength of his faith and the effects of his ideas permeated several generations of those *kleine luyden*, many of whom eventually left the Netherlands during the second great period of Dutch immigration (1870-1920) and came to North America.

When these new immigrants arrived, many gravitated to the fledgling Christian Reformed Church. And they toted with them a freshly ground Calvinism, something specifically brewed by Abraham Kuyper, a slightly different variety of the faith than that brand or style carried along by Van Raalte and Scholte and others who had emerged from the *Afscheiding*. Those differences were both significant and notable, but they did not, at least at first, disturb the quiet growth of the new American denomination.

To understand Kuyper and his influence, it's instructive to listen to him. What follows is an English abridgement of a single devotional essay he wrote in what may well be his most treasured volume of meditations, *To Be Near Unto God*. While his political theory and his theological works are certainly worth reading, we probably meet the essential Kuyper most intimately in his devotional writing. The devotional Kuyper is, of course, the Kuyper most common people knew—and no one should forget that in the late nineteenth century, just as today, it is generally the "little people" who immigrate.

This particular essay meditates on the verse, "No man . . . knoweth the Father, save the Son, and he to whomsoever the Son will reveal him" (Matt. 11:27, KJV). And pardon my interruptions, but I'm going to interpolate occasionally in order to explain the man somewhat.

> *"And to Whomsoever the Son Will Reveal Him"*
>
> *Who can doubt the words of the psalmist: "The heavens declare the*

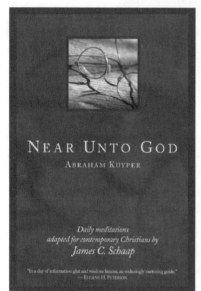

Abraham Kuyper's classic meditations, adapted for contemporary Christians by James C. Schaap.

glory of God; and the firmament sheweth his handiwork" (19:1)? Anyone who's ever taken the time to look knows that somewhere in the glorious majesty of a starry night there is something of God Almighty. Beneath an open sky, even an unbeliever has to take pause.

A knowledge of God exists, really, in the malls of our everyday experience. Breathtaking landscapes aren't the only revelation of his might. Something of God is in us—all of us humans. Paul claims that even unbelievers "show the work of the law written in their hearts, their conscience also bearing witness, and their thoughts the mean while accusing or else excusing one another" (Rom. 2:15). In the beauty of the lily and the machinations of the human mind, one can spy the reality of God.

[Some might beg to differ here, of course. Kuyper's insistence that every last human being is capable of knowing God may not have sat particularly well with those who preferred to believe that only a few were so blessed. In the history of the CRC, a statement like this will lead to a battle royal.]

But then how do we read this verse? "No man . . . knoweth the Father, save the Son, and he to whomsoever the Son will reveal him"? An apparent contradiction?

The subtlety of difference begs clarification. Knowledge of God is accessible all around us and offered to every last human being. Knowledge of the Father, how-

ever, is the exclusive blessing of those who know him through his Son, Jesus Christ.

As we all know, Satan himself has a knowledge of God. If he didn't know God, he'd have had no sinful reason to rebel against the Lord of the universe. Satan had to know God. He knows him so well, in fact, that Scripture tells us he trembles. Satan's teeth chatter at the reality of God; we, God's children, are comforted by the very same reality—because we know him as Father.

Those who know Christ, the Word made flesh, have not only a general knowledge of God but a saving knowledge of his reality. Those who don't believe in Christ don't share that knowledge until they are reconciled in our Savior and thereby come to know God as all believers do—as Father. What Christ tells us is that this saving knowledge of God comes only through him, through his Son, our human link to the Father.

[Not so deeply hidden behind the exploration of the verse is an idea that created a firestorm within the CRC in early decades of the twentieth century—the notion of common grace. To those who know nothing of that old struggle, let's just say that Kuyper's ideas here define the argument. He claims that everyone is capable of an understanding of God (even Satan has that), but not everyone knows God in an intimate and personal way as Father. Some measure of grace, therefore, is common—distributed almost equally across

humankind; but another kind of grace is very special, because it's intimate.]

Now, to refine it just a bit, consider this. Knowing that God came to earth in the form of man and that all revelation begins in Christ, the living Word—just knowing that, in the same manner as we know the law of gravity—isn't at all the same phenomenon as knowing God in one's heart. Head knowledge is not the same as heart knowledge. Only those who have been brought near unto God through his Son really know fully *the truth of the gospel's good news.*

[Perhaps one of the oldest and most difficult breaches in the Christian character is the one that separates mind and heart, knowledge and emotions, reason and feelings. What Kuyper insists here is that a true and deep knowledge of God begins in our nearness to him (the theme of the entire book of meditations), not in our understanding of theology or our ability to recite the catechism. Knowledge of God begins personally.]

We're not just hair-splitting here. Listen to this. Those who really know God, as fully as human beings can, see God even more clearly in a starry night than those who don't. Our nearness to God himself brings his splendid creation to us in Technicolor.

[What he's offering is this idea: knowing God in our innermost beings makes us more acutely aware of the beauty all around us, the glory of his creation. Now watch what he does.]

Free University in Amsterdam.

So what? you ask. Here's the goods. Sometimes those who are recently converted find such spiritual ecstasy in his presence that they want to sing forever of his majesty, to concentrate their lives' tasks on basking in the glory of Christ. That's commendable, of course, as long as it isn't accomplished at the expense of the beauty of the world he loves.

When we are converted through Christ, we need to let that same light of redemption, that light we know in our inner life, shine gloriously on our outer life as well. "In the beginning was the Word, and the Word was with God, and the Word was God" (John 1:1). Those familiar words insist that Christ shines not only in us, but in his world as well.

[That's undiluted Kuyperian doctrine.]

Don't run away from the world—that's the idea. Live gloriously in a creation that is immensely brightened by your knowledge of God. What's important to remember is that everything we see around us looks different as a result of our knowledge of the Father through his Son. Our knowing God—in head and heart—unites the life of grace with the life of nature in a glorious harmony and turns the whole world—all of history and science and art, everything we are and shall be—into . . . you guessed it . . . into one mighty revelation of the Father. Wow! Don't miss it.

The single line of Abraham Kuyper most often quoted by his admirers is one taken from his speech at the Inauguration of the Free University of Amsterdam, a line that goes something like this: "There is not one square inch of the entire creation about which Jesus Christ does not cry out, 'This is mine! This belongs to me!'"

Armed with the vision of a sanctified sinner, Kuyper, the preacher/politician, wished to take back—in essence, to reform—every last segment of the Lord's incredible creation. He wanted Christians to be alive and kicking in every area of life—from farrowing hogs to framing pictures, from running track to running for office. He wanted Christian servants in every profession, and he wanted them rebuilding a world he saw had turned its back on its Savior and King.

During and after the Kuyper years, thousands of "little people" from the

Netherlands came to America and Canada armed with a vision of Christianity Kuyper himself called a "worldview," a means by which to see God *and* the world God had made. Kuyper was not in any sense single-dimensional; but his vision of taking faith into the world is certainly among his greatest refinements of Calvin's theology.

Understanding Kuyper helps us understand some of what might otherwise seem to be historical oddities of history in cities and towns where significant numbers of CRC folks came to dwell on this continent. For instance, this year the Christian school in Oostburg, Wisconsin, the school I attended as a boy, is celebrating its fiftieth anniversary. It was established in 1947, an entire century after Dutch-American settlers cleared forests and set down roots in the sandy lakeshore Wisconsin frontier.

Meanwhile, the Christian school in Sioux Center, Iowa, where I now live, is ninety-three years old, even though the town only recently celebrated its centennial. Only thirteen years after turn-of-the-century immigrants came to American soil here in northwest Iowa, they started working seriously on Christian schools, not because they were disenchanted with existing public schools (which were largely staffed by Christian teachers), but because they were full of enthusiasm for the principle they'd picked up in the Netherlands long before they came to America—the principle that every inch of creation belongs to the Lord.

Before we go on with this story, we need to return to some events in Europe at the end of the nineteenth century that helped create the zeal many turn-of-the-century immigrants—as well as those coming

later—packed with them when they left the old country.

KUYPER AND THE *DOLEANTIE*

Abraham Kuyper was no child of the *Afscheiding*. His father, a pastor in the state church, sometimes chafed under the direction his church was taking, but, unlike the followers of de Cock in northern Holland, he never left. Jan Frederik Kuyper found himself in agreement with those who'd left the mother church, but committed himself to working more diligently within the structure of the *Hervormde* churches he served.

Kuyper himself was a very bright student whose penchant for ideas and literature likely descended from his father as well as his mother, Henrietta Huber, a schoolteacher. In addition, Kuyper spent a significant part of his youth in Leiden, home of one of the Netherlands' finest universities.

When he graduated *summa cum laude* from the University of Leiden, Kuyper was hardly one of the "little people." He had absorbed the rationalistic ideas that made Leiden famous, his childhood faith becoming more moralistic and intellectual. He

---

Letter from J. Vander Mey (Grand Rapids) to Abraham Kuyper (the Netherlands), 1896

As Reformed Christians we face a dark future here in America. People in the Netherlands have no idea how the whole of America drinks from the fountains of Methodism, and the young people in our church also lean in that direction. We scarcely know how to preserve them. If, as many prefer, we choose to remain isolated as Hollanders, we will be signing our own death warrants. But the other option—swift Americanization—often results in more disastrous consequences.

became, in a late nineteenth-century way, a liberal, essentially rejecting the traditional view of a transcendent God, the divinity of Jesus Christ, the reality of miracles and life after death, and the authority of the Bible. He was, in many ways, the kind of preacher the *Afscheiding* folks hated. "For years," he says of himself, "I had entertained notions of modernism."

He entered the ministry armed with the notions of Christianity then current at the University of Leiden, but then things began to change. For instance, he wrote a prize-winning essay comparing the ideas of John a Lasco, a Polish reformer, with those of John Calvin, indicating that even during his stay at Leiden he found Calvin attractive—more attractive, perhaps, than most of his more enlightened teachers might have.

Soon a series of events changed Kuyper's whole notion of Christianity and its profile in contemporary society. A student of literature, Kuyper read the English novel *The Heir of Redclyffe*, a fictional account of the spiritual struggle between an arrogant intellectual Christian and a character Kuyper considered a model of true piety. Kuyper saw himself in the story. The novel, he later commented, "in significance for my life, stands next to the Bible." Kuyper would mark his vital conversion to Christianity by the date of his reading *The Heir of Redclyffe*—1863.

An unmarried peasant woman, Pietje Baltus, also contributed to Kuyper's transformation by regularly challenging the upstart, university-trained pastor. Ms. Baltus wasn't altogether sure that she wanted any part of a liberal preacher; most historians would say she wasn't the only

parishioner so inclined in her congregation. For some time, she was extremely critical of Kuyper's preaching—and, in the bold Dutch way, simply told him so. She felt that his reading of the significant texts had failed to get at the insights of the Reformed confessions. Eventually, oddly enough, the peasant lady convinced the academic theologian, and did so with such thoroughness that when she died years later, Kuyper eulogized her in this way in his newspaper: "The main characteristic of that still young woman was her deep conviction. . . . She stood on the full confession of the faith for which the martyrs had died."

The spiritual conflict of a novel he'd read brought Kuyper to an understanding of himself and his own intellectual arrogance, but it took a young peasant woman to show him the efficacy and power of the Reformed faith. And Ms. Baltus was not alone. In the church at Beesd, his first charge, Kuyper met people unlike any he'd ever known before, people knowledgeable about faith despite their limited education. The faith of these devout and faithful Christians so flourished that, when he compared it to his own, Kuyper saw in himself an intellectually driven commitment not nearly as strong as that of his parishioners. He recognized that his own commitment was to an idea—not to the Lord God Almighty.

When he left the church at Beesd for a position in Utrecht, Kuyper began to make an impact in larger circles. He'd begun to question, for instance, the church's stance on practices related to the Lord's Supper, on public profession of faith, and on candidacy for the ministry. When he moved to

Amsterdam in 1870, he had developed into a powerful preacher with strong designs for reforming the church. His became the voice of renewal in the Dutch state church, the church the *Afscheiding* had left three decades before.

In 1883, when the synod of the *Hervormde Kerk* revoked the requirement that pastors pledge their agreement with the Reformed confessions, the dissension that had been growing for years in Kuyper and elsewhere became public and volatile. Those who, like Kuyper, felt that the Reformed confessions offered the truth about God and his world maintained the necessity of holding fast to the old standards. But the conservatives lost, and soon enough the *Hervormde Kerk* mandated the change, forcing it upon those who disagreed. When dissenters continued to oppose such action, they were simply deposed. Among those removed from the rolls was Abraham Kuyper.

For some time the *Hervormde Kerk* had been losing more and more of its members, and by the time Kuyper finally left, a sizeable number of dissenters joined him, forming another union called the *Doleantie,* meaning "the grieving church."

By 1888 many of the *Doleantie* churches formed a new free church, the Reformed Churches of the Netherlands. Soon enough they were discussing possible mergers with the *Christelijk Gereformeerde Kerk* (the Christian Reformed Church of the Netherlands), which was an outgrowth of the *Afscheiding* and had already formed a presence in North America.

Some in the older fellowship *(Christelijk Gereformeerde Kerk)* were not inclined to give in to Kuyper's powerful leadership.

Some even found certain of his views unacceptable. But many remained in the newly created fellowship, as did Kuyper, who was active in the church as member, pastor, and leader until his death.

All of this is Dutch history, not American history; but it is history that has had an impact on the Christian Reformed Church in North America. Even today, differences remain between those who see personal piety as the very core of the Christian faith (many of them descendants of the *Afscheiding*), and those whose worldview calls for Christian action in society as the centerpiece of the Christian life (many of them descendants of the *Doleantie).* The lines are not always clearly cut or easily seen, but they are there.

In part, the differences between the two ways of thinking are more universal than they are peculiar to the CRC fellowship. At the heart of the issue is personal spirituality versus Christian social action. When people criticize the Christian school movement for robbing the coffers of money better spent on missions, something of our old-standing differences lies at the base. When some fault Calvin Seminary for being too "intellectual," too fastidious about academic preparation for the ministry, something of our old-standing differences lies at the base. When highly cultured CRC members roll their eyes at hands-high praise gatherings, something of our old differences emerges.

What is most important—a personal relationship with Jesus Christ or a deep and convincing understanding of God, the world, and God's grace?

It's interesting to note one additional Kuyper story. He himself would admit that part of what reformed his views on doctrine and life was a visit he took to England, where he picked up on the revival led by the most famous American evangelical of the age, Dwight L. Moody. Abraham Kuyper—perhaps the most significant single individual in the history of the Christian Reformed Church—a man who became Prime Minister of the Netherlands, a prolific writer and social theorist, a brilliant student and profound theologian, and who, along with Groen van Prinsterer, did more to establish a rationale for Christian education than anyone else, "got saved."

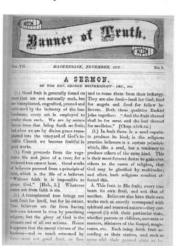

The Banner of Truth.

Which is most important in the Christian life—piety or purpose? Feelings or intellect? Individual faith or a society-wide witness?

The answer, via Kuyper's life story, is not either/or, but both/and.

YEARS OF GROWTH AND DIFFERENCE

While Kuyper steered Calvinistic Christians toward taking stronger hold of the social, educational, and political issues in the Netherlands—and thousands of his followers were embarking, once again, for America—the Christian Reformed Church in North America was experiencing what might be described as its own "golden age," an era of growth and relative peace. The ugly quarreling and sometimes foul accusations that marred earlier periods of our history—and would characterize some of its story

in its immediate future—were, for the time being at least, almost nonexistent.

On the East coast, a group of RCA churches who had left that denomination over a longstanding fight for the right to local ordination, a group known as "Classis Hackensack" in the RCA and the "1822 Secessionists" in the CRC, moved closer to affiliation in the CRC. Their magazine, *The Banner of Truth* (which would later be shortened to *The Banner*), became the most widely read English periodical in the CRC. Their interest in doctrinal purity and absolute orthodoxy made the CRC a likely partner, and in 1890 Classis Hackensack simply merged with the youthful denomination to become its own "Classis Hackensack." While that merger created another round of anti-RCA spirit, it gave the CRC English-speaking congregations in New Jersey and New York, some of which still exist today.

Meanwhile, in the same year (1890), the CRC synod approved special rules by which German congregations in western Illinois, north-central Iowa, and south-central Minnesota could become Christian Reformed. These congregations had been planted by preachers and lay leaders from German regions just over the border from the Netherlands and had undergone their own German secession in the old country, then brought a similar dissent and vision to America. The people called themselves East Frisians.

At the time they joined the CRC, the German churches were distinctive in some ways; for example, their commitment to evangelism and mission appeared much stronger than that of their Dutch colleagues in adjoining classes. But the congregations as a whole were very similar to the Dutch churches that had already defined the American CRC.

In spite of these similarities, the language differences led, understandably, to dissension in some places. As late as 1902, thirty-five years after the entrance of First Wellsburg CRC to the denomination (then, of course, *De Ware Hollandesche Gereformeerde Kerk*, or True Dutch Reformed Church), the congregation suffered internal strife related to a language problem. Even though the people were German, the Dutch language was used in the worship services; even the minutes of the consistory were written in Dutch. Because the people at First Wellsburg hailed from an area of Germany so close to the Netherlands, their German dialect, "low German," enabled them to understand the Dutch language. However, Dutch was not the language they used in their homes. Problems arose—as they did in the few Dutch CRC congregations looking to use English. By 1905, First Wellsburg was using German in their worship, but little more than a decade later they would have to change again—to English, of course.

In 1890 the German congregations were given the title "Classis Ostfriesland," named for the German territory from which they'd come. They were also given permission to sing hymns (a privilege forbidden Dutch-speaking CRCs for another three decades) and were urged to become fully assimilated into the CRC. And they did. Today, Classis Ostfriesland is (mainly) Classis North-Central Iowa, though some of the German-rooted congregations lie outside that area.

CRC MIND-SETS

Within the Dutch-speaking part of the CRC, three different "parties" or "minds" began to form, based on how members viewed the North American experience itself and on what style of Calvinist baggage immigrant folks carried with them into the new country. These mind-sets or parties aren't mere historical relics; each has its descendants among CRC groups today. Various CRC historians have used different terms to designate the different groups. James Bratt's terminology is as follows.

At the turn of the century and even today, the "Confessionalist" mind puts critical emphasis in worship and piety upon correct doctrine, on orthodoxy, often on a commitment to the three forms of unity. For the Confessionalists, any deviation from those standards means the church is loosening itself from its own crucial theological moorings and putting itself at peril. The mind-set finds its roots in the *Afscheiding,* from de Cock and his followers, those who had sacrificed much and suffered numerous hardships in their long and arduous battles with the Dutch state church.

The Confessionalists spot heresy like birds of prey. Deviations from tradition, explorations into new and uncharted areas, or new approaches to Scripture or doctrine were, at the turn of the century, often suspect—and still are today. Descendants of the Confessionalists are evident in the CRC today, although in the last twenty years a significant portion of that group has left the denomination for more conservative fellowships. Confessionalists place a very high premium on their own definition of orthodoxy, raising doctrinal integrity well above a range of other important elements of ecclesiastical life, drawing very clear lines in the sand around those issues and beliefs they consider nonnegotiable.

In the grand scheme of things, Confessionalists have always been the liturgical and creedal archivists, those who have placed abiding value on the denomination's historic documents. Confessionalists may well live most deeply in the legacy of the past, often refusing to step away from its shadow. In the constant push and pull of a changing world, the Confessionalists, stubbornly firm in their views, often rigid in their appraisals of contemporary culture, have played a vital role in continuing to honor a theological definition or confessional identity. In the dialogue that goes on in every church, classis, and synod—and in the dining rooms of our homes—Confessionalists have always held fast against change that appears to threaten unity or occurs too rapidly. One of the difficulties the CRC must face in the years ahead is how to replace its Confessionalists now that so many are gone. The disappearance of their often strident and critical voices may make discussion appear easier in the future, but the outline of what they have traditionally brought to dialogue within the denomination will be missed.

Bratt describes a second party or mindset as "Positive Calvinists" or "American Calvinists." The mind-set of this group was to join America in every Christian way possible—to become, as quickly as possible, a salt in the New World society, a yeast in the rising American culture. To accomplish that task, one may well have to abandon a strictly set theology; thus, doctrine, broadly speaking, at some points may well need to be compromised.

If anyone would be foolhardy enough to call Hendrik Scholte a Calvinist, he might well be the most obvious example of a "Positive Calvinist." After all, within only a few years on the American continent he had rather openly abandoned most of his theological and cultural heritage. But we're drawing too wide a net if we include Scholte in this appraisal. For better or for worse, the relative isolation and determined doctrinal stands of the CRC have not produced a variety of notable Positive Calvinists. Throughout our histories the Reformed Church in America has, generally, been more accommodating to American culture itself than we have (witness the RCA's longtime distrust of "Christian" schools because of the manner in which they separate "Christian" children from the mainstream). Nonetheless, Positive Calvinists have existed in the CRC and continue to exist today. In fact, today their numbers may well be growing. What characterizes that mind-set, according to Bratt, is a sometimes overly optimistic view of culture and society—the belief that things are getting better and better. That view of progress is a tough sell to a mind shaped and molded by Calvinist doctrine—specifically the doctrine of original sin.

But then, Positive Calvinists likely wouldn't invest all that much confidence in the doctrine of original sin anyway—or in any somewhat abstract line of doctrinal inquiry. Which is not to say that Positive Calvinists could be called "liberal." They may well be more pious—at least in appearance—than their Confessional brothers and sisters. After all, Positive Calvinists have always had a deep and sincere belief that Jesus Christ died for our sins. To Positive Calvinists, getting along well in American culture is a far greater calling than simply and obstinately standing apart from it. Where Confessionalists all too often put their faith in creeds and historic theology, Positive Calvinists tend to find such thinking parochial and provincial.

Today, the Positive Calvinists minimize doctrinal differences with other denominations and fellowships, nurture personal piety, and in general find themselves quite comfortable within North American society. Not all Positive Calvinists are affluent, but many have well-established places in the culture; it is, after all, undoubtedly easier to look optimistically at the society around you if you're seated on a sunporch sipping lemonade than if you're hoeing beans on a rented farm in a depressed grain market. Although Dr. Robert Schuller, the RCA's most visible preacher and advocate of "positive thinking," is not Christian Reformed and never has been—although a goodly number of CRC members (me included) wouldn't consider him much of a Calvinist at all—I believe we can use him as an example of what Bratt describes as the Positive Calvinist, a member of a group whose background may

Synod 1894.

well be Reformed, but who can best be described as "outgoing pietists who hoped to lift individuals to a higher moral plane and thereby lead society toward broadly defined virtues" (*Dutch Calvinism in Modern America,* p. 46). Schuller has created a gospel empire and become a friend to a whole series of American presidents. He

Munster CRC, Munster, Indiana, 1899 (church, school, teacherage). First Munster Church has occupied this strategic corner since 1870.

didn't create his Crystal Cathedral by reminding people of their sin.

And let's face it. While the CRC has lost a number of congregations to a Confessionalist mentality—the old way is the best way—it's also lost more than a few to what we might broadly call a Positive Calvinist mentality. It's this second group who argue for the release of a congregation from its denominational family because strictures of the family become too confining—its liturgies too stiff, its church order too calcified, its rules and regulations just too restraining on what these folks might call the "Spirit"—with a capital S. In those fellowships, doctrine is tradition, and tradition is moribund. End of story. We want out.

Whenever pious folks—believers all—eschew the tenets of Reformed doctrine for reasons that have to do with optimism and accommodation to the society at large, especially the evangelical culture at large, one may well find hearts shaped by Positive Calvinism. Historically, Bratt says, Positive Calvinists can best be described as "outgoing pietists who hoped to lift individuals to a higher moral plane and thereby lead society toward broadly defined virtues" (46).

Bratt describes a third group as "Antitheticals," a name borrowed directly from Kuyperian ideas. Kuyper felt strongly that Christians were compelled to counter the reigning ideologies (or *theses*) of the day. To that end, he countered the prevalent ideas (theses) of his day with his "anti-theses," a system of distinctively Christian alternatives in the society at large: Christian schools, Christian newspapers, Christian political parties, and Christian labor unions.

Kuyper's American followers (who were not tightly unified themselves, as we'll see later) also emphasized the establishment of separate organizations. Under the influence of this group, all the Christian schools founded by the CRC were, beginning in about 1892, transferred out of local congregations and placed under the control of "Calvinistic societies." Before that time, they were all parochial, created and maintained by individual churches.

At the turn of the century, leaders of the Antitheticals were outspoken in their demands for separate Christian organizations. By the year 1910, in Grand Rapids, Michigan, Kuyperian Antitheticals, following their leader's initiatives, had created a

Christian political party, although it amounted to little more than a discussion group. In addition, Kuyperians had created a Christian newspaper (Chicago), a Christian labor union, and a network of Christian schools, all following the Dutch pattern envisioned by Kuyper.

Pushed to the limits, the movement for Christian institutions across the broad spectrum of human behavior often proved ludicrous (in some places in the Netherlands, for instance, Christian homing pigeon clubs were created as alternatives for Calvinist kids). The CRC's separate youth organizations—for years called "Calvinist Cadets" and "Calvinettes," still in place, although renamed—are manifestations of a form of the Antithetical vision of things.

In the Netherlands, the movement for separate Christian organizations resulted in a society composed of pillars of separate organizations (characterized by contemporary Dutch historians as "pillarization"). Henry Zwaanstra once called the Antitheticals "Separatist Calvinists" because of their devotion to separating all of society via its religious communities.

Kuyperian Antitheticals were not the only force in the denomination to push for Christian schools—remember that Van Raalte himself carried a vision of Christian education into the Michigan wilderness. But it is important to point out that what some consider the most successful contribution of the Christian Reformed Church to American culture, a strong and growing Christian educational system, is the unique and abiding gift of the Antithetical mind-set in the CRC. Although critics have long claimed that the Christian school was really created to

keep covenant children both out of "the world" and in an environment where marrying each other would seem natural, the continued success of the movement illustrates that parental, Christian education offers something much greater than a haven for bigotry, self-righteousness, or suitable marriage partners.

Cincinnati (Ohio) Christian Reformed Church, 1893 or 1894.

Some would say that today the Antithetical mind-set lives most richly on the campus of the denominational college, Calvin College, as well as those institutions of higher learning less directly affiliated with the CRC—Dordt, The King's, Trinity, and Redeemer. The passion of the Antitheticals has always been something more deeply set in the mind, for instance, than the heart. To talk about a "Christian approach" to history or art or literature or mathematics demands an appreciation for and understanding of those particular academic areas. So those not involved in higher education sometimes consider the arguments of contemporary Antitheticals purely academic, arcane, or even silly. After all, any academic pursuit can be tedious and tangential if it does not appear to affect the lives of real people.

As people like Wheaton College professor Mark Noll have pointed out, there is and has always been a distinct current of anti-intellectualism in the American evangelical world, a current so deep and abiding that for years the academic and unbelieving world itself has simply assumed that confessing Christians are those not yet liberated from the tyranny of ancient superstitions. In some ways, it is easy to allow the necessity of an individual experience with Jesus Christ to define Christianity itself, because that experience is always primary. Knowing Christ intimately is essential—and it always has been. Remember what we just read of Kuyper. But then, taking our new sanctified identities to the public square in any culture requires, in Bavinck's words, a "conversion back to the world," an understanding of what is going on, of whose voices are being heard and what kind of worldview lies behind those voices.

In the twenty-first century, the job of the Antitheticals at the CRC's academic institutions (and elsewhere, since our educational system has produced more than its share of prominent academics) will be to continue to think creatively and Christianly about what it is they study—whether it be physics, computer science, or theology. At the same time, however, their academic pursuits should not become merely "academic."

At the beginning of the twentieth century, the Antitheticals, those who'd lugged along Kuyperian baggage and tried to set up shop on the North American continent, often went to battle with the Positive Calvinists, those who saw themselves as blessed by American freedoms and opportunities and saw personal pietism rather than cultural confrontation as the means by which to express the joy of their salvation. Meanwhile, the Confessionalists, always a significant presence in the Christian Reformed Church, were watching everyone and everything to be sure that nothing foundational would be sacrificed in pursuit of new knowledge or unchristian entanglements with culture.

Furthermore, the Confessionalists and Antithetical Kuyperians entered into a fairly substantial union in the Christian School movement. Both camps could argue for the importance of Christian education—not as a means to separate children from the world but rather as a means to develop a Christian mind and a Christian approach to all areas of learning, from art to zoology. Both minds may well be adamant in their support of Christian education; but, given the significant differences—the contrary views of the culture those mind-sets hold to—keeping peace in the classroom can be difficult.

These significant differences in denominational thinking appeared a century ago, and they've never really disappeared. We can use the Promise Keepers movement as an example. Positive Calvinists love the undeniable success of the movement for a variety of reasons, not the least of which is its stress upon personal piety and evangelical fervor. They're less likely to split hairs about the theology of some of the speakers because they're convinced that the movement itself is good for America, good for their marriages, good for them personally.

Antitheticals, on the other hand, are somewhat wary of this movement; most professors at the college where I teach don't attend, even though very few are likely openly critical. While Antitheticals appreciate the movement's strong emphasis on racial harmony and male servanthood, they often feel the Promise Keepers movement doesn't critique the foundational aspects of American culture and even contributes to gender separatism.

Oddly enough, Confessionalists also maintain a safe distance from Promise Keepers because they feel its popular and rousing speakers tend toward Arminianism, thereby violating a doctrine central to the Reformed faith—the doctrine of God's sovereignty.

Positive Calvinists feel all of those who are critical of the movement are, in essence, thwarting the work of the Holy Spirit. Thus the beat goes on.

Who's right? In a way, all sides. The distinctions being formed in the mind of the CRC at the turn of the century are mind-sets that exist in all communities of Christians. Each of us, after all, is given an independent mind and is shaped by unique life experiences. No two of us—not even twins—are perfectly alike. And each voice has its own legitimacy. The Positive Calvinists appreciate the revival accomplished by the Promise Keepers, not only because it has had an effect on male Christendom, but also because the moral admonitions of the movement have likely affected them very person-

ally. The Antitheticals aren't completely off-base when they criticize the movement's wholesale adoption of football metaphors—packed stadiums, coaches, rah-rah cheers—as images of what is to them an almost repugnant macho male psyche. And Confessionalists are accurate in their appraisal as well: many of the speakers are, according to the confessional stances of strict Calvinist doctrine, quite obviously out-of-line, even heretical.

To be sure, no one wants to be classified, because a classification is, by definition, a limiting process. It would be silly to assume that any individual within the CRC could fit *only* one of these categories. Nonetheless, the distinctions that are noticeable in the "mind" of the CRC, distinctions based in part on the denomination's history, are helpful in understanding the foundations of the arguments we bring to our disagreements. And believe me, we'll come back to these distinctions time and time again.

SUPRA AND INFRA

Some battles, however, disappear. One particularly contentious battle emerged in the 1880s and continued well into the twentieth century. The source of the conflict was rooted in attempts to define precisely the Calvinistic doctrine of predestination. In a nutshell, the battle raged over what we may well regard today as an arcane theological point—the logical order of God's decrees concerning election, creation, and salvation. As in any battle of significance, the baggage carried into the fray is almost as enlightening as understanding the theological lines of argument. Here, as elsewhere, the various mind-sets within the CRC prove useful.

Those who maintained that God's eternal decree of salvation came logically *prior to the fall* were called the "Supralapsarians"; while those who argued that that decree came logically *subsequent to the fall* were "Infralapsarians." From a century's distance, such an argument seems a cousin to the question of how many angels could dance on the point of a needle, but the issues were not insubstantial, considering the historical position of the church.

Supras maintained that because election preceded creation, the elect were redeemed already at birth. The sacrament of infant baptism, they maintained, assumed regeneration, and therefore any experience of salvation (what their American Christian friends would have called "a conversion experience") was merely the individual's mature recognition of what had already been accomplished long before. The Supras felt this belief grew healthily from what they considered the traditional Calvinist emphasis on the sovereignty of God—and not on human choice.

If you're following the whole argument here, it may come as no surprise that the leading advocates for the Supralapsarian view tended to be those who were more closely aligned to Kuyperian ideas about faith and culture, specifically those who tended to be impatient with believers who harbored what they considered to be excessive concerns about the state of their individual souls. The Supras argued that such a position

was, in James Bratt's terms, "sounder scripturally and more fruitful ecclesiastically," since their own major concerns were given to "reformation" of society and culture, the second half of Bavinck's two conversions—the conversion to the world.

But Infras were not easily moved on this point, since they maintained that concerns with culture and society too offhandedly dismissed what they considered to be the greatest drama of all human life—the individual's own testimony to a personal relationship with Jesus Christ. Often, the Infras were historically aligned with the *Afscheiding* movement, individuals who had been reared on the pietism of secession. What's more, some who argued passionately for the Infra position did so for very personal reasons—because they had themselves undergone what they considered to be radical conversions.

One tireless campaigner for the Infra position, Lammert J. Hulst, had spent his early years agonizing over his salvation, and then experienced a powerful spiritual conversion—*after* becoming a preacher. By the time the theological argument arose, Hulst had already gained a significant reputation and following in the CRC by providing leadership in and out of almost every controversy. He was a strong leader, forceful and experienced, a patriarchal figure. Hulst's very life bore witness to what he saw as the truth.

Another major force in the Supra/Infra debate was Foppe Ten Hoor, the man who occupied the weighty position of Chair of Systematic Theology at the

Theological School in Grand Rapids (the school that would become Calvin College and Seminary). When compared to Hulst's tenure in North America, Ten

Hoor's experience was limited. But he'd been a tireless campaigner *against* Kuyperian theology and concerns during his years in the Netherlands. Together—

Six Chairs

༺෴༻

Lammert J. Hulst immigrated to the New World in 1874 after receiving a call from the Danforth, Illinois, Reformed Church in America. In his biography Hulst describes some of the circumstances surrounding that move—revealing that even in the good old days, ministers were sometimes subjected to insensitive treatment.

In the call letter extended to him by the Danforth Reformed Church while he was still in the Netherlands, Hulst explains, he was told not to ship a stove or a kitchen table and chairs. This equipment, the letter said, was part of the parsonage fringe benefit. Upon arrival, Hulst and his family were greeted by the consistory. A tour of the drafty and bleak parsonage revealed that in addition to the stipulated furniture, the parsonage contained six weather-beaten unstable cane chairs. Four of the six were sufficiently in disrepair so that the bottom of the human anatomy would sag downward upon use.

One of the elders, with a jovial and generous gesture, pointed to the row of chairs and said, "This is our gift to you for coming to America." Two years later when Hulst stood ready to leave for Grand Rapids, he and his wife had an animated discussion about what should be done with the wonderful gift of the six never-used cane chairs. She suggested that it might offend the congregation if they left them behind, so they were dutifully packed and sent to Grand Rapids.

Two weeks later an urgent communication arrived from the consistory of Danforth, asking about the whereabouts of the chairs. Nonplussed, but irritated to the bottom of his patient soul, Hulst brought them to the local railway freight station and returned them to Danforth.

When the congregation heard of the outrageous conduct of its consistory (who claimed that there was nothing in the minutes about the chairs being a gift), they rebelled and rejected the first duo for a new minister. Their indignation was so intense that they informed the consistory that they would never vote on any subsequent duo if it did not contain the name of their former pastor, Rev. Hulst.

Lammert Jan Hulst.

With belated wisdom, the consistory acquiesced—and the next duo included the name of the former pastor, who only four weeks before had been installed in his new church in Grand Rapids. The outcome was a landslide in favor of Hulst.

He acknowledged the call, expressing gratitude for their confidence in him, and declined their gracious invitation to return. His letter concluded with a P.S.: "If something like this had not been done, I would never have set foot in your church again." —WDB

arguing from good, strong pietistic traditions—Hulst and Ten Hoor were a formidable force. What they feared, among other things, was that the Supra argument, soft-pedaling the importance of some kind of conversion experience, would spell the end of piety in the CRC. They feared that the kind of earnest speculation concerning the state of one's own soul before a living God, an earnest measurement of self so richly a part of the pietist tradition and the old conventicle ways, would lose out to a theology that took the great question of working out one's own individual salvation altogether too glibly.

On one side of the argument stood those CRC folks who paid great homage to personal salvation; on the other, often enough, stood the Kuyperians, who constantly tried to move the Christian mind beyond what they may have considered its own spiritual myopia.

The Supras judged that Ten Hoor and Hulst may well have been guilty of what they called "dualism." Ten Hoor, in his position at Calvin Seminary, maintained that theology was "the queen of the sciences," the most important single avenue of learning for the Christian. Theology, to Ten Hoor, stood above and beyond every other academic discipline. The Supras, on the other hand, insisted that such a hierarchy created a horrendous split in the Christian consciousness—theology and the world of the spirit on one side (grace), and the world of nature on the other (nature). That kind of "dualism" led to a

Professor Foppe M. Ten Hoor (1855-1934).

conviction, for instance, that there were only certain real spiritual callings in life—the pastorate, mission work, and maybe Christian education; while every other profession was, well, "of the world." The Supras wanted a theology that pressed its concerns into every last area of life and didn't for one moment stand above and beyond the material world.

These more substantial arguments, which may have rarely made their way into the heat of the Infra/Supra battle, were specifically tied to the culture in which its participants lived. As James Bratt points out, accompanying all of the argumentation was a perception of the Christian's place in the society around him. What Hulst and Ten Hoor argued was a variation on the slippery slope—that all confessional fellowships, all churches, all groups of believers tend to fall to the seductions of power and wealth. The Infras (descendants of the secessionists and very deeply "Confessional") saw the Kuyperian movement cozying up to worldly wealth and power, becoming all too comfy with politics, art, and science, and thus moving down the road toward assimilation into a godless culture. The argument of the Infras found its foundation on a cultural fear Bratt locates in the title of one of Ten Hoor's own sermons: "[According to the Infras], if Reformed people wished to remain God's people, they had to remain 'The Worthless of the World.'" Those words would not likely have sat well with Abraham Kuyper, member of the Dutch Parliament and Prime Minister of the Netherlands.

The CRC Synod of 1908 expressed its agreement with the following conclusions drawn by the *Gereformeerde Kerken* in the Netherlands at its Synod of 1905:

- The Reformed confessions assume, but do not explicitly state, an Infralapsarian position.
- This does not mean that the Supralapsarian position should be either excluded or condemned.
- Supralapsarianism should not be touted as the official position of the church.

The substantial differences between the Confessionalist and the Kuyperian minds (as we've try to outline them above) went on to find different issues, but the conflicts that lie at the base of this Infra/Supra argument still exist. Perhaps *battle* is an inappropriate metaphor, but undoubtedly the argument was waged with sometimes boisterous voices and deep-seated antagonism. Once again, we have come to a place in the story where the best answers to the dilemma in question may not be either/or, but both/and; unfortunately, it is almost always more difficult for us to accept the mystery of paradox than the certainty of any single position.

For all the firmly held differences among leaders in the CRC—differences in strategy, in opinion, in emphasis, and in character—there were remarkably few charges of heresy during the period moving up to World War I. Some difficult issues were sorted out to various degrees of satisfaction, but there appeared to be room in the growing denomination for differences of opinion and behavior. Leaders were not laying land mines in the battleground of theological dispute. Synods were not concentrating on heresy-hunting. It was a lively, jumbled time.

CHAPTER 12

To Be in America

In the decades surrounding the turn of the twentieth century and up to World War I, the Christian Reformed Church was growing significantly. Once again, thousands of Dutch immigrants began to come through Ellis Island. Many of them then boarded an ethnic railroad that would eventually bring them, after occasional stops in Dutch quarters in New Jersey, Michigan, or Wisconsin, to the still largely unpopulated West—Minnesota, Iowa, South Dakota, Texas, or Washington. Some new colonies flourished; others barely took root, their settlers quickly moving on. What pulled the new Dutch-American arrivals to certain geographic areas was the same force that drew many other American ethnic groups to certain spots on the broad and relatively unsettled American landscape—the possibility of living in community with others of their own cultural and religious heritages.

Settled extensively by European immigrants in the years between 1865-1917, the American prairies remain today a patchwork of ethnic towns and villages where descendants of European immigrants of Polish, Czech, or German stock still comprise a majority of the citizenry. Chicago stills sells itself as a city made more delightful by its dozens of ethnic enclaves. Canada officially sanctions its diversity and urges its immigrant communities to keep up the traditions of its respective cultures.

Today, the Christian Reformed Church recognizes the superglue that holds immigrant communities together and officially sanctions Korean and Spanish-speaking Christian Reformed churches throughout North America, churches where an ethnic community's language remains the language of worship. In part, that recognition comes from the experience of the denomination's oldest ethnic tradition—the Dutch. For even though turn-of-the-century growth in the CRC was significant, there were few McCalls, Stevensons, or Dobrinskis in the pews. New members had old names like De Vries and Vander Meer. They may have been new Americans, but they found the CRC, as many others did the RCA, a very comfortable fit. Numbers swelled, but the sources of growth were internal—huge families and recruits from "the old country."

THE CRC AND LODGE MEMBERSHIP

One significant reason for the strong growth of the CRC in the late nineteenth and early twentieth centuries is linked to the Old World differences between what

Richard
Kortenhoven,
ca. 1920. Hunting on
a Columbus,
Montana, farm.

is now the Reformed Church in America and the Christian Reformed Church of its time. Many of the new CRC folks—as well as many of those who had been part of the fellowship for decades—were

Pine Rest Chapel.

decidedly opposed to lodge membership. The old Dutch Reformed Church in America (now the RCA) had, by the turn of the century, taken a look at lodge membership and shrugged its collective shoulders. When new immigrants came to this country, immigrants accustomed to fearing "secret societies," they were appalled to find Odd Fellows, Elks, Moose, and Masons right there beside them holding the hymnal.

A few years ago, the community where I live celebrated its centennial with, among other things, a downtown parade. There were marching bands and floats and kiddie groups, but by far the noisiest participant was a gang of go-karters who pulled astounding maneuvers in their

tiny vehicles, meandering in and out of long lines and twisting donuts in the street, all of it orchestrated like a motorized folk dance. People loved their shenanigans, although I have to admit that often as not the parade watchers were laughing *at* the go-karters, not *with* them.

The drivers were adult males, most of them well past forty, I think, about a half-dozen sizes too big for their vehicles. They wore colorful costumes with funny little conical hats, each festooned with a dangling gold cord that slapped all over their heads as they spun donuts. Their maneuvers were fascinating and well choreographed. But imagine: thirty or forty paunchy men in funny hats blitzing around Sioux Center streets in go-karts. It was a hoot—it really was.

They were lodge members, all of them, and proud of it—Shriners out of Sioux City, Iowa. Considering, from this time and distance, all the noise given to lodge membership throughout the history of the CRC, it's remarkable to think that a motley gang of go-kart daredevils could have inspired such antipathy. But once again, one must go back to the old world.

In the Middle Ages, freemasonry was a movement of, well, masons—builders, highly skilled stone carvers. Later, the organization's membership grew when they admitted individuals who didn't share the same occupation. At that time, they uniformly held to a philosophy of work and a view of God as "the sovereign Grand Architect of the Universe." Devoted to enlightened rationalism and political radicalism, they were the "ACLU" or "NOW" of that era in the eyes of pious

Christians. Both on the basis of their definitions and by the manner in which they created and maintained organizational unity, these groups undoubtedly vied with the church for the faith and conviction of their members. By 1900 in the U.S., more men in big cities belonged to these secret societies than to churches. Their wives went to church, but the men had their own fellowship—a religious fellowship. So it's not surprising that lodge membership was banned in the U.S. not only by the CRC, but also by Roman Catholics and strict Lutherans.

Although opposition to lodge membership was already a factor in the establishment of the CRC in 1857, the reasons for that opposition are most clearly outlined in a report adopted by the Synod of 1900. That report listed numerous reasons for the church's continued opposition to "secret societies," groups that synod defined as "an organization which requires of every one who becomes a member unconditional concealment of all that pertains to the lodge, without officially informing the candidate of the contents of what must remain secret; and which at the same time obligates its members to unrestricted, or at least insufficiently restricted, assistance or obedience."

The lodge, synod asserted, is sinful when it commits a person to a concealment of evil, which is a misuse of the oath. By having to swear allegiance to fellow members, members of the secret society, synod claimed, could find themselves oath-bound to a course of action that could be contrary to God's own commands or will. Perhaps most significantly, synod felt confident that "the lodge demands an unconditional promise of obedience by means of which it, in effect, appropriates to itself the honor due only to Christ," and as such is in conflict with, "to a greater or lesser de-

The Lodge Question

The problem of membership in the lodge and in the church did not surface in the very early life of the CRC. But once church leaders became familiar with the nature of the lodge and realized that the lodge had universalistic religious aspects that conflicted with Christianity, they quickly judged these "secret organizations" to be forbidden territory for members of the CRC.

When the lodge issues began to sharpen, they created unrest in the colony in western Michigan and in the western part of the Dutch Reformed Church (later the RCA). In the early 1880s the General Synod of that church refused to condemn lodge membership, leaving the decision to local congregational option. Because of that stance, several congregations seceded from the Dutch Reformed Church and joined the CRC. The most conspicuous congregation to join was the very large and prestigious church built and pastored by Van Raalte, the father of the Holland, Michigan, colony.

The CRC's stance on the lodge issue also finally brought the young denomination support from its secessionist friends in the Netherlands. Abraham Kuyper judged that the lodge embraced a false religion and steered the newer immigrants to the CRC. That swelled the membership of the CRC so that it eventually became larger than the western part of the RCA.

The CRC has consistently held that church membership and lodge membership are incompatible, and that membership in the lodge is forbidden for members of the CRC. There have been attempts throughout the years to change this position, with the argument that candidates for membership who happen to be lodge members should be given time to learn that the lodge is unacceptable and then be allowed to give up their membership by choice. This position has never gained more than minimal support in the church. It is a firm conviction of the CRC that choosing Jesus as Savior involves departing from any and all other ways of seeking salvation. "Lodge membership" is no longer a living issue in Christian Reformed churches. —TEH

gree," the first, second, third, fourth, sixth, ninth, and tenth commandments.

Strong stuff.

Once synod had made its pronouncement about lodge membership, little more was said within CRC circles for the next seventy years. The only exception occurred in the denomination's centennial year, 1957, when a pair of overtures from a northwest Iowa classis asked synod to translate the 1900 report into the English language.

Then, in 1969, Classis Lake Erie asked synod to "study whether it is possible for a person to hold simultaneous church and lodge membership." Central to Lake Erie's problem was their sense that the 1900 rulings, as well as the denomination's history of opposition, no longer reflected the reality of experience in American culture, either with regard to the church or the "secret organizations." Because the church was out of date with respect to the lodge, Lake Erie argued, the denomination's long-time opposition stood four-square in the path of the church's more important call to bring the good news.

The denomination's stand had, in fact, kept folks away from the church earlier in its history. When, in 1906, synod found its eastern-most classis, Hackensack, somewhat lacking in fervor to keep the membership away from secret societies, it warned Hackensack to be more diligent in the matter. But in 1908, that classis admitted a candidate to the ministry who said he had no objections whatsoever to lodge membership. Apparently Hackensack didn't give much mind to synod's warning.

With little advance warning in 1908, synod received notice that seven of Classis Hackensack's ten churches had decided to break off relations with the denomination it had so recently joined. Three churches stayed. But the CRC had lost the majority of its most "Americanized" family members—in part, because of our historic stand on lodge membership.

Perhaps it's understandable that, sixty years later, some new agitation about the issue would come from the East. Classis Lake Erie's overture didn't claim that secret organizations were "Christian"; they simply argued that fraternal organizations were, for the most part, indistinguishable from many cultural organizations that are legitimate fellowships for members of the CRC—say, labor unions, for example. "The present stand does not deal adequately with weakness and inconsistency which are found in everyone, but seems to declare," Lake Erie maintained, "that in this one area all weakness and inconsistency must be overcome before church membership may be permitted." After all, they said, not every last member of the organization is deeply fervent and zealously committed to "the religion of the lodge."

In an extensive report that attempted to define not only the nature of the lodge and lodge membership (including a detailed exposition of some of its own "secret" rituals), but also the biblical teachings concerning church membership, Synod 1974 adopted its own study committee's report and thereby reaffirmed that "there is an irreconcilable conflict between the teachings and practices of the lodge and biblical Christianity, and that therefore member-

Ellis Island—Doorway to the Promised Land

From 1893 to 1924, Ellis Island, a small piece of land tucked under the benevolent shadow of the Statue of Liberty, served as an entry point to the United States of America for millions of immigrants from Europe and Africa. It was a place of heartbreak and hope.

During its heyday Ellis Island was a veritable United Nations, filled with a Pentecost of languages and dialects from all over the world. Immigrants came from the mountain villages of Austria, the ghettoes of Russia, the medieval villages of France, the flat, green countryside of the Netherlands, the blighted fields of Ireland, and a thousand other places. Although most were poor and came from the uneducated peasant class, all shared a common dream— for them America would be the land of unlimited opportunity, the land of their dreams.

Motives for coming to America varied. Some fled bankruptcy or family scandal; others were lured by hyperbolic letters describing a promised land flowing with milk and honey, dotted with "alabaster cities undimmed by human tears." Many came to evade service in some kaiser's or czar's army, only to don the uniform of Uncle Sam a few years later.

The short stay on Ellis Island could be excruciating, since many of the newcomers only dimly understood the questions that surfaced through the haze of their weariness after the long ocean journey. And the civil servants who hustled the immigrants off the ships frequently acted in a most uncivil fashion.

The required physical exam was a nightmare, because there was always a possibility that one family member might be rejected for some physical disability or ailment. That meant a return to the homeland with two or three more weeks of cramped confinement in aging ships. And what do you tell your neighbors? That America does not want you? As tense families waited for the decision, once quiet and clean children became fretful and dirty. Harried mothers seated on long, wooden, backless benches felt the first fearful waves of homesickness.

Imagine the relief when the coveted green card, the token of acceptance, was handed to the head of the family! With that gesture, the family was assured they had taken the first step toward becoming part of the mosaic of America. Gathering their meager possessions together, they rode the rails—Germans and Scandinavians to Minneapolis and Wisconsin; the Irish to Boston and Chicago: the Dutch to Michigan and Iowa; and a hundred other nationalities to a thousand different destinations.

—WDB

ship in the lodge and in the Church of Jesus Christ is incompatible and contrary to Scripture."

In reference to the problems associated with evangelistic outreach toward those who have been lodge members, synod advised the churches to show the lodge member "kindly but firmly" that lodge membership is contrary to the will of God.

Little else has been said about the issue for the last quarter century. The silence may be attributable to the denomination's simple adherence to the old mandates. On the other hand, it's entirely possible that in some quarters lodge membership is quietly tolerated—a CRC version of the U.S. military compromise on gays: "Don't ask, don't tell." I say that because I remember being a member of a city church where a small red marker on a regular member's bumper identified him as an International Odd Fellow. As far as I know, no one ever questioned him or the bumper sticker.

In 1975, I was twenty-seven years old and living in Phoenix, Arizona. Okay, I admit it—I wasn't following synodical goings-on very closely. We were going to have a baby, I was teaching in an urban high school—I was growing up. I still am. It's ironic when I think about it now, but just a year after the Synod 1974 decision, an Odd Fellows representative called to tell me that someone had nominated me for membership in their organization. I knew the Odd Fellows was a lodge, but I wanted to hear more about the whole business, so I told the guy he could visit. He did. He came equipped with a fancy little miniature slide projector that plugged into a socket on my wall and came alive with a sight/sound presentation on the advan-

tages of membership in the Odd Fellows, as well as a long list of their organization's considerable good works.

I listened to and watched the whole thing. The guy was nice enough. To my mind, he wasn't odd at all. When the pitch was over, he hauled out the papers and asked me if I wanted to join.

I had absolutely no idea why my church was against the organization he'd just introduced me to. There was nothing in the little song-and-dance he gave me that indicated anything I thought I couldn't subscribe to as a Christian or a member of the Christian Reformed Church. Had I read the history of the CRC's opposition back then, had I even scanned the synodical reports, I may have been more wary of his pitch. I might have been watching for a twitch or a deftly concealed sneer; I might have assumed the whole show was a pretense to finagle me into a position where I was forced to take a line of oaths that would forever compromise my faith. But I remember the guy. He seemed quite ordinary. He just didn't seem capable of such treachery.

Now you may laugh about this, but I told him I didn't really know why for sure, but I knew my church was against lodge membership. I said I didn't care to join.

The guy looked at me as if I were Martian. "I've been doing this for years," he said, "and no one has ever said no before."

"Sorry," I said.

He left, dumbfounded.

Before you indict me for being a dolt, a follower rather than a leader, let me explain that as a high school teacher I didn't have time, midweek, to come up for air beneath the flood of student papers I had to correct. What's more, I thought it exceedingly strange for anyone to want to be an "Odd Fellow" in the first place. I still had enough of the late sixties hippie in me to distrust anyone over thirty and any organization that even smelled like the Establishment. And this did. In other words, I didn't join the Odd Fellows for a variety of reasons— not simply because the CRC was against it.

Today, fraternal organizations do lots and lots of good work. Often, they're not significantly different from their American descendants—Lions Club, Rotary, or the local Chamber of Commerce. I still think those grown men with deadpan faces and absurd hats doing kitty-butts in go-karts on the streets of Sioux Center were a hoot, and I don't care to be part of their group. But I think we've come a long way from the time when the Moose or the Elks or the Odd Fellows were an enemy force in the culture in which we lived.

THE BAGGAGE OF ETHNICITY

We were, at the turn of the century, defining ourselves in what was still an alien culture, often using Old World definitions in a New World context. For years it was commonplace for CRC members to speak of "Americans" or "Canadians" as if they themselves were not. When a girl from the church dated an "American," it could well have been a Norwegian boy with no greater ancestral foothold in North America than the Dutch girl. To Dutch immigrants—like most immigrant communities—there were really only two designations: themselves and "Americans." Generally, Americans were feared by the immigrants, not because of some presup-

Calvin Seminary class, ca. 1910, with instructor Foppe M. Ten Hoor. Located in the Madison Avenue building.

posed criminality, not even because they were suspected to be unbelievers (in fact, many were Lutherans or Methodists or others from the Protestant family of churches). "Americans," like "Canadians" a half century later, were simply, well, "different." Many felt that close acquaintance with Americans threatened a loss of something profoundly important. Marrying an American could mean becoming "unequally yoked." A major fear of all first-generation immigrant people, not just the Dutch, is loss of identity in a world where personal dignity is obtainable only in the close (and even closed) circle of one's own ethnic and religious community. Holding on to personal dignity is so important in the process of Americanization that today we in the CRC don't ask newly arrived Laotians, Venezuelans, Koreans, or Mexicans to give up the world in which they best recognize their own dignity, the world of their own language and culture.

What is ethnicity? That's a question we've come back to several times in this history, and it's not an easy one to answer. We can begin to answer the question with the word *culture,* but that term is almost equally vague. Culture includes, after all, just about everything we do and know and learn. Today, second-generation Greek boys, like second-generation Vietnamese

First CRC in Ripon, California, ca. 1927.

boys, wear baggy shorts, Nikes, and baseball caps jerked backwards over remarkably similar haircuts. Traditional ethnic dress changes very quickly in the process by which one becomes American or Canadian. Although language is not lost quite so quickly in most immigrant communities, English soon becomes the language of choice among second-generation kids schooled in North America. Diet changes quickly as well, but maybe not as quickly as fashion; what we eat, after all, is more private, less public, more intimate, something we do in the confines of our homes.

For the most part, deeply comprehensive socialization to a new culture takes longer than changes in hairstyles, food choices, and even language usage. Most immigrant groups, even if they don't use a common language or dress in a distinctive way, still socialize primarily within their own groups. They are, after all, linked by a common history as well as family ties.

Culture includes all kinds of behaviors, of course. What is often primary to a certain identity are those values and practices most deeply shared, most intimately central—for Dutch people, for example, a penchant for cleanliness. Maybe you've heard this one. Dirk and Maartje De Witt came back from a trip across America that lasted, amazingly, almost two years. It took them so long because every time they came to a freeway rest stop, they pulled over. After all, the sign said "Clean Restrooms." So they did.

Today, ethnic jokes are a sin against American civil religion. I hope you'll forgive my iniquity; but for thousands and thousands of members of the CRC—both those with a Dutch heritage and those who've lived with us long enough to know us well—that joke probably prompts a smile. I've had people from my own home state say that the cleanest towns in Wisconsin are those inhabited by the state's sizeable colonies of Dutch Calvinists and Dutch Catholics. "Cleanliness is next to godliness" isn't in the Bible, but some presume that the source of this proverb was likely William of Orange.

Ethnicity is a complicated and complex thing, comprised as it is of a whole number of outward manifestations (how we eat potatoes, for instance), as well as less easily defined and more private characteristics and behaviors. There's a certain validity to the admonition Rev. Andrew Kuyvenhoven, a former *Banner* editor, once leveled at the CRC—that it was time to "burn the wooden shoes." But at the same time, kicking off the *klompen* isn't as easy as it sounds. We can burn wooden shoes with a quick dose of gasoline and a match, but it's much tougher to radically change how or where we walk.

Let me offer an example. We are all, as human beings, equipped with a certain propensity to sacramentalize. The walls of my study are festooned with memorabilia of interest, I suppose, only to me. Athletic trophies stand beside my favorite books. Writing awards hang from the walls on either side of my basement window. Just behind me, an old playbill from the rock musical *Hair*, a symbol of my sixties upbringing, hangs in a place where it has embarrassed my kids. These things, and many more, have

meaning. To others, they may mean nothing at all. To me, they are worth more, much more, than their market value.

To sacramentalize is a natural penchant—regardless of ethnic background and the particular religion in which one is raised. Even atheists feel the desire to commemorate, to grant extraordinary meaning to a place or a symbol, to grant that artifact meaning and value far greater than what it appears to have for others.

Years ago I put together a scrapbook about my great-uncle Edgar, a man who was killed in France in 1917, more than thirty years before I was born. As far as I

Pioneer Preachers

The homesteaders on the plains were people of faith, strongly committed to establishing the church as well as their farms. The Home Missions Board was active in sending "missionaries" to minister to the early settlers and to help them organize into churches.

These early ministers were a hardy breed themselves. The work was hard, the way was rough, the remuneration was usually pitiful, and they had precious little opportunity to study and to improve their professional skills. The best reward they had was the knowledge that they were heeding the Lord's call to gather his people into churches.

Home Missionary Menno Borduin was typical of the early "circuit riders" in the CRC. His story is told in *The Strength of Their Years* as follows:

> The outstanding man in the life of the congregation was undoubtedly Menno Borduin, whose devotion and faithfulness made him the epitome of a selfless servant. He was affectionately known as "the old prophet" in the churches he served as home missionary. . . . A large portion of his time was spent traveling from one church to the other, in all sorts of weather, finding his lodging in the generally overcrowded pioneer homes; now with one settler, then with another, for weeks on end. His possessions were meager; his clothing was not always warm enough; on trips in winter he often wore newspaper under his coat to keep out the cold. Yet when the church once owed him $12 for traveling expenses, he gave what was due to him to the young people's society for the purchase of Bibles. But the consistory judged that the parents should buy the Bibles and paid his expenses.

That book also tells a story about James Holwerda of the Manhattan, Montana, church, who was often involved in ministry to the outlying groups who didn't have a minister of their own. Holwerda, recalling his early experiences in Alberta, told of lodging with one of the settlers in Monarch in the wintertime. They had no extra bed for visitors, and it was too cold in the shack to sleep on the floor, so the dominie was invited to sleep with the farmer and his wife, with the farmer in the middle, of course. Holwerda had no recourse but to accept this very generous offer.   —TEH

know, nobody else on earth has any information about his life and death; it's all in my book. That book is not *sacred* to me. But it would take a lot for me to part with it.

We impute value to things we judge worthy of our remembrance and esteem. Is it any wonder, therefore, that one of the greatest difficulties of the turn-of-the-century CRC was moving from the Dutch to the English language? My grandmother, born and reared in the turn-of-the-century Reformed Church in America, once told me that it was absolutely ridiculous for her to have to recite the Heidelberg Catechism in Dutch; she didn't know the language at all. Although she was third-generation American, her church forced her to recite the catechism in a language she didn't even understand.

Ridiculous? Of course. But why the elders would continue to require the old language is understandable. As humans, even as Protestant Christians, we sacramentalize things, and few "things" are easier to sacramentalize than the manner by which we speak of and to the King of Creation and his Son, Jesus Christ. One need only witness the difficulty many fellowships are having over the contemporary movement toward "praise choruses" (some people call the conflict "worship wars"). Church music is being redefined; the new praise choruses often speak in a radically different lyrical and

Henry Beets (1869-1947)

∞

There can, for the CRC, never be another Henry Beets. Between 1904 and 1929 he served simultaneously as *Banner* editor, coeditor of *Missionary Monthly,* Director of Missions, and Stated Clerk of synod. Meanwhile he pastored the LaGrave Avenue and Burton Heights congregations (1899-1914 and 1915-1920, respectively) and wrote over a dozen books, including *The Christian Reformed Church in North America: Sixty Years of Struggle and Blessing,* which remains a standard work.

During the Beets era the CRC was a simpler institution with fewer members, congregations, and programs than today. That fact, however, should not detract from the astonishing combination of energy, intelligence, and dedication that marked Henry Beets's life and career. When he retired in 1937, the CRC tallied a membership of 118 thousand in 286 congregations. More than half of these were organized during Beets's tenure as Stated Clerk, an office he used in conjunction with his editorships to publicize the organization, growth, and achievements of every congregation. He actually knew every CRC pastor and visited nearly all of its congregations. He was a unifying central figure in the CRC who also functioned as its spokesperson throughout North America and the world at large.

—HJB

Henry Beets and his wife, Clara Poel. In 1895 these newlyweds went directly to Sioux Center, Iowa, where Henry Beets pastored First CRC, 1895-1899.

musical language. Conflict follows because few accoutrements of culture—the means by which we practice our lives—become as "sacred" as any medium by which we meet God.

For Christian Reformed churches in the immediate decades following the turn of the century, no issue was so dividing as the issue of what language we use to speak to God. Already in the late 1800s there had been a drive to introduce English to the immigrant church. Founded in 1887, LaGrave CRC in Grand Rapids (then known as "The English CRC") had to call a preacher from Classis Hackensack in order to fill its pulpit with an English-speaking preacher. The man who came to LaGrave was Rev. J. Y. De Baun, who was also then editor of *The Banner of Truth*. When De Baun retired from the ministry, his successor at LaGrave, Henry Beets, inherited not only the English-language pulpit but also the English-language magazine. Meanwhile, for its innovation with the American dialect, LaGrave CRC, despite a long string of essentially conservative pastors, earned an undying reputation for liberalism.

At the turn of the century, English-speaking congregations in the CRC existed, most of them on the East coast. German-speaking CRC churches in Classis Ostfriesland continued to prosper in the Midwest. But the dominant language and culture of the CRC was Dutch. Prompted by those who were descendants of the *Doleantie*, those who wanted to confront the larger "theses" of the time, the CRC was interested in American questions, but the answers it offered were shaped and even limited by its own Dutch experience. As Henry Zwaanstra observed, "During this period the Christian Reformed

ATTENTIE !

De Kerkeraad verzoekt ernstig en dringend aan **de gebruikers van Tabak** om dit in de Kerk na te laten en vooral zich te onthouden van **SPUWEN** en het neerwerpen van Tabak, als niet betamende in Gods huis.

"Attention! Users of Tobacco! The church council urgently requests that you refrain from smoking or spitting in church. That's not fitting in God's house."

Church probably showed more interest in social and political questions than at any other time in its history." But the interest was that of a Dutch spectator.

When members of the CRC, at the turn of the twentieth century, looked at American Christianity, what they saw were two separate movements. First, they saw the "fundamentalists," a term often given to those who stake out a very firm and tight position relative to Scripture's intent, a position that seemed a bit too confining to many members of the CRC. The fundamentalists seemed to want a religion of experience, an individualized relationship with God most clearly evidenced by a perception that Jesus owned the human heart, but not the world around us. For many years, most members of the CRC who cared to give time to the idea perceived fundamentalists to be less than wholly right about the way to understand the gospel's truth. At the same time, however, few would have ever considered the fundamentalists to be totally wrong. There is, after all, enough *Afscheiding* in our blood to make the fundamentalist a cousin,

Memorial Day
church outing, 1921,
Denver, Colorado.

if not a brother or sister, in the Lord. Nonetheless, in the early twentieth century, the CRC criticized fundamentalism—though few, if any, fundamentalists were listening.

On the other side of the religious spectrum, the Social Gospel movement was gaining a considerable American following. Walter Rauschenbush, chief advocate of the movement, insisted that "the religion of Jesus has less to fear from sitting down to meat with publicans and sinners than from the immaculate isolation of the Pharisees." The core of Rauschenbush's gospel was good works. There was enough of the *Doleantie* in us to agree that the kingdom of Christ must be built here and now—but never, we've always contended, at the expense of a personal relationship to Jesus Christ.

For decades the CRC lived between the two major American religious movements of the day, sympathizing and attacking. Neither movement was significantly affected by our many editorials and exhortations; we were, after all, writing and speaking in Dutch to a country that understood English.

Americanization is a process, not an event—or even a series of events. Factors rooted in our ethnic past besides language and even relative size kept the CRC from Americanizing more quickly. More than a decade ago, I interviewed Richard Ostling, then religion editor of *Time* magazine and a member of the Christian Reformed Church, for *CRC Family Portrait,* a collection of stories about members of the denomination. In the process of that interview, we talked extensively about the CRC and its place in the denominational mosaic of North America. His insights were fascinating, drawn as they were from his broad and deep understanding of various religious fellowships on the continent.

At one point in the conversation, we were talking about trends in American Protestantism and what was then the issue of the hour among American evangelicals—inerrancy. With some glee, I brushed the term aside, as I remember, telling Ostling how blessed we were not to have to deal with the inerrancy question and get bogged down in what seemed to me to be a tedious argument about whether or not the Bible had errors. I told him I thought that our own tradition of looking at Scripture, a view drawn from European theology, simply transcended such silliness. I fully expected Ostling to give an amen to my relief.

"It's typically Christian Reformed to think that way," he told me. "The CRC is American now, not Dutch," he said, "and if it's going to be a part of the American landscape, it will have to participate in the issues that are important to American Protestantism. It can't stay aloof."

I felt reprimanded, even if he didn't intend his comments as a slap on the wrist. Ostling was exactly right. The kind of superiority I had offered was not only arrogant, it was separatist. Even though I couldn't speak a word of Dutch, was a fifth-generation American, and had never been a real theologian, Richard Ostling made very clear to me how a species of ethnic and religious insularity had kept me from participating in real-life battles in American Evangelicalism. The year was 1982, three-quarters of a century after the denomination officially battled with "Americanism" by giving up the Dutch language.

While our editors and preachers busied themselves with critiques of American life at the turn of the century, the denomination itself floated in wonderful isolation, perched comfortably above the American scene. So confident of that impermeable isolation was the Rev. J. M. Bosma that, in the preface to his 1907 *Exposition of Reformed Doctrine,* a catechism book used throughout the denomination, he bluntly confessed: "No serious efforts have been made to combat the views held by non-Reformed teachers of religious truths." If his students weren't ever going to face American theologies, Bosma apparently reasoned, why bother them with such matters?

For the most part, the Christian Reformed Church deliberately stayed apart from the mainstream of American life until the United States entered World War I. Our isolation was radically altered by the experience of that war. Americanization came with brutal swiftness and a stubborn staying power.

The war effort created animosity wherever loyalties were challenged. Old country ways and old country languages met with disdain, bigotry, and outright hatred, especially for those whose language, Dutch, passed for German to some Ameri-

Dutch or Deutsch?

During World War I, many CRCs still used the Dutch language exclusively. Some, whose knowledge of linguistics was overshadowed by their hyper-patriotism, concluded that Dutch and Deutsch (German) were, if not identical, at least linked in a common bond of depravity.

On one occasion in Peoria, Iowa, threats had been made against the church and Christian school. These threats became a reality one night when, fueled by liquor and pseudo-patriotism, a group gathered in the dusk and set fire to the church and Christian school. The parsonage was scheduled for a later date.

The pastor, J. J. Weersing, was sufficiently alarmed that he accepted a providentially timed call from the church in Hull, Iowa. In the dark of the night, he and his family fled the precincts of Peoria and took refuge in Hull.

Weersing chose as the text for his farewell sermon, which was delivered not in person but by U.S. mail, "In your struggle against sin, you have not yet resisted to the point of shedding your blood"—a unique choice of a text for a shepherd who had abandoned his flock in their time of crisis.　　—WDB

can ears. Henry Zwaanstra, in *Reformed Thought and Experience in a New World,* makes the problem of being Dutch during World War I very clear:

> *The national loyalty of many Holland-Americans, particularly pastors of [Dutch-speaking] congregations and members of the Calvin College faculty, was seriously questioned. According to [then* Banner *editor] Beets, a Hope College student publication stated that the average Dutch settlement in America was a hotbed of disloyalty. A Grand Rapids newspaper claimed there was great joy in Berlin because many Christian Reformed ministers refused to permit the American flag to be displayed in their churches or patriotic hymns such as "America" to be sung by their members.*

In 1965, the Dutch patriarch of a large clan in Iowa could still remember how he'd driven into town one day during World War I, parked his new black car (one of the few owned by Dutch farmers in his day) in front of a store, and gone in to do some shopping, only to find, when he came out, "Friend of the Kaiser" printed in yellow paint that still dripped from the new finish. Dutch sounded a great deal like German.

Board of Heathen Missions, 1912. Chairman Henry Beets standing, others, left to right, Revs. Johannes Groen, John Dolfin, John Walkotten, M. Van Vessem.

Particularly in Iowa, and to some extent in South Dakota, the Americanization of the churches was, according to Zwaanstra, "virtually imposed by state authorities." Iowa was the only state of the union to pass a language law specifically prohibiting the use of foreign languages in public meetings. Officers of the law sometimes attended church services to be sure that the language used was English. In some places allowances were made, of course; and in others, where people knew each other well and understood not only the language differences but also the degree of patriotism in otherwise suspect peoples, the law was never really enforced at all.

By 1917, according to Zwaanstra, "nearly every congregation in Grand Rapids made some use of English in church worship and education." In fact the shift in language was accomplished so swiftly that Beets confessed in a 1917 editorial that "instead of delegates to classis being unable to express themselves in English, the number having difficulty using the language of the fathers was increasing."

When one considers the enormity of accommodation necessary to change a language, the speed of the change was terrifying. It created its own share of comic moments. After all, the initial changes often came in the package of compromise—an English service plus a Dutch service. The requirement put an additional burden on preachers, some of whom weren't comfortable in English, others of whom weren't comfortable in Dutch. Rev. B. J. Haan, first President of Dordt College, liked to tell stories about

how bad his Dutch really was. He knew it, he said, by the unanticipated giggles he'd hear in the sanctuary when he'd use the old language—when he certainly wasn't telling jokes.

In *Americans from Holland,* Arnold Mulder relates some language bloopers he pulled from an English-language newspaper whose correspondents were Dutch.

> *The youngest son of Mr. and Mrs. Simon Bos who was found unconscious several days ago in the stable there he was kicked by the horse with a scalp wound and a big gash on his forehead and internal injuries and who was given no hope for his recovering is by the prompt medical aid of Dr. J. Masselink that he is reported slowly improving.*

And this:

> *Leonard Kieviet had a nice experience. While driving his auto he met with a collision. The auto and a buggy were driving the same way and when by turning the corner from Maple Street and Main Street Mr. Keiviet drove into the buggy and didn't stop before he was in the cigar shop of Mr. Schulmeyer.*

Many, many CRC congregations went to split services during the era. In Central Avenue, Holland, Michigan, Rev. Lambertus Veltkamp held forth for four sermons every Sabbath, two each in Dutch and English. Rev. Bill Buursma remembers sitting in Centennial Park in Holland as a boy, waiting for the Dutch service to be over so the family could go home; he and his father went to the English service, while his mother and his sisters attended Dutch worship.

For preachers, the language change made Sabbaths look even less like a day of rest. Buursma remembers a time when Rev. Veltkamp, in order to make a point in the English service, told the congregation, "Now in Dutch we would say it this way—." He then proceeded to make his point. But once he was started, the good dominie forgot to return to the English. Five minutes passed, Veltkamp going on and on in the Dutch language. Finally, Elder Oelen made his way to the pulpit, jerked at the preacher's coat, and said, *"Dit is een Engelse dienst"* (This is an English service). Veltkamp, shocked, responded, *"Och, dat is ook zoo"* (Oh, yes, that's right, isn't it?), and smoothly switched back to English.

In many places, of course, the elderly could not keep up with the new tongue. They feared that all they'd built would collapse under the weight of Americanism. The English language was foreign, not to be trusted. They had always spoken to God in Dutch. Changing to an entirely new language, a job difficult enough in everyday life, seemed not only impossible but a violation of something sacred when it was done in the sanctuary of the church.

In serious theological discussion, a major question became, "How do we speak English and remain Reformed?" For those who knew how to express their faith only in the language, terms, and models of the Netherlands—whose whole constellation of saints and sinners were drawn from the old tales of the old country—how to hold on to something good and strong and right when it was communicated in a whole new tongue was a deadly serious question.

SIOUX CENTER'S LANGUAGE WARS

Case in point—Sioux Center, Iowa, the town where I live today. Few visitors could imagine the vicious battles that accompa-

---

The Building of Manhattan Church

The Manhattan, Montana, church is known locally as "the hill church" because it is built on a rather prominent rise and can be seen far and wide. A relatively small congregation built this large rural church in 1912, and therein lies a tale.

The Rev. J. Vander Mey, pastor of the Manhattan congregation at the time, took a very active part in the building program. He sent for a church plan somewhere "in the east," which called for this huge building, complete with stained-glass windows. The planned church building far exceeded the aspirations of the congregation, but Vander Mey was aggressive and persistent, and he got his way. When it came to the stained-glass windows, however, the consistory drew the line and vetoed his plan. "Much too expensive," they said, especially with the burden of paying for such a huge church.

But Vander Mey was not so easily sidetracked. He secretly ordered the windows, and when they arrived at the railroad station in Manhattan, destined for the CRC, there was nothing the consistory could do but accept the windows and the debt. It took the church forty years to pay off its debt for the new building.

Manhattan (Montana) CRC church and parsonage, ca. 1920.

History has vindicated Vander Mey's insights, if not his methods. The day came when this huge church could not hold the crowds that filled its worship services. A second congregation had to be organized in 1960. An old saying may provide a bit of insight into this piece of history: The Lord can strike a straight blow with a crooked stick. —TEH

nied the language change in this town seventy-five years ago. Bethel CRC stands along Sioux Center's Main Street, its stunning vaulted roofline aspiring towards heaven in a modern gesture somewhat comparable to the cathedrals of old. Only a few blocks east, First CRC, marked by an almost Puritanical plainness yet not without its own spacious grandeur, is situated elegantly amid residential homes. If today there is any animosity between members of those congregations, it has nothing at all to do with what happened in the single church they were both a part of following World War I. Yet what happened between Christian Reformed people in Sioux Center back then fractured the community and split the fellowship.

So rancorous was the battle that not until just a few years ago would anyone even talk about it publicly. I am indebted to Louis Van Dyke, who researched the story for his own congregation's anniversary celebration.

But before we start, we should remember that the battles that rend communities rarely stem from one issue alone. While the use of the Dutch language played a significant role in what happened in Sioux Center during the 1920s, no one—then or now—would say that the effort to retain the Dutch language was the only reason God-fearing people went to war. The real reason was an undeniable process—Americanization. Two generations took opposing sides created out of two different mind-sets: one of them, the consistory, was deeply affected by its own Dutch past; the other, the Sunday school teachers, were second-generation, perhaps as American as they were Dutch. One generation put

down its fist when it felt that what was good and proper was at risk; the other put its finger in the face of tradition and charged that if change didn't occur, there would be no future at all.

The motive was grand and good and right—the faith of our children. To those who wanted change in the Sioux Center CRC, the old language and the old ways weren't enough to hold on to the kids, who were becoming far less Dutch than American. When CRC kids started wandering over to the RCA's youth programs—in part because those programs were conducted in English—the progressive forces in the church pushed for change. They demanded that worship, catechism, and Sunday school be conducted in English and—and here's the rub—that some power in decision-making be granted to those who were in authority in those church organizations.

Power. Authority. Whether or not the words are ever said publicly, often as not they're the real glowing embers. The Sunday school teachers didn't have it and wanted it. The consistory had it and refused to give it up. What we need to remember here too is that Sunday school itself was a peculiarly American institution. No Dutch immigrant churches carried a Sunday school tradition from Gelderland, Zeeland, or Groningen. Sunday school didn't exist in the Netherlands. The first Christian Reformed churches to have Sunday schools created them from uniquely American models.

That something as innocent and dear as a Sunday school program could split a church full of believers may seem astounding, but it's understandable. The American

Sunday school movement originated from what we might call the revivalist tradition—tent evangelism, altar calls, testimonies, and "finding Jesus." What's more, when, in some churches, Sunday school classes became more popular than communal worship, some recognized that worship itself, as well as power and authority, was at risk. Some felt confident that the fundamentals of the way we practice our faith were placed in jeopardy.

The consistory of Sioux Center CRC wasn't alone in calling the congregation's attention to the dangers of Sunday school. Synod 1918 recognized that this American church phenomenon could well become a problem in Christian Reformed churches and adopted guidelines for local congregations, guidelines that made clear that Sunday school curriculum should be under "strict church supervision so that an attitude of 'Christianity above differences in belief' does not arise." Sunday school, synod feared, could water down the historical Christian faith, make following Jesus something "cutesy," sell its richness and depth like so much penny candy. Synod 1924 continued the warning, claiming that "our covenant youth" must be safeguarded from the "perils of liberal teaching with which the air is full."

The consistory of Sioux Center CRC took these synodical warnings seriously. When the "Teachers Meeting" (the Sunday school teachers) drew up a constitution in 1919 that allowed them, not the consistory, to choose Sunday school teachers, and then gave that constitution to the consistory for approval, the consistory balked. The consistory was sure that such a move would erode its own power. The Teachers Meeting seemed to be declaring independence from consistorial authority.

So the consistory didn't buy the change. They rejected the new constitution, and the first shots in a long, bloody battle were fired. But the teachers didn't back down. In fact, they set about to buttress their position with authority of their own. They reviewed church order, studied the synodical record, consulted a Calvin Seminary professor, and informed the consistory in November 1919 that they would, like it or not, stand by the new constitution.

Those were fighting words. The consistory recognized mutiny when it happened on their deck, and they fired back. Unless the teachers operated under the old constitution, the consistory insisted, the whole program would be locked up tight and put away—no more Sunday school, period. End of discussion—or so the consistory thought.

Most of the action, of course, had been behind closed doors. But the whole affair came out from behind the curtains at the conclusion of that year's Sunday school Christmas program, when the teachers registered their own formal and dramatic public protest by announcing not only that there would be no more Sunday school, but that it was ending under their protest. There was an impasse between teachers and consistory, they announced. Hand it to the teachers—they knew how to get people's attention. On Christmas Eve 1919, there was likely no "Silent Night" in Sioux Center.

Consistory members, who'd been watching their grandchildren perform, had absolutely no idea that such an announcement was forthcoming. To them,

(Top) Sioux Center, Iowa, ca. 1915, and (below) the city today.

such an open acknowledgment of the problem was a declaration of war, a war they didn't intend to lose. Unfortunately, from their point of view, the teachers' first public shot had been very effective: the consistory had come off looking like dastardly villains.

Immediately thereafter, the consistory found the teachers guilty of violating the ninth commandment, "Thou shalt not bear false witness." The teachers' public announcement was not only inappropriate, consistory said, but entirely inaccurate. What's more, in going public the way they had, they had deliberately sidestepped consistorial authority. Things were getting very hot.

In the next few days, three young peoples' societies closed up shop in protest over the consistory's actions, which only confirmed to the consistory that the mutiny was becoming a conflagration. Sioux Center CRC was burning.

A series of cannonades from either side were fired in the next weeks and months. Some members notified the consistory that they were taking their fight to classis. The consistory demanded that the Sunday school teachers confess their sin of slander from the pulpit of the church.

When the battle shifted to classis, it was a mess. Although classis tried to find some middle ground, they ended up appeasing no one and ending nothing. Classis said they regretted that the consistory had taken actions without making a stronger attempt to work out differences, but they also "severely condemned" those who had opposed the consistory. In addition, they recommended that Sunday school be reopened but failed to indicate under whose control and leadership.

By the summer of 1920, the situation was nearly out of control. At a congregational meeting, the pastor, Rev. Cornelius De Leeuw, opened nominations for church office to the floor, something that had never been done before. The consistory was furious, interpreting the preacher's actions as an attempt to unseat them. Members of the congregation who supported the consistory demanded that the sacrament of the Lord's Supper be suspended until the preacher himself confessed his guilt for the public sin of undermining the consistory's authority. The consistory decided to call in other local consistories to help them evaluate the situation—and especially De Leeuw's leadership.

Just how bad were things? That meeting between Sioux Center's consistory and the consistories of Hull and Rock Valley lasted twenty-nine hours! What's worse, the results weren't very helpful. The only way to retain any kind of congregational unity, the "double consistory" ruled, was for the church to choose officers from both sides—progressive and conservative.

The Sioux Center consistory went along with the recommendation and allowed the congregation to submit written nominations. They did—thirty-nine names for elder and fifty for deacon. Of that extensive list, the consistory found that only two, in their opinion, fully qualified for office. The war was far from over.

Once the progressives looked over the list announced by the consistory and didn't find their candidates, they found the names listed wanting. Protests were registered. One of the consistory's favorite candidates, it was said, slept in church; another was too old; another hadn't been a member of the church long enough. It was well known, some people said, that another of the consistory's good old boys had done some shameful and immoral act on the ship coming over to America.

When these protests came to the consistory by way of well-circulated petitions, the consistory knew they were facing a public and well-orchestrated rebellion. They decided to cancel the congregational meeting altogether.

Right from the beginning the language issue was in the center of the contention. Already in December 1919, two members of the congregation, both of them supporters of the Teachers Meeting, had come to the consistory to request that worship be done in the English language. When nothing was done with their recommendation, a number of members began to voice the opinion that, because of the unrest and turmoil, the church itself ought to be separated by language—a Dutch congregation and an American congregation. The consistory, noting clearly that there were two definite sides in the congregation, decided to ask classis how a church might be justly separated.

The congregation's factions were at an impasse. Irreconcilable differences separated the two sides. More and more protests occurred with respect to the potential office-bearers—who would or who would not be presented as candidates at the congregational meeting that was long overdue. And when the election was held despite the protests, the difficulties continued to deepen.

In late February, five members of the progressive wing of the church protested the consistory's action, claiming that they represented ninety members. "Our beloved Reformed principles are trampled underfoot," they wrote. "They have been stomped into the slime by the Consistory." Not exactly the language of a peacemaker, but the war had been going on already for months.

In March, classis met once again but refused to allow the church to split over the issue of language usage. What was needed, classis said, was reconciliation, not secession. In addition, they ruled that the consistory elected from the consistory's own slate should not take office, but that a new congregational meeting should be called to elect a consistory in a "free election" from nominations taken from the floor of the meeting. To be sure this would be done in good order, classis further appointed a seven-man delegation to supervise the proceedings.

Sioux Center's consistory didn't appreciate classis's work. Even as the proceedings were occurring, they decided to appeal to synod itself. They maintained that the "free election" mandated by classis was contrary to their own Articles of Incorporation. They were right about that, of course. In addition, they claimed that such an arrangement violated Article 97 of the Acts of Synod, 1886.

Before classis adjourned, it called the entire Sioux Center consistory into session and asked if it intended to abide by the decisions of classis. The consistory said it would not alter its stance even if that meant classis might depose the entire consistory. They continued to maintain that the Teachers Meeting needed to publicly confess its own sin of Christmas Eve 1919, because, they said, no reconciliation could occur where there was no repentance.

Classis heard their response and promptly deposed the entire consistory.

The sordid tale doesn't end there. It includes ugly legal wrangling carried on in a public court of law for almost a decade. The split of the Sioux Center CRC left a sordid trail through more Acts of Synods in the next several years, a full stack of classis notes, and many, many more consistorial minutes.

Only time, it seems, could end the hostility. Today there are two churches where once there was one. And today, thankfully, it's all behind us.

Very few people are old enough to remember those battles, and fewer yet care to remember. Some might say we'd all be better off if no one ever brought up the whole unseemly tale again. But if history is at least what the Puritans thought of it—moral and dramatic—then it is not only telling but instructive. And some of us know very well—as does our God—that the tales of the past often return for awkward and ugly repeat performances, even when the issues aren't cut from the same cloth. You can see the truth of that statement when you consider today's battles over women in office and our worship wars over music. History does come alive in our own present-day actions, whether or not we like it, and whether those actions are joyous or sad, inspirational or regrettable.

All of which brings to mind this verse from Psalm 130: "If you, O Lord, kept a record of sins, who could stand?"

And the next. "But with you there is forgiveness. . . . "

INCREASING AMERICANIZATION

In the decades around World War I, the CRC made significant strides toward becoming something other than a European church fellowship. In 1914, as America prepared to enter the war, the *Jaarboek* became the *Yearbook.* The following year, 1915, the *Instructor* for Sunday schools came out in English, and later that year the church order—the Church Order of Dort, nonetheless—made its English debut. An English psalter was also in preparation, and the irrevocable first steps from Dutch to English had been taken.

Meanwhile, CRC boys who'd been raised in Dutch-American homes, educated in Dutch in their schools, and catechized in Dutch in their churches, were called into an American army and thereby socialized in American life in a manner that was to them, ironically enough, totally foreign.

Returning veterans told horrendous stories about persecution for their inability to speak the English language. Boot camp was not only an excruciating physical preparation for war; it also tested CRC recruits emotionally, morally, and spiritually. Their sympathies were often suspect because their language, their inflections, their brogues seemed so very much like "Deutsch." One young man, snatched from the farmlands south of Chicago and dropped only three months

later into the trenches in France, recalled decades later how at night, once the firing would cease, he could understand the words that rose from the nearby German trenches more clearly than the strange-sounding slang of his GI buddies speaking the American idiom.

For the young men who returned from the war, the "Dutch era" of the CRC was gone forever. One of the most popular songs of the time captures the essence of the change in America—and Christian Reformed life: "How you going to keep them down on the farm, now that they've seen Paree?" After CRC boys went to war for America and their families supported the war effort, they had become Americans, like it or not. When they returned, they joined the young Calvinist church groups that had long been a feature of their tradition and formed the "American Federation of Reformed Young Men's Societies" (1919); they also founded a monthly English-language magazine that didn't include a word of Dutch.

In the five-year period from 1914 through 1918, the Christian Reformed Church changed, at least on its face, more drastically than it had since its first steps on the continent. It had been a collection of isolated Dutch immigrant churches; after the war, it was less isolated and less Dutch.

The church where flags and anthems had been excluded in 1914 was not the same church as the one that gathered for the Synod 1918. Zwaanstra describes the scene:

> *The auditorium in which the synod met was beautifully decorated in the national colors. A portrait of President Wilson was displayed in front of a large American flag*

behind the officers' rostrum. At the opening of the afternoon session on the first day the assembly sang the first and last stanzas of "America."

And the synod unanimously decided to send the following telegram to the President of the United States: "Mr. President: The Christian Reformed Church, in Synod assembled at Grand Rapids, Michigan, send you their greeting and pledge you their whole-hearted support in this critical time. We will support the government with our prayers, lives and property in this righteous cause. Respectfully . . . "

The Christian Reformed Church, just a few years earlier a peculiar Dutch tulip on the New World landscape, began to look more and more like some native American flower. But it was not an easy transition, and the conflicts were not safely behind. The denomination was about to enter the most tumultuous decade in its own history.

CHAPTER 13

The Wars of the Postwar Years

It may be helpful to think of the decade from 1918-1928 as an identity crisis of major proportions for the Christian Reformed Church. Identity is, of course, fiercely important. Before the war, we could define ourselves easily as long as we stayed within our ethnic and religious fortresses, as long as we spoke the Dutch language and carried old country attitudes and beliefs. We had our own schools, we kept to ourselves, and we rather liked a good, strong argument—with each other, of course.

Already in 1911, B. K. Kuiper, a major figure in CRC history who we will shortly hear more about, had laid out a position on "Americanization" that stood for years in the CRC, even though it was more difficult to practice than to preach. In a series of *Banner* articles about the change to the English language, he wrote: "We are quickly changing from Hollanders to Americans." But he considered that adjustment "not in the least a problem" because "it is a process that cannot and may not be held back. We shall become Americans, and we must become Americans. It is an irresistible, moral duty." But he also saw a grave danger: "The danger is this, that our people will also lose their Reformed character. And that must not be."

The question facing the CRC in the decade following World War I—and many might say the question it still faces today—was, What exactly is "the Reformed character"? Multiple definitions for that phrase prompted a series of wars that were not only lamentable but calamitous.

DISSENSION ON THE RIGHT: THE BULTEMA CONTROVERSY

Christian believers feel the soaring blessedness of enriching joy when they consider the world beyond our own. The heft of many a hymn draws us toward the divine reality of life in the presence of God's goodness, the cessation of sorrows, and genuine unity of believers in eternal praise to the Three-in-One. The desire for heaven, for consummation with God through Christ, and for an end to sadness, arises not from a wish but a promise—the promise of eternal life made by none other than the Creator of heaven and earth, the King of Glory.

At some moments in any believer's life, those promises seem more assuring and real than they do at other times. Our earthly suffering, whether it comes by way of untimely death, grave family problems, or simply the relentless effects of aging, prompts many to invest their hearts deeply

in the wonders of the world beyond our own. Those longings are, in effect, perfectly natural. Heaven is, after all, the reward of which we've been assured.

Perhaps we need to start with that reality when we look at a decade of strife and bitterness in the CRC. Perhaps we need to start with the very real desire to say, with African Americans, "This world is not my home—I'm just a passin' through." When difficulties arise all around us, we can fall back on our assurance that that other life, that wonderful, eternal life with the Lord, will be there for us.

Rev. Harry Bultema (1884-1952), founder of the "Berean" church after ejection from the CRC because he advocated premillennial despensational interpretations of the "last days."

The people in the CRC needed that kind of comfort in the decade after World War I. No sooner had the "war to end all wars" ended than other battles began, some of them old struggles that were repressed for a time when the more immediate concerns of war threatened. Once the flow of blood in French trenches was finally stanched, once the doughboys returned from the killing fields, once Dutch ways were no longer considered disloyal on this side of the Atlantic, the CRC, still less than a century old, didn't pack away the armaments but aimed them instead at other targets— often enough, each other.

Why fight? Fear is usually part of the motivation, and, as James Bratt points out, during the post-war era "apocalyptic premillennialism was the rage of Dutch-American conversations." For reasons that now seem less weighty than they did then, many members of the CRC looked at the rapidly changing face of American life and world-wide alignments and felt unsure of themselves. Three great European empires had crumbled and the Bolshevik Revolution had installed a Communist regime in Russia. Change, that often scary but omnipresent reality, was occurring too quickly. Radio, film, automobiles, even air transportation threatened our understanding of time and space. Christendom seemed radically altered, the old verities too creaky to carry the load of gospel truth against the onslaught of constant and fundamental alterations in the way people thought and lived.

As an antidote, perhaps, and in a pattern of thinking forever close to the hearts of Christian believers, God's own strong hand of judgment on an unrighteous culture seemed ready to descend; heaven beckoned just around the corner because hell itself seemed all around. We became concerned, then fascinated, then, in some cases, obsessed with "the end times." Oppressed by a world of darkness, we focused on the stream of glory emanating from a long-promised eternal future.

In the world of the church, modernism seemed to be the roaring lion at the gates. It had arisen in Europe more than a few decades before and had slowly found its way to North America, often by way of the mainline Protestant churches. To many CRC members who'd fought this parasite before, Christianity in America appeared in danger of being devoured from within by a loss of commitment to the authority of Scripture and the persistent intellectual questioning, even scoffing, at truths of the Bible—truths like the resurrection or the virgin birth. In general, mainline Protestant churches in America seemed to be falling to the tendency to view the Word of God by the light of scholarship and intellectualism.

Were these real enemies? Yes, of course. Were these enemies worth fighting? Yes, they were. Was scriptural commitment among American Christians on the decline? Yes, it was. Did it seem that there was little hope for the world? To some, any other conclusion was impossible. Was Jesus coming again? Of course. Would he take his own to him? Of course. Would he judge the sinners? They'll run to the mountains to hide. Is he coming? Yes. Praise God.

But the belief that the world is going to hell in a handbasket tomorrow is just as one-sided, just as much half-truth as the American doctrine of progress—that somehow things will always get better and better. Progress was the doctrine being preached by the modernists: as scientific inquiry continued to bring light to our mysteries and erase our superstitious silliness, the modern progressive mind insisted that culture would move ever upward and forward, improving our lives. And there were myriad miracles in the early years of this century to back up that position. Rural electrification, for example, made candles useless and lamps antiques. Author Jim Heynen says he was just a boy on the night when electricity came to his farm north of Rock Valley, Iowa; but he'll never forget the miraculous phenomenon of light, bright light, suddenly all around the yard. Such gargantuan changes can be

difficult and scary. Apocalyptic thinking grew energetically in the fertile ground of American technological and cultural change. In the CRC, apocalyptic thinkers also created interfamilial warfare.

Rev. Harry Bultema carried his assurance about the imminence of the "end times" directly into the tradition from which he'd come:

> Many well-meaning Christians have condemned the fervent anticipation of the future of the Lord as fanaticism or onesidedness. This common mistake has had the result that today in Reformed circles there is little preached or written regarding the return of Christ. While the whole world stands in fire and flames, we still discuss "the doctrine of baptism," and people seem to have no desire to know about the coming of the Lord.

Even today, at the beginning of the twenty-first century, wherever CRC folks see the world standing "in fire and flames," there will be great sympathy for Bultema's Jeremiah-like prophecies. Some who are reading these words at this moment may well think the Lord could raise up no greater saint at present than another Bultema to bring the church to its righteous senses. But the effect on the body of the argument for the imminent return of Christ is often devastating. Its fervor makes rhetoric passionate and unreasonable. It prompts people to question every doctrine they've inherited, and it forces people to take sides. Hence, warfare.

Was Bultema really out to bring down the church? No, in good Reformed fashion, he meant to bring about a renewal of faith and fervor by way of the standard evangelical format—revival. Was he right about the imminent coming of the Lord Jesus? Probably not. Almost a century has passed; the Lord tarries. Does that mean that we shouldn't be aware of the "signs of the times"? No, it simply means that—and this will come as a revelation—we can be wrong. Could Christ come tomorrow? Sure. Shouldn't we be anxious? Sure, but if our passion is aimed totally at the "other world" of eternal joy, we're reneging on our job—to be salt in the world God loves. A long series of Reformed minds would argue that it is amazingly easy for good, fervent believers to abandon their calling for the sake of their scalps.

At Synod 1918, beautifully festooned with patriotic pomp and circumstance, Bultema's views were soundly rejected by a coalition of Confessionalists (those who believed that good doctrine was the most significant aspect of a church fellowship) and Antitheticals (who saw cultural action and worldview as the most important feature of faith). Two years after that initial rejection, Bultema himself, most of his congregation, and many of his sympathizers left the denomination to form the Berean Church. Their departure would be the first exodus of a startlingly divisive decade, undoubtedly the most bloody of the CRC's first century.

Bultema's ideas, overcooked as they may seem to most of us today, held a close relationship to the ideas and passions of American Evangelicalism, both at that time and today. Bultema hailed from Muskegon, Michigan, which had, at the time, one of several conference grounds important to the turn-of-the-century revivalist tradition of American Evangelicalism. That Bultema would be heavily influenced by the Dwight L. Moodys and Billy Sundays, American revivalists of the first magnitude who came to preach just down the road from Bultema's church, is not at all unlikely. The basic belief in Christ's imminent return is not a peculiarly "American" idea. But there can be little doubt that Bultema's ideas about "end times" were shaped by the discussions going on around him in American culture. To a denominational fellowship deeply concerned with preserving the truth but having difficulty determining exactly what was true and what was expedient, Bultema's views may well have seemed symptomatic of the problems resulting from excessive flirtation with American theology—American dispensationalist and Arminian theology.

Bultema's Berean church grew into its own institution, creating Grace Bible College, Grace Youth Camp (near Ludington), and an active worldwide missionary enterprise. Even today many might say that the fellowship he and his followers began is "American Evangelical," meaning, pejoratively or not, *not* Reformed.

DISSENSION ON THE LEFT: THE JANSSEN CASE

At the same time at Calvin Seminary, another controversy was boiling over. According to his critics, Ralph Janssen, professor of Old Testament, was teaching a "higher critical view" of the Bible. They claimed that he was placing reason above revelation in true modernist fashion, subjecting the claims of Scripture to scientific tests and historical analyses.

Janssen was a second-generation American, born and reared in the Holland, Michigan, area. Even though he took his higher education in the Netherlands, he was not an import to the youthful denomination, but was himself a child of the Christian Reformed Church in America. Undoubtedly, though, his education had influenced his academic stance and methodology, which led ultimately to his deposition.

In this situation, as in others, it is difficult to recreate some eighty years later the specific infractions that prompted the judgments against Janssen. What it boils down to is that this professor was accused of leaning toward "modernism." Among other things, Janssen taught that some of the great Old Testament miracles could well have had natural causes—the sun standing still for Joshua, for instance, could actually have been a solar eclipse. His opponents read such a judgment as a repudiation of the supernatural acts of God. They accused him of denying the authority of Scripture and, most abhorrent of all, elevating reason over revelation.

Janssen also claimed that theology, through time, was a progressive science, capable of being changed when our understanding of the world itself changed. What he meant was that our knowledge of this earth changes, as it did with Copernicus, who maintained that the world was round despite Scripture's reference to "four corners." In his own defense, Janssen quoted from Kuyper and Bavinck, who, he claimed, held very similar views.

More than anything else, it was a 1920s "slippery slope" argument that brought Janssen down. Convinced that Janssen's views would usher in more "higher criticism" to Calvin Seminary and the Chris-

Professor Ralph Janssen (1874-1945) taught the Old Testament at Calvin Theological Seminary, 1914-1922, and was ejected when he was accused of advocating higher critical exegetical study techniques.

tian Reformed Church, the Confessionalists (in particular, his colleagues in the seminary) called into question Janssen's orthodoxy—and kept calling his reputation into question until the case closed and Janssen was shown the seminary door.

What's important to remember here is that everyone uses a "slippery slope" argument sometime in his or her evaluation of contemporary culture. As a teacher of literature, it's easy for me to argue that contemporary illiteracy is a by-product of the media revolution; that people don't read anymore, they watch TV. What's more, I could argue that eventually we will become a culture of spectators, a nation of narcissistic individualists, capable only of being entertained by a show in front of our faces, our God-given sense of imagination severely wilted by the medium that carries the message. Will that actually happen? No one knows. What I can do, however, is use the "slippery slope" argument in a fashion designed to make my own position (for literature, against cinema and TV) convincing.

There is no question that the conservatives feared Janssen's teaching—if not in itself, then in what they assumed would occur once its modernistic tendencies reached full bloom in the seminary and the church. What's more, they had some precedent for believing it could happen, since the scenario they outlined had already occurred in other Protestant fellowships. What Janssen was trying to do—bring the study of Scripture into the twentieth century—was something the conservatives wanted to avoid at all costs and feared perhaps more than anything.

The result was suspicion, invective, and condemnation. Once, in the middle of synod's proceedings on the Janssen case, Herman Hoeksema, quoting Psalm 139, rose to denounce Janssen's methodology as well as the advice others were offering about restraint and Christian charity toward those whose ideas didn't parallel one's own: "'Do I not hate them, O Lord, that hate thee? I hate them with a perfect hatred: They are become as my enemies.'" Conflict turned into bloody war.

In 1918, several of Janssen's fellow faculty members brought their accusations against him to the Calvin Board of Regents (now the Board of Trustees). The regents listened to the charges, talked to Janssen, and cleared him. In 1920, Janssen's colleagues pressed their charges again, this time at synod. Synod reviewed the entire matter, discussed Janssen's positions at length with him, examined his testimony once more, and pronounced him clean.

Then, in 1922, when the charges were brought again, synod reopened the matter. This time Janssen rather defiantly announced that he had defended himself as often as he intended to. He wasn't going to participate in another round of inquiry and quizzing. His opting out of the process, while understandable, was likely not helpful to his defense. After he refused to present himself for interrogation by the appointed synodical committee, they wrote this recommendation, which was accepted by the synod: "Your committee judges that Synod is called to the sad task of deposing Professor Janssen from his office, in accordance with the Form of Subscription. . . ."

But here, as elsewhere, at least two additional factors must be understood.

First, let's look once again at the mind-sets of the CRC we've already identified. Janssen, with his interest in the higher forms of criticism, someone who was not in the least afraid of the dangers of the culture around him, seems to fit into the Positive Calvinist camp. It's unlikely, however, that he would have been happy with that stamp, since he saw himself more specifically as an "Antithetical," quoting from Kuyper—on such subjects as common grace and the freedom of science, including theology, from church control—to substantiate his claim that he wasn't parting from the tradition of Reformed scholarship. The Antitheticals tended to side with Janssen too, perhaps because they weren't sure that worldly scholarship and academic inquiry were as dark and sinful as the Confessionalists assumed.

Those who opposed him, for the most part, were the Confessionalists, who were more than happy to insist that Janssen's flirtation with rationalistic methods of scriptural interpretation put him very much at odds with the confessional traditions of the church and orthodox Christianity. Oddly enough, they too used Abraham Kuyper as a reference point, but what they used of Kuyper was his confessional and pietistic writings, specifically those in which he portrayed the antithesis—the radical line of difference between the church (the city of God) and the world (the city of man). Both sides invoked Kuyper; both found aspects of Kuyper's work that would substantiate their claims and positions.

It's important to think of both the Confessionalists, who valued doctrinal orthodoxy above all, and the Antitheticals, who wanted more confrontation with the world, as Kuyperians. They were—and still are—alike in their appreciation for Kuyper and their conviction that Christians have to maintain a presence in "the world."

SOME NEW DEFINITIONS

Let me stop the narrative for a moment to identify the mind-sets of the CRC anew. As we move further along into the twentieth century, the labels we've used to identify the different mind-sets begin to lose some of their meaning. We can do

better. Just for a moment, let's look at three significant and universal characteristics of God's people—not just Christian Reformed people, but believers in general. We'll rename them in a process that may help us understand some of the issues and battles yet before us in the rest of the twentieth century.

But first, a warning. All such divisions are simplifications. Whenever we call a real live person a Confessionalist or an Antithetical or a Positive Calvinist, we're doing that person an injustice. On the very basis of the complex and marvelous humanity given us by our Creator, we're always—each one of us—more than a designation. No one *is* a Republican or a Democrat, a conservative or a liberal. Such labels never define comprehensively because human beings are not sandwich boards; we are a whole lot more than our individual predilections or party affiliations. I say that because I'm about to make some generalizations about people—for purposes of simplification—and that's bound to make me some enemies.

But here we go. I'm proposing that for the rest of this book we use three words to describe the differences that have existed and continue to exist within the body of believers called Christian Reformed: *Inward* Christians, *Outward* Christians, and *Upward* Christians.

Those I've previously identified as "Confessionalists" I'm going to call Inward Christians. Their basic orientation as believers is toward what they already know—hence, *inward*. Inward believers treasure the creeds, the Word itself, the traditions of the people they come from. As I've said of the Confessionalists, they function in the community of believers as archivists, holding onto what has been passed along through the generations. As such, they are not only least susceptible to change, they often oppose it. They know what they are; they are confident of themselves and their sense of truth. They believe that the answers to all of life's greatest questions lie in the Bible, as distilled in the historic creeds and confessions as well as the church order. Their orientation to the world begins within themselves and what's packed away in the history of their fellowship.

Outward Christians don't see things that way at all. If the world we live in teaches us something that makes us question the church order, then Outward Christians feel no great pain in simply changing it. If we've

always read the Bible a certain way—say, with a sense of women's place in the church—but we know that in the world *out there* things are changing fast—then Outward Christians maintain we have to learn to read the text in a different way. Outward Christians put more weight on "general revelation," the way God reveals himself to us in the world as well as through Scripture. Inward Christians put the greatest value on the creeds and confessions; Outward Christians invest their time and interest in the world around them. Inward Christians often feel that Outward Christians are far too liberal; Outward Christians often feel that Inward Christians are far too conservative.

Upward Christians think both of the others miss the point, because to Upward Christians nothing is as important as their experience of God—experience that results in a closer personal relationship with the Lord Jesus Christ. Upward Christians know very well that all the learning in the world means very little to a believer. They know that book knowledge is not the same thing as "knowing" God. Upward Christians long for and achieve personal fellowship with God, an ever closer walk with their Savior. When Pentecostalism visits the neighborhood of a Christian Reformed Church, it usually snags the Upward believers from the pews.

The basic orientation of Inward Christians is themselves—they see themselves as the keepers of the truth, and they meet Jesus through the truth. The basic orientation of Outward Christians is the world itself—they see themselves as God's hands in his world and they meet Jesus through right actions. The basic orienta-

---

The Banner

The Banner (first called *The Banner of Truth*) came to the CRC through our union of 1890 with the True Reformed Dutch Church (or Classis Hackensack). In the years that followed it became the leading official periodical of the church.

Its first well-remembered editor, Rev. Henry Beets, combined his work as editor with serving as Director of Missions for the denomination. In 1939 Rev. H. J. Kuiper became editor while serving as the minister of Neland Ave. CRC. Five years later the editorship became a full-time position, and Kuiper continued to serve in that role until 1956. Since then five additional editors have served the church:

Rev. John Vander Ploeg (1956-1970)
Dr. Lester De Koster (1970-1979)
Rev. Andrew Kuyvenhoven (1979-1989)
Rev. Galen Meyer (1989-1992)
Rev. John Suk (1992-)   —TEH

---

tion of Upward Christians is meeting Jesus through their experience of him—they see themselves on a loving pilgrimage toward becoming closer and closer to Jesus with every passing day.

Now, just a couple of footnotes, and we'll get back to the story. Many of the battles we'll witness in the twentieth-century saga of the CRC are waged between Inward and Outward believers, even though, as I've said, both of these types claim to be Kuyperian. Both of them watch the world closely, as Kuyper asserted Christians must do; but because Inward and Outward Christians distribute their loyalties in different ways, their views on some things are almost necessarily bound to clash. Inward Christians look at life in terms of the historical record of what they believe, throwing out what doesn't square with their creeds and confessions. Outward Christians look at life on its own and are quick to point out that the church has often enough shipwrecked itself by using the Bible to claim that the world has four corners or that the institution of slavery has God's righteous sanction.

Generally, Upward Christians are not really concerned with all that. Their most immediate concern is their personal relationship with Jesus Christ—and their mission is to bring that kind of relationship to others, to preach the gospel of grace—which is why, often as not, Inward Christians and Outward Christians share a common distrust of what they view as Upward Christians' excessive spirituality.

Finally, let me say this. I humbly submit that everyone here has a part of the truth. Is a personal relationship with Jesus Christ central to belief? Certainly. Are our creeds and confessions significant in assessing the world around us? Without a doubt. Do our beliefs change through time and the effects of our own learning? That too is undeniable. No one reading this book believes exactly the same things as his or her great-grandparents did, no matter if those great-grandparents were deeply set within the Christian Reformed Church or not.

Often as not, our own fallen humanity makes it difficult for us to appreciate the significant value in all three orientations. We can't do it. We are loyal to the theology set down in the creeds; we are fascinated by the culture in which we are set; or we seek passionately for a personal relationship with Jesus Christ.

Think of the most saintly human beings you know. My guess is that they are finer composites of the three mind-sets than most of us are or can be. Our sinful humanity, or so it seems to me, is limiting. We can't do or be everything. Why we choose what we do is itself a whole other mystery, but the fact seems to be that within the CRC—as well as throughout all Christendom—believers appear to choose one of these three basic orientations. When stress appears in the family, it works most perniciously at the seams of our relationships—and the seams are where these mind-sets meet.

From here on I'm going to use these designations: Inward Christians—those who put greatest value on what is already known, most specifically on the Bible, or special revelation; Outward Christians—those who place more regard on general revelation, the world in which God has placed us; and Upward Christians—those who seek above all the treasures of a deep spiritual life with the Lord.

A FORCEFUL LEADER: HERMAN HOEKSEMA

Perhaps no single individual was more visible in the CRC during the tumultuous post-war years than Herman Hoeksema. Hoeksema, who had first vigorously opposed Bultema, later led his segment of the church in opposition to Janssen, even though Janssen's form of heresy was almost

Rev. Herman Hoeksema (1896-1965), founding father of the Protestant Reformed churches.

completely different from Bultema's. After his powerful leadership of the opposition to Bultema, Hoeksema was given a column in *The Banner* specifically devoted to church doctrine, a column he used to indict "modernism in general" and Janssen in particular.

There can be no doubt that Hoeksema was a brilliant man. In personality, he stood in the tradition of de Cock in the Netherlands and Koene Van Den Bosch in America—spitfire apologists for their own brand of orthodoxy, men who despised accommodation. There can be no doubt that Hoeksema believed every column inch he ever gave to his distaste for modernism; he was an ideological giant of the first sort, not simply political. His case against Bultema had won him high regard, and his case against Janssen had run the professor out of seminary. By his intellect and by the sheer power of his personality, Hoeksema created disciples, even if he hadn't intended to do so. He was a leader of heroic stature, bright and engaging, decisive in his opinions. Some in the CRC still consider him the most talented and able theologian of his era.

These were the players in the wars of the twenties, players who brought their mindsets to the battle: Bultema, leader of those I'll now call Upward believers; Janssen, certainly more readily understandable as an Outward believer; and Herman Hoeksema, leader of the people I've chosen to call Inward believers. Regardless of the specific charges against Bultema and/or Janssen, what is obvious is that each of these men— as well as Herman Hoeksema, B. K. Kuiper, or Henry Beets—had specific visions of what the CRC should be in a world that was changing drastically after the war. It's important to assert clearly and authoritatively here that no one wanted to destroy the church; everyone wanted to do the right thing. It's a mark of our fallibility, our deeply sinful condition, that even these blessed intentions, all of them accomplished out of commitment and loyalty not only to the church but to our Savior's name, often served instead to bring conflict and even death where there could have and should have been life.

THE CHURCH IS SPLIT: THE PROTESTANT REFORMED BREAK

Those who break from the church, no matter when that break has occurred, like to assert that they never really left, but were abandoned by the church. As children of the Reformation, we would say as much for Calvin and Luther: they didn't leave the church; the Roman Catholic Church, by way of its apostasy, left them. As children of the *Afscheiding*, many of us would say the same thing—when a liberal church departs from its moorings, the mission of the righteous remnant is to return God's people to orthodoxy. During the late nineteenth-century *Doleantie*, those who left with Kuyper would likely have described their actions in a similar way.

I have no doubt that our brothers and sisters in the Protestant Reformed Church will differ substantially with the way in which the story of their departure is told here, just as those who write the history of today's breakaway congregations will write history in a different way than subsequent CRC historians might. We are all influenced by our history and our biases.

In 1898, Abraham Kuyper delivered an immensely popular series of lectures at Princeton Seminary. Those lectures were

later published in both Dutch and English, and they were read everywhere in the CRC during the early 1900s.

In those lectures, Kuyper claimed that there are two kinds of grace flowing from God's throne: particular (or "special") grace, by which we are saved in Christ Jesus, and general (or "common") grace, by which God "maintains the life of the world, relaxes the curse that rests upon it, arrests its process of corruption, and thus allows the untrammeled development of our life in which to glorify himself as Creator."

Ralph Janssen had said as much in his own defense. Specifically, when accused of using "higher criticism," he responded by saying that no one in the Reformed tradition had ever seriously asserted that every miraculous act of the redemption story had to be supernatural in means as well as end. In other words, to use the specific story we've referred to previously, while God acted (divine intervention) to bring about his miraculous ends in the Battle at Gilgal (the Israelites' marvelous victory), the means he used didn't necessarily have to be miraculous (the sun standing still). Then as now, some orthodox scholars would agree with Janssen: whether or not the earth literally stopped its rotation (the sun, of course, doesn't turn), the outcome—Israel's convincing victory, aided by God's own hand—is the miracle and moral of the Gilgal story.

What is important here is how such a view of Joshua at Gilgal can be seen in light of the changes modernist "higher criticism" was introducing within the Christian church. The slippery slope Hoeksema and many others pointed out in Janssen's argument (despite the fact that Janssen was correct in saying he wasn't the only Reformed scholar to insist on such a view) was structured on an "if, then" process. *If* Janssen could question the Bible's veracity about the sun standing still in the book of Joshua, *then* what was to stop him or some other scholar from saying that Jesus Christ didn't really need to be born of a virgin either—that such a tale was simply another scriptural myth? *If* the means to God's ends didn't have to be supernatural, *then* did one really have to believe that Jesus Christ literally rose from the dead? No.

The attack on Janssen was aided and abetted by the assertion of exactly those views by biblical scholars in liberal circles in the CRC, both in Europe and America. What Herman Hoeksema and others saw in Janssen's teaching was a first modernist step toward denial of the central tenets of

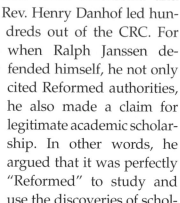

Rev. Henry Danhof
(1879-1952).

the gospel, and that's what caused the firestorm.

To understand both sides in this crucial battle is to begin to understand the nature of the split that was to come when Hoeksema and Rev. Henry Danhof led hundreds out of the CRC. For when Ralph Janssen defended himself, he not only cited Reformed authorities, he also made a claim for legitimate academic scholarship. In other words, he argued that it was perfectly "Reformed" to study and use the discoveries of scholars and theologians from outside the Reformed family and even from outside the body of believers. Not to do so, he might have said, is to back away from an understanding of our world, which, thanks to science and scholarship, continues to grow throughout human history. To pay no attention to the cutting edge of discovery and research is to emulate the Amish, who are often thought to assert that what believers must both know and practice was revealed in its entirety by the late nineteenth century. Janssen was manifesting Outward Christianity.

Was Janssen wrong? Not really. Not so many years ago we spent our summer vacations in the Black Hills of South Dakota. On one trip, we visited the sight of a dinosaur excavation. My children were fascinated. We watched as college students, volunteers, worked at brushing away dirt and stones from the outlines of massive bones that had laid in the ground for centuries. It was a marvelous display, a fascinating archaeological dig; but I felt guilty. Way, way back in my earliest childhood education—both at home and in a Christian school—I remember being taught that dinosaurs were nothing but a hoax, something dreamed up by atheist scientists to refute the Bible's own record of creation, something to cast doubt on the biblical record.

It's likely that some of the archaeologists who made claims way back then for the reality of dinosaurs were Christians—but when I was a kid, I was confident that they could be nothing but card-carrying atheists, bound and determined to wrestle my faith and the faith of every other believer throughout the world down to the ground of this broken world.

So there I stood in South Dakota watching my son's eyes light up as he noted the careful excavation going on, watching huge, club-like bones emerge from the rusty grit in which they had lain for centuries. Even though I'd long ago decided that what I was taught as a child simply wasn't true, seeing that archaeological work before my eyes still made me uncomfortable—a truth I'd accepted so zealously as a child was obviously dead wrong. Dinosaurs were not a hoax. I had been a victim of energetic and well-meant zeal in the defense of faith—zeal, not reason.

But we are at the point in the history of the CRC where the denomination split, where some hundreds left. In order to understand why they left, it is important to allow some legitimacy to both sides in this crucial argument. Our fiercest arguments are rarely a matter of "either/or"—both in the past and in the present, all sides of a conflict hold elements of the truth, but no one side holds the whole truth.

Janssen argued for an *outward*-looking Christian life that refused to turn away from what was happening in the world—in his case, the world of biblical scholarship and scientific research. He claimed that a relationship between the Christian and the unbelieving scholar was thoroughly "Reformed." But the understanding Janssen was after wasn't limited only to scholars. The real question in the debate was, How seriously do we take an unbelieving world? Can those who are not Christians be trusted to provide real beneficial service to the world—and to Christians themselves? What Janssen was arguing for was what seemed to many to be an unholy alliance between the Christian and the non-Christian, a covenant relationship with certain restrictions.

Danhof and Hoeksema claimed that such a union could never be blessed. They were confident that whenever believers cozy up to contemporary culture, they become unequally yoked. Even Kuyper had warned against believers becoming too comfortable with the world in an old orthodox theological argument often referred to as the antithesis—the idea that believers always see clearly before them two *different* worlds, the city of God and the city of humanity. There was, after all, the kingdom of darkness and the kingdom of light. Augustine argued from that premise; Calvin followed in Augustine's steps. Believers were children of light. According to Hoeksema and Danhof, orthodox Christians throughout the centuries have always maintained that Christians need to be highly critical of the kingdom of darkness in all of its manifestations. By getting too comfortable with the world of biblical scholarship, in their opinion, Janssen was toying with the fires of hell.

Yet Janssen was simply saying that Christians can't pretend that good things—advances in medicine, innovations in technology, beauty in art and literature—cannot be accomplished by those who deny God. And because we can't say that, we must not slap blinders on our eyes. We are "in the world," after all, although we may not be "of " it.

At its core, the issue forces the question, "How does God relate to the church and the world?" If God deals graciously with the whole world—sinners as well as saints, police forces as well as congregations—then there is a common ground where the church and the world can meet. If God brings judgment only upon unbelieving humankind, even in this life, then we'd better stay away completely.

I remember a time when I went to juvenile court to speak on behalf of a young man from our congregation who had been convicted of breaking and entering. The kid was guilty; that was not in question. I was, at the time, a first-term elder, and I never questioned whether going there and arguing for leniency was the right thing to do—after all, isn't loving the sinner a significant task of the Christian? Outside that courtroom, I met a CRC lawyer, a friend of mine who had been practicing law for decades. He saw me and smiled. "The thing about the church," he said, "is that they always seem to believe that the courts don't work in their favor—as if my job as a lawyer is something I do totally apart from my profession as a Christian. Sometimes you've got to trust that what the courts are doing is operating in the interest of all involved—that's our job."

To me, it was a lesson in the wars we sometimes wage with the culture at large. In standing up for the kid, I had simply assumed that the court would, unless it

The Age of the Big Meeting

∞

During the interval between World War I and World War II, one of the characteristics of the Christian Reformed family was the popularity of mass meetings. Thousands of men gathered for the annual meeting of the Federation of the Reformed Men's Societies. Mission fests attracted young and old to forest groves and city parks. Young Calvinist conventions were popular, and society life in the church was flourishing.

A typical example of this phenomenon was the annual Christian School Rally Day, held on the 4th of July at Kardux Beach near Holland, Michigan. Prominent speakers from within and outside the denomination were featured, including people like J. Gresham Machen, Peter Eldersveld, Henry Schultze, and, in a real coup, the Rev. Dr. Walter A. Maier, radio preacher of the immensely popular Lutheran Hour. I'll never forget his long-awaited appearance at the event. Even children and young people turned from their sports and games to hear this internationally known supporter of Christian education.

There was one hitch, however, that put a slight pall on the day. Before he could speak, a certain protocol was deemed essential. Local Christian Reformed clergy were permitted to welcome the audience and to announce the singing of patriotic songs and appropriate psalms and hymns. However, they were not permitted to share the pulpit with the eminent Lutheran divine. All that the chairman (the Rev. Dr. Ralph Danhof, pastor of the Fourteenth St. CRC of Holland) was permitted to do was introduce the youthful pastor of the local minuscule Missouri Synod Lutheran Church, who led in prayer and introduced Dr. Maier.

I can still see the frustrated scowl on Danhof's face as he descended the steps to join the *hoi poloi*. Strangely enough, this Lutheran intolerance actually comforted some of us in the audience, helping us realize that we were not alone in our self-chosen ecumenical desert. The speech was a huge success!

—WDB

Women's Missionary Union gathered in Chicago, 1927. Meetings of this sort flourished until the 1970s, when women began to work outside their homes.

heard from us, act in a less than just way toward him. Unless checked by the church—the salt of the earth—the courts would turn this kid into even more of a problem than he was already becoming, by simply writing him off and sending him to a penitentiary bursting with hardened criminals. I had not stopped to think that maybe the court might be operating in the best interests of the kid. I had simply assumed that unless good Christian folks were there to plead for mercy for the kid, the godless authorities would throw the book at him and call for the next case. What my friend the lawyer taught me is that the court isn't always godless.

Once more, it's the old question—how do believers in Christ Jesus relate to the world? If we assume that no good can come out of the court system or public education or non-Christian social workers, then we assume only the righteous (us) can do any good. But if only Christians can write good literature, then why is so much bad literature written by Christians?

On the other hand, if we simply assume that we're all alike—that non-Christians see the world as we do, that non-Christian judges have the same standards of justice we do, that atheists are fully capable of teaching our children ethics and moral principles—then we're in a sorry mess. It is true—forever true—that something radically different separates the believing and unbelieving world. In my own profession, I am convinced that the teaching of literature by an individual committed to eternal truths creates both a methodology and a mission in the classroom that are not at all the same as the theory and practice of someone who sees the world as entirely

separate from biblical meaning and cause. Once again, at a time when taking a side may appear much easier, what's important is to understand both sides. Both sides can legitimately claim some truth here.

The Janssen case is important in itself, but also instructive in the way it sets the stage for the biggest battle of the post-war era. Hoeksema, then pastor of Eastern Avenue CRC in Grand Rapids, and Danhof, of First Kalamazoo, attacked the idea of common grace time and time again, and did so with fists raised. Both in a *Banner* column ("Our Faith") and in two books, these two bright preachers blasted away at a church gone "soft" on worldliness, that softness clearly attributable to an unholy dalliance with "common grace." We'd simply cozied up to the world far too intimately, they claimed, and thereby lost our peculiar Christian essence.

The whole denomination was swept into the fray. My mother-in-law remembers Sunday afternoon on the Iowa prairie, listening to her father (who became CRC when he married his wife) and his father (who'd become PR with the split) waging war over *algemeene genade* (common grace), a phrase she'll never forget from a long series of arguments, as much a part of the whole Sabbath ritual at her home as the Saturday night bath. These men were not learned professors; they were largely uneducated. But they were participants in the battle nonetheless, and they knew where the lines were drawn.

My mother-in-law claims that in her home those arguments were heated but never divisive. Her father and grandfather would lock horns, then finally simply agree to disagree. Perhaps her family was unique. All over the denomination, similar arguments rarely ended in mutual respect. All over the denomination, battles turned bloody in an uncivil civil war that split the denomination, and—as all schisms do— put families gravely at odds with each other. Many who have deep family roots in the CRC can point to family arguments that took years, sometimes generations, to heal—if they ever have. Our own sinfulness is vividly realized in the legacy of theological disagreements that almost always end in animosity and bitterness, rarely in mutual respect.

The Outward believers were no less pointed in their criticism of Hoeksema and Danhof than the Inward believers, led by Danhof and Hoeksema, were in their assessment of what they considered the liberal forces taking the church rapidly down some precipice. In the pages of *Religion and Culture,* an old "Antithetical" periodical, John Kuizinga, one of its leading voices, issued what James Bratt calls a "declaration of war" against Hoeksema and Danhof after Janssen's dismissal from the seminary: "We ought to tear up by the roots the various forms of Separatism, Dualism, Pietism, Anabaptism—the whole brood whose tendency is to tear Redemption loose from Creation [and] shrink down theology to mere Christology."

Throughout the era, the arsenal was largely emptied of weapons and ammo, all of it spent on fellow believers.

Eleven pieces of correspondence dealing with the issue of common grace appeared on the synodical agenda in 1924. Several asked for a study; two asked for an immediate judgment *against* Hoeksema and Danhof. Outward Christians were claiming that to deny common grace was to deny, in effect, the entire Reformed confessional heritage.

Ultimately, Synod 1924 boiled down the complex issue to just three questions:

- Does God show grace not only to the elect but also to the non-elect?
- Does God, by way of the work of the Holy Spirit, restrain sin in society in general?
- Can the "unregenerate" still perform some kind of "civic righteousness"?

To all three questions, synod said yes. Danhof, a delegate to that synod, said no.

The deliberations of Synod 1924 did nothing at all to cool the heat. If anything, dissent and quarrelsomeness grew. Danhof and Hoeksema fought the decision with their sermons and their pens, showing a healthy contempt for synod and basing their continued divisiveness on the argument that orthodoxy itself was at stake here. Like Luther, they could not do otherwise.

Heeding the synodical rulings, their separate classes began disciplinary proceedings against them, at which point the two led their congregations out of the Christian Reformed Church. Eastern Avenue CRC split over the issue; a bitter dispute over the church property followed. Hoeksema and Danhof attracted a number of congregations—especially in Michigan and Iowa—to their newly formed Protestant Reformed denomination. Today, the Protestant Reformed denomination has two classes, twenty-seven churches, and somewhere close to 6,500 families.

Synod's rulings never completely resolved the issue of the nature of God's grace. Perhaps the best questions are the best questions *because* no human being can offer completely satisfactory answers. A half-century later, the so-called "Dekker controversy," in which another faculty member at Calvin Seminary was accused of being too generous in his attitude towards the world, raised related questions. Harold Dekker taught that God loves all people, including unbelievers, and we can tell them so. It is not difficult to plot out more recent accusations in a similar outline— those against Howard Van Till, who teaches that we must interpret our understanding of creation in the light of scientific discoveries with respect to such things as the age of the earth; and those against Hessel Bouma, who raised questions about synod's ethical pronouncements on abortion.

And if it's true that the issue at the heart of the controversy about women in ecclesiastical office is our dalliance with feminism, then, once again, dissension on that issue emerges, at least in part, from the very same tangle: how important to our confession are significant changes occurring in the culture around us? In short, how should we regard "the world"? The answer isn't easy, perhaps because the issues are not insubstantial.

While working at Eastern Avenue CRC some years ago, Rev. Peter Niewiek scrounged through old minutes and

THE
FOURTH DAY
HOWARD J. VAN TILL

What
the Bible
and the Heavens
are telling us
about
the Creation

Howard Van Till, pictured with the Calvin College telescope.

(Above) His controversial book (1986) that explained his theories about science and creation.

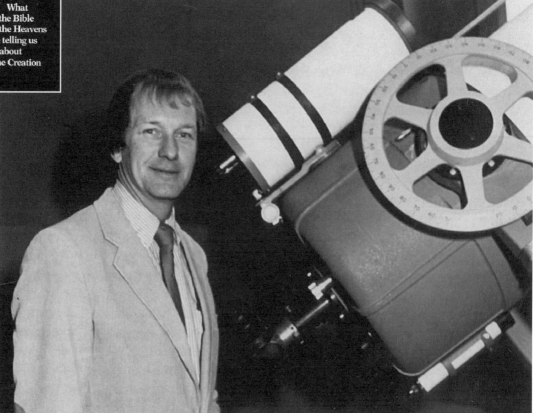

records left from the battles of the twenties. Later, he summarized the difficulties in historical perspective. Before the turn of the century, Niewiek writes, Eastern Avenue "had this batch of rough immigrants of separatist mentality who were afraid that the 'transplanted flower of the Reformed faith was not going to flourish in American soil' unless kept in a greenhouse."

Then he goes on to explain the direction of the church under a new minister:

> Then [Rev. J.] Groen, an avowed Kuyperian, accepted a call in 1900. He hired [Johanna Veenstra] to do evangelism and pastoral care among young working girls in Grand Rapids factories. He hired an Italian "premillennialist" evangelist to minister to the Italian-speaking sector [of the community]. He championed women's suffrage. He became involved in labor organizations. He tried to maintain the "in" as well as the "not of" the world.

That was the church Rev. Herman Hoeksema found when he came to Eastern Avenue in 1920. It is not particularly surprising, then, that Hoeksema would almost immediately charge his predecessor with bringing "the world into the church." It may not be entirely coincidence that the very same year, 1920, Johanna Veenstra made a bold decision to leave for Africa.

In 1985, in an issue of *The Banner* given to a look at the Protestant Reformed church, Rev. Homer Hoeksema, son of Herman, drew the denomination's portrait in a fashion that illustrates clearly the identity by which they understood themselves:

"And who is the Protestant Reformed Church?" he wrote. ". . . [A] center and a refuge for all who want to be genuinely, consistently, confessionally Reformed."

Capital *R*.

Not long ago, I happened to meet a young CRC minister in western Michigan. I asked him about the state of the denomination in the area where he was ministering. He was upbeat and generously optimistic. When I asked him what people thought of when they used the word *Reformed*, he grimaced and told me that among the laity the word is generally associated with quarrelsomeness, intractability, and in-fighting. Most people would rather not use that word at all, he said, sitting right there in a fast-food restaurant in Van Raalte's hometown.

Personally, I find that sentiment sad. However, there are altogether too many moments in our history when the word *Reformed* is clearly at the base of struggles that have brought more heat than light into our pilgrimage as God's people. And all too often, that heat has turned Uncle Henry away from Uncle Jack; it has set barriers between Mom and Aunt Jen. Friends split. That kind of heat has gutted congregations across the continent—sadly enough, ironically enough, in the name of truth and in the name of being Reformed.

CHAPTER 14

1928: Putting Some Distance Between Church and World

L ast night my son, a college student, watched *Hardcore*, Paul Schrader's 1979 film about a tough Dutch Reformed father who is humbled and broken in the pursuit of his runaway daughter. My son had been to Best Buy; amazingly, he'd found the video in a sale bin. No film Hollywood ever made features Christian Reformed life as specifically as *Hardcore*. Schrader, long considered one of Hollywood's most thoughtful filmmakers, grew up in Michigan in a Christian Reformed home, graduated from Calvin, then went west to Los Angeles. His film credits are impressive.

My son is very interested in film. Early this summer, I told him that if he wanted to collect all the Schrader films, I'd pay for them. It's a risk, I know. But Peter De Vries and Frederick Manfred, two nationally known former CRC novelists, played consequential roles in my life when I was my son's age, helping me to understand myself, the people I had come from, and the faith they carried, not always successfully, into their lives.

In some ways, the portraits drawn by Manfred, De Vries, and Schrader are similar; Schrader's medium is film, but his analysis of his own religious past in *Hardcore* isn't much different from De Vries's look at the CRC a generation earlier in the novel *Blood of the Lamb*—or Manfred's in *Green Earth*.

Hardcore is terribly offensive, full of nudity and vulgar language, and I'm not recommending it here, even though I did to my son. The story is a chase, a quest—a father's search for a child who has gone badly astray. George C. Scott plays Jake Van Dorn, a successful Grand Rapids furniture maker and widower who leaves the comforts of his home to pursue his daughter, Kristen, who'd run away from the Young Calvinist Convention in Bellflower, California. He discovers that she's fallen into the world of hardcore sex—pornographic films of the worst sort.

The law is of no help to him—kids run away all the time, after all—so, in an effort to find her, this persistent, iron-tough father goes undercover, so to speak. He begins to dress and act in the sleazy manner of the sex-peddlers to get himself into the world his daughter has reportedly become part of. His sole purpose is to find his runaway daughter.

Hardcore is the only Hollywood movie to feature an exposition of the Canons of Dort. In a memorable scene in an airport, Scott runs through the five points of Calvinism (T-U-L-I-P: total depravity, unconditional election, limited atonement, irre-

TICKET OFFICE

Adults 40¢

Comedian Buster Keaton (1895-1966) waits outside a ticket booth in a scene from the film *Sherlock Junior*.

sistible grace, and perseverance of the saints) for a street hustler, who says, once he's finished with the explanation, "I thought I was crazy."

Jake finally finds his daughter at a level of hellish horror even Dante didn't imagine. But right then, surrounded as she is by horrendous ugliness, she tells him to his face—and in horrible language—that she wants no part of him. His moment of triumph turns into a meeting that mutilates his soul, and the moral equation of the film suggests itself clearly. She tells him she's not going back to Grand Rapids. She intimates that, as a child, what she'd experienced from him—his plastic Christianity,

Film director (*Taxi Driver, Hardcore, The Last Temptation of Christ*, etc.) Paul Schrader.

his superficial pietism, his unbearable self-righteousness—was to her simply a different kind of "hardcore" life, another form of lovelessness. In running away, she was merely trading one kind of obscene life for another. In L.A., she says, at least some people love her.

Jake Van Dorn breaks down. His search for Kristen has ended in a way he could not have anticipated. What he had never before confronted—in addition to the world of pornography— was his own sin, his own spiritual pride. And that's what he discovers in her vile rejection of his offer of deliverance. That discovery breaks the man in pieces. His tears are wrung from a purging of his soul, a recognition that he's lived his life dead wrong because he's never really taken the time to love his daughter.

And yet, the movie ends in triumph, at least from an orthodox Christian point of view—and, maybe ironically, from a Calvinistic point of view. Not only does Kristen reverse her ground and go back with him, but in a very "Christian" way, his recognition of his own sin is itself a moment of triumph, a moment such as James Joyce once described this way: "First you fail, then you fall, then you feel." Van Dorn has been to the depths of hell—not in sleazy porn studios, but in self-recognition. Now he knows his sin. He has nowhere to go but up. His relationship with his daughter will never be the same—it will be better. This successful businessman, this pillar of what Schrader calls "the Dutch Reformation Church," has been leveled, not by the

Author Frederick Manfred (Feike Feikema 1912-1994) signing autographs at Calvin College homecoming.

dreary dungeons of hardcore sex, but by his daughter's personal rejection of her father's own hardcore values.

Last night, my son watched that film alone. We were upstairs with friends. I didn't watch it with him because I knew that would have made him uncomfortable—and it would have made me uncomfortable too. There are scenes in that film I wish no filmmakers would make. The film itself is hardcore, the language sinful, atrocious. My parents would be mortified, I think, to know that I suggested their grandson watch the film. My grandparents, like my parents, like Jake Van Dorn himself, could not have imagined what my son would see on a TV screen in our own basement. And I let him do it. I even encouraged it.

But this is not a confession of sin. As much as it scared me to think of him watching all that ugliness—not only the world of pornography, but also Schrader's violent slap at his own people, my son's own people—I believe it was the right thing to do. My son is interested in film, interested in story, and if he is ever going to understand it and get good at it, he has to know it, inside and out.

If you understand some of the major themes that are forming in this story of the CRC, you will, at this moment, identify me clearly as an Outward Christian of the first order. I am not as readily identifiable as Inward or Upward. I would like my son to study film, to learn it, to master it—and to use his profession of faith, his belief in the God of creation, the God of life itself, to understand film, to critique it, and even, if that's where his interests go, to do it—in the language of the Antithetical Kuyperians, *to do film Christianly.* I believe that

Peter De Vries (1910-1983), author of *Blood of the Lamb* and many other novels.

to study film for the kingdom, he needs to study film, period. There—1928 synodical prohibitions or not—my cards are on the table.

But I'm not so arrogant that I don't worry about being wrong. A few years ago my daughter went to a movie with some friends. The next day, when we asked her what she'd seen, she pulled up her nose and described some trashy horror flick she knew she wouldn't like the moment she'd bought the ticket. Then why did you go? we asked. Because the other kids wanted to. Their parents didn't want them to, she said.

At that moment I wondered about my child-rearing theories. The parents of the kids she'd been with laid out for their children a black-and-white code of right and wrong—preached it so vividly, in fact, that their kids knew very well they were violating something big in watching the movie. My daughter's more liberal parents had drawn no such lines. She went, even though she knew from the get-go that she wouldn't like the movie.

Delegates to a meeting of the leadership of the American Federation of Reformed Young Men's Societies in Passaic, New Jersey. A quick survey of the representatives indicates that many pictured had been drinking deeply from the fountain of youth without significant success.

The advantage we had over other parents the day after our kids watched the film was that our daughter talked openly about it. We took some comfort in our daughter's rejection of the film on its own merits, and her being able to talk with us about it. But I wondered then—as I wonder today—whether my open and forthright attitudes toward the world we live in—my Outward Christianity—was the best possible policy for bringing up kids. I'm not sure. I'm proceeding by faith, as we all are. And if you think I'm sure of myself, you're wrong.

The dilemma I'm outlining is perfectly human. One does not have to be born and reared in the Christian Reformed Church to wonder whether simply forbidding certain behavior is the best way to approach child-rearing. One does not even have to be Christian to know that dilemma. Atheists might well forbid their children watching TV preachers or attending Billy Graham crusades. Few feminists buy their daughters Barbie dolls. How do we keep our kids on the straight-and-narrow—or is it possible at all? Maybe the better question is how do we help them find the straight-and-narrow for themselves?

Synod 1928 adopted the famous Christian Reformed position on "worldly amusements," condemning gambling, movies, and dancing, and it did so ten years after Bultema left with his Berean premillennialists, six years after Janssen was fired for his modernism, and just four years after Hoeksema and Danhof led hundreds out of the CRC for a new home, the Protestant Reformed Church. Ironically, as David Snapper says in an unpublished dissertation, while Herman Hoeksema lost the battle (and his pulpit in the CRC), for the most part he won the war. At the end of the decade we still call the Roaring Twenties, synod became certain that worldliness was a conflagration, burning up denominational life like a prairie fire, destroying righteousness in its path, just as Hoeksema had warned it would. The way to deal with the flames, they believed, was to set up fire breaks—prohibitions, guidelines, specific rules and regulations designed to keep people safe and secure behind holy walls.

In 1928, we identified ourselves by what we didn't do—or shouldn't.

In wrestling with Bultema's dispensationalism, Janssen's "higher criticism," and Hoeksema and Danhof's rejection of common grace, the CRC was slowly and definitely defining itself anew in a country where, after World War I, it could no longer hold back the world, despite the ethnic walls it had carried over from the Netherlands. While each of these struggles were internal, each had external dimensions; while defining ourselves from within, we were also identifying ourselves from without. And we did it in 1928 by constructing a list of activities we wouldn't do.

According to Outward Christians, "the world" is not the stronghold of the enemy, but rather potentially occupied Christian territory. (Although militaristic metaphors may be inappropriate here, they are, for better or worse, typically Calvinist.) Our role as Christians is not to run away from the world but to go in, guns blazing, and take it back for Jesus Christ. That view may well be fanciful and idealistic, but it is the view of many a Kuyperian, many an Outward believer.

But Herman Hoeksema, his Protestant Reformed Church, and a still-significant segment of the Christian Reformed Church (a segment we might label more inward-looking) lean toward a different Kuyper, a Kuyper of the antithesis. They too are interested in what is going on in society and life around them, but they take an obviously different attitude toward that culture. That inward-looking Kuyperianism can be seen, for instance, in a recent series of articles in the Protestant Reformed *Standard Bearer,* a series written by Professor Herman Hanko.

Hanko commends Kuyper as "a Reformed theologian, unsparing in his attacks on the 'liberals' whose hatred and fury he incurred, and unwearying in his defense of the Reformed faith." Furthermore, Hanko admires Kuyper's regard for his followers and his theological tradition.

Kuyper, Hanko says, "was a theologian of the people. He taught and wrote in a way which could be understood by the least educated of the church; he could make the most profound truths unmistakably clear; he rallied the scattered sheep of the church

Calvin College students Marie Schaap, Augusta Schuurmann, Thersa Storm and Luenna Prins prepare to take a dip.

of Christ around the banner of the Reformed faith."

So far, so good. Yet, Hanko says, Kuyper's work as a theologian was "somewhat limited." He introduced ideas that were "often outside the mainstream of the Reformed faith of the past and innovative in the sense that they could be challenged as unbiblical, unconfessional, and, therefore, wrong." Chief among his errors is, of course, the heresy of common grace.

Hanko admires Kuyper, another Kuyper, a Kuyper with whom he is much, much more comfortable: "Kuyper was a man of the antithesis. He believed strongly that the antithesis required absolute separation of the church from the world in all areas of endeavor, to the point that he himself labored mightily for a Christian labor union, a Christian political party, a Christian system of education free from any government control."

The key phrase here is "absolute separation." Hanko, from an Inward believer's mind-set, sees Kuyper's interests in Christian education, for example, as an expression of the man's desire that Christian students be in Christian schools for "absolute separation" from the world. When I urge my son to watch *Hardcore,* I'm not for a moment suggesting any kind of "absolute separation." I am hoping and praying that he learns to view the world as a Christian should view it, but I am not trying to isolate him; just as by enrolling him in a Christian school, I never for a moment wanted him to feel anything close to "absolute separation" from the world. I wanted him to learn that the world belongs to God.

Both sides—the Outward-looking Antitheticals and the Inward-looking Confessionalists—claim their own version of Kuyper. They do so because both have grasped a worldview; both are concerned with the world around them. Inward believers know the evils of the world so well that they want "absolute separation." Outward believers, convicted of a "common grace" bestowed on all bearers of God's own image, don't want to separate but to transform. I would love my son to bring a Christian witness to the world of film.

It may well have been easier to hold the kind of Outward view I have before 1918, a time when the CRC had little contact with the American world. CRC folks were less likely to fear the world because an invasion

would have been almost impossible, so fortresslike were the walls of language, custom, and tradition. Our schools kept our children safe, after all. Had they been in public schools, the outside world would have been much more of a presence, in fact, inescapable. The kind of outward-looking theorizing I like to do could be practiced safely because there was, for the most part, little real contact with American culture.

But the demise of the immigrant language made it impossible to keep the outside world outside. Suddenly, "our people"—a phrase that hasn't been used in years—were vulnerable to the winsome attractions of a world we'd only lived beside for several generations, a world that, before World War I, we'd never really known at all. Suddenly, the threat of "worldliness," a sometimes-synonym for "American," was not only substantial, it was everywhere.

That perception prompted Synod 1928, despite Herman Hoeksema's absence, to try to construct walls once again, walls that would keep CRC folks in a condition of "absolute separation" and, at the same time, define who they were.

With great daring and strong conviction, Synod 1928 decided to bring a halt to "worldliness" by creating guidelines by which ordinary believers could more clearly identify both sin and righteousness. Although it would be wrong to call the guidelines on worldly amusements definitive, that was, in essence, what they became. For nearly half a century thereafter, Christian Reformed people identified themselves as both *Christian* and *Reformed* by Synod 1928's addendum to the decalogue, a short list of no-nos that would be destroyed only by the rebellious, turbulent 1960s.

For more than a generation, the CRC defined itself by what its people couldn't do. From the thirties through the sixties, the inward-drawn Confessionalists, joined by upward-looking pietists, ruled the denominational roost with a brand of moralism designed not only to keep people righteous but to prescribe the behavior of the tribe. It was a gallant effort and well-meant, created to help fearful members of congregations all over the country clearly identify the earmarks of Christianity at a time—the Roaring Twenties—when the sober Christian life was definitely at peril. Avoid dancing, cards, and movies, the guidelines suggested, and you're not only avoiding real evil, you're establishing residency in a fortress where "absolute separatism" is the straight and narrow way.

The Antitheticals and the Confessionalists—both of them raising the banner of Abraham Kuyper—had agreed to oppose Bultema's Upward extravagances. But they disagreed about Janssen and then fought brutally over common grace, resulting in schism. Nonetheless, despite the departure of Hoeksema's followers, synod's 1928 declaration on "worldly amusements" was a victory for those who continued to define what it meant to be *Reformed* and *Christian* as a matter of behavior that would separate them from the world. No movies, no gambling, and no dancing. Abstinence became, even if synod itself didn't intend it, the litmus test of orthodoxy.

Today, it's difficult to imagine how fervently the denomination at large carried out synod's warning. One quick story.

Once upon a time there was a movie theater in the town I live in, Sioux Center, Iowa. At the conclusion of World War II, some residents put up a screen in a building on Main Street and showed movies, an enterprise that created great consternation among CRC community members, deeply influenced by the 1928 synodical prohibitions. Eventually, via public opinion, the theater ceased its operations. The Reverend B. J. Haan, a young, passionate orator, was instrumental in its demise and was even pictured in *Life* magazine in his Prince Albert preaching garb, holding forth, an image that caricatured him for years—but that's another story.

The moral war over the legitimacy of movies in this town created a dilemma in the minds and hearts of many of its residents, including its kids. Roger Visser, then a little boy and today a successful agribusinessman, remembers hearing his friends talk about all the great things they were seeing at the theater. He remembers thinking that seeing a movie really couldn't be all that evil. He'd heard Rev. Haan preach, had him as a catechism teacher in fact, and respected him a great deal; but the fascination he felt for what his non-CRC friends were talking about was simply too persuasive. He says he'll never forget grabbing a dime out of his savings bank, warily walking downtown one Saturday afternoon, and, after looking in both directions like a timid jaywalker, sneaking into that Main Street theater, confident he hadn't been seen.

He took a back seat, he says, a spot where no one would notice him, and there he sat in the dimly lit world he'd been warned so frightfully about. Simply being there made him scared. Confident he hadn't been seen and sure his parents knew nothing of his whereabouts, he tried to settle back into his seat—but he couldn't. It was dark and forbidding in that theater, a place many people claimed was a den of iniquity. His palms itched, his legs wiggled, and he couldn't stop shaking. He had no idea what was going to happen. Guilty fear bristled in him; every minute noise blasted away in his ears.

Then, suddenly, up in front of him, without warning, the entire wall lit up in a burst

B. J. Haan (1917 - 1994)

Bernard J. Haan first achieved fame in the denomination and beyond in April 1948, when a large picture in *Life* magazine portrayed him in tails and other appropriate ministerial garb, shaking a menacing finger at his mesmerized audience. The occasion of his "righteous indignation" was a proposed theater soon to be functioning in Sioux Center, Iowa, where Haan was currently serving as pastor of the First Christian Reformed Church. Haan's appearance on the pages of *Life* was received with mixed emotions among the faithful.

Far more important was B. J. Haan's dream—a dream that was fulfilled beyond his expectations. Haan envisioned a Calvinistic college in the middle of the prairies of Iowa. Working against nearly insuperable odds, he steadfastly challenged the Iowa community to join with him in the dream. The result was Dordt College, an institution that has gained the respect of academics everywhere and has sent hundreds of graduates into society with a world-and-life view based on the Scriptures and the insights of Abraham Kuyper and other Reformed theologians. Haan served as president of the fledgling institution from 1963 until his retirement in 1982.

His career, which began with tilting at theatrical windmills, ended as the father and primary proponent of higher Christian education in Northwest Iowa and far beyond.   —WDB

B. J. Haan in a photo that appeared in *Life* magazine, April 19, 1948, with the following caption: "Reverend B. J. Haan, a hellfire-and-brimstone preacher, does not claim to have seen any movies but says he knows all about them. He approves light drinking, smokes, plays golf himself."

of light and movement that shook him to the bone, frightened him so completely that without even considering what he was doing, he charged out of that theater, scared to death of what he'd almost fallen into. He never saw a minute of the show. Flushed out of his back-row seat like some ring-necked pheasant from a strip of unpicked corn, he flew home and never again wished he could see a movie—well, not until high school.

Several years ago, I was surprised to see Harold Aardema, editor of the *Doon Press,* show up at Dordt College for a movie. He told me that the reason he came was simply to go to a movie at the college B. J. Haan was so instrumental in founding, a man whose opposition to a theater in this quiet little village on the western edge of Iowa made national news. Just the irony, Harold said.

A decade or more ago already, *The Banner* reviewed new movies on a regular basis because CRC people were hoisting dollars up to the ticket counter. Today, Dordt College—like all the other denominationally related colleges—offers movies for the entertainment of its students. Christian Reformed professors (myself among them) teach film and film technique.

My, oh my, how we've changed!

When Synod 1966 adopted a report titled "The Church and the Film Arts," it ended the prohibitions that CRC members had felt for almost forty years. Many might still ask—have we done the right thing?

After all, last night, thirty years after the demise of the synodical guideline, my son watched *Hardcore* in the privacy of our own home. I'm confident that I will not see more movies in what time the Lord gives

me on this earth than my children have already seen in their short lives. That's how far we've come. Synod 1928 had no idea what kind of world my kids would be exposed to when they watch movies today—the gratuitous sex, the constant

The Church and the Film Arts

In the early history of the CRC three worldly amusements were frequently singled out as dangerous and off-limits to Christians: theater attendance, card playing, and dancing. Synod 1966 took a close look at one of those amusements, theater attendance. Instead of making judgments about "good" movies and "bad" movies, synod made rather a forthright commitment to the principle of Christian liberty. That principle had long been espoused in the CRC in theory; after 1966 it was a reality.

An interesting sidelight of synod's action was the near unanimity of its vote in adopting the new guidelines. There was virtually no opposition to the proposed action. However, the next day a ministerial delegate to synod preached vociferously about how the church was slipping and pointed to the movie decision of Saturday morning as evidence for his contention. Ironically, he had not said anything against it while at synod.

In retrospect, it seems there was a downside to this quantum shift from perpetually warning against worldly amusements to sanctioning involvement in the same. It resulted in dulling the church's voice of warning against the secular involvement of church members in modern cultural activities, especially the evil aspects of television. —TEH

vulgarity and profanity, the lusty violence. If synod could have seen what cinema would be like in the last several decades of the twentieth century, their prohibitions would have been more than guidelines. *Hardcore*, after all, is not *Mr. Smith Goes to Washington.*

Are those immense changes good or bad? Undoubtedly the answer to that question says much about the manner by which the answerer sees the world. But once again, the best answer is likely yes—and no. Or maybe no—and yes.

THE KUIPERS

The differences in the mind-sets of the CRC are clearly identifiable in those who played leading roles in its development during this time. For instance, the Kuipers. One cannot know Christian Reformed history without meeting them, their name spelled with an "i" (unlike Abraham Kuyper). Three prominent Kuipers played important roles in the story of the CRC in the first half of the twentieth century, and they are remembered, in what seems good Christian Reformed fashion, by their initials.

We need to begin with Rev. Klaas Kuiper, an immigrant CRC preacher who had two sons who also became ministers—B. K. and R. B. The first son, B. K., was something of a renegade; more on him later. R. B. was less

rambunctious and infinitely more traditional. He became a popular preacher and served stints as professor and then president of Calvin College and, years later, of the Seminary. He also taught at Westminster Seminary in Philadelphia, an institution to which the CRC has maintained, until recently, very strong links. Westminster became the intellectual headquarters of the Orthodox Presbyterian Church in the mid-1930s, and the OPC has always been—again, until recently—a friend of the CRC in North America. R. B. was thoughtful, engaging, and patently CRC.

The third Kuiper is H. J., who, despite his name, came from a different Kuiper clan altogether. H. J. was named editor in chief of *The Banner* in 1928 and became the most dominant single personality in CRC history for nearly three decades, holding that position until Eisenhower was in his second term. James Bratt calls Henry J. Kuiper the

Rev. Klaas Kuiper family. (seated, from left to right) Mrs. (DeBryn) Kuiper, Dena, Rev. Klaas Kuiper. (standing, from left to right) Herman, John, Henry, Anton, Rienke B., Berend K.

"preeminent Christian Reformed spokes-man" for the nearly three decades he edited the denomination's magazine. "Kuiper," Bratt says, "made *The Banner* stronger than it ever had been or would ever be—the authority on all matters of truth and morals, a voice whose every word was to be eagerly awaited, treasured, and—most of all—heeded." Ordained at twenty-one, the youngest preacher ever in the CRC, Kuiper's conservative voice both created and reflected the mind-set of the CRC during his long stay at

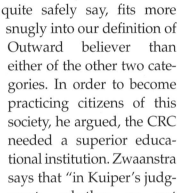

B. K. Kuiper
(1877-1961).

The Banner. Kuiper was Antithetical (or an Outward believer) in his willingness to assess society's problems; but he remained much more Confessional (or Inward) in the way he faced those difficulties. (Already we can see how difficult it is to categorize people.) For better or worse, H. J. Kuiper saw gigantic threats to the solidity and life of the CRC from aggressive forces outside the church and the stealthy movements of change within. Change was as difficult for H. J. as it was for the denomination he served.

Berend K. Kuiper was, if anything, immensely colorful. He was brilliant, erratic, given to curious views on a variety of issues, and constantly in denomina-tional hot water. In 1903 he published what Henry Zwaanstra calls "one of the most significant documents ever to have appeared in the history of the Christian Reformed Church," something he titled "The Proposed Calvinistic College in Grand Rapids." By way of that piece, B. K. sounded the first clear call for a full-fledged CRC college. B. K. argued that Reformed Christians had a God-given obligation to place themselves in the main-stream of American life, to become full-blooded, practicing citizens of this society. B. K., we can quite safely say, fits more snugly into our definition of Outward believer than either of the other two cate-gories. In order to become practicing citizens of this society, he argued, the CRC needed a superior educa-tional institution. Zwaanstra says that "in Kuiper's judg-ment, whether or not Reformed Christians would become known and influential in America would depend on what Calvin College would become." In some ways, were it not for B. K., humanly speaking there would be no Calvin College at all.

Although B. K.'s dream of Calvin College did begin to take shape, the next two decades public support for B. K.'s view of Christian higher education became thinner and thinner within the ranks of the CRC. After the trauma of World War I, when English became the dominant tongue and fear of worldly amusements took hold of the denomination, B. K.'s per-spective seemed not only worldly, but something akin to heresy. It wasn't only B. K.'s view of Christianity and culture that created his checkered career in the CRC, however, it was also B. K. himself.

When Rev. John Groen of Eastern Avenue CRC was threatened with suspen-sion for having led a women's suffrage march down the streets of Grand Rapids, no Christian Reformed leader would defend him. Except one. B. K. came to his defense, wrote editorials (he was editor of *De Wachter* at the time) supporting him, and went to classis on Groen's behalf.

In 1926, B. K. was named to a chair in historical theology at Calvin Seminary. His appointment was contested by H. J., the man who would become, in two more years, the long-standing editor of *The Banner,* and who was at that time president of the seminary board. H. J. accused B. K. of complicity in the sins of the expelled Ralph Janssen. In typical B. K. style, he had come to the defense of Janssen when he felt his colleague was being unfairly accused. But H. J.'s charge against B. K. was a form of guilt by association; the attack against Janssen had been led and engineered by H. J. himself. What's more, B. K. had published a tract called "The Janssen Case and Something Besides" in which he had taken a few broad swipes at the full range of Janssen's persecutors, including H. J. There was no love lost between the two men. But to appease H. J. and get his appointment in 1926, B. K. had agreed to write an apology—which he did, twice. The first draft didn't satisfy H. J. The second did, and B. K. got his post at the seminary.

Two years later B. K. came up for reappointment. Before synod convened, the Board of Trustees received a letter from an elder (reputedly a member of H. J.'s congregation) who complained that he'd seen Professor Kuiper enter a theater in downtown Grand Rapids. At first, B. K. denied the scandalous charge, offering the strange explanation that he had entered the cinema merely to adjust his new dental plates. The explanation didn't wash, and the whole matter was sent to Synod 1928.

When discussion of his appointment came up, B. K. knew that how the synod acted on the question of "worldly amusements" (including movies) would likely dictate how it would act on his case. He asked that the synod act first on "worldly amusements." It did, and it condemned them. He then asked that he be allowed to defend himself on the floor and that the synod meet in public session.

B. K. went to the floor of that synod and adopted precisely the position on worldly amusements that the synod had just finished condemning. For no less than three hours, B. K. told that synod where it had gone wrong. When his speech ended, so had his life in the seminary.

The CRC had lost another of its dissenters—Bultema, Janssen, Hoeksema, and B. K. Kuiper. We were continuing to define ourselves by standards we were confident were biblical. But B. K.'s departure once again illustrates the temporary triumph of what I've been calling the Inward Christian, the Confessionalist mind, in a power struggle that continued to grow throughout the next decades in the CRC. The Inward Christians' control of the church would last for more than a generation.

I know I've said this once before, but it bears repeating here. Historians of the American Puritan experience like to say that the beginning of the end of the Holy Commonwealth occurred only a few years after the experiment in Christian living had begun on the new continent. One of the signals of its demise was the necessity of law, for nothing so illustrates the end of a dream as the requirement to objectify, then mandate, its ideals. When New Englanders were required by law to attend church, one can safely presume that the original vision had faded.

Synod's ruling on "worldly amusements" suggests a similar loss of a central defining vision. No matter how well-meant at the time and no matter how godless the society may have looked in the Roaring Twenties, those guidelines illustrate, rather painfully, that many CRC members were so afraid of the change occurring all around them that they felt they had to draw the line somewhere and define clearly what it was that made them believers. That attempt to codify righteous living was, among other things, an indication of the cessation of a deeply shared sense of identity. God's love, like his rule, is always much bigger than our human perception of it.

Our attempts to create laws and regulations outlining God's righteousness will always fall short of what God knows and expects from us. We are not his chosen on the basis of certain prescribed behaviors; we aren't stronger candidates for his grace simply because we don't dance, don't watch movies, or don't send our kids to public schools. Attending Sunday worship twice doesn't by itself make anyone a saint. Raising our hands in praise to God doesn't make us a dime's worth better in the sight of our Father in heaven. Being able to share our innermost selves in a small group discussion may make us emotionally healthy, but it neither verifies nor gains for us our salvation.

On the other hand, our purity will not be proved either by our work to redeem literature or art or politics or education. My urging my son to watch *Hardcore* is not an act that gives others proof of God's grace in me. A life spent writing fiction that brings praise to God won't merit a day in glory. Preachers

fall, after all. Murderers rise. The most despicable of criminals may well greet us one day in glory—along with King David the adulterer, Rahab the harlot, and Thomas the doubter. Grace is that amazing.

All of our penchants, our pet behaviors, our personal prohibitions are not sufficient unto righteousness. A deep commitment to Reformed doctrine doesn't buy eternity, but neither will revival fires or memorizing the gospel keep us from perdition itself. Look at Peter, rising to the defense of his beloved Savior with almost comic gestures. "I won't let them take you," he told Christ when Christ predicted his own demise. Jesus turned to him and said, "Get thee behind me, Satan." Our best deeds . . .

Synod 1928 did its best with "worldly amusements," but they couldn't create a new Christian (or Christian Reformed) identity with a list of rules and regulations. It didn't work.

One more thing about *Hardcore* and the era we're now discussing. I may not like the movie; I may despise Schrader's characterization of the people with whom he grew up. But I'm not blind to the fact that the film offers this truth: We can all be humanly strengthened by the prescription of certain behaviors; it's likely that Jake Van Dorn found comfort in meeting the standards set by the prohibitions of Synod 1928. He didn't go to movies, he didn't dance, he didn't play cards. But what he learned is that he didn't love either. That's the obscene film's own messy lesson, the truth Schrader brings home in a movie I'll recommend only to a few. It's much easier to wear a form of godliness than to commit, wholly and deeply, to the power of love.

CHAPTER 15

The Thirties

During the 1920s the Christian Reformed Church dismissed many of its own who held differing views on the Judgment Day, higher criticism, and common grace. In the process the denomination became more unified, more lean and trim perhaps, and, by our own estimations at least, more capable of negotiating the still troublesome American waters that lay ahead.

By 1930, a more crisply defined CRC may well have anticipated the next decade as an era of peace and growth—growth at least from within. But even those members most sure that the final judgment was just around the corner could not have predicted what was to follow—first, an economic depression steep enough to wilt resolve and test faith; and then, a decade later, another World War, this one drawing many more members of CRC congregations into a ferocious conflict that nearly spanned the globe.

If there were ever a time conducive to the rigors of Calvinism, the thirties and forties would be the decades of choice. Neither Calvinism in general nor its Dutch hybrid in particular have ever been accused of frothy shallowness. If we are as dour as the stereotype we have created for ourselves, then that seriousness—the perpetually wrinkled brow, the hand held meditatively up to the chin—should have served us well in those decades on a continent we had only recently begun to call home.

The story of the CRC is always far larger and far greater than a recitation of the events transpiring in Grand Rapids synods or a tally of the body bags picked up after our theological battles. Throughout North America today there are Christian Reformed people worshiping and praising the Lord—not only on Sunday—who are almost oblivious to this history. Those ordinary people existed fifty and one hundred years ago too. After a war-torn decade like the twenties, it's tempting to say that churches capable of staying out of the fray were the ones most blessed.

It's a dangerous argument to make, but there is often a subtle blessing to theological dispute, a silver lining to the dark black clouds of conflagration. For better or for worse, as the denomination entered the thirties it had defined itself by what it wasn't—it wasn't premill, it wasn't modernistic, and it wasn't about to drop its belief in a certain level of grace given to all people of all cultures and all times. Bloodied and weary, it had, in a sense, defined itself by the battles it suffered. And struggling so intently over what it meant

Wall Street during
the stock market
collapse.

to be Reformed had the effect of redoubling everyone's commitment to that tradition.

But again, we do well to remember that not every member of the CRC suffered through those battles, because not every member had the time, the opportunity, the inclination, or even the ability to sift through often difficult theological issues. Throughout the denomination, people were living—falling in love, taking new jobs, raising kids, playing softball, laughing, and getting along. At this time especially—after the stock-market nosedive that marked the beginning of economic depression unlike anything ever seen in North America—remembering the day-to-day lives of our members may well be an

especially good exercise. So here are some Depression stories.

For weeks, sometimes months, the Maatman family couldn't get to church in Roseland, Illinois, twenty-five miles north of where they lived. They had a car, but no money for gas. Russell, a boy at the time, remembers a time when there were three cents, total, in the house. His parents made plans to move him, an only child, to some friends' homes when their food was completely gone, but the deacons would bring money occasionally so they always had something to eat. Russell says that to him the deacons' gifts were, and still are today, an act of God.

In Oostburg, Wisconsin, Harry Dirkse, my grandfather and the town blacksmith,

would come in from his shop for supper at night, eat what food my grandmother had prepared, and then lead his family in devotions. My mother remembers his anxious silences; he didn't know where the next dime would come from, even though he was working constantly. Few of his customers, local farmers, had any money at all. Not to do their plowshares and horseshoes would mean they couldn't get their own work done. Sometimes after praying, my mother says, he put his head in his strong blacksmith's hands and cried right in front of the kids.

One Sunday after church in rural South Dakota, Hattie Los and her husband, Pete, looked up at the sky and thought they saw rain. It wasn't rain at all, but dust—a storm of dust. By the time they got home, the kids' clothes—she'd had those clothes laid out on the bed—had almost disappeared beneath a blanket of dirt. Daily, the dust choked machinery and blinded livestock. Every day Hattie swept an entire pailful from the house, no matter how hard she tried to keep it out, how closely she locked the place up. Then the grasshoppers came and ate everything, even the onions still in the ground.

In Manhattan, Montana, Christian Reformed families hung wet sheets over their windows to try to keep the dust out. It didn't work. Eventually, they couldn't tell the color of their kitchen linoleum. One family tried to cook rice in a closed oven so that they wouldn't be eating dust, but the fine, blowing sand got in anyway. Cattle sold for six or seven dollars a head, and one milking of one cow made a dairyman a nickel. Millions of army cutworms crossed the land in a straight line, making the ground shiver eerily. Everything those cut-

worms came upon, they ate. And there wasn't much to start with.

In Leighton, Iowa, Rev. Cornelius Witt didn't receive enough salary to pay for coal, so his congregation kept him supplied with firewood. Young people remember going over to the parsonage to sing on Monday nights because Witt loved music. Those were great times, but in the winter those who sang so joyfully were always shivering because there was never enough firewood to light *both* the furnace and the kitchen stove. For the kids on Monday nights, Witt chose only the kitchen stove.

Grace Wierenga, a child in Neerlandia, Alberta, dreamed of a doll she'd seen in Eaton's catalogue—it cost a whole dollar. She had no dollar, of course, and neither did her parents. But after seeing her dream day after day, they promised Grace that if they ever got a dollar, they'd buy the doll. One day a man who owed her father a dollar paid him back, and true to their promise, they bought Grace the doll. It took her decades to understand the incredible price of that single gift.

On a small farm near Ocheyden, Iowa, John and Henrietta Hoftyzer worked themselves to the bone, only to have their entire corn crop go to rent payments—and even that wasn't enough. When the landlord walked right into the house to see what more he might collect, he reached for the popcorn Henrietta had hung up to dry. She wouldn't let him have it. In fact, she chased him out of the house with a broom handle.

Nellie De Jong, of Orange City, Iowa, remembers wearing out her shoes. No one had money for new ones, nor was there anything extra to pay for repairs. Her mother would cut out pieces of cardboard to substitute for leather soles. It worked, sort of.

In addition to grasshoppers, dust, and horrible farm prices, a huge hailstorm hit Tonnie Kadyk's family in North Dakota. So much hail fell that it was still scattered all over after the family did the afternoon milking. Someone had the great idea to get out the ice-cream maker, then gather cream, eggs, sugar, and vanilla and make ice cream. They did, and that night they ate as much as they could possibly eat. After all, it was summer, and the ice cream would not keep. Manna, almost, it seemed.

Lou Van Dyke remembers not being allowed to go trick-or-treating in Ireton, Iowa—he was a preacher's kid, after all. But his father would give him a nickel instead, almost as if to buy his favor. Lou was just a little boy, but he knew he had a choice. If he bought a wonderful triple-dip ice cream cone, the delicious pleasure would be gone in less than an hour. So he stood forever in front of the candy counter, deliberating on how to spend that nickel. Five cents worth of candy, he knew, would last a week.

Gil Baker, who lived in Ripon, California, during the Depression, remembers a farmer who responded with good grace at a time when egg prices fell to a measly twelve cents per dozen. "At least my figuring is easy now," he said. "One more egg, one more penny."

In the middle of the Depression, Grace Beld fell in love with Gerald Vander Veen. Soon enough they were married, but they had no money—and their biggest wedding gift was nine dollars. When they looked around the South Dakota land-scape, they realized there was nothing there for them; so Grace killed and dressed all her turkeys, sold them for what she could get, and the lovers, married only two weeks, headed for California in a car that held only their wedding presents. They had forty-three dollars to their name.

In 1923, Reka Van Es, of rural Orange City, Iowa, bought a new dress for her son Gerald's baptism. Then came the Depression. In 1941, when Gerald graduated from high school, she wore that same dress once again—the only dress she'd ever bought.

Rev. John Hoogland, of Decatur, Michigan, had no money for shoes for his family. He prayed. And his daughter Helen will never forget the answer to that prayer. A family in the church with relatives in Chicago claimed their cousins were just a bit older than Hoogland's kids. "Maybe you could use some shoes," those people said. A miracle.

Henry Vander Giessen of Lynden, Washington, was one of a family of seven living on next to nothing. His father owned a nursery. For their only present one Christmas, each of the children was given an orange. He claims that the orange seemed to him, that Christmas, nothing less than pure gold.

A Christian Reformed farmer near Struble, Iowa, was advised by a neighbor that the only way to protect himself against the chicken thief who was stealing his chickens by the burlap bagful was to position a shotgun ready to fire once the coop door was opened. Chickens were, after all, a major source of what little food the family had. That night, a Saturday, the thief came again, but not until Sunday morning, Easter morning, in fact, did the farmer discover the body. The man had bled to death in the middle of the yard.

Dick Zwagerman and Cornie Granstra of Hospers, Iowa, made their only income by carting roadkill—squirrels, coons, and anything with fur, along with car parts or whatever they could find along the road—to Sioux City for bounty or whatever they could get for whatever they could find.

In order to get enough wood to heat the church for Sunday worship during the winter, Herman De Jong and Lawrence Ringling would drive a team of horses fourteen miles one way from flatland prairie around Platte, South Dakota, all the way to the river. It was such a long trip that they had to rest the horses, up and back, several times.

Jennie Tinklenberg, of Edgerton, Minnesota, had one good dress. She wore it every day to school and church. On Saturday, she'd wash it. Every week.

Peter De Boer remembers wintry days on snowy hills in Prospect Park, New Jersey, days when all his boyhood buddies went skiing down the long slopes with homemade skis fashioned from curtain rods. He never really knew his family was poor. They just "made do." Years later, he learned that there were times when the bank nearly foreclosed on their house. Even though they had little money, he remembers his mother saying how blessed they were never having to go on relief.

In Doon, Iowa, the congregation simply couldn't pay the pastor, Rev. Joseph Betten, his annual wage. One day Case Harthoorn told the rookie, city-slicker preacher to have a look at his hogs. "Which one do you think is the best of the lot?" Harthoorn asked. Betten pointed to one that looked exceptionally strong and healthy. Harthoorn told the dominie that that was the one he'd butcher and deliver to the parsonage. Mrs. Betten learned how to can meat very quickly.

In Whitinsville, Massachusetts, the Whitinsville Machine Works understood very well the economic difficulties its workers were facing, so they allowed their help to charge essential household items like washing machines to the company's account, expecting someday to be repaid. "It was a time," Fritz Bosma says, "when we made sure we wasted nothing."

These were the experiences CRC members brought to worship on Sunday during the Depression. One senses that prayer, in these situations, may well have come more easily than it does for some of us today.

BANNER EDITOR REVEREND H. J. KUIPER

No single individual may ever again come to speak so much both for and with the mind of the CRC as did longtime *Banner* editor Henry J. Kuiper. Today it is inconceivable that any single person could lead the denomination so completely. Many looked to Kuiper's words as if they were Holy Writ. We may well have more educated people in the denomination today, as well as some who are more loving or more wise; but no matter what sterling qualifications any single individual brings to the task of leadership in the denomination, the CRC today can no longer be as unified or as efficiently led as it was at the time of Kuiper's editorship.

Why? There are many reasons. We'd already lost many who'd disagreed; we were, therefore, more unified. But we were substantively closer in the 1930s anyway; much of the CRC was nothing less than a grid of interlocked extended families, the vast majority of them Dutch-American, with a common history and culture. We were less educated than we are today; often one of the goals of education is independent thinking. Also, our culture today is more individualistic than it was back in the thirties; we've become, like the society around us, more interested in our rights than our responsibilities, in our own needs than in the needs of others. Not long ago, I sat with a number of college students who insisted, without blushing, that worship in local churches wasn't good enough for them because it was not "meeting their needs." That's exactly what they said. Not that many years ago kids would have been reprimanded for such brazen egotism, whether or not they were right.

But there's another reason for Kuiper's strong influence too, a reason that is quite obvious when we consider the specific character of the thirties and forties: pure stress. It's not their word, of course—*stress*. It's ours. This generation has created a score of new professions out of our own obsession with stress—how to avoid it, how to deal with it when you can't. But consider for a moment the stress of the Depression—where is the next meal coming from? And the stress of the war—will Johnny come home? When we consider those times and contrast them to our own, our stress today seems cheap.

If Christian Reformed people all over North America grabbed *The Banner* from their mailboxes eagerly during those two decades, one important reason for their eagerness was the anxiety of the times. People wanted leadership because they needed leadership. When there is no money, an orange is a blessing. Selflessness was the very marrow of the war effort; giving, not getting, was the quality that would make America strong, and everyone knew it. The rigor of the times made people shut up and listen, and do so willingly. What today's tremendous North American prosperity has proved convincingly is the truth of the old adage—money doesn't buy happiness. Today stress comes in wholly different packaging.

In 1940, *Banner* editor Kuiper opened the new year with a lengthy analysis of the

H. J. Kuiper and a *Banner* from his time as editor.

preceding three decades. He argued that the buoyant revival of Calvinism, which had inspired the CRC before World War I, was over. "Unless we retrace our steps and dedicate ourselves anew . . . to the development of everything in our Calvinistic heritage," he declared, " . . . we shall gradually become a conglomerate of religious groups, each working for its own pet cause." He went on to identify what he considered to be the splintering factions in the denomination: one of them, he said, was "clinging to historical Calvinism," another "espousing a sort of fundamental evangelicalism," while a third followed meekly behind "the liberal, socializing modernistic churches of our land." Kuiper's analysis of the minds is a familiar theme by now. Obviously, what he was talking about even before World War II was the push and pull between mind-sets we've already played with throughout the story of the CRC. The arrangement he offers is slightly different than the distinctions Bratt uses, but the two of them are not far apart. Kuiper would have included himself in the first category; his editorials would bear witness to his claim. He was undoubtedly one of those who was still "clinging to historical Calvinism," what Bratt calls a "Confessionalist," and we've called the Inward believer.

The second mind-set he locates is an Americanized hybrid, a group "espousing some kind of fundamental evangelicalism." What these people were looking for in the practice of their Christian faith was something that looked and felt more American than Dutch, something tough enough to be orthodox yet sweet enough to be emotionally endearing—something

Rev. Frank De Jong (1900-1993)

Frank De Jong, born in northwest Iowa, prepared for the ministry and served two congregations before volunteering as a home missionary for the CRC in southern California just prior to World War II. He was one of the first home missionaries to serve when the CRC was just breaking into what might be called the second phase of church planting.

With his musically gifted and hospitable wife Ruth, De Jong was a very effective church planter. A gregarious man, he made friends easily and preached the profound gospel message simply and effectively, using his considerable "people skills" to bring members into the church.

His method was also simple, practical, and effective. He would find a place to live, get a telephone installed, and begin to call all the Dutch names he could find in the telephone book, inviting all to meet for Sunday worship. Some of those he called had previous CRC connections, but most did not. Amazingly, some responded who had not been in a church for years.

Rev. Frank De Jong (1900-1993) and wife Ruth (1899-1997), World War II military service pastor, 1930-1944; home missionary and pastor to churches in California 1938-1962, paying special regard to the large number of Dutch immigrants who settled in California during the fifties.

In these days of telemarketing, team ministry, and in-depth surveys, it may be tempting to mock De Jong's method as "rounding up Dutchmen," but his approach had the advantage of being low cost and very effective.

Remarkably, the congregations started by De Jong all developed into stable and productive churches. —TEH

that engaged the emotions but didn't slight the antithesis. They found these things in the growing movement we now call American Evangelicalism. These people came to represent the mind of piety, those we've called Upward believers.

The third group, those "inclined to follow in the wake of the liberal, socializing modernistic churches of our land," looked to mainline Protestant denominations in America for their source of inspiration and leadership. Today, CRC conservatives would say these are the folks who chum far too intimately with feminism, for instance, or those who flirt with evolution. They're Outward believers.

But wait a minute. I've already touted myself as an Outward believer, but I certainly don't want to "follow in the wake of the liberal, socializing modernistic churches of our land." I don't look to mainline Protestantism with its slowly emptying sanctuaries as any kind of pattern of ecclesiastical rectitude or cultural vision. To me, mainline Protestantism shows definite signs of becoming, if not being, theologically bankrupt. I know there are good, strong believers in the fellowship of mainline Protestantism, but with all due respect, I don't look to the Presbyterian Church U.S.A. for a definition of how to be a church in the twenty-first century.

Kuiper's analysis and warning were as valid for his day as they are, in part, for our own. But people who think like I do are missing in it somehow. By my estimation, the Kuyperian forces in the American CRC are not really distinguishable in his analysis. Confessionalists, liberals, and pietists are duly represented, but the Kuyperians don't have a specific place in Kuiper's out-

line. That may be because immigration had largely ceased following World War I, and the fresh supply of Outward-looking Christians had dwindled. So it could well be that there were fewer Kuyperians in H. J.'s era.

But it may be beneficial for all of us—me included—to take editor Kuiper's warning to heart. If I do, then I must admit that my own position as an Outward believer, one who places significant emphasis on the Christian's place in the culture at large, risks becoming exactly what Kuiper's analysis and warning indicates. That was and is the soft underbelly of the believer whose basic orientation is toward the world. When that orientation dominates my attention so fully that neither adherence to doctrinal integrity nor a personal relationship with Jesus Christ registers great importance to me, then my own mind-set—like all of us Outward Kuperian types—begins to resemble nothing more vitally Christian than the agenda of the most progressive wing of the American Democratic Party. Then, indeed, something vitally essential to the Christian life and the Calvinist worldview has been lost. That's what this Kuyperian father who tells his son to watch *Hardcore* needs to understand. Like all of us, I stand in need of the Lord's guidance in every area of my life. And with respect to my own place within the mind-sets we've been sketching out now for some time in this story, I need to remember that for me, as for all of us, a strength can become a weakness through single-mindedness.

While we've already described Kuiper as a Confessionalist or Inward Christian, it's important to note that he would have thought of himself as an Antithetical. He clearly identified himself with that mindset. But he parted company with those Kuyperians who, like Johannes Groen, advocated greater participation in American labor unions and other institutions of American society. At the same time, he praised denominational efforts like the Christian schools, deaconal concerns for Christian mercy, city missions—even the structure of men's and women's societies—and attributed all of those successes to the influence of Herman Bavinck and Abraham Kuyper's Neo-Calvinism. "Our deaconate would likely have begun to fade into the perfunctory and useless thing it is in most of our American churches," he argued in an editorial. "Our societies for young men and women would have been swallowed up by the Christian Endeavor Movement, a nationwide organization on which modernism already has a firm hold." Instead of men's and women's societies, he insisted, we would have only "adult Sunday school"—by which he meant fluff, silliness, shallow faith, and cheap grace. These abiding strengths of the denomination, Kuiper would have argued, are a legacy of its Kuyperian vision.

At the same time, however, H. J. himself remained deeply devoted to confessional purity. Although he felt that across the spectrum of society—church, school, and the culture at large—a specifically Reformed witness still beckoned, during his initial years as *Banner* editor he devoted far more attention to maintaining the purity of the church than to expanding its visionary potential, what Kuyperians would have called "the kingdom"—the

Henry Stob (1908-1996)

Henry Stob represents the contribution of the Chicago community to the life of the CRC. He came out of a tradition of deep appreciation of the Reformed heritage when it still bore all the marks of its Dutch ancestry. But in Henry Stob the tradition took on an American character that made him a remarkable leader in the CRC as it sought the kingdom of God in its North American context.

Henry Stob (1908-1996), professor of philosophy and ethics at Calvin College and Calvin Theological Seminary 1939-1975.

Stob's Americanization began during his brief stint in the business world before his studies at Calvin College and continued in his broader study of philosophy. He became a world citizen through his doctoral studies in Germany and was further broadened by service in the U.S. Navy from 1943-46. He was assigned to the Department of Religion and Education as a commissioned officer and rose to an important position in the occupation of Japan under General MacArthur. There he was placed in charge of all matters concerning Christianity in the reconstruction of governmental forces in Japan after the armistice.

Stob returned to teach philosophy at Calvin College. There he mentored several young ethicists and philosophers who went on to become leading Christian lights in the academic world, among them Nicholas Wolterstorff, Alvin Plantinga, Lewis Smedes, and Richard Mouw.

Stob spent a large part of his career in Calvin Seminary where he taught Christian ethics and apologetics. He made another significant contribution as one of the founding editors of the *Reformed Journal*, a periodical that for several decades articulated a progressive approach to life in the kingdom.

His autobiography, *Summoning Up Remembrances*, reveals the life and times of a man of great personal and spiritual integrity. He is another of our heroes of faith. —TEH

march of the gospel into every inch of creation.

The editor asserted that the most characteristic virtues for the CRC were distinctiveness, purity, and discipline. If we fail in these, he wrote in 1931, "we shall fail everywhere." Christian schools, mission work, interchurch relations, and every other facet of denominational life required the test of distinctiveness, and on that account the majority of H. J.'s editorials sounded.

Longtime Calvin Seminary professor Henry Stob once characterized the intellectual posture that Kuiper encouraged as "the mind of fear and safety." Even if Stob may have been too close to his contemporary to see the complexity of H. J.'s positioning, *fear* is an important word in any analysis of his long and distinguished career as *Banner* editor and of the nature of the denomination at the time. Fear was, in fact, an important weapon in his assault on the dangers facing "our people." In 1931 Kuiper devoted an entire column to "the wholesomeness of fear," because "one of the most serious phenomenon in modern society . . . is the breakdown of authority." Besides, he argued, fear "can be wholesome—fear of God, parents, government, and the courts—but not slavish or disabling fear." Endless repetitions of the maxim that God is love, he asserted, could distort the balance of biblical truth that proclaims, "The fear of God is the beginning of wisdom."

To derail the gathering forces of worldliness and impurity, Kuiper insisted, the best antidote was the Christian school. At all levels—primary, secondary, and college— *The Banner* encouraged the expansion of Christian schools. Throughout the thirties, Mark Fakkema's reports on "Our Christian Schools" chronicled the development of every facet of the educational enterprise. He claimed that in 1931, 70 percent of the Christian Reformed Church used the private Christian schools.

No matter how enthusiastic he could be, Kuiper could always find danger lurking, even in Christian education. Some teachers, he warned, might have selected Christian schools without full commitment to Reformed ideals. Some school boards might be appointing faculty members because they were sons and daughters of their local communities and not because of those individuals' devotion to Reformed principles.

Higher education—college specifically— carried the greatest potential to derail orthodoxy. Independent-minded students and professors could, and most certainly would, corrupt confessional integrity. The greatest danger to the fellowship, he maintained, came from those who disagreed with the church but refused to leave it, a particularly disturbing problem in a denomination where, then as now, family and ethnic ties sometimes run deeper and stronger than theological affinity.

The suffering of ordinary church members during the Depression is not documented on the pages of either *The Banner* or *De Wachter* during the 1930s. Perhaps people neither needed nor wanted to be told about the difficulties most of them were going through. Perhaps many didn't know they were poor until some cultural analyst told them they were later. Maybe the editors operated under a different theory of journalism than do editors today, a different definition of what is news. Perhaps H. J. Kuiper's own penchant for negation is itself a means

BANQUET of the
HIGHLAND CHRISTIAN SCHOOL ALUMNI
May 24, 1939   Highland, Ind.

1939 Alumni Banquet of the Highland, Indiana, Christian School.

by which he—and his readers—dealt with the stress and strain of the Depression era.

Let no one assert, however, that during Kuiper's reign as *Banner* editor, he deliberately avoided discussion of the political issues of the times, nor that his perceptions, pet projects, and peeves dominated the discussion in the pages of the magazine and in the denomination. Kuiper not only tackled some of the tough questions of the day, he also provided space for opposing viewpoints. For several months in 1935, Dr. Peter Berkhout, a physician from New Jersey, dueled with Kuiper on the issue of pacifism. That same year, Kuiper's good friend, J. Gresham Machen, a remarkable man and powerful leader of the Orthodox Presbyterian Church, publicized his opposition to the Child Labor Law amendment. Machen's argument, mainly a defense of state's rights in contrast to federal power, was vigorously challenged by Amry Van den Bosch, a Christian Reformed professor of history at the University of Kentucky. Throughout the thirties and beyond, E. J. Tanis, a frequent contributor to the *Banner*, published independent views in "The World Today," views that often offered alternatives to H. J.'s assertions.

Nonetheless, *The Banner*'s social and political perspective was firmly conservative. Even in the depths of the Depression, socialism, to say nothing of communism, was dismissed as unworkable and unchristian—unworkable because it destroyed self-initiative and unchristian because it required the theft of private property to redistribute wealth and opportunity. Using ideas from Abraham Kuyper, H. J. Kuiper and others argued that governmental intrusion into family and economic life violated the principle of sphere sovereignty—that each area of our lives (home, school, church, labor, etc.) needed to operate Christianly on the basis of its own definitions and foundations. Government, Kuiper argued, should be restricted to arbitration and law enforcement. Even the postal service, he noted with satisfaction, lost efficiency under governmental supervision.

But capitalism also took some lumps. E. J. Tanis, together with longtime denominational stated clerk Ralph Danhof and H. J. Kuiper himself, repeatedly asserted that free-enterprise capitalism required alterations, and they did not reject the whole of Roosevelt's New Deal. Kuiper favored profit sharing, while Danhof highlighted the organic character of society as a balancing antidote to excessive individualism. Tanis declared that the Bible provided no economic road map and that Christians could function under any economic system—communist, socialist, or capitalist. The profit motive, he continued, could not be a Christian's primary economic concern, and all private possessions must be governed by the ideals of Christian stewardship. H. J. added his own warnings: "We fear the robber barons and financial dictators produced by modern capitalism. Something must be done to clip the wings of our unscrupulous 'money changers' and to curb the power of the 'malefactors of great wealth.'" "Without change," Tanis warned, "our economic order will be destroyed by the weight of its own corruption."

We might add another reason to the list attempting to explain the *Banner*'s prominence, leadership, and popularity during the thirties: it seems to have been a remarkably lively magazine.

FOUR NOTABLE DEVELOPMENTS

During the thirties, four notable developments signaled the CRC's continuing efforts to broaden its influence in North America. In 1935, *Calvin Forum,* a new periodical specifically devoted to the discussion of significant cultural issues, emerged. Calvin Seminary professor Clarence Bouma announced the editorial vision of the *Forum* in this way: "We welcome controversy. . . . The intelligent person cannot live without it." But to consider the new periodical *controversial* requires a bit of a stretch. Bouma continued, "Conservatism by itself leads to stagnation and petrifaction; progressivism cut loose from history is like chasing a rainbow." H. J. gave his enthusiastic support: "The need for such a magazine," he wrote, "is apparent."

Though edited and largely written by the Calvin College and Seminary faculty, the *Forum* also printed contributions from a wide range of Calvinistic scholars. Its content ranged across the cultural spectrum— evolution, the age of the earth, social justice, mission strategies, and economic issues, among others. In the first issue, Peter Berkhout presented the case for pacifism and conscientious objection. It was that particular argument that led to his disagreements with H. J. Kuiper, all of which resulted in a healthy debate in the more widely circulated *Banner.*

Another new journalistic venture was *The Christian Labor Herald,* established in 1935, a periodical that proclaimed its dedication, in fine Kuyperian tradition, "to the service of God in the sphere of labor and industry" and to the "Lordship of his Son in the social and economic life of the nation."

Another notable development of the thirties was the founding of the Reformed Bible

Johanna Timmer (1901-1978)

Johanna Timmer was one of the most outstanding women ever to serve in the fellowship of the CRC. She was born in 1901 in Graafschap, Michigan, where her grandparents had settled early in the life of the colony. At age twelve this very precocious child knew she would do something special in the kingdom—likely be a missionary.

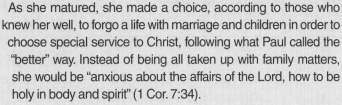

As she matured, she made a choice, according to those who knew her well, to forgo a life with marriage and children in order to choose special service to Christ, following what Paul called the "better" way. Instead of being all taken up with family matters, she would be "anxious about the affairs of the Lord, how to be holy in body and spirit" (1 Cor. 7:34).

At age seventeen she was teaching school, and at eighteen she was a student at Calvin College, studying Greek to prepare herself for missions. She became the first woman graduate of Calvin to win the coveted University of Michigan Scholarship.

Because the missionary challenge didn't open up for her, Timmer continued teaching. At age twenty-six she was appointed to the faculty at Calvin College; she became the first

Johanna Timmer (1901-1978).

dean of women and the first woman ever to set foot in Calvin's all-male faculty room. Timmer gained an awesome reputation as an outstanding and powerful speaker and a teacher with no-nonsense expectations for her students.

When Timmer became restless at Calvin, she began to think about training others for mission service. In 1940 she became one of the leaders in the formation of the Reformed Bible Institute (now Reformed Bible College), also serving as its first director and an inspiring teacher of future missionaries.

From this position she also led in the organization of the American Federation of Reformed Young Women's Societies to equalize the opportunities of young women's societies in the church—opportunities the boys had enjoyed at the federation level since 1919. As director of the federation, she traveled extensively and worked long hours, all in addition to her work at RBI.

Officers and Central Committee of American Federation of Reformed Young Women's Societies, October 1937, meeting at Prospect Park, New Jersey. The question marks indicate persons who could provide local conference information. The committee constituted a significant portion of the CRC's most prominent women from 1930 to 1970.

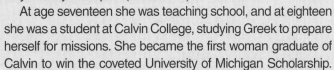

With compassion and vision, Timmer encouraged two of the women graduates of RBI to begin a ministry to unmarried mothers and fatherless children, a ministry that persisted through difficult times to flourish as the renowned adoption and family ministry of Bethany Christian Services.

After joining Corrie ten Boom and helping her set up a school in the Netherlands on the model of RBI, Johanna returned to teaching and school administration, first in Ripon, California, then in Philadelphia. She retired in 1963 and busied herself teaching Bible studies to numerous women's groups in the Holland, Michigan, area until her death at age 77. —TEH

Institute in 1939, an event H. J. Kuiper cited as additional evidence of Neo-Calvinist vigor still alive in the CRC. Some might argue, however, that the Institute (or "RBI," as it came to be known) was perhaps more a child of the Confessionalists than the Kuyperian Antitheticals, functioning as it did as an alternative to America's Bible schools, specifically Chicago's Moody Bible Institute. When young CRC men and women went to Moody for preparation for the mission field, Confessionalist believers (as well as others) felt strongly that those students were in danger of losing Reformed doctrines. RBI was therefore a necessary alternative to schools steeped in Arminian and premillennarian doctrines. Whether the establishment of RBI was more of a progressive step into American culture than a defensive maneuver designed to retain the Reformed orthodoxy is a question Inward believers and Outward believers could debate, then and now, for hours. What is clear, however, is that RBI was designed to instill Reformed doctrine into students preparing themselves for mission work both at home and abroad.

Perhaps the Bultema controversy of the early 1920s had muted the discussion of premillennarian biblical interpretations within the CRC, but the attraction of that theology did not abate completely with Bultema's departure. What's more, the new Scofield Bible, which explained such views clearly, was attractive enough to push Kuiper and the *Calvin Forum* into yet another defense of Reformed theology. Kuiper characterized premillennarians (as well as a growing number of "nondenominationalists" within American Christendom) as hopelessly at odds with Reformed ideas. "Their ranting against denominationalism comes close to religious quackery," he once wrote.

The threat of nondenominationalism loomed just outside the gates of the CRC when, in 1929, Rev. M. R. De Haan defected from the Calvary Reformed Church of Grand Rapids and opted for a more typical American fundamentalist theology, claiming the baptism of infants unbiblical and the Scofield Reference Bible his Scripture of choice. When the Reformed Church in America deposed De Haan as an apostate maverick, many of his followers, Dutch Grand Rapidians from the southeast side, left with him. Moody represented one kind of threat, but De Haan's defection from the RCA, gathering its force and power from the neighborhood of the CRC, was acute and scary.

De Haan, Kuiper asserted, was "cock sure, but dead wrong." He then proceeded to call up a new list of enemies, drawn, in total, from the camps of other confessing Christians. "Some of our own Christian Reformed folk," he wrote, "have been swept along with [De Haan-like] movement[s] . . . which may be characterized as fundamentalist, premillennial, baptistic, and sensationally evangelical." With these labels, Kuiper castigated the species of American Christianity De Haan represented and continued to lay out the distinctions by which he meant to keep his listeners both scriptural and Reformed.

It's not surprising to hear Kuiper hold forth against American fundamentalism; what is surprising is to hear the echoes of some CRC voices even today in his critique of its excesses. More than a half century later, the CRC has still not resolved the dilemma posed by what many of us still call "American Evangelicalism," whether the movement is led by Robert Schuller, Billy Graham, or James Dobson. In one sense, such believers are our Christian brothers and sisters; in another sense, historically at least, we come from different stock. Here is H. J. on the evangelicals of the 1930s: "We dare say that if . . . American Christianity had not been so individualistic, if the churches had depended less for their growth upon spasmodic, revivalistic campaigns and more upon Christian parental training, Protestantism in America would not be as weak as it is today."

A half century later, many contemporary Kuyperians, Outward-types like me, feel a little shaky about claiming H. J. Kuiper as one of our own. However, many of those same Kuyperians (again, me included) would raise a hardy "amen" to editor Kuiper's description of his evangelical comrades in the faith.

THE BACK TO GOD HOUR

De Haan's own acerbic individualism eventually fractured his Calvary congregation, but he went on to found the Radio Bible Class, a program that gained a national audience and has now been adapted for television under the direction of one of De Haan's sons. But De Haan was only one of many preachers CRC folks could pick up on their new radio sets during the thirties.

Soon enough, CRC congregations began to broadcast worship services—for shut-ins primarily, but also with the hope of reaching members who had fallen away. These efforts, both in Chicago and Grand Rapids, encouraged Synod 1928 to appoint a study committee, which urged a subsequent synod to appoint a denominational radio minister in 1930. H. J. Kuiper himself was incensed when synod rejected that proposal. "Let us make use of the radio to propagate the true gospel of Jesus Christ," he urged, for "we believe that our Reformed doctrine is the purest interpretation of the gospel. We believe that our Calvinistic world-and-life view is the only hope of the modern world in its intellectual bewilderment and moral confusion."

"Bewilderment," particularly in religious broadcasting, required, again in good Kuyperian fashion, a Reformed alternative. "False religion" and "sects of all kinds" spend "huge sums for the propagation of their principles," Kuiper noted. "Religious ideas of the most fanatic and absurd kind are being sent over the airwaves and are contributing to that lamentable and ever-increasing confusion of thought on religious subjects, which is one of the characteristics of religious life today—especially in our own country." By 1939, the proponents of a denominational broadcast succeeded in founding the Back to God Hour, and it reached its first audience from station WJJD in Chicago.

Not at all unlike the computer or the television, radio offered dramatic new possibilities, some of them glorious, some of them not so glorious. While it beamed the gospel to all corners of the world,

The Voices of the Back to God Hour

In the fifty-year span of Back to God Hour broadcasting, only a handful of men have served as radio ministers of the CRC.

The first was Rev. Peter Eldersveld, who completed nearly twenty years of service before his untimely death in 1965. Peter was gifted with a magnificent voice and the ability to use this instrument to God's glory as he enunciated for millions of radio listeners the good news of salvation by grace alone. He functioned as a prophet for his time, preaching sermons that were relevant to the day as well as faithful to the Scriptures. Much sought out as a convention speaker and loved by the "common folk," he made an impact for the CRC on listeners worldwide.

Dr. Joel Nederhood, who served from 1965 to 1996, was Eldersveld's immediate successor. Like Eldersveld, Nederhood was a gifted and effective voice for radio broadcasts and later a competent, well-groomed presence on "Faith 20," the agency's television program. According to Rev. Esler Shuart, radio pastor since 1952 and a seminary classmate of Nederhood's, "He was the right man at the right time to succeed Rev. Peter Eldersveld—and I thought Eldersveld was irreplaceable. Joel demonstrated unusual gifts for a multifaceted ministry. He showed a beautiful consistency over the years of standing on the Bible; all of his talks came out of the truth of God's Word."

Rev. Peter H. Eldersveld (1911-1965), first full-time radio minister of the Back to God Hour. During the fifties and sixties this radio broadcast was so prominent that the CRC was known as "the church of the Back to God Hour."

Rev. David Feddes, who accepted the assignment in 1996, is the current minister of the English language broadcast. Cal Bremer is the director of ministries for the agency. These men continue to do the work that Eldersveld and Nederhood did, proclaiming the good news of God's redeeming grace in Christ Jesus for the Back to God Hour.

Rev. Joel Nederhood served as radio minister for the Back to God Hour for more than thirty years, demonstrating "unusual gifts for a multifaceted ministry."

radio also carried the world into kitchens and milking barns, parlors and garages. Writing in *The Banner,* Egbert R. Post, longtime principal of Grand Rapids Christian High School, sounded a warning that might well be interchangeable with contemporary warnings about television or the Internet. "We have never before been in such intimate contact with the world," he wrote. "Most of us have never before known what attractions [the world] offered, nor known to what extent sacrilege and defiance of God have gone." Post then begins another variation on the slippery slope argument we've heard before. The "demonic thrusts" of radio, he says, shock us initially, but

> *later we become more and more accustomed to it, and though not yet calloused, we merely shrug our shoulders. Still later we meet an especially clever joke with an appreciative twinkle of the eye, the next one with a smile, and after having laughed heartily at the final spurt of humor on the program, we hopefully turn our dial in quest of another menu of Broadway hits, dance melodies and vaudeville wisecracks. This may not be the invariable experience, but we are only reminding you of possible dangers.*

Most of us may chuckle at his seeming paranoia when we consider that he's talking about nothing more villainous than the radio we can't do without in our homes and cars. But instead of lowbrow humor or the seductions of Broadway music, substitute, for instance, today's television violence or vulgarity and test the argument yourself.

Elsewhere in his lengthy article, Post claims that much of the material of radio programming (which is far different today than in the thirties) is "decidedly sacrilegious, profane, immoral and degrading," and aired with "the avowed purpose of advertising attractions at the local theaters . . . giving samples of what may be heard in the vaudeville houses during the coming weeks."

The link between Post's comments and contemporary life and culture are interesting, but what is most important to the story of the CRC at this point is a reality we can infer from the article: radio had circumvented synodical efforts to proscribe worldly thought and behavior. No walls were thick enough to stand against this new medium, riding sound waves perfectly unseen as it did. No matter how hard synod might argue and even pray for isolation from worldliness, the radio—and later the TV, the videotape, and the personal computer—made that isolation impossible.

Even those who opposed the radio could not deny its value. It carried news, weather, and market reports, classical music, and even the gospel. But its abuse "threatened," in Kuiper's words, "the collapse of Christendom."

Of course, that hasn't happened. But in the thirties, the radio brought mainstream American culture into every Reformed home, into every Reformed community, and, as a result, into most every Christian Reformed church. Even though its influence did not diminish the church's opposition to dancing, games of chance, or movies, every last Christian Reformed church member who tuned in, simply by listening, became more decidedly American.

Especially difficult for the church was its lack of control over how its members interpreted what they heard—whether it was news, entertainment, or religious programming. The fact of the matter was that radio waves found their way into CRC homes before any Reformed editor could tell Dad, Mom, or the kids how to listen. No Reformed preacher could weed out trash or falsehood, show by show. No Reformed analyst could explain world events or argue the theology that emerged from the set. Radio was instantaneous, unchecked, pervasive, and—above all else—unabashedly American.

Radio continued a process that had begun with Van Raalte and Scholte's first steps on the continent almost a century earlier—the process of Americanization. In addition to hastening the complete loss of the Dutch language, radio, parked in the center of people's lives, carried American culture into Grand Rapids living rooms, into workplaces in Lynden, Bellflower, and Paterson. Once the ethnic characteristics of language, dress, and diet disappeared, CRC people became more indistinguishable, at least by a quick appraisal, from their American neighbors.

Yet, beneath their American exterior, CRC parishioners remained basically Dutch-Americans. Even though they were now more capable of talking about everything from the stock market to the plight of the Chicago Cubs, they maintained and even enlarged the institutions their grandparents had established. From cradle to grave—with churches, mental hospitals, recreational facilities, homes for the aged,

cemeteries, and an adoption agency—the ethnic community still kept the boundaries of its enclaves secure.

What's more, much of the CRC community still reflected the institutional pillarization of the Netherlands, where Calvinists, Catholics, socialists, and other ideologically cohesive groups created separate and often parallel institutions to advance their own ideals. By contrast, most American institutions shunned strictly religious or ideological identities. While some North American churches and some schools maintained denominational characteristics (Lutheran and Roman Catholic schools, for instance), the YMCA, Boy Scouts, Rotarians, labor unions, and political parties preferred only vague, if any, religious identities. Even with *Amos & Andy, The Shadow,* Edward R. Murrow, and even Franklin Delano Roosevelt coming into CRC homes, the fundamental character of the Reformed people was still being shaped by its own institutions, institutions quite obviously different from those of the American mainstream.

For a long time such a broad network of institutions virtually insured that the majority of the children of the Christian Reformed Church would court, marry, and then baptize their own children into the inherited social structures. Some would insist that same medley of institutions operates in a very similar fashion still today.

Even in the thirties—with the nearly complete loss of the Dutch language, the beginning of a powerful new media revolution, and the burgeoning power of our brothers and sisters in American Evangelicalism—it's impossible to say that the Christian Reformed Church had become fully Americanized.

CHAPTER 16

War Again: Viewed from Two Perspectives

During World War II, my grandparents, Rev. John C. and Gertrude Schaap, lived in the parsonage of First Christian Reformed Church, Oostburg, Wisconsin, a massive, square, perfectly manse-like home that still stands downtown, even though the old church that once stood beside it is long gone. Five stars decorated the front window of that parsonage, because during the four years of American participation in that war, my Grandma and Grandpa Schaap had five children in the armed services and overseas.

Uncle Jay served on a Navy hospital ship that cleaned up beaches after some of the bloodiest battles in the South Pacific. Aunt Agnes, an Army nurse, worked in a hospital in Germany after the Battle of the Bulge, along with her husband, my uncle Al Groth. Calvin, my father, spent his years in the South Pacific aboard a tugboat that hauled pontoon and supply barges to South Pacific ports. Uncle Marinus Goote, an army chaplain, spent his term of service duty in Burma. All five were overseas.

Perhaps it is remarkable that every one of the Schaap children returned, none of them wounded physically. Millions, of course, didn't return from overseas. My mother-in-law lost her fiancé the moment

he stepped from a landing vehicle craft off the Normandy coast on the morning of June 6, 1944. You can read the names of those who died on brass plaques in cemeteries and on marble memorials all over the United States and Canada.

Cemeteries in Europe, Asia, and North America are seeded with the bones of those who died in what some refer to as a "good war"; the most traumatic result of war, after all, is death. World War II was a worldwide war. From East Asia to England and Alaska's Aleutian Islands, the conflict ruptured the routines of ordinary life and laid its print on each region differently.

Today, members of the CRC hold strikingly different memories of World War II. Some of them, like the Schaap family, recall the story of military power that crossed oceans to engage the enemy. To American and Canadian World War II forces, the war was "over there."

Others remember the war differently because it was fought in their pastures, on the streets of their villages and cities, and in the darkness of the long, long night of Nazi occupation. About 27 percent of CRC members reside in Canada today; the vast majority are descendants of Dutch postwar immigrants who remember the same sweet joy of victory their American and Canadian friends do, but whose stories,

when they can be told, belong to a whole different genre. North Americans remember V-E Day and V-J Day; Dutch immigrants remember, just as fondly, liberation.

When Hitler invaded Poland and then turned west to occupy France and the Netherlands, the pages of *The Banner* and *De Wachter* registered outrage. Nonetheless, the CRC's official publications, like most Americans themselves, favored neutrality and isolation as late as 1940. Even in northwest Iowa, a place where the Dutch language was often still used in worship and on the streets, the *Sioux Center News* warned its readers, many of whom had relatives in the occupied Netherlands, to beware of involvement in a war that wasn't ours. As national policy progressively edged toward an alliance with Great Britain, denominational spokesmen cautioned that when President Roosevelt gave destroyers and war materials to England, his action made a mockery of our supposed neutrality.

H. J. Kuiper, the leading voice of the CRC, noted Hitler's aggressiveness with dismay but was not at all convinced that the United States should join the fray. "We hate Hitlerism," he wrote, "but we have no reason in national self-interests to go to war."

Others, among them William V. Muller, a minister and missionary to Brazil, disagreed and argued that the U.S. had "the moral right to go to war" because "Hitlerism . . . is more than an attack on certain European countries. It is an avowed

attempt to wipe out all democratic institutions." Both Kuiper and E. J. Tanis favored defensive preparations such as military conscription. Kuiper declared, "It is foolish to trust in the Lord if we do not keep our powder dry."

When Japan bombed Pearl Harbor on December 7, 1941, the debate about neutrality and preparedness evaporated. The loss of almost 2,400 lives and the tremendous damage to the U. S. Pacific Fleet galvanized the nation in a surge of patriotism. There were no more sides to the argument. The U.S. was in, and the nation mobilized for war. Germany and Italy declared war on the United States, and four days later, December 15, the U.S. Congress extended military conscription laws for men between the ages of 20 and 44.

The CRC responded to the crisis with a single voice. H. J. Kuiper quoted the President, "We need God's guidance that this people be humble in spirit, but strong in the conviction of the right: steadfast to endure sacrifice and brave to achieve a victory of liberty and peace."

The *Young Calvinist,* a periodical aimed at young people, had been addressing its readers in military training camps long before Pearl Harbor. After December of 1941, however, the magazine devoted much of its space to "the Boys in Service." Already in the opening issue of 1942, Earl Strikwerda, professor of history at Calvin College, counseled the draft-age generation on the ironies of history with its recurring cycles of war and human self-deception. Richard Postma, well-known as "Uncle Dick" from his frequent *Banner* contributions for kids, editorialized this way in the *Young Calvinist:* "The United States enters with clean hands and noble purpose. Fully aware of the magnitude of the task awaiting us, conscious of the sacrifice we must make, we enter the fray courageously and with the determination to bring the war to a successful end."

In retrospect, such a sentiment is remarkable. The *Young Calvinist* unflinchingly suggests that some of its readers will likely have to die for a cause nearly everyone understood to be good and right. As I type this line, thousands of CRC young people are gathered for their annual convention. Praise God no one has to say anything similar to what Richard Postma said back then; praise God that for years now we've been able to live without another world war. But it's difficult to imagine anyone at this year's convention talking as seriously to young people about the absolute necessity of sacrifice and the imminence of death.

After Pearl Harbor, there was no need to justify or encourage patriotism as there had been in World War I. On the contrary, an entire nation inclined toward what some might consider excessive patriotism. Thus, while Henry Beets wrote editorials extolling national loyalty in 1917, in 1942 E. J. Tanis, H. J. Kuiper, and others sounded a cautious note. While they—and the church along with them—were fully committed to the nation's war policy, they urged their

readers to beware of the unholy alliance of faith and nationalism. "Love for one's country is a real virtue," Kuiper wrote. "It is the fruit not of special grace, but of common grace. We should add, though, that the purest patriotism has a Christian root, namely love for God, and it is cured of excesses and directed . . . by the influence of the Word and Spirit of God." In the *Calvin Forum*, Clarence Bouma called for "a new patriotism, one that is neither militarist nor pacifist."

The "mighty passion of patriotism"—H. J.'s phrase—was not easily directed and could never justify personal hatreds. When the government-approved film *Hate the Enemy* was distributed, *The Banner* criticized the work severely. "We should hate sin, not the sinner," the editor said, then argued that government authorities would do better to elevate a sense of justice than feed a thirst for

---

Packed and Ready

With touchingly humble pietism and naivete, Thomas Y. Nelson from Paterson, New Jersey, described the weapons of spiritual warfare that accompanied him on his adventure in World War II: "Anticipating certain leisure hours, I wondered how I would be able to fill them with useful reading. A small Bible, a pocket-sized copy of the *Psalter Hymnal*, the official songbook of my church, the Second Christian Reformed Church of Paterson, New Jersey, Professor L. Berkhof's *Systematic Theology*, and Professor W. Hendrickson's book *More Than Conquerors* were all that my suitcase would hold."

—WDB

revenge. In 1943 Kuiper quoted from a military publication:

> *War is the business of killing and being killed. . . . an eye for an eye says the old Mosaic law, a tooth for a tooth. The —— with that! Two eyes for one. A whole jaw for a tooth. One enemy taught the world a savagery that most of us thought had died with Attila the Hun. They must be paid for it."*

Kuiper snapped back, "The spirit revealed in the above article is precisely the spirit of devilish hatred which accounts for the Japanese atrocities," he wrote. "If we retaliate in their own spirit, in what respects are we better than they?"

Throughout the war the CRC's print media persisted with efforts to separate legitimate from illegitimate hate. In the *Young Calvinist*, Earl Strikwerda noted, "Too many of our cartoons picture the Japanese soldier as a partially toothless monster. . . . We refuse to believe that human nature is as fundamentally different as sensational journalists would lead us to believe." Furthermore, he said, "Public morale is better served by a healthy respect for the enemy than a blind senseless rage."

The obvious dangers of war—to the country and the branches of the military—dominated the nation's attention, but also the attention of its churches. In the conflict's heat, religious groups were easily tempted to subject their independent voices to the goals of the state. Along that line, E. J. Tanis noted the appearance of an advertisement in the *Baptist Watchman Examiner,* which urged, *"To keep the Bible*

Uncle Dick Postma (1891-1976)

Richard Postma, born in 1891, emigrated to Roseland, Illinois, in 1915 as a young single man to begin a teaching career in the New World. He likely taught in both Dutch and English at Roseland Christian School before coming to Grand Rapids, where he took on the English language full time. As the principal of the Grandville Avenue Christian School, he was deeply involved in organizing the American Federation of Reformed Young Men's Societies in 1919, and later became its president.

Eventually, in the early forties, a Federation of Reformed Young Women's Societies also came into being under the leadership of Johanna Timmer. When the two groups joined to form the Young Calvinist Federation, Postma became its full-time director and editor of its periodical, *The Young Calvinist.*

Postma may best be remembered for his "Uncle Dick" columns in *The Banner.* He set his mark on several generations of young people with "Our Indian Cousins" and "Pen Pals." Uncle Dick was an enthusiastic, positive, "can-do" kind of leader. He was a feisty, five-foot-five dynamo, with a great voice that never lost a bit of a brogue. He kept all aspects of his life under the umbrella of his Kuyperian Calvinism. His faithfulness to the Reformed tradition is the legacy he so tirelessly worked to transmit to young people during his watch in the struggle for the kingdom of God.　　—TEH

Richard Postma.

open, buy war bonds." "Let us not," Tanis warned, "belittle the Bible to win the war." God did not need the aid of the United States to preserve his eternal Word, Tanis asserted.

General Douglas MacArthur was also cited for misleading sentiments when he comforted grieving civilians after the Bataan invasion by declaring, "I only say that the sacrifice and halo of Jesus of Nazareth has descended upon these [dead heroes] and that God will take them unto himself." *The Banner* commented, "MacArthur is undoubtedly a military genius, but that does not make him a safe guide in the field of religion."

Whatever its excesses, the war did create a unified sense of purpose in churches and denominations, and, for the war's duration at least, many distinctions and animosities were shelved. There was simply little time or emotion left to argue about "end times" or common grace or even modernism. War dominated everyone's life. Commonly held beliefs from sources as diverse as Karl Barth, General Douglas MacArthur, and Bishop Fulton J. Sheen found favorable notice in *The Banner*. The CRC joined forces with the National Association of Evangelicals in 1943 and thereby proclaimed compatibility with Arminians, perfectionists, and even pacifists like the Mennonites. The NAE's opposition to modernism kept the CRC aboard until 1951, when the increasing fundamentalism in the organization led the denomination to part company with them. But during the war, the church was inclined to emphasize areas of agreement within the evangelical community.

As victory came nearer, E. J. Tanis reported that even in Russia religious freedom had gained a measure of respect. He recommended a more tolerant attitude toward the U.S.S.R. because the Russian people "have been in bondage to a corrupt church and a despotic state for hundreds of years." "It was only thirty years ago," he noted, "that Russia moved out of despotism into communism, and Russian communism is a mixture of totalitarianism and democracy." Though communism remained corrupt, Russia was our ally, and Henry Schultze argued that because Hitler was a greater enemy than Stalin we were fully justified in joining the Communists to destroy the Nazis.

The columns of the *Calvin Forum* and *The Banner* repeatedly declared that our enemies were not German, Italian, and Japanese people, but their demonic beliefs. And on that level the Allies were also tainted. H. J. Kuiper detailed the problem. "There is a difference between fighting Nazism and the Nazi. . . . We must fight the Nazis with modern armaments, but Nazism can only be fought with intellectual and spiritual weapons." Such a strategy had domestic implications, he told his readership. "We have to wage war against many in our own borders—not aliens, but 'good Americans' who have not recognized the fundamental falsehood of the Nazi philosophy and are themselves tainted with the pernicious doctrine of an omnipotent State." He added that the doctrine of racial superiority could also be found in the U. S., where "some preach white supremacy because they are alarmed by the progress of the negroes among us." Kuiper went on to chide all bigoted Americans. "The Germans," he wrote, "have no monopoly on intolerance, hatred and cruelty. The worst of human vices are latent in all human beings. War unleashes the wild beasts in the human heart."

THE RISE OF THE CRC CHAPLAINCY

Such "wild beasts" could also find lodging among the CRC's young people, and that fear motivated urgent calls for military chaplains and service pastors, as well as solemn warnings about spiritual dangers. The commonly recognized moral pitfalls of military life—grossly obscene language, alcohol abuse, and sexual promiscuity—demanded attention. In clear but tender exhortations, the *Young Calvinist* urged its readers, in Rev. J. M. Ghysels's words, "that there be no Pearl Harbors in their lives." Dr. Jacob D. Mulder of Pine Rest Hospital wrote authoritatively of "many ex-soldiers who were hospitalized due to venereal diseases contacted in a state of alcoholic confusion."

The *Young Calvinist*, with over 5,500 subscribers, reached into every CRC community and was mailed to every young woman and man in the armed services. Regular columns by editor Richard Postma, Earl Strikwerda (in "Current Events"), and service pastors offered advice, information, and encouragement. Peter Eldersveld and others crafted homilies. The many letters from military personnel and the regular reports of service pastors like Harry Dykstra likely provided the most-read features of the *Young Calvinist*. In these columns some parents discovered words from or about their own children. By publishing the location of CRC recruits,

the magazine often brought its own young people together in military training camps. "Gold Stars" reports, numbering at least 275 by the end of 1945, symbolized the war's deepest and most enduring wounds. For everyone, though—parents, wives, and friends—the *Young Calvinist* forged a link between the denomination and loved ones at war.

The path for CRC chaplains was created already before the war when Dr. Henry Beets, then Director of CRC World Missions, visited the National Committee on Army and Navy Chaplains and discovered that for as small a price as fifty dollars the CRC could become a part of the effort. He reached into his pocket and paid the fee himself.

While there had been talk about preachers becoming chaplains at the conclusion of World War I, and while Synod 1922 had even adopted an overture from Classis Muskegon allowing ministers to join the reserve corps of chaplains, it was not until 1942, after the U.S. entered the war, that the fifty dollars Beets had paid (annually!) was paid in full by the denomination, who that year appointed an official Chaplaincy Committee.

It's altogether possible to see that action itself as basically protective once again. After all, the primary motivation for creating a CRC chaplaincy was not to preach the gospel to men and women on the field of battle, but rather to protect CRC servicemen away from home and significantly distanced from "Reformed" witness. But what happened on the battlefield was altogether another matter. Harry Boer acknowledged that the mission was to minister to our own, but he also made very clear, in a *Banner* article he wrote fifty years later, that, from the beginning of his experience as a military chaplain during World War II, he "felt quite ecumenical." Boer, who was involved in the battle of Saipan from beginning to end, claimed that throughout the effort he saw only one CRC boy. "Chaplaincy taught me," he said, "to minister to the needs of many people."

Likewise, Chaplain Henry Van Til made a deep impression on synod when he cautioned them in 1944 about the lack of opportunity most soldiers had to maintain satisfactory church attendance while in the middle of battle, then urged a much more ecumenical attitude from the denomination, and finished with a challenge to young ministers who were capable of joining the corps to do so.

Boer and Van Til were only two of many young CRC pastors to opt for the chaplaincy. By the end of the war, 10 percent (twenty-six chaplains) of the denomination's ministers were serving as military chaplains. Despite that number and their proximity to military action, none of them were killed in action.

When the war ended, the Chaplaincy Committee was reduced to three members, and no one pushed for the CRC's continued membership in the military. As a result, most of the ministers who were part of the corps left the service for parish ministries.

Marinus Goote, who had served in Burma during the war, reflected on his wartime experience in a series of articles in the *Calvin Forum*. Goote expressed sadness about the way in which some men who considered themselves Christians could so glibly shirk their responsibilities toward God and fall into moral darkness in the service. At the same time, he claimed to have been enriched by the experience of meeting vibrant Christians of other confessions in other lands. He comments that those experiences were difficult for colleagues who hadn't served to understand. "Re-

---

Servicemen's Homes

During World War II, thousands of young men and women were drafted or enlisted in the great crusade for freedom from dictatorships. Anticipating the needs of these homesick teenagers, the CRC developed service homes near military bases across the country. Staffed by ministers, these homes offered a place of retreat from the violence, profanity, and blasphemy of boot camp or basic training.

A typical example was the home of Rev. and Mrs. John M. Vande Kieft in Raleigh, North Carolina. Each weekend soldiers from a nearby base took the long bus trip to the Vande Kieft's home. Saturday night was devoted to long conversations and getting acquainted with first-time visitors. Some of the men came fifteen to twenty weekends in a row.

On Sunday morning, sleepy men awakened to the smell of coffee, and a hearty breakfast followed. Then Rev. Vande Kieft led the entire group to a large Southern Presbyterian Church, where we sometimes filled four rows.

After church we were treated to a wonderful home-cooked meal at the Vande Kieft home. Then, at 2:00 p.m. we assembled in the tiny Baptist Church for a regular Christian Reformed worship service, where we used the *Psalter Hymnal* and dutifully observed the 1928 order of worship. After the ample Sunday dinner, most of the GI's fell asleep right after the pastor's introductory sentences. Our guilty consciences were somewhat assuaged when we noted that the pastor's family suffered from the same malady.

Time to head back to Fort Bragg came all too soon. The seventy-mile bus ride (usually standing up) seemed endless. The prospects for the week under the tender ministrations of the drill sergeant were foreboding. Already in our mind's eye, we were anticipating the weekend and our return to the loving embrace of our fellow Christians at the home of Dominie Vande Kieft. —WDB

---

turning chaplains were frequently looked upon as the champions of the movement to break down denominationalism," he wrote in those articles. Yet, he said, in some circumstances the truth was exactly the opposite since his work "revealed that many who were Protestant were no longer protesting. Too many," he wrote, "were fearful of offending anyone by expressing religious convictions. The mood was toleration. Consequently, some realized that unity would be at the expense of truth."

Being outside the confessional circles of the CRC, Goote said, made him more specifically conscious of the basic outlines of the Christian life.

In some ways, the experience of the military, even in the extremes of war, paralleled life in community with other Christians before and after the war.

Synod 1947 gave Home Missions the task of evaluating the possibility of "industrial chaplaincy," or ministries to industry, but Synod 1949 decided against entering

San Diego Servicemen's Center

Rev. Gerrit Boerfyn entered the ministry just before World War II, serving as a home missionary in San Diego at a time when thousands of soldiers, sailors, and marines—many of them from the CRC—were passing through on their way to the Pacific war zone. In addition to his work of church planting and evangelizing, Boerfyn became involved in pastoring these young men and women.

San Diego Servicemen's Center, Rev. G. Boerfyn, pastor.

He soon recognized the need for a servicemen's ministry to provide fellowship and support for the young people while they were in area camps. So in 1943 he and his wife, Nellie, and the small nucleus of Christian Reformed people in the San Diego area created the Servicemen's Center. The center, which provided lodging, meals, worship services, and counsel to hundreds, was managed by the Boerfyns, one full-time domestic helper, and the volunteer ministry of the families of the San Diego church.

Boerfyn kept detailed records of all the young people who passed through the center. Every Monday he wrote a personal letter to the parents of each service person who had been there for the weekend—all this in addition to preaching twice each Sunday and caring for the needs of his small church. Rev. Peter Eldersveld once rated him as "the best home missionary in the Christian Reformed Church."

The center closed at the end of the war in 1946. It was reopened during the Vietnam War to minister to military personnel until the number of bases in southern California was reduced. The center closed again in 1991. —TEH

Seaman's home in Hoboken, New Jersey (ca. 1925).

that work because "the task of bringing the gospel to sinners belongs to the Church of Jesus Christ and not to industry." Furthermore, synod felt that the industrial chaplain's first loyalty would always have to go to management: "Experience teaches that the industrial chaplain is expected to serve management first."

The Korean War activated interest in the chaplaincy again, but only for a time. Some war-veteran chaplains returned to hospital chaplaincy, especially in Veterans Administration institutions. Rev. Edward Heerema, for example, became chaplain at the Christian Sanatorium in Wyckoff, New Jersey.

Not until 1955 did the denomination officially approve the Chaplaincy Committee's request to look into "institutional chaplaincy." Today chaplains define themselves as pastors in specialized ministries in a largely secular setting. They find themselves in the middle of action in the military, in prisons, in hospitals, in detox centers, and in industries. Today a total of eighty-seven full-time active chaplains, as well as twenty-one pastors who serve in congregations or education, comprise the CRC chaplaincy corps. Seventeen still serve in the military, twenty-five are in institutional settings, sixteen do their work in health care, and eleven are pastoral counselors. The rest of the corps work in the Veterans Administration, in hospice work, in prisons, as Clinical Pastoral Education supervisors, and in industrial positions. They carry out a vital role of the ministry of the Christian Reformed Church, just as they did in the heat of the action of World War II.

HIROSHIMA AND NAGASAKI

Near the end of World War II, a new and even more terrifying reality altered human perception for years afterward. The bombing of Hiroshima and Nagasaki ended the war but opened the curtain on the Atomic Age. First reactions included both joy and fear. No war would ever be the same, and even the dreary images of World War II paled before the potential annihilation that this new force exhibited to all the world. Debate about the wisdom of its use sprang up immediately. The *New York Times* declared that we had "sown a whirlwind," and H. J. Kuiper agreed. "Suppose," he wrote, "that within twenty years this frightful weapon will be used against New York, Chicago, . . . and other fair cities of our land?" History gives us, he said, "no reason to believe that the most frightful weapon ever devised will restrain nations from declaring war. As long as men hate they will fight."

In that same *Banner,* E. J. Tanis declared, "We must not be so naive as to think that these bombs will not be dropped on American cities in future warfare. We are fortunate in living one or possibly two generations too soon to see American cities bombed to pieces."

The bomb also had defenders, and the main lines of debate were quickly established. Rev. Ring Star, for instance, argued that the enemy used criminal tactics—the bombing of noncombatants in Rotterdam, suicide missions, and concentration camps. Did those evil tactics not justify the bombing of Hiroshima—a single blow to stop further bloodshed and destruction? If yes, then the indiscriminate slaughter of civilians could be justified in every war.

H. J. Kuiper, while disagreeing with Star's defense of the bombing, proposed that the atomic bomb, as well as flame throwers, poison gas, and germ warfare, "be outlawed forever by the United Nations." He concluded, "Why should humanity destroy itself in the name of war?" As every reader knows, these fundamental questions continued to haunt American life for the next forty years and have abated in intensity only with the fall of the Berlin Wall and end of the Cold War. More recently, India and Pakistan's testing of nuclear weapons raises these same questions again.

DENOMINATIONAL ISSUES DURING THE WAR

The war dictated much of the denomination's agenda as issues ranging from Sunday labor to the practice of open communion in the military forced the church to adjust its views.

The justification of Sunday defense work required immediate attention because the overwhelming demand of ammunition and war machinery had launched the industrial sector into seven-day weeks with double and even triple shifts. It is possible that no single behavior of Dutch-American CRC members was so central to their own sense of religious identity as Sabbatarianism. Among older members of the church today, few cannot relate an anecdote or two about the old prohibitions, some of them solidly biblical, some simply legalistic, and some, by today's standards, silly, if not absurd. War was a powerful foe to Sabbatarianism. A sense of duty and commitment, many times to one's own family members "overseas," conflicted with the old strictures of "honoring the Lord's Day."

Church leaders throughout the country tried to find some middle ground to establish the legitimacy of Sunday work without giving up on the principle laid out by the fourth commandment. Generally, Sunday work came to be regarded as "work of necessity," but throughout the denomination many warned that the emergency could become a cover for abuse. Surely, H. J. Kuiper argued, not everyone was required to work seven days each week and even among those who did, none should do so consistently.

Classis Hudson issued a declaration on the matter that acknowledged the necessity of Sunday labor, but warned of the pitfalls that accompanied its continued practice. The classis cautioned its members about the potential of losing sensitivity to the "sanctity of the Lord's Day" and succumbing to "the desire of the love of money." To assist those who sought relief from excessive Sunday labor, Classis Hudson formed a committee that pledged itself to intercede for conscientious workers with their managers.

During the war, the CRC's long-time association with the Lord's Day Alliance (since 1926) gained increasing strength. Affiliation with the Alliance bound the CRC with twenty-two other American denominations representing some 30 mil-

Servicemen's board from Alpine Avenue Christian Reformed Church in Grand Rapids. A familiar sight in most churches during World War II.

lion parishioners. Together they petitioned national authorities to minimize Sunday labor for the military and encourage Sunday observance throughout the nation.

Other ecclesiastical concerns focused on maintaining proper church order for the denomination's members in military service. The general practice of open communion troubled both the church and its chaplains. Even though the War Department manual asserted, "Chaplains will conform to the requirements and practices of the particular denomination to which they belong," everyone acknowledged that close communion was neither possible nor preferable amid the smoke of the battlefield.

Though they often discussed rules of behavior for chaplains, synod did not provide precise rules for them. But the chaplains were committed to maintaining the spirit of true communion, even in war. Harry Boer recalls that during his chaplaincy he always announced the availability of special communion services for those who truly loved the Lord and sought to serve him. During basic training, Boer also conducted classes in Bible history and doctrine, classes that attracted clusters of students to his tent five nights a week.

War created a wide range of new questions. May servicemen and women make profession of faith without consistorial participation? And furthermore, may they do so to chaplains of unknown religious convictions? The answer—yes. But such professions required repetition when the soldiers, sailors, and nurses returned to their home churches.

The Banner warned repeatedly that alcohol abuse threatened lives and morals.

Both at home and in training camps, the dangers of "mixed" marriages loomed larger than ever. With potential husbands at war (some never to return), young women were tempted to marry unbelievers; servicemen were similarly attracted

Harry R. Boer

Harry R. Boer was born in Hillegom, the Netherlands, on April 4, 1913. As a lad in his early teens, he immigrated with his family to Holland, Michigan.

Boer attended Hope College, Calvin College, and graduated from Calvin Seminary in 1942. He became a chaplain in World War II, serving with the U.S. Navy and the U.S. Marines in combat in the South Pacific.

Upon returning to civilian life, he served a brief term as missionary to Nigeria but was called to the Chair of Missions at Calvin Seminary in 1951. Embroiled in an ongoing controversy in the seminary, he and three other professors were released from their assignment in 1952.

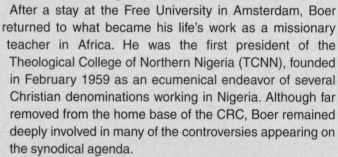

After a stay at the Free University in Amsterdam, Boer returned to what became his life's work as a missionary teacher in Africa. He was the first president of the Theological College of Northern Nigeria (TCNN), founded in February 1959 as an ecumenical endeavor of several Christian denominations working in Nigeria. Although far removed from the home base of the CRC, Boer remained deeply involved in many of the controversies appearing on the synodical agenda.

Almost from the beginning of his ministry, Boer was concerned about the ecumenical responsibilities of the church.

Harry R. Boer.

He was also sensitive to the need for reaching out and gathering in those who did not know the Lord Jesus as Savior. The fruit of this concern was a somewhat controversial book entitled *Compel Them to Come In.*

Boer was a frequent contributor to *Reformed Journal*—on its pages he urged that the form of subscription be rewritten to avoid ongoing hypocrisy from those who signed with fingers crossed and silent reservations.

A lifelong bachelor, Boer threw himself into the theological fray with enthusiasm and did not always follow the ponderous protocol for those who expressed dissent from prevailing positions.

However, his controversy with official church positions and those who disagreed with him never led him to personal bitterness and rancor. He is the "happy warrior" personified.

—WDB

into unfortunate marriages. For such the advice was simple: Don't do it!

The inclination to join neutral labor unions also caused renewed concern during the conflict. Obligatory employment in defense plants brought additional church members into the American Federation of Labor (AFL) and the Congress of Industrial Organizations (CIO), and Rev. John Gritter urged the denomination to clarify its opposition to such union memberships. Synod 1943 reviewed its history of deliberations on neutral labor union membership and concluded that church discipline could not be leveled against neutral organizations. Parishioners and churches were instructed to follow the advice of Synod 1930, which required thoughtful examination of the various unions and discipline for those members who spread Marxist notions. In short, synod refused to condemn the AFL or the CIO and referred the disciplinary question to local congregations.

None of the wartime issues resulted in momentous changes in church politics, and, on the home front at least, the church sailed along during these years without confronting major divisive storms. Reviewing the events of 1943, H. J. Kuiper concluded, "This year has been one of denominational peace and of financial well-being for our churches, schools, and denominational projects. Not a few of our institutions have canceled their debts or are laying up funds for future expansion." He added, "Much attention is being given by the denomination and . . . individual congregations to the spiritual welfare of their men and women in military service."

With battles raging all around the world, the church had neither the time nor the inclination to wage wars of its own.

THE WAR IN THE NETHERLANDS

Once again we travel back to the Netherlands at this point in the story. That may be surprising to some members of the CRC today, but another trip is mandatory, even though by the 1940s the denomination was a bit more than ten years from its first American centennial, and despite the fact that Van Raalte and Scholte had led their flocks to this country almost a century before Pearl Harbor.

Going back to the Netherlands isn't simply an exercise in nostalgia; neither is it something we'll do simply because the story of the Nazi occupation of the Netherlands is so memorable. We need to return to the occupied Netherlands because in the years following World War II, the ranks of the CRC grew immensely when thousands of newly arrived Dutch immigrants made their way to Canada and the U.S. Any discussion of who we are or were has to include the thousands who joined us only a half-century ago.

The denomination many of those new immigrants joined wasn't so much a mother to them as a distant relative. The CRC had created a number of "mission" endeavors in Canada to help new immigrants in the years immediately following World War I, but when the number of Dutch people coming to North America declined during the thirties, the greater part of that effort had dwindled with the flow. There were not many fully established Christian Reformed churches in Canada following the war, but strong congregations did exist in Chatham, Hamilton, Holland Marsh, Nobleford, Sarnia and Windsor, Ontario; as well as Winnipeg, Manitoba; Granum, Lacombe, Monarch, Neerlandia, and Edmonton, Alberta; and Houston and Vancouver, British Columbia. These churches, with the aid of the CRC in the United States, looked forward to the new wave of immigrants and provided much-appreciated support to the thousands who came.

But the new immigrants were different than the "old-timers" in Canada and the U.S.—often much different, even though they may well have shared a common theological heritage. The process of Americanization (and Canadianization) produces fossil remnants, no matter which ethnic immigrant group one considers. For some years following immigration, the cultural values and practices people take with them from their native land become stuck in time, the Old World habits calcified by the necessity of retaining identity in a New World flux.

Take language, for example. The language Dutch nationals use today is simply not the same as the language used by those who immigrated years and years ago. And so it is with a whole gallery of beliefs and behaviors. The Reformed churches in the Netherlands are no mirror image of their sister church in the U.S., the CRC. Dutch laws are different today than they were fifty years ago. Christian education, one of the finest gifts of the CRC to American culture, is today a much different enterprise in the Netherlands than it is in North America.

Often Dutch people traveling in the United States today can't help but laugh at Tulip Time in Holland, Michigan, or Pella, Iowa. Many Dutch travelers, people whose roots may even reach to the same great-grandparents as their American or Canadian relatives, also have to chuckle at the attitudes North American Dutch people take towards, say, marijuana or homosexuality or premarital sex, attitudes they judge as, well, quaint. Because cultural values change through time in any country, after a decade or so emigrants can never really go back to the home they came from.

For people from the Netherlands, the war was not "over there"; the war was in their streets.

All of that needs to be said before we introduce the significant number of new members who joined the CRC upon their arrival in the U.S. and Canada after World War II. The post-World War II immigrant changed the face of the CRC and affected its character immensely.

How so? We need to begin with the war we've been considering. The immense suffering undergone by American families whose sons and daughters did not come home from Europe or the South

Pacific cannot for a moment be understated. What those who stayed on the American continent gave up for the war effort can never be minimized. War exacted sacrifice. It took the lives of millions, changed the lives of millions more. Perhaps the Swiss assumed that they came out of World War II in good shape; but fifty years later, after the revelations about their banks' fraudulent use of Jewish savings, even they now understand that they weren't left untouched by the war just beyond their borders.

It is fruitless, always, to compare suffering. Who faces a more difficult life—the man who loses a leg or the woman who loses an arm? Both suffer.

The important factor to consider is that the North American experience of the war was wholly different from the Dutch experience. For people in the Netherlands, the war was not "over there"; the war was in their streets and on their country roads. Faithful Christians in the Netherlands could express themselves truthfully only in secret, private gatherings, and even then the truth itself was always dangerous. Resistance workers didn't want to know anything more than they absolutely had to know to function. They didn't want to know the real names of their accomplices, or how some things were acquired, or who was hiding where. From the *Gereformeerde Kerken* alone, 106 pastors were imprisoned; 20 of them died. Many more members of the *Gereformeerde Kerken* defied the Nazis and managed to protect and hide at least 3,000 Jews. At the same time, tragically, almost 110,000 Jews were transported to death camps, their decimation reducing the Jewish populace of the Netherlands by

80 percent, the highest percentage of loss in Europe.

During the occupation, Dutch Calvinists were more operative in the Resistance against the Nazi oppressors than any other segment of Dutch society, with the exception of the Mennonites and possibly the Marxists. When scholars today attempt to assess why certain people took on the danger of Resistance work while others chose not to, they can't help but notice certain facts. As David Gushee says in a recent article in *Holocaust and Genocide Studies*, "A disproportionate number of rescuers emerged from among the Reformed." But why? Gushee claims that some elements of Calvin's theology made association with the Dutch Jews easier for Calvinists than others.

> Most prominently mentioned in rescuer research is a strand of Christian thought that tended to produce a strong sense of religious kinship with Jews. This religious philosemitism particularly characterized rescuers from the Reformed (Calvinist) tradition, predominantly in the Netherlands and among the Protestants in France . . . , though occasionally it could also be found elsewhere. A strong sense of the chosenness of the Jewish people, of the value of what Christians call the Old Testament, and of God's covenantal involvement in Israel's past, present, and future marked this view.

Many of the immigrants who came to North America had firsthand experience of the dangers of Resistance work. Looking back on these events in 1945, a Christian schoolteacher wrote,

> We have now had almost four years of German occupation, and the terror which has been leveled against the populace in some segments of the country has been exceedingly bad. Thousands were shot to death because they tried to serve their country by illegal activity. . . . Tomorrow eleven young men will be buried in Burgentheim, and four of them are former students of this school. They were taken as hostages a few months ago and then shot to death. Tens and even hundreds of thousands of Netherlanders have been transported to Germany to work in the war industry, and who knows how many of those will ever return? Virtually all the Jews have been transported from Holland—most of them to work in the mercury mines of Poland where, by now, the greatest portion has probably been buried. Here in Holland almost every farm family has hidden some young folk who refused to work for the Germans.

This young schoolteacher, writing during the war, did not know the whole truth. Most of his Jewish neighbors were not being taken to mercury mines, but to Auschwitz, Buchenwald, and Bergen-Belzen. Perhaps the most famous Dutch Holocaust story is that of Anne Frank, a Jewish girl who wrote an unforgettable diary while hiding in a loft behind her father's business in Amsterdam. Like a hundred thousand other Dutch Jews, Anne Frank died in the camps.

World War II began more than a year earlier in the Netherlands than it did in the U.S. The May 10 invasion of the Netherlands in 1940 forced capitulation in just four days, but not before the heart of Rotterdam, a powerful port city, was obliterated by air bombardment. The Dutch monarch, Queen Wilhelmina, escaped to England with little more than her life and established a government in exile. Her country, meanwhile, suffered under a police state that enforced progressively greater restrictions on every facet of life. During the last hard winter—the Hunger Winter—of occupation, thousands of civilians died from hunger, cold, and exposure.

The Haring De Jong Family

The Haring De Jong family emigrated to southern Alberta in 1949 to work in the sugar beets in Iron Springs and soon joined the CRC. Years later their son Durk became a successful businessman in Calgary.

Durk recorded his memories of World War II in Friesland, offering a glimpse into the reality that many Dutch immigrants lived with during the war. He described the thud of German boots in the street and the soldiers nosing around the neighborhood for people who opposed the occupation. Because Durk was quite young when the war broke out, he didn't know until much later that his parents were hiding Jews right in the house where he lived and ate and slept.

Haring De Jong, Durk's father, served as a contact person for the Resistance. Once, much to his chagrin, a large box of guns and ammunition arrived without his foreknowledge. The boys opened it and were delighted: Now they could take on the Germans! Haring quickly hid the box under the coal in the shed, and although the Germans came searching for people in hiding, they didn't discover the cache.

Another resistance worker ran a woodworking shop that contained a lathe and a pile of sawdust. He was also involved in gathering intelligence for the Resistance, which included monitoring British radio broadcasts that carried coded messages. It was a crime for anyone to be caught with a contraband radio.

One day he was busy at his lathe when he heard German soldiers approaching. He quickly grabbed the radio he had been listening to, pushed it into the sawdust pile near his lathe, and was busy at work when the Germans entered and began interrogating him. He nonchalantly continued to run his lathe, but the vibration of the machine caused the sawdust pile to shake down. There, to his utter consternation, he saw the corner of his radio making its appearance. At that point all he could do was pray and attempt to keep the Germans' interest focused on himself. Fortunately it worked: the soldiers left and the man escaped with his life and the lives of his family. —TEH

When Canadian and other Allied troops captured the last German stragglers on Dutch soil in 1945, the Netherlands was a bankrupt wasteland. Flooded fields, gutted factories, and crumpled churches were all that was left on what once was a peaceful and picturesque landscape. Soon the initial euphoria of liberation gave way to the hard reality of reconstruction.

All of Europe was a charnel house. The crematoriums of Dachau were thrown open. General Dwight Eisenhower visited them and then exploded: "This makes me ashamed to be of German descent." A vast displaced populace trekked the roads and fields of western Europe, their eyes glazed from hunger and grief. Millions were dead.

North America responded. From the U.S. and Canada a huge relief effort took shape. Several agencies—the Red Cross, the National War Fund, and the United Jewish Appeal—poured aid into Europe. The United Jewish Appeal alone distributed over $122 million in aid between

The Dutch have continued to be grateful to Canadian troops for their part in the liberation of the Netherlands.

1946-47. Two committees of the CRC gathered about $430,000 to assist sister churches in the Netherlands, and many Dutch-Americans sent "care packages" to the Netherlands.

Private aid mailed across the ocean from cousin to cousin reestablished family bonds that had been neglected. The gratitude and goodwill that such assistance provided lingers even today. After receiving a gift package from the George Brinkerhof family in 1945, the Kor Kee family wrote back: "You have surprised us enormously. What delicious food and what beautiful dresses. . . . My wife danced around the room with the face soap because we had nearly forgotten that it existed. Again and again we had to sniff the aroma of the coffee beans. You have done very much for us. We don't know how to thank you."

For the people of the Netherlands, although the privations of war were the worst of many difficulties, liberation did not end their troubles. The Netherlands had had no significant reprieve from the worldwide Depression of the thirties, and shortly after the war, in 1949, the Dutch colony of Indonesia revolted and gained independence. Some 300,000 Dutch Indonesians and their sympathizers, who had lost the war, were permitted to resettle in the Netherlands, where many of them had never lived and therefore felt strange or odd. What's more, these newcomers joined a rapidly growing post-war populace who suffered inadequate housing and limited opportunities for economic growth.

War wounds didn't heal quickly. When some of those people the Resistance fighters considered Nazi sympathizers were either not punished or else found their way back into important and influential positions after the war, disillusionment grew into outrage. The future of the Netherlands seemed dismal, and a full third of the population considered emigration.

Ultimately 425,000 Dutch nationals left the Netherlands to resettle in Canada, Australia, the U.S., South Africa, and New Zealand. The Canadian and U.S. contingents (140 and 80 thousand, respectively) arrived between 1946 and 1952. About 20 percent of these were "orthodox Calvinists," people who, by profession, sought similar church fellowships in Canada and the U.S.

When the flood tide of Dutch immigrants rolled into Canada after the war, the CRC was able to expand its existing services and offer both Dutch-speaking pastors and some financial assistance to newly organized churches. Between 1947 and 1957 Canadian congregations multiplied from 13 to 107. By then post-war immigrants accounted for about 25 percent of the CRC's total membership. The denomination faced a new era, with a fresh supply of new members, many of whom had been shaped by wholly different personal experiences.

CHAPTER 17

Americanization and Canadianization

The 1997 *Yearbook* of the Christian Reformed Church states that Abbotsford, British Columbia, has six Christian Reformed churches. The city itself sits like a jewel in beautiful rolling foothills at the southern edge of the province, just a few miles north of the American border. Lynden, Washington, a quiet little town growing quickly and trying to market its nearly century-old Dutch heritage, sits just a bit south and west of Abbotsford, no more than a half hour away. The same *Yearbook* lists seven Christian Reformed churches in Lynden, a village of less than 10,000 people, considerably smaller than Abbotsford.

In 1995, fifty years after the end of World War II, I was part of a group who toured parts of Washington and British Columbia to perform *Things We Couldn't Say,* a readers theater version of the book by the same name—the story of Diet Eman, a Dutch Resistance worker during World War II. Because time was a factor in planning our performances, we tried to find a place on the national border where members of the Christian Reformed communities in both Abbotsford and Lynden could view the performance together, the distance between them being so small.

What we discovered was that planning for an event to bring a dozen or more churches from the two communities together wasn't simply a matter of transcending those few miles. It would be difficult to get a significant number of Canadians to come to Lynden, we were told, but it might well have been more difficult to get a significant number of Yankees to cross the border to the north. Even though hundreds of CRC members lived within a twenty-five-mile radius of the U.S./Canada border, rarely did their paths cross or meet.

It wasn't simply the necessity of packing a passport or birth certificate for the short jaunt north or south that kept the two communities—and fellowships—apart. The distance between Lynden and Abbotsford can be explained better in cultural terms than in geographical distance or national boundaries, for Abbotsford is what many in the CRC might still call "an immigrant community" today, nearly a half century after Dutch immigration ceased for the most part. Lynden, on the other hand, is a descendent of late nineteenth-century Dutch immigration, many of its first Dutch-American settlers having made their way west to the far edges of the continent after suffering through a series of dry and unproductive years in Charles Mix and Douglas counties

Families arriving from the Netherlands.

on the Great Plains of South Dakota a century ago. For the most part, Lynden folks belong to families that have been Americanized for more than a century; Abbotsford's Dutch-Canadian CRC members have been Canadians for no more than fifty years.

As we move into the most recent decades of the story of the Christian Reformed Church, we cannot simply assume that the tremendous growth of the denomination after World War II was a matter of statistics. It wasn't. What postwar immigration brought to the CRC was, in many ways, a collection of old-fashioned Calvinist views of Christianity that weren't really so much brand-new as they were refurbished and reupholstered to look like something else altogether. Theologically, many of the new immigrants were as Christian and Calvinist as the descendants of Scholte and Van Raalte; what's more, they shared a deep allegiance to Abraham Kuyper with those who'd come to America at the turn of the century. But culturally, they were so different that there remains more than a national border between Lynden and Abbotsford.

I hope you'll excuse what I'm about to do, but sometimes when I sit here, my fingers bent over the keys, I tell myself I've already written what I'm about to say, already tried to think this whole business through on paper. And I've arrived once again at one of those moments. What I'd like to do here in the story of the CRC is take time out to tell the story of two different CRC cultures with a personal essay I wrote years ago. It's a tribute to a woman I knew very well, Helen Hegeman, a Dutch immigrant who died a decade ago here on

the eastern edge of the American Great Plains. Following her funeral and committal, I read this to those who had gathered at our church. It's not a eulogy, but rather something of a meditation, I guess, on what I've come to understand is at least part of the explanation for the distance that lies between Abbotsford and Lynden, between St. Catharines and Pella, between Toronto and Grand Rapids.

"THE IMMIGRANT"

I was reared in the old way: as a child I was to be seen and not heard. But the old way has some perks, even for kids. Occasionally my attentive ears were privy to adult conversation, because to be seen and not heard is close to being completely forgotten. I remember one coffee-and-cookie conversation on a Sunday morning after church—it was late spring, maybe 1953 or '54. I sat there quietly with my cookie, listening to my folks talk about Calvin College with a pair of students from my hometown who were home for the summer.

"There's so many wetbacks around there now," one of those kids said, sneering.

My mother didn't understand. I could see it in her eyes. So did the college kid.

"We call 'em wetbacks—the Dutchies—they're just off the boat, ja?" he told her, laughing. He thought it was funny. So we all laughed, probably because laughing at supposed inferiors comes easy to just about everyone, especially when we don't really know who we're laughing at.

When the students were gone, I asked my father what a "wetback" was.

"An immigrant," he said, "somebody just over from the Netherlands."

Today we've buried an immigrant; we've laid her body in frozen prairie earth in a village cemetery thousands of miles from that woman's childhood, an ocean and more away from the world of her parents. Her own children are all grown now; they have their own families. They've developed homes and established roots of their own. But her husband is left here, and he is still an immigrant. Today he is alone.

"We should have come to Canada," she told me once, nodding as if there were absolutely no question about the fact of their mistake.

The comment was not an indictment of the United States—no vindictive condemnation of political principles or cultural values. She said it because she knew she was a "wetback," an immigrant, someone not entirely at home here in the U.S. She knew that Canada has more immigrants than northwest Iowa, more folks like her husband and herself, more kindred souls sharing the odd limbo of an immigrant life—strangers only awkwardly at home in what remains for them a strange world.

I didn't know any immigrants when I was a boy. There was only one old lady in our church whose speech was warbled by an accent, and she was something of a witch to me, not a good-looking woman, slightly eccentric, in fact—a woman my father claimed had never really shaken the Old World idea that she was upper class. So when I was growing up, I knew nothing about immigrants, except that immigrants were something of an embarrassment to those of us who weren't—"wetbacks," those college kids had called them, "Dutchies."

Then, during my own college years I met immigrants personally. In the late sixties they generally had a less extensive wardrobe than most Americans, so they didn't dress quite up to snuff. Often they had peculiar accents and laughed at strange things. They smoked more—men and women, in a time when only really tough girls lit up. Often they were more bold in the classroom, more determined to understand and less driven by grades than we were. Many of them seemed to carry a whole different attitude toward college, as if it were really something of a calling—and yet not so. I think they were more serious about ideas, ideas for ideas' sake. Most of us considered college a kind of high school with homework.

Canadian Immigration and the CRC

In 1945, with the onset of European emigration after the war, Canada opened up its doors to thousands of Dutch immigrants, many of whom were Reformed. Most of those Reformed immigrants came from *De Gereformeerde Kerken*, a denomination with very close historical and ecumenical ties to the Christian Reformed Church. The Dutch were particularly attracted to Canada because the Canadian army had a major role in the liberation of the Netherlands.

Paul De Koekkoek, an American and pastor of the First CRC of Edmonton, Alberta, challenged the CRC to use this opportunity to launch a major ministry in Canada. A visionary and an activist, De Koekkoek carried on his crusade for ministry to the prospective immigrants through a personal publishing venture, *The Canadian Calvinist*, a mimeographed, two-page, single-sheet paper that he put out monthly and financed by personal gifts. Each month he presented new ideas about what ought to be done, urging the denomination to establish a distinct denominational committee on immigration.

His message got through. On the recommendation of the board, the Synod of 1946 approved the establishment of the Immigration Committee for Canada, exactly as De Koekkoek had urged.

—TEH

Through the years I listened to them explain what they called "the Perspective"—some kind of unifying philosophy they used to measure ideas and even people—a kind of tool for determining righteousness. To me, a perspective was simply the view from a high hill. *Perspective*, I learned, was something more than a scenic overlook to them. I'd never thought about philosophy before college. I'd been too busy playing basketball. They thought playing basketball was dumb. I hadn't really known kids who thought playing basketball was stupid.

And they had the language, of course. Sometimes, these children of the immigrants would laugh at word jokes no American kid caught. And sometimes I knew they were laughing at us—the Americans—for our own ways, maybe for simply being American, something I'd never laughed at myself.

My grandmother was a lifelong member of the American Legion Auxiliary because her brother was killed by a grenade in France just a couple months before Armistice Day, 1918. My own father spent two uniformed years in the Pacific theater during World War II, away from his young wife and children. To me, being an American meant being the recipient of a heritage that, by their estimation—and they were more than willing to tell me so—wasn't always in harmony with that weapon they called "Perspective." There was nothing really wrong with being an American as far

An immigrant family in Iron Springs, Alberta.

as I could see; but to them there was something wrong, terribly wrong, with thinking like one. I had never been aware that there could be a difference between "being one" and "thinking like one," and my first reaction to their criticism was that they were the strange ones. They were thinking like Hollanders—"Dutchies"—not Americans at all. It took years for me to understand that what they called "Perspective" had little to do with nation of origin.

In the company of my immigrant friends at college, I sat through hours of war stories, stories of the Nazi cancer eating away at the vitality of the occupied country where their parents had lived. I heard about hiding Jews and lying righteously. I heard about murders and Nazi vengeance. And then I heard about immigration. Over coffee richly creamed, I heard countless stories of what it had been like to come to North America with no money and no language—I learned firsthand about the cultural poverty created when a people lacked the commodity of words.

Slowly the mind of the immigrant began to emerge from the caricature I'd picked up as a boy. Slowly that mind shaped my own, forced me to question my loyalties, pushed me to look at a world larger than the four-square dimensions of a quiet and supportive village of mirrors where the greatest theological enemies were the folks in the church down the street, the one you didn't attend, a village where the gymnasium sometimes seemed far more important than the church.

The woman we've buried today once told me this story. She became very concerned about a strike somewhere in the area—maybe it was the Iowa Beef Packers.

One day she told a lady from her church— "We ought to be in prayer about that situation," she said.

Her friend looked at her. "But there's no one from our church involved in that strike, is there?" her friend said.

The world of difference between those two comments is itself a portrait of the new world faced by many Dutch Reformed immigrants who entered a religious culture that simply didn't see themselves, their world, or their place in that world in at all similar ways.

At least three forces shaped the immigrant mind in ways that Americans don't clearly understand. First, Abraham Kuyper and his followers—professors Dooyeweerd and Vollenhoven, professors of philosophy at the Free University, Amsterdam. From Kuyper and his followers—the neo-Kuyperians—those immigrant students gleaned what they called their "Perspective," a philosophy of life and a philosophical system, something few Americans had ever thought about.

Second, the Nazis—who devoured everything but the spirit of their Dutch hosts. The Netherlands was occupied during World War II, occupied by a brute force that ground Dutch life to a halt for five years. This woman's tearful confession of stealing in order to stay alive during those years is something I will never forget.

And third, the experience of immigration. Immigration can sound so noble when it happened to ancestors whose sepia-toned pictures collect dust on our library shelves. But immigration is displacement of the first order—a willful severance of family ties, national loyalties, and the heritage of home, and an immersion in a culture altogether new and foreign and sometimes even hostile. Immigrants are, let's remember, wetbacks, and many of us who are Americans, established on North American soil for a century or more, felt little but disdain for what we might have considered their dowdiness.

My own immigrant great-grandfather is buried a dozen miles from here in another village cemetery. More than a century ago he took his family across—wetbacks. So for more than one hundred years my family has been American. Today, Terschelling, the Dutch island he came from, is to me nothing more than a fond memory of a two-day visit a few years ago. Four generations of Schaaps have settled into this country. America is, for better or for worse, my home; in these flatlands are my own ethnic and familial roots, as well as those of most of this immigrant woman's children.

Only a few months ago I sat on a long wooden bench in a museum in Philadelphia. The bench had been taken from Ellis Island, New York, the first stop for millions of European immigrants in the late nineteenth century. At one time ancestors from both sides of my family must have sat on those very benches waiting for some American official to call out Dutch names he couldn't hope to pronounce correctly.

Sitting there on that bench thrilled me, took me back to what must have been an anxious and fearful time in my own family's history, a time I could only imagine, sitting there as they must have. But try as I might, I will never know the cross-currents of being adopted into another country—of being an immigrant.

Today we laid a body to rest in frozen earth that is for her no more a home than this

Iowa prairie ever was, the same cemetery where just yesterday two grieving parents left an infant child in some adjacent plot. It's helpful, finally, for us to remember that we are all immigrants—no matter how far back we can trace our proud ancestry. No one stays here for long.

I remember a plaque that used to hang upstairs in my childhood home. The words were in English, but this woman we've buried today knew its lesson in two languages. "Only one life will soon be past," it said; "only what's done for Christ will last."

That "perspective," rooted in Christ's gift of grace, turns us all into wetback pilgrims.

IMMIGRATION

The CRC's dual nationalities became increasingly obvious as Canadian congregations grew and multiplied in the postwar years. The number of churches north of the border leaped from 30 in 1949 to 158 in 1970. New arrivals, about fourteen thousand families during this era, overwhelmed the thirteen Canadian congregations that had organized before the war.

While earlier Canadian settlers had exerted little influence on the denomination, the postwar group, by its sheer size as well as its tenacious hold on neo-Kuyperian principles, created all kinds of effects on a denomination that was itself just recovering from the experience of war. Many Canadian Calvinists were determined to mark their adopted land with a Kuyperian stamp; they had well-established ideas about Calvinism's potential for influencing national values and institutions. Some of these folks had fought Nazis hand-to-hand; they'd carried out armed robberies after asking the

Memorial to a First Church

❦

The spot where the first CRC in Canada was built is marked by a huge memorial rock in full view of the final resting place of the pioneers. The rock was placed there in a cooperative effort of the Nobleford CRC and of the province of Alberta.

On October 10, 1992, as a bone-chilling wind swept the prairie setting, the rock was dedicated to the memory of the pioneers who established the Monarch Christian Reformed Church. The brass plaque reads as follows:

> *Original Site of the First Christian Reformed Church in Canada. The founding members came from the Netherlands, many of them via the United States, to claim homesteads which had become available here near the turn of the century. The congregation was organized by the settlers on November 16, 1905, as the* Nijverdal Christelijke Gereformeerde Kerk. *The frame church, dedicated on May 20, 1909, as the Monarch Christian Reformed Church, has been preserved and restored in the Prairie Tractor and Engine Society Park south of Picture Butte. The congregation has relocated in the town of Nobleford.* —TEH

Lord's blessing on their endeavors. Some had hidden Jews at their own peril, and, under cover of darkness, ferried Allied pilots out of occupied Europe. They had watched their friends be murdered by Nazi henchmen. Most of these people had felt the jackboot at their necks.

And when they came to North America, what they found was a denomination fearfully obsessed with the danger of a movie marquee, a deck of cards, and a step or two on a dance floor. They'd had to fight to stay alive during that last horrendous "hunger winter" of 1945, but what they discovered here was the deep fear that a local grocery store might stay open on Sunday. They'd risked their own families' health and well-being in order to hide Jews, people whose Christ-denying faith they overlooked for the sake of their common humanity, and what they discovered here was people who thought using a common vulgarity for excrement was a mark of real sin. They were—many of them—a rough-hewn and independent people, folks who'd snubbed their noses at the SS. And when they came to North America, what they found was a denomination full of smilers, sweet people whose piety they couldn't help but judge as being superficial at best, nonsensical at worst.

It's no wonder that, even today, the distance between Abbotsford and Lynden is much greater than it seems on a map.

So why did they choose to affiliate with the Christian Reformed Church? Three reasons. First, because in confession and creed, the CRC, in Canada especially, was much closer to what they'd come from than the Lutherans or the United Church of Canada. For example, the GKN and the CRC recognized each other as sister churches. Second, because of the language. What the American

François Guillaume (1905-1972)

For François Guillaume, coming to Canada was somewhat of an accident. As Dutch ministers began serving in Canada, churches discovered that older men were having a difficult time learning English—an important requirement for carrying out their task. So Canadian churches established a general rule that the ministers they called from the Netherlands had to be under forty. The counselors for calling churches were to see to it that the "rule" was carried out.

When Guillaume appeared on the scene as the minister-elect of Rehoboth CRC of Toronto, the colloquium doctum discovered that he was already forty-eight! But he was also in Toronto, along with his wife, children, and belongings. There was no thought of sending him back, so the colloquium proceeded, and he was admitted to the ministry of the CRC in Canada.

Rev. and Mrs. F. Guillaume and family. Second and third from the left are Mr. and Mrs. J. Vande Veen, the son-in-law and daughter of the Guillaumes, who remained in Amsterdam.

It was clear that the Rehoboth congregation was set on calling Guillaume, for he was a man of great reputation: he was a genuine hero who had suffered in the German death camp of Dachau. But it was also clear that he did have a struggle with the language. In order to present an acceptable English sermon he would write it in Dutch, translate it into English, and then have his manuscript edited by the local Presbyterian minister.

One Sunday he was to preach on the petition of the Lord's prayer, "Give us this day our daily bread." Being a very practical sermonizer and given to striking and catchy themes, he chose to preach on *"De brandende brood vraagstuck"*, which he literally translated as "The Burning Bread Question"! His Presbyterian friend wrote in the margin: "What is that? Toast?"

Eventually Guillaume did learn the language and became, as did many of his Dutch colleagues, an outstanding pastor and leader. People in the area said Toronto had three ministers, one of whom was *de dogmaticus* (the dogmatician), one *de boetprediker* (the fire-and-brimstone preacher), and Guillaume, *de trooster* (the comforter). Given his experience in Dachau, perhaps that's not surprising.

—TEH

CRC was able to put together was a means to bring this new generation of immigrants into fellowships led by Dutch-speaking preachers who'd been born into the CRC in the U.S. Third, because the CRC helped them through the difficult process of immigration.

Emigration, after all, took a toll. There was, first of all, the leave-taking. If not all members of any particular family were determined to leave the Netherlands, family strife almost inevitably followed any talk of emigrating to Canada or the U.S.

But even if everyone in the family agreed to go, problems were inevitable. Money, for example. The Dutch government believed that difficulties and changes in agriculture in the Netherlands would inevitably lead to surplus workers, so, in 1948, they inaugurated a system of minimum financial support for families choosing to leave. That helped. But some individuals and families needed to put all their resources into emigration, which meant that they often arrived at their new country penniless. Some learned that restrictions on how much money they could take out of the country adjusted their economic status significantly downward when they came to Canada.

Then there were health restrictions. What happened if a family decided to go, but then discovered that one of them couldn't pass the necessary health inspections? Did the entire family stay? Should one be left behind? Families tried to assure Canadian officials that the one member would never be a ward of the state or a tax upon the system, but the law was clear and held to tenaciously.

Even though the war itself had taken an incredible toll on Dutch life, immigration meant abandoning some of the most valuable artifacts of one's life. Every last possession had to be evaluated; many of them discarded. The farm had to be sold, equipment auctioned. And then there were the farewells. The excitement of possibilities was negated, at least for a time, by the woe of having to say goodbye to so many old friends. The emotional peaks and valleys were immense and unforgettable.

The beginning of Canadianization was made easier for postwar immigrants by the efforts of individuals called "fieldmen," who were almost always members of the Christian Reformed Church. Most fieldmen assumed that economic viability was the first step toward making immigrants safe and happy. They often kept the people in particular areas, sometimes even bringing more new settlers into a region or area than could be supported; but they did so with an eye toward the eventual establishment of a church, a community.

Occasionally, clashes occurred. Christian Reformed fieldmen were sometimes criticized by the immigrants themselves for being *too* interested in establishing a church; in contrast, some in the denomination felt the fieldmen were far too interested in the physical well-being of the immigrants, and not as profoundly concerned with the state of their souls.

But Herman Ganzevoort says, "It was clear that Dutch Protestant immigrants desired to retain their religious heritage in their new land," an attitude verified by the establishment of Christian Reformed churches in Canada during this period. "Without the American concern, financial support, and staffing of missionaries and ministers," Ganzevoort says, "the Dutch Protestants in Canada would have had an extremely difficult time maintaining their traditional beliefs."

Nonetheless, the strain of finding new jobs—sometimes far down the economic ladder from prior occupational experiences in the Netherlands—was very difficult. Establishing new businesses in a new land was adventuresome, but terribly risky and always scary, especially when an entire family's livelihood depended upon economic success. Poverty ceaselessly threatened. Oral histories of the first postwar immigrants to Canada are memorable, replete with both tragedy and triumph.

While the CRC in the United States was gradually pulling itself together after the war, its neighbors to the north were establishing themselves in a foreign country, creating livelihoods, putting down roots, tending their families. These newcomers—from the moment they came ashore—and their established ethnic relatives to the south were brothers and sisters in the faith, but their radically different experiences would never make them much more than kissing cousins.

As someone who has taught for twenty years at an educational institution closely related to the CRC, as someone who went to college with the children of immigrants myself, I must admit that distinguishing between Canadian and American kids becomes more difficult every year. It used to be almost obvious; today, in a class of twenty, even after they've been seated in their chairs for three weeks and I've read some of their essays, I may not know which is which. Certainly, one of the major themes in the story of the Christian Reformed Church in North America is Americanization. One can't tell the story without referring to the power of acculturization in a new nation. That same process, with a different name—Canadianization—is now occurring north of the border. Despite the significant differences between the Canadian and American Christian Reformed churches in history, culture, and experience, their children are slowly becoming less distinguishable.

THE POSTWAR ERA

Historians may be inclined to overemphasize the significance of wars, but World War II did change both national and international conditions profoundly. During the postwar era from 1946 to the late sixties, the world was polarized between East and West, while the dismantled colonial empires of the nineteenth century became the Third World. When the war ended in 1945, the United States stood unrivaled in both military and industrial power, and until the sixties the nation experienced a unified vision of itself and its mission in the world. By contrast, Europe, including Russia, was in shambles. Although the first meeting of the United Nations in 1946 suggested a hopeful future, within three short years the Berlin blockade and airlift symbolized new tensions that led directly to rearmament. Large populations already displaced by war were again set afoot by the Russian occupation of Eastern Europe and fears of another war.

By 1949, after Russia had already tested its own atomic bomb, NATO was organized to curb further Russian expansion. Between 1949 and 1952, the U.S. expended over 30 billion dollars for European recovery and rearmament, while China moved into the Russian orbit. The Korean War broke out in 1950, and once again Western troops assembled in the Orient, this time to enforce the Truman doctrine of Communist containment. With that, the postwar era assumed the bipolar contours that remained entrenched until the fall of the Berlin Wall and the eventual demise of the Union of Soviet Socialist Republics in 1991.

The rhetoric of that era—which branded Russia as atheistic, tyrannical, and anti-Christian, and the U.S. as democratic, generous, and Christian—also persisted. Such extreme characterizations cannot accurately describe whole peoples and nations, but there was no disputing the atheism of Russian Communism or the religious tilt of the U.S. toward Christianity. So America's churches, among them the CRC, enthusiastically supported anticommunism; in that arena the government's policies seemed entirely compatible with the advancement of the Christian religion.

These perceptions intensified the national loyalty of an already patriotic CRC. All of the denominationally related publications (*The Banner, De Wachter, The Canadian Calvinist, Calvin Forum,* and, after 1951, *Reformed Journal* and *Torch and Trumpet*) opposed communism, for on that issue their general views were alike. The facts seemed obvious: the New World, Canada included, had preserved Western democracies, but a new and even greater challenge demanded a thorough discrediting of Marxism and the containment of its practitioners. In that effort North America and its NATO allies were considered righteous warriors in a worldwide struggle with a virtual Antichrist.

With these assumptions, the CRC in the United States embraced, as it never had before, a main tenet of American civil religion—that the U.S. was a nation chosen by God to represent God's truth around the world. That theme originated among New England's Puritans in the seventeenth century and was secularized by the patriots of the Revolutionary War. The creed of that secular faith was embedded in the Declaration of Independence and the U.S. Constitution. Wars, from 1812 to Korea, had sanctified the creed with successful efforts to preserve the Constitution and spread democracy at home and abroad. Over the years U.S. policies and Christianity became so intertwined that patriotism and national loyalty were virtually linked with Christian doctrines.

Still, throughout much of its history in the U.S., the CRC resisted the assumption that America was, like Israel, a chosen nation. Even during World War II, the CRC's leading journalists criticized the nation's foreign policies and leaders. Though the church was loyal to its country, Christ was its master, and he had established independent values and priorities that could and did conflict with national policies. Henry Schultze, H. J. Kuiper, E. J. Tanis, and others advised their readers to view the conflict from a Christian rather than exclusively nationalistic perspective. But during the Cold War these same authors expressed little concern as the CRC increasingly linked its identity with the nation's.

Objections to such an exclusive nationalism came from the more recent immigrants, a new and rapidly expanding segment of the denomination. Already in 1942, a *Banner* correspondent in Lacombe, Alberta, objected to language used in denominational reports that described Canadians as "foreigners." S. G. Brondsema correctly noted that from his perspective the U.S. was also a foreign land. He urged the elimination of terminology that emphasized the national segments of the church, "rather than our unity in Christ."

Because of the close friendships I've made with Canadian CRC members, because I've heard them bristle at rampant nationalism in Christian Reformed churches, I understand what they feel. It is impossible for me to worship comfortably in an American CRC around either Memorial Day or Independence Day, to hear someone play or sing "My Country 'Tis of Thee" or "The Battle Hymn of the Republic," and not be ashamed of our acceptance of the basic tenets of American civil religion. But I know that many, many Americans would bristle just as fully at that criticism. My grandmother, whose only brother died in France in 1918, would be livid if someone suggested that the flag and "The Battle Hymn of the Republic" had no place in church. Many Canadians visiting south of the border feel uncomfortable in a church where the American flag stands proudly behind the pulpit; some Americans would leave the church rather than remove the flag from the sanctuary.

The matter of the CRC's dual nationality became increasingly obvious as Canadian congregations grew and multiplied, thereby increasing their size and strengthening their voice at annual synods. No longer simply objects of Yankee CRC aid, the Canadians became, increasingly, their own substantial power force in church politics. Differences in voting patterns became evident. Almost immediately the politics of synod changed drastically—the Canadians were often of one mind on issues while the Americans

---

The Sarnia Connection

It is amazing how some very modest initiatives at times develop into very striking and cherished realities. Such was the case with the pastorate of Rev. A. B. C. Hofland in Second CRC, Sarnia, Ontario. Hofland was a GKN transfer to the CRC who took with him a well-developed Kuyperianism with a Dooyeweerdian connection. His influence, and that of others who were disciples of H. Evan Runner, made of Second Sarnia "a veritable hotbed of Reformational thinking," to quote Bert Witvoet, editor of *Christian Courier.*

As a result several young people, none with any university training and all self-educated in their philosophical thinking, began to develop an intense interest and involvement in Christian labor unionism and Christian action in general. In the early sixties they became involved in the Christian Labour Association of Canada.

In fact, six members of this group from Second Sarnia rose to leading positions in the CLAC: Gerald Vandezande, Harry Antonides, Stan de Jong, Ed Vander Kloet, and Co Vanderlaan were all CLAC agents in the sixties; Jim Joose became the first chairman of the CLAC board.

Some of these men went on to have significant careers in other kingdom service. Jim Joose was ordained as a CRC minister. Gerald Vandezande took a leadership role in the Committee for Public Justice (in Canada). Stan de Jong became the publisher of *Christian Courier.* Harry Antonides served as director of research for the CLAC and as director of the Work Research Foundation for twenty-five years, researching Christian perspectives on industrial relations and economics.

All this came out of the resourceful study and reflection of new Canadians who, as good Calvinists, began to seriously apply their faith to life. That they were new to the land and minimally educated did not deter their efforts to claim the ground for Christ.   —TEH

Andrew Kuyvenhoven

Although there is only one Andrew Kuyvenhoven, he is, in a unique fashion, an excellent representative of the post-war generation of Dutch Christians who have affiliated with the Christian Reformed Church. A surprising number of current denominational leaders came to us from the Netherlands after World War II.

Andrew came to Canada in 1952 at the age of twenty-three, and candidly admits that the most prominent reason for his immigration was an infatuation with Ena Heerema, who had immigrated to Alberta with her family. Later Ena would become his wife.

Before immigrating Kuyvenhoven had completed studies at the Free University which would have led him to the legal profession. That training is still evident in his writings and preaching.

Not long after his arrival in Canada, Kuyvenhoven changed directions and left law for training in the gospel ministry at Calvin Seminary. Like so many of his peers, he was quickly assimilated into North American culture. In contrast to previous generations, the post-war immigrants spent far less time looking back to the old world and quickly adjusted to a new culture, a different society, and the English language.

After graduating in 1958 from the seminary, Kuyvenhoven served five Canadian churches in thirty-four years of active ministry. As a preacher he was colorful and candid, frequently giving evidence in his delivery of a droll sense of humor. He was thoroughly Reformed in his application of Scripture, a pastor who set the spiritual development of his parishioners as a goal. Disdaining cloying sentimentality, he, nevertheless, maintained a mystical bent. With Kuyvenhoven, it was substance, not style. In an age when even in the church politics was rampant, he remained straightforward and guileless.

Kuyvenhoven's gifts were recognized by the denomination. He served Christian Reformed Church Publications in the Education Department from 1971-1976. Then, after a brief pastorate in Clarkson, Ontario, he returned to Grand Rapids to serve as *Banner* editor for ten years.

His *Banner* editorials were lucid, insightful, sometimes controversial. Particularly famous is one of his early editorials in which he asked for a self-ignited holocaust by suggesting that it was time to "burn the wooden shoes" as a symbol of too much one-sided ethnicity in the Christian Reformed Church. His editorials never straddled the fence. His readers always knew where he stood.

Kuyvenhoven published several exegetical Bible studies and books of meditation, including *Daylight* and *Twilight*. He also wrote a commentary on the Heidelberg Catechism entitled *Comfort and Joy*. In retirement he is much sought after as a speaker at rallies and conventions.

The CRC is a richer church for having Andrew Kuyvenhoven in it.　　　　—WDB

were rather obviously and even equally divided—which, in turn, put the newest members of the CRC in a power position. Life in the decision-making sectors of the CRC would never be the same.

In addition, the new immigrants' more commonly held worldview inspired them to look closely and critically at Canadian culture and to organize parent-controlled schools at all levels, Christian labor organizations, political parties, and a Reformed press. Similar objectives had also inspired the stateside CRC, particularly between 1900 and 1920; but apart from the Christian school movement, the Kuyperian institutions in the States enjoyed only sporadic success. On that account, the Dutch-Canadian Calvinists often found their American brothers and sisters deficient—and told them so.

The Canadians were also chagrined by the paternalism they experienced in affiliating with the CRC. Until they became organized churches with independent classes, the Canadian congregations were supervised by the CRC's Home Missions Board. That arrangement dated from 1926, when the small and widely scattered congregations of Canada could more legitimately be perceived as mission churches. But the huge influx of Dutch immigrants after World War II included many active and experienced church officers who certainly had never considered themselves the objects of missionary activity.

In 1979, Rev. Andrew Kuyvenhoven, a postwar immigrant, recalled the early days of Canadian immigration:

> *We will always remain grateful to the Home Missionaries and fieldmen who picked us up at ship docks, railroad stations, and airports, and who took us to our first Canadian homes. It is true that some of us were irritated that these American ministers called themselves "missionaries," as if we were unchurched and unChristian, but all of us have a warm spot for them. Those men and their wives were our founding fathers and mothers.*
>
> *The goals of the missionaries and fieldmen were simple and straightforward: the immigrants needed jobs, houses, churches, and schools, in that order. They carted and bused and raked us together, so that we would talk together, live together, worship together, and build together. These clear but short-range goals have now been reached. We got our jobs, houses, churches, and schools. Within twenty-five years we got it all. Let God be praised.*

PRESSURES AND TENSIONS

But while they were "getting it all," many Dutch Canadians never forgot that they were direct descendants of the *Doleantie,* and, even more importantly for some of them, a revitalized neo-Kuyperian vision. Described variously as neo-Kuyperian, Reformational, or by the phrase "the philosophy of the law idea" or *Wetsidee,* this movement attracted zealous followers in the Netherlands and North America. By 1952, a major segment of neo-Kuyperians clustered at Calvin College and Seminary, where they were preparing for careers in education and the ministry. Their leading spokesperson, Professor Evan Runner, had been schooled at the Free University of Amsterdam, where notable professors like Herman Dooyeweerd and D. H. T. Vollenhoven devoted their intellectual efforts to the further development of Abraham Kuyper's theories. Following his studies with Dooyeweerd, Runner joined Calvin's faculty. Together with his students of a similar mind, he became, as we've said before, a virtual missionary for neo-Kuyperian ideals. The Groen Van Prinsterer Club founded by Runner and his students discussed strategies for teaching and implementing neo-Kuyperianism in Canada and the U.S.

The Groen Club, though, did not encounter an immediately receptive audience because the CRC had already adjusted its own Netherlandic and Kuyperian tradition to North America. In one sense, the different cultural tradition of the Groen Club members kept them at odds with peers who might well have been like-minded; sadly, within the church or without, a species of bigotry kept American Kuyperians aloof from the neo-Kuyperians. On the other hand, these neo-Kuyperians, perhaps in response to being patronized, took a sometimes arrogant attitude toward the Americans sitting across the table. During my college years, I remember hearing frequent claims that Calvin College was not at all Reformed. That criticism came not so much from confessional conservatives, who had their own reasons for picking apart the denominational college, but from neo-Kuyperians, who didn't think at all about Calvin being "liberal," but often judged it just as harshly for being "not Reformed."

Cutting through that rhetoric was difficult for me—and for many others. In light of where the CRC has gone since the fifties—and where it may be heading—it's instructive to piece together something of a scorecard here, in terms of the mind-sets we've already established.

When the CRC in the U.S. began to regain its composure following World War II, two camps, already in place during the denominational wars of the twenties, began to form once again. One of these camps, the Confessionalists, or those we've characterized as Inward-looking believers, created their own journal to reach those who were of like mind. That magazine, *Torch and Trumpet,* called its readers to the idea of the antithesis, the distinctions between the Kingdom of Christ and the kingdom of the world. Above all else, *Torch and Trumpet* valued orthodoxy, that is, strict commitment to the doctrines and creeds of the Reformed tradition. Its leaders were wary of making ties to contemporary cultural movements and wanted to deemphasize the significance of the old common grace argument. They saw compromise with the world as compromise with sin, and found worthy opponents in those who would, for instance, open stores and restaurants on Sundays. Like their Kuyperian colleagues on the other side of the political spectrum, they defined being "in the world" as taking a part in its development; but unlike the descendants of the century's earlier Kuyperians, they tended to zero in on those conflicts in which the creeds and traditional beliefs of the church were most obviously threatened. Sometimes they cared more about

Sabbatarianism, for instance, than economic systems. And they were not alone; they found willing and able allies among the Orthodox Presbyterians and other conservative Calvinist fellowships whose roots grew more fully from American Calvinism than European Calvinism.

At least at first, the neo-Kuyperians, the more recent immigrants, found the *Torch and Trumpet*'s investment in tradition and confessional orthodoxy wearying and pietistic. They would have said that while such conservative Confessionalists called themselves "Kuyperians," their fear of dancing as a growing problem facing the CRC was ludicrous. To waste energy on opposing dancing while the culture of narcissistic individualism was taking everyone to hell was "majoring in the minors." The rhetoric became even stronger. To preach strict Sabbatarianism when materialism was clouding Reformed minds through the growing strength of the media was, to some of the more ardent neo-Kuyperians, nothing less than sin. And they weren't afraid to say so.

On the other hand, a score of thoughtful CRC academics, assuming that God's common grace to all humanity provided a vehicle for cooperation with secular culture, created the *Reformed Journal,* a publication that pulled denominational thought in a wholly different direction from the *Torch and Trumpet.* For the *Reformed Journal* crowd, existing political parties, labor

The Reformed Journal,
a progressive voice in the CRC.

unions, and social reform movements were potential allies in an effort to inject both Christian and Reformed influences into national culture.

The neo-Kuyperians north of the border never felt particularly comfortable with their more progressive American CRC brothers and sisters; they often considered the *Journal* crowd far too willing to forsake the principles of a truly and deeply Reformed critique of society. What's more, they associated that group with snobbish and pseudo-sophisticated, affluent Grand Rapids culture, specifically with those individual scholars who joked most deftly at the expense of people whose more "Reformational" views they perceived as silly and idealistic, based too firmly on Dutch culture. The neo-Kuyperians understood, with some validity, that the *Reformed Journal* crowd found them not sufficiently "American."

All of this may seem esoteric, but what's important in the story we're telling here is the split (and eventual weakening) of the mind of those who came to represent the Kuyperian or *Doleantie* tradition in the CRC. All three—the new immigrant neo-Kuyperians, the more academic *Reformed Journal*ists, as well as the *Torch and Trumpeters,* considered themselves soundly within the Calvinist tradition of looking at the big picture—the kingdom—as opposed to simply looking at one's personal relationship with Jesus. Ironically, all three wanted to build community. All three were interested in a more definitively Christian society.

But their visions were different. The neo-Kuyperians considered *Torch and Trumpet*'s Confessional Kuyperians, with their emphasis on the old prohibitions against "worldly amusements," far too pietistic for the brave new world everyone was facing. Meanwhile, they called the *Reformed Journal* crowd "unReformed." The *Torch and Trumpet* Confessionalists considered both the neo-Kuyperians and the *Reformed Journal* people too liberal. The *Reformed Journal* folks agreed with the neo-Kuyperians about the silliness of the Confessionalists' preoccupation with issues like dancing, but thought the neo-Kuyperians were "Johnny-come-lately"

idealists, with downright embarrassing brogues.

What's more, as time went on, the relatively solid mind that characterized the Canadian CRC began to break apart. The views of the American Confessionalists—the Inward-looking believers—began to find a more receptive following among Canadian CRC people, nurtured, at least in part, by what many of them considered the growing apostasy of the Dutch church they'd left behind, as well as the excesses of what they considered their own fine educational gift to North America, the Institute for Christian Studies in Toronto.

Throughout the fifties and the early sixties, these separate mind-sets kept picking and picking at each other, setting

The Institute for Christian Studies

The Dutch immigrant movement into Canada after World War II swelled the number of Canadian CRC congregations from twelve to well over one hundred in a few short years, bringing many idealistic Kuyperians into the membership of the CRC. It was their goal to claim all of Canada for Christ's kingdom, beginning with the field of education. That meant establishing Christian schools immediately and a Christian university as soon as possible.

Four men met in October 1955 to talk about a university: two ministers, François Guillaume and Henry Venema, and two businessmen, Peter Speelman and Casper Vanderiet. Less than a year later the movement that would one day give birth to a university was officially organized. For the next ten years the Association for the Advancement of Christian Scholarship (as it eventually was called) promoted its ideals through the sponsorship of study conferences throughout Canada. By 1967, twelve years after the four men first met, the Institute for Christian Studies was founded in Toronto with one professor, Dr. Henk Hart. A few other students about to graduate from the Free University of Amsterdam were eager to join the Institute. All were protégés of Dr. Evan Runner, a professor of philosophy at Calvin College and an ardent follower of Professor Herman Dooyeweerd of the Free University. They included Bernard Zylstra, James Olthuis, and later, Arnold De Graaf, Calvin Seerveld, and C. T. McIntire.

In 1975 the Institute granted its first Master of Philosophical Foundations degree to six graduates. Eventually the ICS was able to offer a Ph.D. program, with instruction given in Toronto and a formal degree granted by the Free University of Amsterdam.   —TEH

the stage for the warfare to come in the last twenty years of our history. More on that later.

Apart from philosophical differences, any discussion of international affairs included Canadian/U.S. relations. The economic dominance of the U.S. fueled discontent among the Canadians. For the Canadian immigrants, but especially for their children, nationalism became a potent fact of life. In that context, the 1966 organization of the Council of the Christian Reformed Church in Canada was a predictable development. Though short of an actual regional synod, the Council was pledged to "speak with a strong voice on many contemporary national issues." Its agenda includes official contacts with the Canadian government, spiritual attention for members in the military service, and interdenominational relationships.

The binational character of the CRC is, however, a distinctive and wholesome feature of the denomination because it restrains excessive nationalism and reminds us that the church of Christ is universal. Andrew Kuyvenhoven spoke perceptively to that issue when he declared, "I cannot help warning you and myself against the feelings of nationalism. Nationalism is an old enemy of the church. It has made fools of godly people. We must be thankful that we have an international church and do what we can to preserve it."

The immigrants of the fifties arrived during an exceptionally prosperous era. From the war's end and well into the sixties, economic growth and wages rose steadily. Both in Canada and the U.S.,

family incomes doubled between 1950 and 1969, while inflation averaged about 3 percent. In the U.S., the gross national product grew from $250 billion in 1949 to $934 billion in 1969. Canada experienced a similar growth rate as its GNP mounted from $17 to $83 billion.

This amazing prosperity affected the CRC quite directly. In Canada alone about 140 congregations acquired or constructed sanctuaries, and their parishioners also organized sixty-four Christian schools. In the States, over 200 new congregations organized during this era, and they built 112 new schools. In all, then, the CRC gained 240 congregations. The number of denominational families grew from twenty-nine thousand in 1945 to sixty-two thousand in 1969.

DENOMINATIONAL MINISTRIES: OPPORTUNITY AND GROWTH

In the 1950s and '60s, major denominational agencies expanded greatly as both domestic and foreign programs blossomed. Foreign Mission Board employees, scattered from South America to Japan and Africa, grew from a scant dozen in 1945 to over 150 in 1969. Similarly, the Calvin College and Seminary faculty expanded from 30 to 180. The denominational budget also soared as the $19 quotas—now called "ministry shares"—of 1945 grew to $118 per family in 1969—a six-fold increase.

For one agency alone, the Back to God Hour, quota allotments rose from sixty thousand dollars in 1945 to seven hundred thousand dollars at the end of the sixties. That growth was due largely to the abilities of radio minister Rev. Peter

Calvin College Radio Choir of the Back to God Hour, ca. 1955.

Eldersveld, who joined the fledgling radio effort as announcer just as it began a weekly schedule of broadcasts in 1944. In 1947 Eldersveld was selected as the CRC's full-time radio preacher, and within one year's time his sermons were carried across North America on the Mutual Broadcasting Network. Many lifelong CRC members will not remember the Sundays of their youth without the radio voice of Peter Eldersveld and the radio choir singing "By the Sea of Crystal" in the background. While they may have been designated as outreach, the Back to God Hour's initial years served—just as certainly as H. J. Kuiper's decades of editorials had—to bring together God's people who called themselves Christian Reformed. Many congre-

gations identified with the radio program and prominently advertised themselves as churches of the Back to God Hour.

Eldersveld's goal was to become a radio evangelist who repeated unvarying appeals for conversion. The Reformed tradition that had molded his life structured his perceptions of the ministry itself. His preaching, he knew, would certainly reach some non-Christians, but the radio sermons would more probably attract new, poorly instructed, or vaguely committed Christians. For these the Reformed tradition offered well-formulated biblical teachings with implications for social, economic, and political activities. The radio pastor declared, "We must be on Main Street with our Calvinism, for Calvinism is a main-street religion."

With that perspective Eldersveld spoke to North America and gained a solid audience. By 1954, the Back to God Hour reached three million listeners; by the sixties, the broadcast claimed the attention of an international audience of five million. They made no appeals for funds, avoided emotional harangues, and refrained from peddling religious trinkets. That policy kept Eldersveld—and his successor, Joel Nederhood—on the air while other religious programming was dumped by their carriers for sensationalism. Eldersveld despised such strategies, for, as he wrote in *The Word and the Cross,*

> *There seems to be a determined effort to make Christianity big in the eyes of the world. The Gospel is presented by super salesmen in a way that will make everybody like it. . . . The result is bestseller religion . . . which builds beautiful statistics. We ought to be ashamed of what we are doing to the Christian church today . . . aping the methods of salesmen and showmen, competing for an audience and the counting house. This is far beneath our dignity as Christians.*

Similar sensitivities led Eldersveld, in 1948, to oppose the CRC's continued affiliation with the National Association of Evangelicals (NAE). His minority report that year convinced a subsequent synod to disaffiliate with the NAE. Although that ecumenical link offered the CRC some influence within a segment of American church life, a majority of Synod 1951 was convinced that they should adopt an independent and more purely Reformed identity.

But synod also doubted that the CRC could influence the NAE and declared, "The cocksureness of the fundamentalist temper, coupled with its anti-intellectual outlook, does not leave the fundamentalist very susceptible to our influence. On the other hand, that section of our own constituency that has any anti-intellectual strain is an easy victim to fundamentalism." Fears that the CRC could easily

Ralph J. Danhof (1900-1971)

Ralph Danhof was a unique representative of a class of ministers who did mountains of work while serving the denomination in singular fashion. He became the minister of Neland Ave. CRC in Grand Rapids in 1945 and was immediately chosen to serve as Stated Clerk of the CRC, replacing a retiring Henry Beets. For a whole decade he combined the duties of Stated Clerk with serving as the sole pastor of Neland Ave.

In 1956, the CRC recognized that the position of Stated Clerk was full time, and Danhof was asked to continue serving in that role. He was soon involved with church-sponsored immigration to the U.S. and was also active in representing the CRC in Washington, D.C.—all with the help of a part-time secretary. It was not unusual to see him in his office laboring over his typewriter, using the "hunt-and-peck" method to compose a letter. That says something about the times, but it also says something about the man. Danhof and others like him did a prodigious amount of work during a time in which the denomination was thriving and growing.

Part of the Danhof legacy stemmed from his deep sympathy for the plight of his uncle, Rev. H. Danhof, who left the CRC with Herman Hoeksema in 1924. Danhof's congregation in Kalamazoo lost its church property when it left the CRC. Ralph considered that very unfair and worked to have the articles of incorporation of CRC churches changed so that congregations leaving the CRC would keep their buildings. Synod finally went along with Danhof, likely assuming the denomination would never suffer another schism. —TEH

drift into the fundamentalist orbit were an additional reason for synod's decision to leave the NAE. The report noted, "Our association with the NAE is almost certain to accelerate an alarming drift toward fundamentalism in our own circles. . . . If we risk our Reformed integrity by joining hands with fundamentalists today, it may be that we shall have very little of the Reformed heritage to pass on to the next generation."

In cutting its links with the NAE, synod declared a kind of ecclesiastical independence but remained vigorously evangelical. The denomination's Home Missions ministry, which dates from 1879, grew rapidly after the war. While that ministry had once focused mainly on tending the newly arriving immigrants from the Netherlands, during the sixties it broadened and changed. Nonetheless, many of the immigrants who had joined the CRC over the decades were converts who came to the New World with only tenuous religious commitments. Today, many devoted Christians can testify that their families were brought into the church through the work of home missionaries. Thus, although ethnically focused, the Home Missions effort has always been evangelical.

Since 1962, Home Missions programs have been redirected to reach with the gospel a broad spectrum of the North American populace and bring a wider ethnic diversity into the CRC. Several denominational agencies, including the Indian mission work in New Mexico, have been consolidated under Home Missions' guidance. There, they joined a growing agenda for work among African Americans, immigrants from the Pacific rim, Appalachian people, the urban poor, and university students. Reflecting this radical transition, Home Missions' quota rose from about $1 in 1957 to $36 in 1969—and $120 today.

This financial reorientation reflects the CRC's efforts to achieve goals that were already announced in 1947. That year the General Committee for Home Missions gained a full-time secretary and adopted a lengthy report, which declared,

> *We are now readying to welcome the Dutch immigrants of our own household of faith in Canada. Well and good. But we shall not be free from the blood of those teeming millions—sharecroppers, Oakies, migrants, under-privileged submerged classes of our society who are driven to substandards of living. Nor may we neglect . . . the sophisticated upper classes moving out of the cities to dwell in suburban homes.*

Today, the Home Missions ministries of the Christian Reformed Church in North America provide leadership assistance for evangelism and discipleship to forty-seven classes and more than nine hundred Christian Reformed churches in Canada and the United States. The agency attempts to implement the denominational vision for outreach and church development under a mandate called "Gathering God's Growing Family," an endeavor to be active in "seeking the lost and discipling the found . . . all for God's glory."

Last year nearly three thousand people were received into the CRC through evangelism, a number that compares to about a thousand each year during the 1960s. In addition, Home Missions carries out its mandate by helping churches develop prayer ministries, offering training and consulting for church leaders, and developing strategies and studies to help people and churches grow by reaching out to others. Currently, forty-three established churches, fifteen campus ministries, and three Red Mesa schools are supported through Home Missions' partnership funding.

Bringing the gospel to such a varied North American crowd has not been easy, but the effort has achieved significant success and altered the face of the CRC. Through the efforts of Home Missions—as well as the individual efforts of thousands of CRC members—the process of becoming a North American church has continued, as the efforts to bring the gospel to our neighbors in the U.S. and Canada have grown and blossomed.

The prosperous growth of Christian Reformed World Missions' ministries must be mentioned here as well. Before 1950, denominational mission history looked altogether different than it does today; of all the areas of the world where CRC mission work goes on today, only one—China—has roots that grow deeper than the last half-century.

The very first mission enterprise of the turn-of-the-century CRC was undertaken in New Mexico among the Navajo and Zuni peoples. Synod 1888 made the decision to begin this ministry, but the mission was not begun until eight years later. In 1896 the CRC sent Rev. and Mrs. H. Fryling to the Navajos, and Mr. and Mrs. A. Vander Wagen, a layman and his wife, to the Zunis. Our denominational mission bill for that year was just under $7,500—which included salaries for missionaries and interpreters, as well as the purchase of a house, rent for another, and other minor expenses. The CRC is still vitally connected to its now century-old mission in New Mexico, although the

Date: c. 1929-1930 Rev. Smit's residence, Jukao, Kiangsu province, China. Headquarters of the China mission
Standing men Rev. Albert Smit, Rev. Harry Dykstra, Rev. John De Krone, Unidentified, Mr. Soong (Bible man), Mr. Shao (evangelist in Jukao), Dr. Beets, Mr. Wang (evangelist of Rev. Smit, co-worker), Unidentified, Unidentified, Rev. Sam Dykstra, Rev. A. Selles
Seated, women (left to right) Miss W. Kalsbeek, Mrs. A. Selles, Miss Lillian Bode, Mrs. Harry Dykstra, Mrs. Albert Smit, Mrs. Sam Dykstra, Mrs. John De Korne, Unidentified, Mrs. Shao, evangelist in Jukao (wife), Mrs. Ruby Liu
Children, on laps Peter Dykstra, Harvey Smit, Evelyn Dykstra
Children, front Jeanne Dykstra, Eunice Smit, Cornelia Dykstra, Andy Dykstra

Rehoboth building complex.

(Below) A student at the Christian school in Rehoboth.

work was transferred to Home Missions in 1964. Today, the New Mexico ministry has a staff of more than fifty, a budget of more than a half-million dollars, and a host of places on the long plains of New Mexico where it brings witness to God's unfailing love.

New Mexico was the first undertaking of the denominational agency once called "The Board of Heathen Missions"—the name changed, for obvious reasons, in 1926. At the time of World War I, a flood of requests came to synod from those desiring new missions work "among the heathen abroad." Between 1918 and 1920, the question of which new field was narrowed down to two possibilities—Central America and China. Synod 1920 chose China, and three missionary families began work there—Rev. and Mrs. John De Korne, Dr. and Mrs. Lee Huizenga, and Rev. and Mrs. Harry Dykstra. But a series of civil wars made progress very difficult for the CRC pioneer mission families.

In 1930, a letter from Miss Johanna Veenstra, who was already serving as a missionary in Nigeria, asked for church support for her work in Africa. The church didn't fully comply with her request until 1939, when the Lupwe-Takum-Wukari area of the Benue Province in Nigeria was officially added to denominational ministry. By then, Johanna Veenstra had already been dead for six years. Yet because of the powerful work she started in Nigeria, she may well be the most celebrated missionary in denominational history. Today her efforts, blessed by the Creator, have resulted in a multitribal Christian Reformed Church of Nigeria of 165,000 attenders.

World War II brought many changes and developments to countries around the world, and the mission enterprise of the denomination learned significant

Johanna Veenstra

∞

"Her body lies buried in a cemetery not far from Vom, but the memory of her self-forgetful life will never fade in that part of Africa. . . . That there is still a steady stream of African Christians going forth from her own missionary field to preach the gospel to the tribes in Nigeria is her continuing reward."

With those words biographer Winifred M. Pearce describes the impact that the remarkable Johanna Veenstra had on the beginnings of the Christian church in Africa. Born in Paterson, New Jersey, in 1894, Veenstra was a rebel in her youth, strong-willed, with little spiritual sensitivity. Then God intervened in her life through the work of her pastor, and she became a changed person who nurtured a dream of serving Christ.

Johanna Veenstra, pioneer
missionary to Nigeria
(1899-1933).

Enrolled at the Union Missionary Training Institute, she decided to become a missionary. At that time there was little missionary enthusiasm in the CRC. So after working briefly in city missions, Johanna volunteered for service in Africa under the sponsorship of Sudan United Missions.

Her first assignment was to the Dzompere of the Cameroon Mountains, a tribe notorious for having practiced cannibalism. The area had many natural hazards as well. According to Johanna, the area where she worked "is considered one of the most dangerous places in the world for white people. Isolation, tornado storms, insects, wild beasts, fever, and overwork all help to cause the nervous system continual strain" (*Pioneering for Christ in the Sudan*).

Even though she served under a board not connected with the CRC, Johanna caught the imagination of the denomination. She urged others to join her in the great task of preaching the gospel to the people of Nigeria. And her letters added to the enthusiasm for outreach in the CRC. Before long, she was joined by Jennie Stielstra, Nell Breen (who later became Mrs. Edgar Smith), Bertha Zagers, and others. Following these pioneers were hundreds of teachers, preachers, nurses, and agricultural experts, many of them household names in the CRC.

Johanna's career as a Nigerian missionary was tragically short. Her ministry in Africa lasted only thirteen years, and she passed away at the age of thirty-nine after an appendectomy performed in primitive facilities. But in that short time Johanna altered the face of the CRC by turning it in the direction of missionary outreach. And her preaching, teaching, and leadership in the infant church brought into being by her labors helped to provide a foundation for the church of Jesus Christ in Africa.

The work begun in such weakness and with limited resources has blossomed—in 1998, there are approximately 75,000 Christian Reformed people in Nigeria. More than 200,000 are in attendance on a given Sunday at the 414 places of worship. In addition, some 500,000 attend the Church of Christ in the Sudan among the Tiv.

—WDB

lessons—specifically, that the life and work of the people of God are inextricably bound up with the life and work of the world around them. Changes in government and culture within the countries where we have worked to bring the gospel profoundly affect both the manner by which we bring the Word of God to the people, and the very opportunity for ministry. World Missions has had to learn to be mobile as a result, capable of moving and changing with alterations in the social climate.

But the ministry has grown immensely in its geographic commitments. In the last quarter-century, World Missions has opened new fields in Nicaragua (1973), Liberia (1975), El Salvador (1978), the Dominican Republic and Belize (1980), Costa Rica (1982), Mali and Guinea (1984), Haiti and Hong Kong (1986), Kenya (1988), France (1989), Hungary and Romania (1990), Ecuador and Zambia (1991), Mongolia, Russia, and the Ukraine (1992).

Today the ministry of Christian Reformed World Missions to proclaim the gospel includes preaching, evangelism, development efforts (in the areas of agriculture, health, and the like), Bible translation, literacy training and linguistics, and the production of Christian literature and broadcasting. In addition, World Missions workers start and lead Bible studies, disciple new believers, train church leaders, start Christian schools, and teach in local seminaries—all as a means by which to help in the process of developing churches.

World Missions now operates in thirty countries, creating indigenous denominations and building congregations throughout the world. But their basic mode of operation hasn't changed: their mandate remains to glorify God by leading sinners to salvation, building God's church, and extending God's kingdom here on earth.

After such growth and success, does World Missions see the end of its own endeavors? Not as long as nearly four billion people in the world do not know Jesus Christ as Savior. As long as the denomination continues to fund its work and support it with its enthusiasm and prayers, the almost three hundred individuals—full-time, short-term, spouses, and seminary interns—who staff World Missions enterprises around the world will continue the work begun a century ago among the Navajo and Zuni peoples.

In a time when denominational loyalties seem to be waning, it is important to remember how effective and powerful the CRC's agencies and ministries have been in taking the Word of the Lord into every square inch of God's world.

CHAPTER 18

The Sixties

For several weeks in the Christian school I attended as a child, kids in my classroom prayed for the people in Hudsonville, Michigan. It was the 1950s, and there'd been a tornado there, a bad one. Lots of people had suffered; several had died. I lived just across Lake Michigan from Hudsonville, and although I was vaguely conscious of having relatives in Michigan, once I began to hear—even on national news—about Hudsonville, the recitation of familiar Dutch-sounding names helped me to realize that some link other than tragedy was drawing people together in prayer. People from "our church" had been killed or left homeless. The concern I saw registered on the faces of my parents and the people in my church was something unique and new. The people who suffered in Hudsonville were somehow close to us.

That year, likely there were tornadoes in Texas, Arkansas, Oklahoma, and South Dakota; but not one of them triggered the deep concern this one had. Something was different here; this one had hit "our people." Even today, I flash back to those elementary-school prayers when I hear the word "Hudsonville." I think, "tornado."

Somewhat typically, the Christian Reformed Church's initial forays into a ministry for the diaconate began with deep concern for "our people." It was those tornadoes in Michigan, ravaging floods in Holland Marsh, Ontario, and killer floods in the Netherlands that prompted the CRC to attempt a means by which to offer disaster relief. Already in 1950, Second CRC of Denver had overtured synod to "consider the advisability of appointing a Synodical Diaconal Committee" to do works of mercy and "provide the diaconates with an overall picture of the needs of the poor."

Benevolent work among the needy other than "our own" had begun at about the same time, when, in 1951, the Grand Rapids Deacons' Conference assumed responsibility for relief work in war-torn Korea. But starving children couldn't be fed from denominational coffers without synodical discussion, of course—a game plan, a strategy, and a statement of position. In response to concern about the projects in Korea begun by the Grand Rapids Deacons' Conference, Synod 1953 created an orderly means by which relief could be given to the thousands suffering there. It specified a difference in ministries. Despite cries of "dualism" from the denomination's Antitheticals, synod declared that from that time forward two separate ministry efforts would exist in Korea—a material ministry and a spiritual ministry—and

it appointed the Grand Rapids Deacons' Conference as the synodical committee responsible for "material" relief.

In 1959, the Grand Rapids Deacons' Conference asked synod about the possibility of a creating a worldwide relief organization. The Christian Reformed World Relief Committee (CRWRC) was created in 1960, in the words of an ambitious mandate chartered in 1962, "to minister in the name of the Lord to man distressed by reason of the violence of nature, the carnage of war or other calamities of life, and to relieve the suffering of the needy of the world."

There is no question that CRWRC brought some muscle and visibility to the office of deacon in the CRC. For years, the tradition of officebearing in the CRC had created a long-standing joke that brought laughs because it sounded so accurate: men became elders after serious training in the diaconate, just as deacons became deacons after serious training as ushers. The whole system seemed drawn directly from professional baseball's minor leagues.

But the work of CRWRC altered that perception somewhat. For the first time in denominational history, a bona-fide CRC ministry was staffed by laypeople. In addition, almost shockingly, its board was created with largely lay leadership. For that reason, from its inception CRWRC was unique in the denominational offices. Even though its roots stretch clearly back to the fifties, it became, undeniably, a child of the CRC in the sixties.

Throughout the history of the CRC, most denominational discussions were led and even carried on by clergy. For years, preachers occupied the positions of highest authority and power in the church and community—after all, Scholte and Van Raalte did far more in their communities than preach the gospel. Until the sixties, that kind of hierarchy remained in place.

But few institutions of society remained intact after the assault of the "revolutions" of that era, and even in the CRC a hierarchy that had been established for generations took its licks. "Dominies" or "Reverends" became "pastors" as more and more preachers asked their parishioners to address them by their first names—as in "Pastor Rick."

CRWRC became the denominational darling during the sixties—in part, because our own hierarchical attitudes began to change. For the first time in denominational history, an entire ministry was staffed and run by laypeople. Preachers weren't necessarily falling out of favor as much as they were simply losing ground to the sustained pressures of a changing of the guard. A new attitude looked to greater lay participation in all denominational and congregational ministries by people who had become much more educated than they were in the early years of denominational history.

Is that change good or bad? Some might say that any erosion of the traditional hierarchy marks the beginning of the end times in the CRC. Others would disagree vehemently. Lay leadership was long overdue in the CRC, they'd say, pointing at a hefty tradition that included the old conventicles, the lack of clerical leadership during the earliest years of the denomination, and Abraham Kuyper's own firm trust in the "little people."

Another reason CRWRC became so popular and grew as astoundingly as it did in the sixties has to do with the fact that traditional mission work became somehow suspect. We in the West woke up to the fact that we had entered the post-colonial era. It was a time when the reputation of Western Europe, which had once considered colonization to be the "white man's burden," suddenly became tarnished. Europe's colonizers were accused of being the purveyors of a nationalist bigotry that enslaved and destroyed native cultures, using the name of Christianity to mask their economic exploitation. Novels and films like James Michener's *Hawaii* portrayed missionaries as charlatans and self-righteous zealots more concerned with making converts British or American than Christian. Even in the CRC we wondered if our efforts among the Navajo and Zuni in New Mexico weren't a species of misguided colonialism, the mission town of Rehoboth, in fact, looking far too much like Holland, Michigan, or Orange City, Iowa.

Along came CRWRC, a ministry of deed, of self-help, a well full of cold water for thousands of cups. A missionary was no longer someone in a long black coat holding his Bible up closely to his nose while half-naked savages sat supine at his feet. CRWRC actually fed people, made them healthy, and showed them how to make a livelihood. Something about those efforts made CRWRC appear somehow basic, a first step we'd heretofore missed completely.

By 1965, Louis Van Ess, CRWRC's first director, announced a change in direction for the organization. "While the mass distribution of food and clothing is provided

A holy drug deal. CRWRC pioneer Louis Van Ess (center) and Ted Clousing (left) deliver pharmaceuticals and food to bring healing to suffering people, 1963.

in cases of emergency and disaster," Van Ess claimed, "it is far more effective to help in a manner whereby those helped can be trained in self-help endeavors." With that change in focus, the CRC began an agriculture program as well as an adoption program in Korea. CRWRC became a ministry devoted to more than storm-related relief. It put itself in a position to help wherever and whenever needed.

There's at least one more reason for CRWRC's sudden and dramatic rise in prominence. By the late sixties, what was happening "in the streets," as we used to say, was undeniable. The evening news showed it all. What the good times of the fifties had seemingly either failed to recognize or deliberately denied were poverty, racial discrimination, and real human suffering, causes now championed by forces calling themselves "countercultural." In

1969, when CRWRC inaugurated new programs in North America among poverty-depressed people in Appalachia, for instance, it took its ministry home to our own streets. Vietnamese refugees needed help after the horror of Vietnam; CRWRC responded. Mississippi Christian Family Services was created to work with handicapped African Americans in one of the most economically depressed areas of the U.S.—the Mississippi delta. The CRC was doing highly visible work among those identified in the sixties as the forgotten and dispossessed.

After Vietnam, world hunger became the moral issue of choice in North America. Once more, CRWRC was in a position to respond, creating programs in Nicaragua, Sierra Leone, Niger, Honduras, and Guatemala, attempting to work with local organizations in agriculture, health, literacy, income development, and church outreach.

For years, with denominational favor so decidedly tilting toward the various programs of the CRWRC, other ministries

Trinity Christian College, a Chicago initiative, opened in 1959.

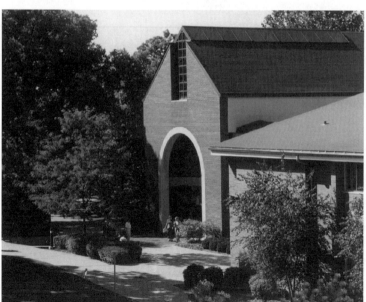

appeared to be left in the dust created by all the enthusiasm. Those kinds of rivalries eventually rose to a point that a new and more comprehensive organizational structure was required to manage denominational operations.

Meanwhile CRWRC, despite its relative youth, did much to fulfill its original and ambitious mandate; it did what it promised, alleviating suffering at dozens of points around the world. But its very success is attributable, at least in part, to the times in which it grew. The CRC was responding to societal needs created by poverty and discrimination, needs made suddenly more visible by the sixties themselves. CRWRC prospered, in part, because of what was happening in the world.

The other great cultural revolution identified with the sixties, the sexual revolution, was something CRWRC was not as capably outfitted to handle. The denomination would have to find other ways to deal with the changes in the status of women in society. No agency could help us with that one. Rest assured, we'll come back to it later. That story is not yet behind us.

THE SIXTIES COUNTERCULTURE

I'm not sure if the founders of Dordt College studied demographics before they broke ground for a new Reformed college in northwest Iowa, but my guess is that they likely did. After all, a CRC group in south-suburban Chicago bought an old golf course and turned it into Trinity Christian College at the very same time. What both parties likely saw in the post-war years was what everyone else who looked at the North American populace couldn't miss—a swarm of kids whose sheer numbers would tax everything from infrastructures to educational institutions. Once World War II ended, the U.S. and Canada had reason to celebrate. Their booming economies verified what the war itself had already proven—we were *numero uno*. It was time to settle back, have families, and live the good life of peace and prosperity.

If part of the motivation for new CRC colleges was the swarm of young people soon to be applying, then the Dordt College planners didn't read the numbers as accurately as they should have. Even more students came to the new college than its planners had envisioned. But then, no one really guessed at the effects this huge generation would create.

Soon enough the new Iowa college was short of room. The story of the sixties I want to tell takes place in a room no one assumed would ever be a classroom, a basement room of a thirteen-year-old college. It was the lunch room when the college opened in 1955. A decade later, it still seemed more fit for tables and chairs and cafeteria trays. Its ceiling hung very low, given its size—big enough for fifty or sixty student desks—and foundational pillars arose everywhere, often blocking views. Professor Cornelius Van Schouwen was teaching a class in Reformed doctrine in that basement room—a class that likely doesn't even exist in the catalogs of any of the five CRC-related colleges today. Van Schouwen's class was, to be truthful, less than mesmerizing; but it's helpful to remember that back then no one assumed education had to be fun. The great attraction of the curriculum, Reformed people thought, was teachers who were biblical,

not necessarily charismatic. It helped if they were good teachers, but we were far more "confessional" ourselves in the fifties and early sixties; what really mattered was our perception of biblical truth. That someone was teaching Reformed doctrine was more important, perhaps, than that it was done entertainingly.

Students understood that arrangement of priorities. Pedagogy was not all that important at the beginning of the television age. While most students would have preferred a more challenging presentation of the material, no one complained—it wasn't our place to, after all. *We* didn't matter as much as the material we were learning did. It was a privilege to go to college. For many of us, higher education was less the fulfillment of our own aspirations than it was the realization of the dreams of our parents.

We were legion, and we were pampered. The Depression was a memorable incubator, as was the war our parents had fought. Children of my generation were raised in a different world than the one our parents were raised in, a world in which the greatest glories, the greatest joys, the greatest sorrows and tragedies took place not on battlefields but in high school gymnasiums. We marked the epochs of our lives by proms and banquets, by the summer we broke up with Angie or Fred or Tami. We'd suffered no dust bowls. We were raised by our parents, but we weren't like them.

Our story was only in its opening chapters. In that basement theology room, a young woman who sat beside me wrote daily letters to her boyfriend in Vietnam. She told me the class was a snap; she'd graduated from a Christian high school, she said, where she'd already heard most of Van Schouwen's lectures. I was a public high school graduate, and the class wasn't that easy for me. To be honest, it wasn't that interesting either. What did I care, after all, about Reformed doctrine? I was more interested in my girlfriend—and sports.

But what happened in that class one day has stayed in my memory longer than any other classroom discussion from my college years. It was 1968, and the young woman next to me wasn't the only girl with a boyfriend in 'Nam. There were few, if any, African Americans at Dordt that year, but unless your head was poked

deeply into the sand, you couldn't help but notice smoke rising from rioting inner cities all over the country. "The times, they were a'changin'," even in a place as remote as Sioux Center, Iowa.

Van Schouwen was lecturing on sphere sovereignty, a principle he lifted directly from Kuyperian theology. I wouldn't have known that then, and I wouldn't have cared. Today, the whole business is fascinating to me.

He said that the place of the preacher was the pulpit—and only the pulpit. I wish I could quote him, but I can't, and now he's gone. A preacher had a place in his sphere, but nowhere else—that's what he insisted in that sometimes garbled and tinny voice of his. He said it was wrong for preachers to take to the streets, to lead marches for civil rights or protests against the war in Vietnam. He said the preacher was called to open the Word of the Lord in the visible church, to hold forth with the gospel, to practice humility and love and administer the sacraments. He said preachers who moved out of their sphere were violating something ordained by God. He said preachers who marched in Selma or Washington or on college campuses throughout America, those who protested government policies concerning the war in Vietnam, were preachers who'd abandoned their role and, quite flatly, done wrong in leaving their sphere.

I don't remember what the girl beside me did at that point, whether she put down her pen or even looked up. I wasn't really concerned about what the others did, but what Professor Van Schouwen said struck a very tender nerve. In fact, the word that came to mind at that point can't be written in this book, even though it refers to a substance that filled cattleyards in every direction around that classroom. I was hardly militant, but I'd already seen enough of life to know that that outrageous idea being sold to dutiful young Reformed students copiously noting every word seemed flat wrong. To me, what motivated the professor's saying it was not God's Word but plain old cultural politics. The man was using God to cover his own political views. Besides that, he was wrong.

"Wait a minute," I said. "You're saying that it's wrong for preachers of the gospel to be part of political rallies—it's wrong for Martin Luther King, Jr., to lead marches because he's a preacher?"

It will come as a shock to many born after the sixties, but to much of perfectly white evangelical America at the time, Martin Luther King, Jr., wasn't so much a Christian as he was a communist. I don't doubt that Van Schouwen shared in that view.

But he didn't bite back at me. In his typical way, he merely repeated what he'd said, as if my not hearing it in the first place was due to some circuit breakdown in my brain. He put his finger down on his notes to help him remember where he was and then simply repeated what he'd said before as if that should be enough to satisfy my complaints. I was supposed to say, "Yes, sir. Thank you, sir." He likely translated my silence as the end of the conversation.

He was dead wrong about that too. I didn't buy what he said—not for a minute. Still don't. But unlike college students all over the U.S. at the time, I didn't push him. I let it be. The class was humming along just fine—even if some seemed uninterested. I wasn't going to make a scene. But

Demonstrators protesting the war in Vietnam.

to me, already deeply affected by the counterculture around me, Van Schouwen was simply convincing evidence of the fact that the CRC itself was a dinosaur. Van Schouwen was out to lunch.

Not only that, his views were typical of a mentality I'd seen too much of in 1968 at Dordt College, a mentality that had staged a demonstration in Sioux Center's Central Park, a demonstration meant to counter the prevailing counterculture. It was a rally where politically conservative kids and professors, while they didn't exactly support the war, held it up in prayer. Such a holy undertaking must have made parents proud. (Please excuse my rather characteristic late-sixties sarcasm.)

But there was no middle ground in 1968, and if you didn't oppose the war, if you only prayed for its participants, you were, in effect, supporting the bloodshed—nearly five hundred young Americans per week. For whatever reasons—some of them good, some of them sinful—I had been as embarrassed by the rally as I was shocked by Van Schouwen's condemnation of Martin Luther King, Jr.

It's unlikely that anyone else in that class remembers my single comment because what I'd said wasn't marked by bitterness or anger. I didn't scream out obscenities, or throw down the book and stomp out of the room. I didn't try to lead the students in open rebellion with a raised fist. But something happened in my head that day that was likely far worse: I learned, sincerely, to doubt—not only Van Schouwen, but the whole hierarchal system he personified. What had begun, perhaps, with the Bay of Pigs fiasco, was continued by freedom marches throughout Mississippi and the rural South, was heightened by antiwar sentiment growing exponentially with the rising number of body bags. What all of this taught some of us was that there was something rotten at the heart of American society, something obviously missing from our fragrant and compelling American dreams. Van Schouwen's response simply didn't wash with me and what I'd learned in the streets.

Many men and women from my generation can tell a similar story. Maybe theirs isn't something that happened in a classroom or even on a college campus. It may have happened in an apartment, Janis Joplin belting out a song on the stereo or Crosby, Stills, and Nash singing a tribute to those massacred at Kent State. It may have struck them in a rice paddy. However and wherever it occurred, many of the kids of World War II veterans began to doubt the very tradition their fathers fought to preserve. The glorious way of patriotism and nationalism began to seem more like the way of lies.

Every institution of culture was suspect. When Professor Van Schouwen insisted that preachers stay off the streets, he lugged his generation, his patriotism, his way of life, all of Dordt College, and even his faith into question in my mind and soul. The whole business seemed a house of cards. I was confident that the whole thing—the "system," the "establishment"—would come Humpty-Dumptying down. The lie about Vietnam, about race relations, about Watergate extended even into the CRC, which I began to think of as similarly reactionary and Neanderthal, totally out of touch with reality—not to mention, as I've said, flat wrong.

I tell that story not because I'm trying to explain myself but because it is emblematic, I think, of the time. In that basement classroom, the whole regimen of my parents' faith not only came under scrutiny but was nearly undone. If I was learning something that far from the truth in a class titled "Reformed doctrine," then I couldn't help but believe that Reformed doctrine itself was not only seriously flawed but completely outworn, dead in the water.

I was at a Christian college my parents hoped would not only preserve my faith but strengthen it with an education grounded in the truth of Scripture. What I heard created exactly the opposite effect; it made me distrust everything. Professor Van Schouwen and I couldn't have been farther apart. It wasn't a liberal professor who made me doubt; it was a conservative.

Thirty years have passed, time enough for history to do its work and reveal something of the theological and cultural forces that created the chasm separating the two of us that morning. I know now that Professor Van Schouwen was as much a man of his generation as I was a child of mine. He'd been shaped and honed by his experience of war. One of dozens of CRC preachers called to military service as chaplains in World War II, Van Schouwen was a legitimate war hero. I didn't know that then. He'd seen people die in combat. With the troops to whom

The Gene Proctor Family

∞

There were very few non-Caucasian members in the CRC until well after World War II. With the movement of the Black community in Grand Rapids into the "southeast Dutch ghetto," the churches were faced with the challenge of neighborhood evangelism that involved large numbers of African Americans. That challenge was met by First CRC under the leadership of Rev. Marvin Beelen and resulted in bringing Gene and Virginia Proctor and their six children into the CRC in the early 1960s.

Gene was a uniquely gifted businessman with theatrical abilities who became a leading representative of his race in the CRC and in southeast Grand Rapids. When the Baxter Community Center, formed in the old Baxter Christian School building, faced leadership problems, the board turned to Proctor. He left his business and almost single-handedly turned the fortunes of Baxter to make it a flourishing and highly-respected service center. Today Baxter, among many other things, houses a medical clinic where eight doctors, several dentists, and an optometrist donate their services.

Gene's family has also served nobly in such ventures as Camp Tall Turf, a summer camp for children that operates in close relationship with Baxter Community Center. —TEH

Gene Proctor today.

The Gene Proctor family, early African-American members of First CRC in Grand Rapids.

he'd ministered, he'd opened the gates of a concentration camp to the most unforgettable images of that war. He'd watched as bulldozers ungraciously buried thousands of emaciated bodies in mass graves. He'd seen what no human should ever see; firsthand, he'd experienced horror far beyond anything I will ever know, the Lord willing. I know now that I was a pup compared to what he'd seen and experienced. Even though I still think he was absolutely wrong about Martin Luther King, Jr., my youthful arrogance is, in some ways, appalling to me today.

Rev. Stephen M. Jung

❧

Stephen Jung, born in Hong Kong, was a very successful owner and operator of a dress factory in Los Angeles in the fifties. Through contact with Rev. Paul Szto in New York, he became aware of the CRC and was attracted to its clear presentation of the gospel of sovereign grace.

Stephen Jung (center), missionary pastor to Chinese in Canada.

When he made contact with the CRC, Jung was directed to Classis California South. In 1963, the small independent church the Jungs belonged to joined that classis and became a CRC congregation, with Jung as its leading elder. Ten years later Jung, who had a B.Th. degree from the former Toronto Bible College, and who was judged as having exceptional spiritual gifts, was ordained as a minister. Rev. Jung served the Crenshaw CRC in Los Angeles for six years and then took the call to plant two Chinese churches in Richmond and Abbotsford, B.C. He retired in 1988. —TEH

A relative of Van Schouwen's once told me that my theology professor was so successful as a military pastor that Douglas MacArthur once requested him to be his personal chaplain, a task the chaplain refused because, I was told, Van Schouwen claimed he wouldn't work for someone who so vehemently took God's name in vain. Van Schouwen had also lost a wife to sickness and suffered the deep accompanying grief. He was, even though I didn't know it at the time, a scarred veteran of life's tragedies.

Dordt College itself was an adolescent, still feeling its way along the path toward becoming a Christian institution of higher learning. Like any thirteen-year-old, it was still confused about who it was, what it would be. I didn't know it then, but the faculty and administration were already beginning a debate about identity that would lead to the most severe crisis in Dordt's history, a debate made more difficult by the tenacious conflicts of the sixties.

To Van Schouwen that day I was a kid who had too uncritically absorbed the ethos of a godless generation, a generation whose aspirations meant to destroy absolutely everything he'd fought for through his years as a preacher, as an army chaplain, and as a father. I was precocious and impudent. He'd seen men die in battle; what did I know about the price of eggs? Besides, he recognized very well the system of thought I carried to the classroom skirmish that day. He knew that my understanding of truth began with what I saw around me—not with the revelation of Scripture. And that way of thinking made me—if not personally, by ideology at least—as formidable an enemy to faith as Nazism had been. From

Van Schouwen's point of view, there was much from which I needed to be disabused.

But who was I thirty years ago? I was a kid who knew from the dialogue of my own generation that something awful had gone wrong in society. I'd been reared, like tons of other CRC kids, on Marian Schoolland's book of children's Bible stories, which included a reading of the Genesis 9 passage that suggested that African Americans were the descendants of Noah's son Ham, and ordained by God, therefore, to be servants—a reading not at all unique at the time. I'd been reared on the equation that government, instituted by God, was to be questioned only when government fiat banned worship and faith itself—look at Russia, for example. I'd been reared with the belief that America was a Christian nation, its laws and traditions somehow sanctified by its own God-fearing populace.

But when I looked around, I saw people like my grandfather, deeply pious folks so capable of knowing their sin that the evidence could stream down their cheeks. He was a believer—good night, he was a believer, a strong Christian. But he was also a racist. No question about it. He was quite openly anti-black. I was too much a child of my time not to see that something here was dramatically off-key; the Christian life seemed dysfunctional to me. I'd listened to people I was supposed to respect call every last protestor a communist, every smidgeon of criticism of the Vietnam War downright anti-American. I felt real doubt, and doubt turns, oh, so easily, into cynicism.

Van Schouwen's perceptions emanated from a world I couldn't belong to. I suffered in that basement classroom the kind of sweet horror that always accompanies our most significant urgings toward freedom. In parting company with Van Schouwen, I was liberating myself from his narrow-mindedness, yet I was very much alone, horrifyingly alone, in my search for identity. What was I if I didn't buy Reformed theology? Who would my friends be?

My only choice, of course, were the long-hairs—the shaggy hippie-types who raised two fingers of peace as quickly as farmers here in Iowa flick up a wave when you meet them in their pickups. Once Van Schouwen had answered my question by repeating what he'd said initially, what lay before me was a cultural choice many of us faced: the culture of the CRC, with all its blemishes and unforgiven sins, or the culture that seemingly put a premium on love and peace and eradicating injustice, that decorated the barrels of M-16 carbines with roses. One of them certainly looked much more like a culture of love than the other—and it wasn't the church that came out on top.

What makes such a choice seem strange to kids today is the real depth of our belief at that difficult time. Bell-bottoms may well be making a comeback nowadays, but they won't be worn with the same ideology as they were in the sixties, when many, many kids truly believed that they could do something to change "the system." In backing away from the culture of Van Schouwen, I was not backing away from commitment and into some self-imposed ghetto of cynicism—not in the least. I was forcing more commitment upon myself. That was part of the motivation for me to go to Washington myself a year or so later and join the hundreds of thousands protesting the war. The sixties were not a time for backing away. Honestly and truly, idealism flourished.

The incredible divisiveness between the generations was created, in fact, by the depth of feeling on both sides. Both Van Schouwen and I considered each other not just incorrect but dead wrong. The sixties created a cultural and generational conflict that still hasn't sorted itself out, even though today both sides have changed and been changed. Idealism waned eventually. For me, the sixties ended in the summer of 1970, when, by choice, I was living a long way from any Christian Reformed church. The bomb of a protestor killed a graduate student at the University of Wisconsin in Madison, just an hour north of where I lived. Grace had departed from the movement.

But at its aegis, the countercultural movement beckoned many students with visions of justice and love. In the process, it blindsided a whole conservative wing of the CRC, who simply lacked the tools to understand what was happening. I don't think Van Schouwen ever did really understand what the whole time was about. I'm not sure that I do. All I know is that by our respective ideologies, we were pitched against each other in a pattern that many on both sides could and did read as the very black-and-white paradigm of the antithesis.

I tell this story because it is ours. Despite views to the contrary, CRC kids weren't, in the sixties, deeply secluded by the walls of an ethnic/religious fortress. The fact that I'd listened to my own youth culture made me choose against the church. If Americanization is what we were still after in the church, ironically enough, I'd become the ideal—as American as I'd ever be. In 1968, I had a clear choice, and I chose the sixties counterculture.

In his poem "Sioux Center, Iowa," poet Jim Heynen, from his perspective as a child of the sixties, vividly describes the way life was lived within communities like this one at the very onset of the sixties revolution. But wherever Christian Reformed folks lived in any prominence, our fellowships often fit a similar characterization. Ethnocentric, moralistic, and self-righteous, we seemed, all too often, simply unpleasant at best. Listen to Heynen.

> *Home of the Christian Smile.*
> *Not a center for Sioux.*
> *The Dutch. A sub-*
> *culture of yah's. Calvin-*
> *istic and clean. Deep*
> *winter. Sustained*
> *by corn and thick*
> *Holsteins, creamy*
> *grins and providential*
> *care. Straight*
> *furrows surround*
> *the town. No mote,*
> *no dike to protect it.*
> *Only the creamery and grain*
> *elevator, the old hatchery,*
> *truck stops and bristling*
> *steeples.*
>
> *Do you think the people are nice?*
> *The people are not nice.*
> *The people are right.*
> *Do you think the people are clean?*
> *The people are clean.*
>
> *Pictures of lonely hands praying.*
> *Pictures of large horses.*
> *Mosquitoes and white lawn chairs.*
> *Miniature German Shepherds*
> *in back windows, their eyes*
> *blinking the turns.*

Do you think the people like baseball?
The people like baseball.
Do you think the people love?
They love what is right.

John Deere and snowmobiles
and predestination for those
whom it hurts. Polished saddles.
Salads with whipped cream
and marshmallows. Thick
steaks.

Do you think the young people
drive in circles with new cars?
The young people
drive in circles with new cars.
The young people drive in circles
with new cars until they are aroused.
The new cars stop near cornfields
and graveyards and rock
in their tracks.

Do you think the people know the
*   Beautiful?*
A daughter in a white gown
who can play the church organ.
Do you think the people drink whiskey?
The people drink whiskey
in the next county.
Do you think the people would like
*   you?*
The people would not like you. You
are not one of them. But you
are important
where you are. God
loves those
who stay in their place.

—"Sioux Center, Iowa" from *Voices on*
the Landscape: Contemporary Iowa Poets,
Michael Carey, ed. (Parkersburg, Loess
Hill Books, an imprint of Mid-Prairie
Books). Used by permission.

That poem will delight thousands of readers who have always seen northwest Iowans in exactly that way. But the picture Heynen presents isn't simply regional. In the mid-eighties at the University of Indiana Writers Conference, I read a story of mine that featured Dutch Reformed folks from northwest Iowa. Two women from western Michigan came up to me afterward and told me how much they liked it. They were from Muskegon, they said, and wondered if I'd ever heard about people called "Christian Reformed." The people they'd known by that name, these two women told me, were very, very strange. I told them I was one of them. They apologized.

What I'm trying to establish here is how we were seen for many years, and how we were seen even by our own—by Jim Heynen and hoards of others who left what they considered an unduly self-righteous and suffocating fellowship. I believe that the caricature Heynen creates in the poem is quite accurate to the flavor of many churches and communities in the fifties.

What the sixties did to the denomination was drive a wedge into an already existing fissure. The decade produced a generation—just as it did everywhere else in American culture—who wouldn't buy the goods in the old packages. It forced change in the church in ways that often seemed violent and confrontational. With the gradual departure of a number of charismatic neo-Kuyperians, deep and ugly conflicts erupted at Trinity Christian College; and a very similar battle surfaced just a few years later at Dordt, when

Our Family Album

a number of professors left or were asked to seek employment elsewhere.

Calvin was bigger, more diverse, perhaps less significantly affected by postwar neo-Kuyperians than its younger siblings. It may well be true that at Calvin more folks understood the violence of crosscurrents roiling the cultural waters. But it was Calvin students who wrote, directed, and produced the most controversial piece of street theater of the time, a publication titled *The Bananer.* No single event during the sixties better character-

izes the whole raucous and confrontational era than the events surrounding the publication of that immaculately composed parody of the denomination's own voice.

When it was first placed at distribution points on campus, few bothered to pick it up because the issue so clearly resembled *The Banner* itself. Even the cover photo was somehow familiar, a cropped version of U.S. Marines hoisting Old Glory up on a mountain on Iwo Jima. But the photo was altered. Old Glory had become a dollar bill, the implication itself a jibe taken directly from late sixties rhetoric: the glory of the U.S. was not freedom but money. Once students began looking closer, once they picked up this facsimile *Banner,* the remaining copies vanished. It was an almost perfect parody created by the Calvin College *Chimes* staff at the very end of the spring semester of 1970.

But the tempest the *Bananer* created did not arise from its critique of American imperialism or its shot at the "military-industrial complex." What raised the hackles of the denomination's traditionalists was its lampooning of *The Banner*—and, almost by extension, the denomination, if not righteousness itself. The Christian Reformed Church became the "Philistine Rewarmed Crutch," and the cross set in the triangle of the denomination's familiar logo was replaced with a crutch.

From cover to cover the *Bananer* so completely resembled the layout of the denominational magazine that even at second glance one wondered whether it was the spoof it seemed to be. All of the

(Top) Calvin's Franklin administration building, where good foundations were laid (1917-1960). (Bottom) Calvin College's Knollcrest campus, a vision realized.

weekly columns were there, as were feature articles that seemed, at first glance, to be the *Banner*'s ordinary fare. But it wasn't the *Banner*. Not by any stretch of the imagination.

Every last word of the spoof was a joke—to some hilarious, to others tasteless, and to still others vile, scurrilous, and evil. A full-page ad on the back cover ridiculed Dordt College ("Warp College," Slough Center, Idawa) by asserting that no CRC parent needed to fear a word of what was taught within its hallowed halls. What's more, the ad suggested, at Warp "the odds are good"—presumably for spouse-hunting.

Page after page offered similar lampooning. An ad for fieldglasses offered a means by which to "view the Second Coming." La Brave CRC asked for promissory notes because the congregation was undertaking plans to complete "our first country club unit and recreational facilities." The CRC's ethnic provincialism was spoofed by countless shipwrecked Dutch names—Vander Balm, Vander Vander, Mousen, and William Vander William. Some of it was silly, some of it questionable, some of it suggestive, some incredibly good; but the whole of it—its achievement as a mock *Banner*—took one's breath away. It was that close to real. It was unquestionably the work of absolutely brilliant kids—but kids nonetheless.

Rev. John Vander Ploeg, then editor of *The Banner,* found the parody of the denominational magazine neither humorous nor amusing. Like Dordt's Professor Van Schouwen, Vander Ploeg was a child of the Depression, of World

Parody of *The Banner* published by the Calvin College *Chimes* staff in the spring of 1970.

War II, and of two long decades of an ecclesiastical life so hierarchical that his predecessor at *The Banner*, H. J. Kuiper, functioned as if he were the pope of the CRC. His was a generation that believed in structure and respect, in piety and holiness. His was not a generation capable of producing a *Bananer*.

Vander Ploeg was horrified. In a four-page response on the editorial pages of *The Banner,* a deeply frustrated Vander Ploeg brought his fist down squarely on the entire enterprise. "The [*Bananer*] is deplorable," he wrote, "a disgrace to Calvin College, and at times nothing less than blasphemy."

And then, filled with righteous indignation, he asked, "Who are the perverted minds that dreamed up this devil's brew?" He knew very well, of course. The staff at the Calvin College *Chimes* had brewed it up, so Vander Ploeg took off after them, and not as if they were spitwadding catechumens or naughty children who needed their mouths washed out with soap. In his mind, the perpetrators were of a different sort—they were, in short, demonic. "The humor(?) of *Chimes'* mock issue of *The Banner*," Vander Ploeg stated, "is so disgustingly off-limits that it reeks with the stench of the demons."

Right from the onset he made his righteous discernment clear. "By this time, the reader may conclude that I am angry. Well, frankly I am. There comes a time when there is nothing else to do but tell it like it is. . . . The Bible does tell us: 'Be ye angry, and sin not . . . ' (Eph. 4). Anyone who thinks that our Lord never became angry does not know the Jesus of Scripture." To Vander Ploeg, *The Banner,* the CRC, and he personally were well-organized on the Lord's side in all of this; on the other hand, quite literally, sat the *Chimes* editors, recruited into the host of the enemy.

Because his analysis drew the line between saint and sinner so deeply, Vander Ploeg assumed that any *Bananer* readers who would laugh at such mockery, such blasphemy, had themselves compromised the faith. "It is utterly beyond me," he wrote, "to be reliably informed that one of

John Vander Ploeg,
a conservative editor.

our ministers can rise to the defense of this blasphemy by saying that it's too bad if we can no longer laugh at ourselves." To Vander Ploeg, such a "nauseating" work provided a litmus test of personal righteousness. He listed a number of Bible verses to warrant not only his rage but also his condemnation of the individuals involved.

One of those verses may well be most telling: "Knowing this first, that in the last day mockers shall come with mockery, walking after their own lusts (2 Pet. 3:3)." Whether or not we can determine Vander Ploeg's exegesis by this usage is uncertain; what is clear, however, is that his intense hatred of the *Bananer* was generated at least in part by an apocalyptic perception of the end times the church was facing. He saw a vision of the coming of the Lord to punish the unbelieving perpetrators while delivering the rest of us from the manifold sin of the generation who had created this damnable thing.

In his long editorial, Vander Ploeg examines three parts of *The Bananer* as "nauseating examples" of its depraved goals. The first was a story meant to mock *The Banner*'s own youth page, a story that included the photo of a distraught, pregnant girl crying in front of a church. The second, from the Boys and Girls department of *The Banner,* featured a dot-to-dot puzzle, which, when connected, revealed the bunny insignia of Hugh Hefner's *Playboy* empire. The third referred *Banner* readers to the *Banner*'s lampooning of the weekly "Announcements" department, where once again Vander Ploeg charged the *Chimes* editors with barely disguised sexual innuendo. "Just how dirty can one become!" he railed.

While he undoubtedly hated other parts of the *Bananer,* Vander Ploeg's three-pronged attack at the openness by which the editors referred to human sexuality illustrates the point at which he was most offended. Although today, thirty years later, the "dirty" references he cites seem tame and even restrained, what was at issue for Vander Ploeg and others was an adroit fear of the sexual revolution of the sixties.

But the story that Vander Ploeg quotes from most extensively in his horror at the suggestiveness of the *Bananer,* the story of the young pregnant woman, has its own history. The *Chimes* editors, like most of us who'd grown up in the CRC of the fifties and early sixties, had experienced an obvious warp in the nature of church discipline. I remember young women standing up in front of the congregation to confess their sin against the seventh commandment—and many times it was *only* young women. Their sin, after all, was public, prominently displayed, and therefore necessitated a public confession, a ritual of forgiveness—in theory wonderful, but in practice often misused and abused.

That the concept of church discipline was poorly served by the way it was practiced cannot be argued. No Christian Reformed congregation I know of continues to march its unwed mothers and fathers to the front to respond to charges of sin; that practice disappeared within the lifetime of the late sixties generation. But back then, what seemed obvious to my

generation, at least, was the fact that across the denomination the seventh commandment became the only ordinance from Moses' law that was verifiably transgressed. There may well have been sinners brought before the congregation for being covetous or having other gods or even desecrating the Sabbath, but I don't remember any. The vast majority of sinners in the CRC, at least those recognized by its own rituals, were kids who'd had intercourse out of wedlock—and then, mostly the young women.

The highest ideals of church discipline were compromised by a practice that turned into what some saw as a public lynching. The church undoubtedly meant well, meant to bestow forgiveness and bring the lawbreakers back into the loving joy of community. But the practice failed because it created a perception that sex was the only sin horrifying enough to merit public condemnation and because women bore a disproportionate share of the exposure and punishment.

That injustice is the history behind the parody "I Saw the Devil," a phenomenon that editor Vander Ploeg, convinced of the righteousness of public confession of sin, likely never understood. But the sixties generation, pushed along by their culture of song and dance, couldn't help but examine every last move of the "establishment" authority. From the angle of the *Chimes* editors, the manner by which seventh-commandment violations were dealt with was indeed worthy of their finest satiric efforts.

Was the *Bananer* dirty? For John Vander Ploeg, undoubtedly it was. For those of us who looked upon the rules and regulations laid down by the church and saw only

William Spoelhof

William (Bill) Spoelhof gained great distinction as the president of Calvin College. He was born in 1909 of immigrant parents and reared in a devout and staunchly Christian home. A good ear might still be able to detect Spoelhof's New Jersey roots in his impeccable English usage.

Spoelhof attended Calvin College with some very brilliant young people, including Don Stuurmans, Calvin's only-ever Rhodes scholar, and famed authors Peter De Vries and Feike Feikema (known as Frederick Manfred). He graduated as a historian in 1931, just when the Depression was making life difficult for young people seeking employment. But he soon began his teaching career in the Christian schools. He met and married Angeline Nydam while teaching in Kalamazoo, and also completed his studies for a doctorate in history.

William Spoelhof, distinguished president of Calvin College (1951-1976).

The war brought Spoelhof into special counter-intelligence duty for the Office of Strategic Services, the forerunner of the CIA. To carry out his duties he was given a commission in the Navy. He was stationed in the European theater of operations and became deeply involved with the Dutch Resistance at a time when the German army still occupied the Netherlands. Because of his service, Spoelhof was knighted by Queen Juliana into the Order of Orange Nassau of the Netherlands.

On his return from the war, he was appointed to Calvin College as a teacher of history. Five years later, in 1951, he was nominated along with Dr. Henry Stob to be the next president of Calvin College. Contrary to even his own expectation, he was chosen by the synod of the CRC. To the credit of both Stob and Spoelhof, their deep friendship survived that very difficult test.

Spoelhof's contribution to the life and welfare of Calvin College and of the CRC can only be alluded to here. He brought modernity and maturity to Calvin College. He reorganized its administration, and skillfully negotiated and guided the college and the church in the purchase of the Knollcrest campus and its development.

Spoelhof sensitively and wisely guided the college through the crises of his time, including the student unrest and rebellion produced by the war in Vietnam and Cambodia, that was highlighted by the Kent State shootings. He carefully and successfully handled the *Bananer* incident, an event that even a few of his board members looked upon as a demonstration of great journalistic aptitude and high humor. With wise insight he supported the development of what might have been seen as rival Christian colleges in the context of the denomination. Throughout his tenure he was able to hold the love and loyalty of the CRC and the respect of the more progressive elements of the college community.

—TEH

repression in its motives and practices, it was wonderfully to the point. During my years at Dordt College, visiting hours in the dorms didn't exist. The administration seemed to be so driven by their perception of the darkness of the human soul that they simply assumed that if a boy and girl occupied the same space for any prolonged length of time, they would, invariably, "do it." A rebellious generation, spurred on by its own burgeoning youth culture, couldn't help but notice that such prohibitive rules were motivated less by righteousness than plain old repression.

There was a war in Vietnam, a war in the inner cities of America, and any number of wars in the culture at large, all of them wars Rev. John Vander Ploeg and Rev. Cornelius Van Schouwen never really understood. But equally crucial to the story is the fact that the editors of the *Bananer* generation never really understood the Vander Ploegs and Van Schouwens either. Affluence and privilege characterized our lives. Every youthful generation finds history irrelevant, but few generations believed that with such passion. Innumerable popular songs spoke of the new time in the history of humanity, the dawn of the age of Aquarius. We were a pampered and affluent mob, bigger than any other generation and raised by our parents in joy and the collective happiness of world peace and a promising future. American life had been made clean by the blood of patriots who'd destroyed the totalitarianism of Nazi Germany and imperial Japan. We were its glorious future. Maybe we were the first generation in American history to be, well, spoiled.

In his editorial, Rev. Vander Ploeg goes on to explain what happened following the publication of the *Bananer*, quoting extensively from documents prepared by both the faculty and the Board of Trustees of Calvin College, documents admonishing the *Chimes* editors. Quite obviously, however, the scolding given the students was not sufficient. "The meekness and mildness of this reprimand," Vander Ploeg wrote, "when the need for a stern rebuke is so obviously in order, hardly seem like virtues in view of the seriousness of the situation."

Calvin College President William Spoelhof had visited him, Vander Ploeg says, not only to brief him on the whole story, but to give him—and here he quotes Spoelhof's own rendition of the meeting—"an assurance that the incident should not be regarded as a personal attack by the students upon the editor of *The Banner*." Furthermore, editor David Dykhouse had sent him a personal letter. "I want you to know," Dykhouse wrote, "that [a personal attack] was not at all our intention."

But Vander Ploeg, by predilection and mind-set a strong Confessionalist (he would, after his retirement, write editorials and articles for the *Torch and Trumpet* and its successor, *The Outlook)*, could not help but see the whole issue as just that—a personal attack. After all, he was named throughout the parody as Rev. John Vander Phlegm. Furthermore, he may not have been wrong in sensing that Dykhouse's personal apology was at least in part contrived to meet the demands of the Calvin administration.

"Let us be truly fervent in prayer for those persons who have given such grave offense and sinned so grievously," he wrote in conclusion, "for the Calvin faculty, students, President, and Board of Trustees; and also for our other institutions of Christian education in all their many and pressing needs."

With that request no one could demur; the needs were certainly there in the late sixties and early seventies, and Vander Ploeg wasn't wrong in sensing that something strong and pure and orthodox to him and the church he loved was mercilessly unraveling.

There are no bright and shining heroes in the story of the *Bananer,* but neither do horribly demonic villains fill the stage. It is not my intention to defend the *Chimes* staff or to laud them for the sheer creative genius of their undertaking. The *Bananer* was the first of many such parodies attempted in later years at Calvin College and the progenitor of many offspring in the almost thirty years since its publication. Some of its sequels may have been more imaginative or brilliant in execution, but none of them would make the denomination quake as abundantly as the original had. The times were, as they say, ripe.

Fear of Calvin College and its influence on covenant children was alive and kicking long before the *Bananer* editors laid those first copies out across campus. There had long been suspicion of Calvin—which is to be expected. In a way, education (even Christian education, and some would argue, *especially* Christian education) delights in the confrontation of ideas and beliefs. The *Bananer* bred that suspicion into a contagion, into fear of what was going on at "our school." In the eyes of those devoted followers of John Vander

Ploeg's sense of things, the *Bananer* was ample proof that the ideals of truly Christian education had been abandoned to the perils of U. C. Berkeley-type "free speech." The history of higher education in America included chapter after chapter detailing how institutions sold out their Christian birthright once liberal professors began to preach the secular faith. Not only was the *Vrije Universteit* in Amsterdam—the university created by Kuyper himself—no longer Reformed; it was more than happy to say it wasn't. Calvin was going down that same road—or so thought some in the wake of the *Bananer* controversy.

President Spoelhof was saddened by the vitriolic tone of Vander Ploeg's editorial, told him so, and then published his own rejoinder, in which he tried to tell the *Banner* editor that his response was less than just. "Your reading of the parody was excessive, and your reaction was inordinate," his published letter said.

The differences between the two men are obvious, and the contrasting views they carried eventually wreaked havoc on the denomination. Vander Ploeg loyalists, who would follow him to the *Torch and Trumpet* after his term as *Banner* editor, looked upon Spoelhof's rejoinder as a further indication of unholy toleration of sinful, blasphemous behavior.

Spoelhof's followers, for the most part residents of the intellectual communities of the CRC, shook their collective heads at the Vander Ploegs as recalcitrant traditionalists given to excessive moralism, tired and fearful people who lacked the ability to laugh at themselves. They were angered by the imputation that to sympathize with the

Calvin students was to take the side of Satanic forces. Such condemnation, they assumed, came from people so sure of themselves that their arrogance itself seemed a sin.

The *Bananer* opened divisions in the CRC so wide that when substantial differences on issues yet to come descended upon the denomination, it would be

---

John H. Kromminga (1918-1994)

John Kromminga was one of four children of Rev. Dietrich H. Kromminga, who served first as a minister and then as professor of church history at Calvin Theological Seminary. John walked in the footsteps of his father, becoming a minister and specializing in church history in his doctoral studies. He was prepared and available when the church called him to teach in the wake of the seminary debacle in 1952, when four of its six professors were dismissed. Four years later Kromminga was appointed president of Calvin Theological Seminary and served in that capacity until his retirement in 1983.

John Kromminga was a leading figure in the life of the CRC in his time. He gave the seminary steady and consistent leadership in the midst of struggles and dissension in the seminary and the church over issues such as the inspiration of Scripture (1959), the love of God (1965-67), and the nature and extent of biblical authority ("Report 44" in 1972). Kromminga was involved in many synodical study committees and helped produce several important reports, including "The Nature of Office and Ordination" in 1973.

Deeply committed to seeking the unity of the church, Kromminga was always active in ecumenical affairs. He served several terms on the Interchurch Relations Committee and was instrumental in setting forth the concept of Churches in Ecclesiastical Fellowship (1974) as well as the writing of the Ecumenical Charter (1987). He often served the Reformed Ecumenical Synod (Council) as a delegate and as one deeply involved in its ongoing life and ministry. He played a leading role in the CRC's discussions with the GKN and with the churches of South Africa.

Upon his retirement, Kromminga became president of the fledgling International Theological Seminary, mainly for Asian newcomers, in Los Angeles. He also involved several other retired professors of Calvin Seminary in that ministry.

The real quality of John Kromminga as a Reformed churchman came clearly to light during his one-year interim coeditorship of *The Banner*, just before the devastating attack of cancer that quickly took his life. His editorials were written with great insight into the life of the CRC. He forthrightly focused on the issues in a critical time with an honesty that rang true and with a passionate pastoral concern for the peace and unity of the church.

During all of those years of service, John and his wife, Claire, served literally hundreds of visitors and representatives of other churches as semiofficial hosts for the CRC, opening up their home and their hearts to strengthen the bonds of unity that join the people of God as one. —TEH

John H. Kromminga, a true churchman.

almost impossible for the two sides to get along, to give each other mutual respect.

No single document in the mid-century history of the denomination better illustrates the continuing process of Americanization in the Christian Reformed Church. The *Bananer*, in a very real sense, torched its own era's wooden shoes. The critique of the church embedded in its satire did not reflect deeper and wider foment in the denomination at large; rather it was a witness to a generation that had idealistically bought into the cultural changes of the sixties, into movements of "liberation" from racial stereotypes, Victorian sexual attitudes, and various other restraints imposed by almost any "establishment" institution, including (especially in the Christian Reformed world) the church.

It's instructive to remember that the *Bananer* editors were products of Christian Reformed churches, of Christian schools, of Cadet and Calvinette organizations, and of young peoples' conventions; but they were also children of their own long-haired, bell-bottomed American generation and marked, therefore, by their own ethos. They were shaped by the music and thinking of the sixties culture—all of it generated by a political motivation best characterized by what we might call "hippy-dippy" idealism. Late sixties kids really believed, for a while at least, that they could change the world; but in order to accomplish that, the "establishment" had to be destroyed—"burn, baby burn." To CRC kids—especially those most conscious of what was going on in the world

around them—no more strategic target could be found than *The Banner*, the traditional mouthpiece of the CRC, the voice of its own authority.

If the major theme of the story of the Christian Reformed Church in North America is its inevitable Americanization, then the story of the *Bananer* and its subsequent conflicts offers us an opportunity to locate another milestone in that process. A few Calvin students created the *Bananer*, but almost every CRC student, at least those in its academic circles, had the opportunity to read it; and when they did, their reactions were telling. If they simply thought the *Bananer* hilarious, they'd been shaped deeply by the broiling social milieu all around them. If they growled, they were as fundamentally and traditionally Christian Reformed as editor Vander Ploeg. Most of them, unlike Vander Ploeg, likely did a little of both—laughed, sometimes uproariously, but winced at times, even felt a little sad.

Editor Vander Ploeg's profound distress illustrates nothing more or less than the celebrated "generation gap" of the late sixties. That gap stretched across the CRC too; its effects blindsided some of us, emerging as it did from our own affluence and seemingly endless opportunities. Even though we are still, in many ways, licking the wounds of the late sixties, it's foolish to assume that that generation, or the *Chimes* editors themselves, were demonic villains.

Spoelhof remembers those days, on campus and denominationally, as very, very trying. With good reason.

CHAPTER 19

The Challenges of the Present

Synod 1973 surprised many people—some pleasantly, some not so pleasantly—by urging the U.S. government "at the earliest opportunity" to grant amnesty to those individuals who, "by reason of their Christian conscientious objection" to the war in Vietnam, were then parked somewhere in Canada or imprisoned in the U.S. or by some other means "deprived of the full rights of citizenship."

We can be thankful that some issues eventually—through God's gift of time itself, perhaps—clear our rostrums and our kitchen tables. Twenty-five years later, it may be hard for some to imagine how an issue like amnesty could have been as rancorous as it was. In a subsequent *Banner*, editor Lester De Koster analyzed the whole "emotion-laden" issue as well as synod's stand in a three-page editorial replete with sharp questions about the nature of conscience and the whole question of a "just war." Coming as its decision on amnesty did on the heels of one of the most tempestuous eras in American and Christian Reformed Church history, synod at least attempted to begin to heal the differences that the Vietnam War and all its baggage had created.

But there were more issues at Synod 1973, many more. In fact, while denomina-

tional historians may never call that synod a decisive or watershed gathering, what seems obvious from the perspective we've gained is that that particular synod dealt with some significant issues that certainly have not disappeared from our attention since.

Take Pentecostalism. The denomination felt pressured by many of its churches to deal substantively with the heat created by a much more charismatic gospel experience than that to which it was historically accustomed. The church, synod said, must examine itself and thereby realize its own weaknesses: a "painful lack of assurance exhibited by many of its members, the limited display of joy and power in the service of Jesus Christ, and the widespread lack of appreciation for a full-fledged covenantal life in Christ as the Bible speaks of it."

While the report itself warned against the excesses of religious enthusiasm—speaking in tongues, healing ministries, and other attributes characteristic of the practice of Pentecostal Christianity—it also made very clear that some of the fire of experiential Christianity was a very good thing and sadly missing in the spiritual experience of many members of the CRC.

But the agenda in 1973 included more than amnesty and Pentecostalism, as if those weren't sufficient matters to handle

Two women await
synod's crucial 1984
decision.

in one two-week period. To think clearly about the difficult issue of homosexuality in the church and to help the church properly discriminate between the sin and the sinner, Synod 1973 developed a new term, "homosexualism." Homosexuality, synod said in a decision that still stands as denominational policy, is a condition about which the homosexual has no particular choice. To resist the temptations inherent in this condition, synod stressed, gay Christians need the loving concern of the church itself. So long as gay Christians remain celi-

DeKoster, Boomsma, and Vander Ploeg, leadership of *The Banner*, 1970.

THE BANNER
OCTOBER 16, 1970

bate, in other words, they can and should be active participants in every aspect of church life.

The word *homosexualism* was created by Synod 1973 to characterize active sexual practice between members of the same sex, which synod said is condemned by Scripture.

Homosexualism is, flatly, sin, and just like every other sin, it must be acknowledged by repentance, then forgiven by the body of believers.

Synod's vote on the matter was nearly unanimous. It's fair to say that opinions on the matter today vary somewhat more widely.

I am isolating these two issues—Pentecostalism and homosexuality—because they have never really disappeared from the landscape the way amnesty for conscientious objectors has. Even though few would campaign hard and long for the necessity of Pentecostal experience in the church at large, today we still can go to battle on the matter of the necessity of a "religious experience." Contemporary liturgy is often the battleground for those who disagree on this point. Should our worship and our Christian lives be characterized by the passion of religious experience? Or should our emotions always play a kind of second fiddle to those aspects of devotional life that seem more intimately connected to our reason: a commitment to doctrine, justice, and the development of a Christian worldview in every inch of this world? Can we have one without the other? Which is most important?

In the culture at large, there can be no doubt that the last quarter century has

Rev. Clarence Boomsma

∞

Few ministers have rendered such distinguished service to the CRC as Clarence Boomsma. Born in De Motte, Indiana, in 1917 and reared on a farm, he began his preaching career in Imlay City after graduating from Calvin College and Seminary in 1943. In 1948 he became the pastor of Calvin CRC in Grand Rapids where, thirty-five years later, he completed his pastoral ministry. For much of that time Calvin Church was the largest congregation in the CRC, and for all but nine of those thirty-five years Boomsma was the only minister serving the congregation.

Boomsma is generally regarded as one of the best pulpiteers in the history of the CRC—a fine and insightful theologian, an omnivorous reader, and a sensitive pastor. But his contribution to the life of the church went far beyond his pastoral charge. He was a regular delegate to synod and elected president of synod four times. He served for six years as chairman of the denomination's Publications Committee, which supervised the production of *The Banner* and *De Wachter*. When that committee was joined with the Sunday School department and became the Board of Publications of the CRC, Boomsma served another six years as president of the unified board. For twelve years he was the official contact with the editor of *The Banner*, often in very stormy weather.

In other areas of service to the church, Boomsma served the Interchurch Relations Committee, presided over the Reformed Ecumenical Council, worked to bring the churches in South Africa to a more Christian attitude with respect to Apartheid, and led the denomination's discussions with the GKN in an attempt to maintain a relationship that was in deep distress. —TEH

brought more respectability to gays and lesbians. This year, a television celebrity "came out," both in real life and the life of her sitcom. Human rights, which emerged in issues having to do with race and then transferred to issues of gender, have now moved decisively into issues that arise out of the difficulties that homosexuals have encountered through their history. As a denomination, we live in a culture in which attitudes are changing; there can be no doubt that those attitudes affect our own perceptions of the whole issue. Like "experiential Christianity," the issue of homosexuality has not disappeared from our concern—and, it seems, will not quickly fade.

For our purposes, however, we need to look at one more item on the agenda of Synod 1973—women in ecclesiastical office. As large as the issues I've outlined may loom before us today, no single issue has been as divisive in the last quarter century as that of the place of women in the church. What did Synod 1973 add to that discussion? To answer that we need to go back a ways and provide the foundation for a fight that would eventually lead to the loss of tens of thousands of CRC members.

Where are we today (if, in fact, we can even use that singular, plural pronoun)? Where is the Christian Reformed Church of North America? Where is its head, its soul, its mind, its strength? Where are its people? In part, the answer to those questions may best emerge from an understanding of the most recent and most agonizing of our long history of denominational battles.

WOMEN IN ECCLESIASTICAL OFFICE

The Christian Reformed World Relief Committee, the darling of denominational ministries for the last twenty years, became so, in part, because it dealt so specifically and effectively with high-profile political and cultural issues identified and politicized during the sixties. Antiwar protests had been canceled by the Vietnam War's end in the mid-seventies, but other sixties issues stayed on the front burner. Poverty didn't simply stop, after all. Biafra made it clear that Vietnam was not the only place on the globe where children went hungry. And after Martin Luther King's murder, we discovered that racism isn't something that disappears once public restrooms are no longer marked "colored" and "white," or kids bused hither and yon around the city for purposes of integration.

Two additional sixties-type "liberation" issues—both of them initially addressed by Synod 1973— had similar staying power. That's true in part, I'm sure, because they were connected intimately to what might well be the most pervasive revolution of the sixties era—the sexual revolution.

Those issues are homosexuality and the status of women in society. For the most part, the manner by which we deal with homosexuality remains somewhere out on the horizon. But the matter of the status of women is not "out there" somewhere; the issue of women in ecclesiastical office cre-

ated such a substantive storm that we'll never be the same.

Let me take you back to my college days once again. We had rules—good night, did we have rules! Men could not visit the women's dorm—or vice versa. Simply could not. No exceptions.

We didn't even have a "one foot on the floor" rule, like some colleges. On the Dordt College campus of the late sixties, there simply was no visitation. Zero. Zilch. After all, you never know what might happen!

In addition, women had hours—10:30 on weeknights—rustle them up and lock the doors. Men, on the other hand, had none. The operating theory was drawn directly from barnyards all around the campus: if the cows were locked up safely, the bulls wouldn't be much of a problem. Strange.

Guys weren't terribly ecstatic about the women being inaccessible come 10:30, but there was a trade-off: nobody checked on us.

But that's not all. Women were required to wear skirts or dresses to class—*required.* Before you say, like President Clinton, that a dress code is a good thing in education, let me describe an Iowa winter. Snow doesn't fall in Iowa; it hits the skin like a ratchet, blown horizontally by winds that begin on the ice crags of the Yukon and don't lose a step all the way through Alberta. For entertainment, we used to sit in our dorm rooms and watch young women trying to hold themselves upright in that wind, while slipping and sliding and more than occasionally going bottoms up on the icy sidewalks on their way to class. What I'm saying is that January in

Iowa is neither the time nor place for dresses. Had the Israelites wandered in the Great Plains, you could read that law in Leviticus somewhere, I'm sure.

Dresses were proper, of course. Dresses and skirts were, well, female. And nobody knew it better than the guys behind the windows in the dorms, for the sixties also hiked up the hemlines. As absurd as requiring dresses in sub-zero weather was, the rule was even more lunatic when you consider that mid-thigh was the standard back then, even in Sioux Center. At times, we males sympathized with women students for the discrimination they suffered; but if the truth be known, we rather preferred the hiked-up skirts.

The quality of mercy for female students was strained all right, but a bit of relief came by way of campus radio. If at 7:00 a.m. the temperature down there was close to freezing motor oil, women could wear slacks. Reprieve. But only then. Thus saith the Board. Incredible.

My children are nonplussed to hear things like that. Last year, Dordt College did away with dorm hours altogether. I'm sure that college authorities won't be happy that I'm saying this, but twice, when lining up chairs for adult Sunday school, I had to wake up sweetly sleeping couples from love seats in the college Student Union Building—on Sunday morning. If that had happened thirty years ago, we'd have been tossed out on our ears. In addition, lots of constituents would have been more than happy to point specifically at the eternal fires blazing away down the road where the entire college was heading.

But there's more. Academically, women were, in effect, offered two courses of study—teaching and nursing. And many young women never made it to college; their parents, brought up in the aftermath of the Depression, simply assumed the expense far too great when its potential benefits would likely be wasted anyway, since marriage and family were simply a bygone conclusion.

Who needed a costly college education when all you were going to do was diaper kids? Even in the late sixties, many young women were tacitly not permitted to go to college.

To deny that the change in the status of women in the CRC is really an outgrowth of the feminist movement is downright foolish. Of course it is! Thank goodness it is. Without women themselves challenging the limitations on their roles and behavior, few men would have. Any institution, religious or secular, including the CRC, grows comfortably into its own *modus operandi*. It's easier, in many ways, to keep women out of the consistory room because it's so much easier for men to shuck-and-jive with the guys when women aren't present. I know. I'm one of them, and I've been there. There's something forever comfortable about home—about the way things have always been done.

What's at issue here is perhaps the most pervasive change of the whole gamut of sixties "revolutions." While there has been a dramatic increase in the number of middle-class African Americans, racism remains, thirty years after Dr. King's murder. And while some areas of the globe have made it through the hard times with the help of international food and aid, we still see far too many gaunt and fly-ridden children in places where war and famine never quite pass away.

To many who study such things, the most drastic and pervasive change of the late twentieth century occurred in the status of women in our society. Even there, we've not reached equality or even parity, but the world of the nineties is simply not at all like the world of the fifties. Even in Sioux Center, the vast majority of mothers whose children attend the Christian school work, at least part-time, *outside* the home. On the farms of rural America, something almost as definite as barbed wire often separated the kitchen from the barn; but in suburbia, there are no fences keeping genders out or in.

Nelle Vander Ark

Tall, even statuesque; dignified, even stately; confident, even a bit dogmatic—Nelle Vander Ark is a remarkable woman.

Born in Montana during a time when some people in the area still went to church with horse and buggy, and a woman's place was in the home, Nelle has lived to see tremendous changes in society and in the church. Lillian Grissen, in her volume *For Such a Time as This,* calls Nelle a compassionate critic. Without question, Nelle deserves that designation. Gifted with remarkable intelligence, an insatiable desire to learn, and a commitment to justice and righteousness, Nelle's influence in the CRC has been noteworthy.

Although not a proponent of the extremist feminist position, Nelle took a firm stand in favor of the ordination of women early in the controversy over the role of women in the church. Synod 1988 recognized her intellectual gifts and steadfast but gracious convictions and appointed her to a committee to examine the meaning of headship.

In her earlier years, Nelle taught in various Christian schools, the fifth Vander Ark in her family to join the profession. Her first class was in Manhattan, Montana, a one-room country school. After three years, she became a Christian high school teacher at Manhattan.

Nelle Vander Ark served effectively in a "man's world."

She also taught at Oakdale Christian School in Grand Rapids and South Christian High School in Cutlerville, Michigan. In 1969 she became a member of the English department at Covenant College, Lookout Mountain, Tennessee. After a five-year stint at Covenant, she taught until retirement at Reformed Bible College in Grand Rapids.

Nelle was a born teacher and perfectionist. Now in retirement and not far from eighty, she maintains a pace that would be the envy of many women a quarter of a century her junior. She speaks to adult education classes, teaches five different Bible classes, and occasionally entertains by giving Yankee Dutch readings.

Today Nelle is a member of the Calvin Seminary Board of Trustees and speaks her mind forthrightly on issues facing the school. Although a strong supporter of women in all offices, she has not become embittered at the long and twisted path the church has taken to reach a conclusion. She respects highly those who differ with her and cherishes her role as a servant teacher in the church.

—WDB

One quick but priceless anecdote. The local Christian school has had a soup supper fund-raiser for so many years that some think the event ordained by Old Testament law. Anyway, for years women did the whole thing—still do. They not only made the soups and sandwiches and pies, they also served it all. The soup supper does what it's supposed to do—it makes money for the school. In addition, it has become a community event; the whole constituency comes out. But through the years, something fascinating happened. Few women today have time anymore to bake pies; yet pies are, by Christian school statute, part of the very identity of the soup supper.

I'm going on too long, but this is delicious. Today, the local bakery takes out an ad in the paper come soup-supper time. It offers women the service of not only baking their pies for them (for the soup supper, the ad says), but actually carting those pies over to the Christian school gym in their name. It's a wonderful service, because today, here as everywhere, your typical Sioux Center Christian School mom has more money than she has time. Case's Bakery is more than happy to be the means by which she deals with both her responsibility and her guilt. The moral of the story is that times have changed significantly, even among CRC folks in rural Iowa.

It was inevitable that the sexual revolution would affect a fellowship like the CRC, not only because women's roles were changing all around, but also because of who we are. It's important to remember that taking the world's issues seriously is a tradition as venerable as Calvinism itself; Kuyper, the preacher/politician, spent most of his life wading chest-high and deeper into cultural affairs. What's more, a Reformed view of Scripture tends to place the Bible's great themes above and beyond individual texts and wordings. It's a thoughtful tradition of reading the Bible—too thoughtful for some, in fact.

But there is more to the mix. At the same time that society itself was reexamining women's roles, the old structures of church life were also changing. A combination of the American democratic impulse and the assault of a sixties mentality brought all authority into question. I remember my father's joy when the Oostburg CRC council decided elders and deacons no longer had to sit together in two specially marked pews during worship services. Really, that was no small change. The simple event of a group of men walking down the aisle and filing, together, into a single row had considerable symbolic power. It created an image of an esteemed and exclusive group, people who were seated separately because they were leaders. When that processional stopped (so that husbands could sit with their families), the liturgical prominence they held previously ended, for the most part. What the demise of the processional suggested was that family office was, at least in terms of perception, more important than church office. Some CRC family therapists might argue that such a change was beneficial to CRC families. Undoubtedly, they'd be right.

In addition, the office of deacon was changing, becoming more prominent. While the rise in the visibility of the office of deacon was important in the establishment of CRWRC, there was an equal and opposite reaction to the phenomenon: the rise of CRWRC brought more visibility and power to the office of deacon. When the women-in-ecclesiastical-office issue first began, one of the spin-offs was a reexamination of the office of deacon itself. That reexamination did not diminish the office.

So have a look at the directions indicated on this chart: women's roles changing toward more visibility and authority in a wider variety of places in society; elders' roles becoming less authoritative; deacons' roles becoming more defined and substantive. We exist in a church where social issues are taken seriously and where the Bible is treasured more fully for its themes than its word choice. All the ingredients are there for a storm—and a big one.

Change, significant change, was already occurring. Those of us who have been Christian Reformed for a long time remember that by the late sixties the practice of house visitation began to change—when it occurred at all. No longer were the children quizzed on the Heidelberg Catechism; *huisbezoek* still aimed itself at heartfelt examination, but its austere methodology had been softened. I also remember my father returning from house visitation one night and telling my mother that something very sad was happening in the church. A teenage boy at one of his stops sat there all night long cleaning his toenails—while the elders were there! The times, they were a'changing.

And it's instructive to note that those changes weren't occurring only in CRC sanctuaries and consistory rooms. Already in 1963, the Reformed Ecumenical Council (then called the Reformed Ecumenical Synod), a group of churches to whom the CRC belongs, had appointed a committee

to study "the general Reformed practice of excluding women from the various ordained offices in the church." When that committee's study was considered in 1968, the Reformed Ecumenical Synod passed a motion that "it is the plain and obvious teaching of Scripture that women are excluded from the office of ruling and preaching elders." But the vote tally was very close—25-22. There was no unanimity on the subject.

THE SYNODICAL RUNNING SCORE

That study prompted the beginning of the formal denominational study of the issues connected to the issue of women in ecclesiastical office. When the denomination's representatives on the Reformed Ecumenical Synod reported to the CRC synod, they asked for a study, citing the variety of different opinions on the subject and pushing for some official stand.

Seven people—five men and two women—were appointed to the first of many committees and told to report in 1972.

That report was delayed—and for good reason. Once the committee began its deliberations, it ran head-on into a related and difficult question: what exactly is "ecclesiastical office"? Since synod had already appointed another committee to study that issue, and since that report was scheduled to be brought to Synod 1972, the newly formed committee asked for and received permission to postpone their report until 1973, so that they would have time to consider the ideas of the committee studying office and ordination.

Concurrent to the opening rounds of this discussion, another related thread needs to be mentioned. Synod 1957 had indicated that women could vote in congregational meetings. In other words, the CRC allowed women to vote but hadn't required it in individual churches. An overture in 1972 asked synod to do just that—require all congregations to give women members the power of the vote. But synod demurred, citing the conscientious objections of some individual consistories.

The synod we've been talking about, Synod 1973, was going to be a crucial gathering. Not only would it hear reports on the nature of church office, it would also listen to the very first report of a committee specifically drawn to look at women's roles in the church. There is no question but that the two reports of that year need to be seen together.

The report on church office dealt substantively with words like *service* and *authority. Office,* they said, means "service" or "ministry," and it refers to activity the entire church participates in, not to something undertaken or carried out by only a select group of individuals. Christ calls everyone to service, they pointed out.

But there are certain jobs that only some do—what about the tasks of elders and deacons and preachers, for instance? Once again, the synodical report maintained that these special ministries are functional and are characterized by service, not by status or dominance or privilege. There is no essential distinction, only a functional difference, between ministers, elders, deacons, and all other members. And the reason for the lack of distinction is obvious from the Word of God: we all live and serve under the authority of Christ. Nobody is,

by nature of a particular office, holier or more righteous or closer to God than others. We all serve.

In the context of that report, the committee asked to study the status of women reported to Synod 1973 and offered these principles concerning women and ecclesiastical office:

> a. *Christ's redemption and restoration result in a new equality between the sexes and does not allow for any discrimination in the congregation (Gal 3 :28).*
>
> b. *The Scriptures warn repeatedly against the idea of complete sameness between the sexes and their roles and functions in the church.*
>
> c. *During the times of biblical history women have, in fact, officiated in many ways and in many offices.*
>
> d. *The Scriptures stress continually the way (modus) in which women should function in the church. This way may not give offense and ought to be conducive to the ministry of the church.*

These principles were not so much new as scary. After discussing the ideas themselves, synod referred the entire report back to the churches for study and reactions, well aware of the fact that any change would require patience, deliberation, and care. For many conservatives, a highly significant change in the way the church did its work loomed suspiciously behind the platitudes and scriptural references.

Synod also created another committee (four men and one woman) to study and evaluate the report and to receive reactions from the churches. Their mandate was simply to study the place and role of women in the Christian church, and they were instructed to report to Synod 1975.

Two years later, the committee had received 165 communications, the vast majority of which were critical of the 1973 report. Following the 1973 committee's lead, the 1975 committee evaluated the crucial texts once more in a way which, if I'd try to summarize, would make this chapter even bulkier than it's going to be. With the reactions of the churches in hand, however, and with a new, wider view of Scripture's principles, the 1975 committee concluded that

> *the church should not now open her offices to women. . . . To invest a woman with the authority of the offices of the church under present conditions involves the unacceptable risk of conflict between her authority as officebearer and her husband's authority as head of the home. Some of us are convinced it may be possible for women to hold ecclesiastical office in the future, while others of us are convinced it will never be possible.*

What is obvious from the committee's conclusions is that synod judged the principle of unity in the church more crucial than what supporters of change would have called the principle of equality or justice for women. The overwhelming response of the denomination had been negative, no matter how strong the argument for opening church office, no matter how passionate the claims of those want-

ing change. But what had been made clear from 1973 was made more apparent by 1975: there were two bona fide motivations going to war here—those who wanted, above all, to hold on to a view of women they perceived to be prescribed by the apostle Paul; and those who wanted, above all, to seek justice for women. There were two diametrically opposed sides praying fervently to the same God for two wholly different outcomes. The battle then only beginning was not going to be fought by forces of good on one side and evil on the other; both sides had legitimate and righteous arguments. Both could allude to principles of Scripture. Both could use images drawn from the life of Jesus Christ—prophet of justice, prophet of righteousness. And neither was about to back down.

But the 1975 committee extended the terms of the discussion by bringing in issues having to do with a previously unexamined theme of Scripture—namely, the issue of what might be called "creation order." Not only was there a kind of hierarchy established in creation (Adam first, then Eve), but that very idea is alluded to and sharpened by Paul himself, who, in 1 Corinthians 11, speaks of woman being created for the man. The 1975 committee asserted that this important theme—an idea not pursued by the 1973 committee—needed further study. Suddenly, a new word became part and parcel of the whole discussion: *headship.*

The word itself first surfaced when, in 1975, synod was discussing the male/female relationship between husband and wife. Synod argued that, at least in marriage, the Bible's view is relatively clear: the husband exercises "headship" over his wife. A problem would therefore arise if women were given church office; that would violate not only what Paul commands about women in church, but also what synod thought of as a more basic principle—the submission of a woman to a man.

The issue wasn't about to go away, one direction or the other. Two committees were appointed by Synod 1975. The task of the first was to help churches find new ways of using women's gifts in ministry— short of women occupying church office, of course. The second was given the task of studying "the hermeneutical principles which are involved in the proper interpretation of the relevant Scripture passages." And so another new word found its way into the discussion, *hermeneutics*.

Anita Vissia (1914-1995)

Born in a minister's family, Anita Vissia was exposed to the work of missions by attending mission fests with her family. Johanna Veenstra, pioneer missionary to Nigeria, spoke at one of

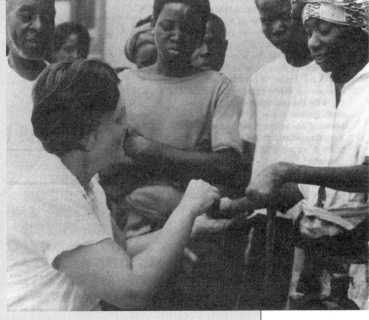

them. The teenaged Anita was so impressed with what she heard that she dedicated herself to mission service.

To prepare for this work, Vissia attended nursing school and, after graduation, spent time at Moody Bible Institute to gain insight into the missionary task. She was appointed by what was then the Board of Foreign Missions of the CRC and commissioned for service in Nigeria in 1941, just before the U.S. entered the war in Europe. She would spend her whole life of service there.

Vissia began her ministry in Nigeria by almost single-handedly serving a leper colony. When new medications basically solved the leprosy problem, she began to minister to the need for maternity care deep in the heart of the Nigerian bush. In her forty-plus years in Nigeria, Vissia delivered over four thousand babies and

Anita Vissia, missionary to Nigeria from 1941-1979.

cared for their mothers until they could return to their huts. The only help she had was from natives she trained in their duties. In the midst of this work she was often faced with abandoned children, whom she cared for until a better solution could be found. She kept one baby girl in her foster care until the child was fully grown and educated and able to serve herself.

Anita Vissia was also active in bringing the gospel to the people of Nigeria. When asked if, being a woman, she ever preached in those churches, she chuckled slyly and said, "Oh yes, but there was no one else to do it." —TEH

Committee for Women in the Christian Reformed Church

Hardly anyone would challenge the statement that the controversy concerning the role of women in the CRC has been more divisive than any other in the history of the denomination.

At the prompting of the Reformed Ecumenical Synod, the CRC was asked to study the question of whether women could serve as officebearers in the church of Christ. In 1975, to the dismay of many, a synodical study committee came to the conclusion that there were no biblical reasons for excluding women from office in the denomination. Realizing how volatile this conclusion would be, the committee also cautioned the church by indicating that, in their judgment, the denomination was neither ready nor willing to implement this radical change in policy. At that point, many women in the church said that they were, indeed, "ready and willing."

To assist them in presenting their case, the Committee for Women in the Christian Reformed Church was founded. In 1977, Joan Flikkema became vice-president and later executive secretary of that committee. Other significant leaders and spokespersons included Neva Evenhouse, Claire Wolterstorff, Carol Rottman, Dorothy Van Hamersveld, Gertrude Beversluis, Irene Konyndyk, Donna Sieplinga, and Lillian Grissen.

The goal of the organization was to do public relations advocating the ordination of women. The committee held public meetings, published a newsletter, and sponsored retreats. Outstanding speakers such as Rev. Neal Plantinga and Rev. Melvin Hugen addressed the concerns of the committee at yearly banquets with the theme "Partnership in the Gospel."

In 1980 the committee initiated a scholarship fund for Christian Reformed women enrolled at any Reformed seminary. Some one hundred women benefited from this effort.

After many years of "yes," "no," and "maybe," Synod 1995 opened all offices to qualified women. In the year 2000, this subject will be revisited. At this writing, there are four ordained female ministers in the ranks of the CRC clergy, although several more have been approved for candidacy.

Commenting on the struggle for women in office, Joan Flikkema ruefully reflects on winning the battle but not yet conquering in the war. She says, "The door has been opened. However, it is still difficult for many women to go through the door. This will likely hold true for our generation. We have been blessed with some opportunities; future generations must expand these opportunities."

Flikkema also mentioned a few of the highlights in the synodical debates. She recalls the day when the "reverend fathers" who were delegated to synod adjourned for dinner. Their seats were taken by the women while the delegates were "out to lunch." The officers of synod wisely requested the women to leave, which they did silently.

At another synod, a large number of women, dressed in white robes, passed from one to another a ceramic white bird with a broken wing as a symbol of the handicap facing the women in the church. The group created quite a stir. One minister returning from synod could not repress his indignation, and, after an exegetical homily on the unscriptural behavior of the women, he came to the application, saying, "When you get home, your husbands ought to spank you."

—WDB

Hermeneutics comes from a Greek word meaning "to translate, explain, or interpret"; generally it is the study or science of deciding how we might interpret or explain a body of literature. When the second committee created by Synod 1975 reported to Synod 1978, the bulk of their report had to do with how we read Scripture. Once again, this newer committee read through the important passages of Scripture and discussed those passages in ways that Synod 1975 had not. Occasionally they begged to differ with the prior synod's assessment of meaning. And on the newest issue, headship, they departed quite definitely from the prior synod's understanding, arguing that headship is a principle that can easily be overdone, both in practice and in light of what Scripture says elsewhere about the relationship between men and women.

But at that point the committee studying hermeneutics parted ranks. A majority asserted that, in light of their own findings, there was no reason *not* to allow women to serve as deacons. A minority agreed that women could be deacons, but felt that that would be possible only if the work of the deacon were easily and clearly distinguishable from the work of an elder. What's more, they stepped a bit further into the quagmire that was yet to come: "There is no evidence in the Bible for opening the offices of elder and minister to women," they said. Their reasoning stemmed from the argument that no women were to have authority over men.

Synod's own advisory committee accepted the recommendation of the study committee on hermeneutics and proposed opening the office of deacon to women. Synod itself agreed, but added that women's role as deacons must be kept entirely clear of elders' work. (The most significant block remained this business of headship. Just exactly what authority did Scripture seem to allow for all men to have over all women?) With that stipulation, synod changed church order. After 1978, voting women into the office of deacon was just fine, as long as the two offices were kept distinguishable.

But as with other major decisions, the 1978 ruling, even with its limiting stipulations, had to be ratified the following year by Synod 1979.

There are hundreds of elders and preachers in the denomination who remember those sometimes rancorous synod meetings. Rarely in contemporary denominational history did an issue so fully ensnare people's attention. Often enough, delegates would come in from lunch or dinner to see the galleries at Calvin College's Fine Arts Center full to overflowing. At times, the crowds were boisterous and impolite, as if the decisions handed down by synod after synod might be somehow affected by sheer noise. The atmosphere in and around many of those synods, passionate and unflinching, was not pretty.

A year after Synod 1978 had opened up the office of deacon, with stipulations, sixty-four communications came from individual congregations concerning what had happened the summer before. Most of them minced no words—they were against the decision, and they asked Synod 1979 to turn the church around. Some argued for postponement or withholding ratification, but once again it was clear that the denomination itself was at logger-heads. Some churches simply went ahead on their own and elected women to the office of deacon, infuriating other more conservative fellowships.

Synod 1979, sensing no clear mind on the issue, formed what had come to be the fourth study committee on the matter and presented that committee with a mandate that looked very similar to the ones that had come before: study and define the office of deacon, review the '78 report and decision, have another look at "headship." This newest offspring, composed of seven men and two women, was told to report back to Synod 1981.

It would be wonderful to be able to say that suddenly in 1981 or 1987 or 1994, everybody came to see things in the same way. That didn't happen. For more than twenty years already the votes on the issue of women in ecclesiastical office have been split, the synod fractured, the denomination halved. While each report likely shed a little more light on the issues of women in office, the nature of office, headship, and hermeneutics, one by one churches began leaving the denomination, convicted that the path of the argument was leading the CRC away from its fundamental beliefs and truths and toward worldliness, modernism, and the end of orthodoxy.

Synod 1981, sensing the high surf of con-gregational unrest, merely postponed deci-sion-making. When an elder delegate pro-posed that the whole business be studied more deeply, especially the thorny busi-ness of "headship," synod agreed. You see, successive synodical committees had run stuck on a perplexing dilemma: while the Bible makes it clear that men and women

are equals, it seems to say quite explicitly that men, on the basis of "creation order," are vested with authority over women. Just exactly how the genders could be both equal and not equal at the same time was vexing, and eventually proved to be the undoing of the whole headship thread of the women's issue.

Nonetheless, in 1981, synod's postpone-ment of a decision didn't stop them from creating a new committee to go after this headship business once again. "What is the meaning and scope of headship in the Bible?" synod asked the new committee. "Does headship carry authority for the church, for society, for anything other than marriage?" Five men and two women were appointed to go back to the drawing board, then report to Synod 1983.

The succession of turnovers and post-ponements did nothing to quell what amounted to righteous anger throughout the churches. All during this time, more and more meetings were held with the avowed purpose of looking into the future of the denomination and trying to assess whether or not faithful believers could stay with a denomination that seemed so reluctant to see what was noted so obviously by so many of its members: that they were dead right and the other side was dead wrong. We were hopelessly split, and successive synods seemed powerless to do anything about it. Not acting only provoked the extremes more viciously—both the right and the left.

Acting one way or another meant surely alienating a huge chunk of the denomination.

Synod 1983 came, and there was no report. There was no decision. The com-mittee asked for more time. The denomi-

Lester De Koster

Lester De Koster can truly be called "one of a kind," a real individualist. He was a product of conservative Zeeland, Michigan, where he did not attend the Christian school. As a youth he was a spiritual rebel at a time and place in which there were no young rebels. He gave his pastor, William Kok, ample reasons for despair.

After graduating from Calvin College, studying at the University of Michigan, and doing a stint in the U.S. Navy, De Koster contacted Dr. Henry Stob, mended a few of the breaches remaining from his college years, and was appointed in 1946 to teach speech at Calvin. He was now part of the establishment.

But the establishment was not yet comfortable with him. De Koster was an erudite critic of the "political right" and gave expression to his views in his evaluation of *The Road Ahead,* written by John T. Flynn. Flynn, on the other hand, was championed by the editor of *The Banner,* H. J. Kuiper. The argument grew so heated that Kuiper labeled De Koster as a "pinko," a light shade of Communist Red.

As the director of Calvin Library, De Koster continued to gain the trust of the establishment. He became one of the leading lights of the more progressive wing of the church. His power as a speaker and orator grew with the years, and he became a renowned Calvin scholar and spokesman and a vigorous critic of Marxism.

When the Board of Publications was looking for nominees to replace John Vander Ploeg as *Banner* editor, De Koster was suggested as a candidate and was elected. *The Banner* had its first non-ordained editor, and the progressives were enthusiastic about its future.

Lester De Koster.

But things did not develop as the progressives had expected and hoped for. De Koster began to take very conservative positions, especially where theological issues were concerned. In the context of the discussion of the nature and extent of biblical authority and the women in office issue, the subject of hermeneutical principles came to the fore. De Koster had little confidence in hermeneutics and began to ridicule "Hermen Neutic." It became clear that De Koster was committed to a literalistic reading of the Bible. When someone pointed out that the church does not demand that women be "covered" in worship nor that they refrain from cutting their hair, as set forth in 1 Corinthians 11, he responded by saying that this indicated how far we had fallen away from the truth.

Because of his conservatism, De Koster lost the support of all those who had been most enthusiastic about his appointment as editor, including the Calvin faculty, a reality that grieved him deeply. As a result he became isolated from his former support base and from the life of the church.

While De Koster did not actively promote the schism of the nineties, he did bless it. His writings were used by schismatics to fuel the attack on the church and to strengthen their position. When the option of allowing women to be ordained finally opened up, De Koster joined the break-away Seventh Reformed Church in Grand Rapids.

There is another reality to the enigma that is De Koster. His tight circle of friends includes his very conservative pastor and Richard Rhem, a minister disciplined by the Reformed Church in America because of his liberal views. It also embraces the Universalist-Unitarian Duncan Littlefair with whom De Koster has, in a sense, everything, and nothing, in common.

It all leads one to wonder if there is another development waiting in the wings of the future of Lester De Koster. He really ought to come home.

—TEH

nation continued to hemorrhage from rifts that were turning bloody.

The fifth report, a ninety-four pager from a committee called "Headship and the Bible," was lugged to Synod 1984, offering an interesting variation on the theme: headship was a biblical principle that extended beyond marriage and beyond the church and even into society itself.

Simply stated, men, on the basis of what the Bible said, were to exercise authority over women in all areas of life.

In retrospect, it's almost unbelievable that clear-minded, able people could argue that position seriously, but they did. The committee noted, for example, that the church has not really preached that kind of directive outside of its own system of governance; that's why society doesn't look like the biblical model. "It is our conviction that the Scriptures teach the relevance of headship for the whole of life," the report argued. "The church must teach and proclaim it as such."

The committee was not blind to the boldness of its own argument. This directive to the church—to shape society by the headship principle—was not going to be easy. The issue raises, they said, "innumerable questions of application in such areas as education, business, politics, and so on." To say the least. To reduce the argument to its own logical end, however, was to see the irrelevance of the directive: any man has authority over any woman in any situation—so says the Bible.

How could thoughtful people really believe such a thing? We need to remember a few things here. First, the church was coming apart at the seams. The committee's attempt at finding a middle ground took a

scriptural principle very seriously and yet allowed for significant change.

Headship or no headship, the committee recommended that women could become deacons in a biblical church, because the office would not—as the offices of elder, preacher, and evangelist certainly would—put a woman in a position of authority over a man.

What the committee had negotiated, in other words, was a middle road, a compromise. The left gets women in the office of deacon; the right gets a firm commitment to the biblical notion of headship, as well as a hermeneutic that's orthodox. We take Scripture's words seriously and take the changes in society seriously too.

The committee's recommendations were a kind and merciful and even loving middle way.

Unfortunately, its findings weren't beyond question, even to the members of the committee itself, for by the time the committee brought its headship report to synod, it was signed in three different ways. The majority report—which made a case for the universality of the headship principle—was signed by four of the seven committee members. One committee member created a minority report that argued that even the office of deacon would have some authority, and that therefore no woman should be placed in that position. Rather, that member argued, women should be placed in a new position—"assistants in ministry."

A second minority report, signed by two committee members, simply didn't buy what the majority report offered, not in the least. "There is not sufficiently clear evidence from Scripture to warrant the conclusion of a 'headship principle,' holding that man's rulership over woman is a creation norm," that report argued. With that in mind, the second minority report suggested the local option—let the churches do what they want to do in their own way.

Synod 1984 took close note of the work of its latest study committee, read through its three reports, and affirmed the headship principle once again—but in its own way. Headship, synod said, is a firm biblical principle in the marriage relationship; furthermore, the biblical principle is so deeply a part of Scripture that it extends beyond the marriage relationship. But then, contrary to its own 1928 directives on worldly amusements, Synod 1984 was forced into dancing. For while they felt that the headship principle was pervasive and authoritative throughout Scripture, and while it therefore had to extend farther than marriage, synod was very much unwilling to say that such a principle actually had authority in schools, governments, and businesses. "There is insufficient scriptural evidence," synod said, "to warrant the conclusion that a headship principle holding man's rulership/primary leadership and direction-setting over woman is a creation norm extending over the whole of human life." What they faced was a horrendous quandary: to deny the principle of headship was to reconfigure dozens of Scripture passages; yet, to say such a principle was directive for society was to see unrighteousness everywhere, even in one's own family. Should there be women teachers, women lawyers, women business executives? Can a woman teach adult church school? Should I, on biblical grounds, tell my daughter that she should not go to medical school? And is some future synod going to sit down and draw up the list

Two women hug after hearing Synod 1993's vote on women in office.

of exactly which professions women can and can't enter? And if they do, can there even be a woman on that committee?

The arguments were strained and sometimes, from our vantage point, even bizarre. But everywhere—from St. Catharines to West Michigan, from southern California to New Jersey— CRC people were fighting, going to war once again. To be in attendance at synods throughout the last two decades was to bear witness to a church that often seemed at permanent odds. At the same time, many of those synods were marked with a pious fervency that all sides couldn't deny. More prayer was offered on the floor and behind the walls of Calvin's Fine Arts Center than long-time synodical observers remembered. Despite their significant differences, all sides wanted to deal substantively and fairly with the issue—and keep peace back home.

If the committee work and synodical deliberations sometimes took sudden turns that appear odd or strange, if attempts at compromise look gerrymandered, we have to remember that participants often wanted, more than anything, to keep peace. Right from the beginning of the controversy surrounding the issue of women in office, two mutually exclusive and equally righteous mandates propelled the opposition platforms. We've said this before, but it must be said again and again. On the one side stood a view of Scripture that took Paul's injunction to keep women silent more literally. On the other side stood a view of Scripture that wouldn't give an inch on Galatians 3 : in Christ there is no male and female. The conservatives shot the big guns of tradition and the history of Christianity; the progressives returned fire with the inescapable changes occurring in society, changes not dissimilar to those the church had horrendous difficulty acknowledging in the past. Viciousness and demeaning rhetoric filled the air from both sides.

What Synod 1984 did, in principle, was to reaffirm the decision of 1978—women would be allowed to become deacons in the CRC. With that in mind, they went on to adopt the ratification of the necessary changes to the church order occasioned by that decision. I'm sure there were delegates who left Grand Rapids thinking that something good and solid and workable had been struck.

They were wrong. In the next year, five overtures, fifty protests and appeals, and five personal reports made very clear that there was no peace in the land. Synod 1985

adopted the motion that the headship principle "implies that only male members of the church shall be admitted to the offices of minister and elder."

Didn't help. Overtures, protests, and appeals continued to stream into the synods of the next two years, until in 1987 one more study committee was appointed. Synod 1987 considered four overtures concerning the headship principle, the idea that had become a kind of watershed for the entire issue of women in office. What was needed, synod argued, was a thorough and comprehensive study of "the biblical and confessional basis for extending the 'headship principle' from marriage to the church."

While previous study and synodical committees had argued well for the extension of the headship principle into culture at large, Synod 1987 felt that the case hadn't yet been made definitively for the extension of that principle into the church itself. In other words, previous synods had simply assumed that that relationship was there— that the headship principle was operative in church as well as society. Synod gave this fifth study committee a mandate in two parts: first, to provide clear biblical grounds for extending the headship principle from marriage into the church; and second, to clarify exactly what that might mean in terms of the various functions people carried out in the church—for example, teaching adult church school.

In 1990, the committee responded by saying that the second part of the mandate presumes that there is a link, which, they claimed, had never been firmly established. For the first time, a study committee reported what had been obvious already for years; on this issue there would be no middle ground. The only solution that might lead to a cessation of warfare would be something like the local option. What the committee reporting to Synod 1990 offered was not so much a simple solution as a recognition of the deep split in the denomination. There are two legitimate ways to look at things, the committee suggested. It's clear that both ways have warrant, both have some biblical foundation: "While weighty arguments can be credibly adduced in their support," the report said, "other weighty arguments can be raised against them."

If a house divided against itself cannot stand, then the CRC was tottering. On the other hand, what had become painfully obvious was the fact that neither side in this old and increasingly bitter debate was about to back down. Both sides thought God was seated on their side of the aisle. Both sides prayed with equal fervency and frequency to a God who, were he human, would have been humanly befuddled. Both were convinced they were doing the Lord's work, establishing the work of his hands, being righteous.

For the first time, synod was confronted with trying to hold together a church that the study committee wanted to recognize as holding two completely different, yet completely legitimate views towards Scripture itself and the issue of women in office. Once again synod created a split report, the minority arguing for more study. The majority, however, offered no prescription for what the church should do in the whole headship matter. What they said, simply, was that sincere Christians differ sincerely. Good believers can come to conclusions that seem to be almost polar opposites. With that portrait

before them, the majority asked synod to "permit churches to use their discretion in utilizing the gifts of women members in all the offices of the church."

And they had precedence. After all, way back in the fifties when the denomination ruled that women could vote in congregational elections, synod didn't make that rule mandatory. Local option had operated in local congregations for thirty years or more without problems. The matter of women in ecclesiastical office too, the committee bargained, was an issue that could best be handled by congregations. Some churches would have women as deacons, others would have them as elders, still others would likely have women preachers. And some would have women in none of the offices.

The report also reminded the delegates that Synod 1989 had declared the issue of the ordination of women to be a "church order" matter and not a "creedal" matter. The choice has more to do with the manner by which an individual church chooses to order its life as a congregation than it has to do with matters essential to salvation.

Deliberations on the issue at Synod 1990 went on for more than eight hours, and when it finally was over, the vote was taken. The majority committee report—asking that the determination for including women in all church offices be made by local congregations—was passed by a tally of 99 to 84. It was not a landslide, and it showed no clear and visible consensus. But suddenly the headship principle was gone; what was left—almost shockingly—was a blank check. It wasn't simply the office of deacon now; every office of the church had been opened.

But not for long. Synod 1992, besieged by dozens of overtures and personal communications, reversed 1990's decision by ruling against the change in church order required by the acceptance of women in all church offices. The grounds were simple: first, biblical support for the change, synod found, simply was not there; and second, ratification "would aggravate the current unrest and divisiveness in the church, and therefore . . . would not be prudent in the current polarized situation." Yet, as other synods had, Synod 1992 continued to urge the churches to use women's gifts "to the fullest extent possible in their local churches." Specifically, their objectives for that goal stated that the gifts of women members would be used "to teach, expound the Word of God, and provide pastoral care, under the supervision of the elders."

But once again, the issue would not go away. The word *expound* in *Acts of Synod 1992* had created more disagreement, for while the conservatives were happy in blocking ratification of church order, they were unhappy that synod had left a window open. Did *expound* mean the same as *exhort?*

Synod 1993 came back strong and hard, using the very grounds Synod 1992 had used to justify their action—divisiveness in the church. For while conservatives had been shaking their heads vehemently over the 1990 decision, progressives were equally chagrined—and vehement—over what Synod 1992 had done in once more shutting the door to women. Furthermore, they claimed that the word *expound* had muddied the waters even more. Since Synod 1992 had not defined the word, nor given guidelines for establishing what the word meant, a kind of local option had already been created. Because of that fact, the advisory committee of Synod 1993 dealing with the issue of women in ecclesiastical office recommended that the church, in essence, return to the 1990 decision and give "councils and churches the option to nominate, elect, call, and ordain qualified women to the offices of elder, minister, and evangelist."

Once more, the recommendation passed, with twenty-one elders and ministers in opposition registering their negative votes. One of the delegates, Rev. Warren Lammers, attached his grounds in this statement, along with his negative vote: "I wish to have my negative vote registered on the basis that this decision is contrary to the holy, sacred, infallible, and inerrant Scriptures, which speak very clearly to this matter. . . . This decision today is a violation of Scripture and merely a knuckling under to the current trends in Western culture."

On Tuesday afternoon, June 21, during the fifteenth session of Synod 1994, the del-

Nearly every day of Synod 1993, a group of white-robed women filed into the gallery and sat in silence. One woman held a clay bird with a broken wing on her lap. The bird was described as "an artistic petition from CRC women whose spiritual gifts are denied or restricted."

egates faced once again a decisive vote, this one also concerning the change in church order that would allow women access to the offices of minister, elder, deacon, and evangelist. Once again, synod reversed the course it had set only a year before by voting with a substantial majority against the necessary change. Once again, dozens of delegates recorded their negative votes, and several added their personal protests. Gerald Gabrielse, an elder delegate, registered his complaint in this way: "An insensitive assertion that Scripture is clear on this matter, despite a twenty-year discussion and biblically defensible alternatives, does not make it so." The issue itself had become a shuttlecock. From outside the portals of Calvin's Fine Arts Center, what was happening inside was becoming, after a fashion, a comedy of errors.

With scores of overtures and communications weighing down their folders once again, the Synod 1995 advisory committee dealing with the issue of women in office went back at the issue and noted, in the preface to their recommendations, what had become painfully obvious: "It is apparent from the overtures, as well as from the long history of debate on the possibility of opening the offices of elder, minister, and evangelist to women, that our denomination is divided on the interpretation of the Bible's directives on this issue."

What the advisory committee asked synod to recognize was that there were two different "perspectives and convictions" on the issue, both of which "honor the Scriptures as the infallible Word of God." In light of those significant and obvious differences, the advisory committee offered the possibility that "a classis

Women react to synod's 1994 decision not to ordain women as elders, ministers, or evangelists.

may, in response to local needs and circumstances, declare that the word *male* in Article 3-a of the Church Order is inoperative and may authorize the churches under its jurisdiction to ordain and install women in the office of elder, minister, and evangelist."

New to the issue was the introduction of the classis as a separate and independent governing body of the denomination capable of handling this issue. In effect, what synod offered the church was a more governable form of local option.

On Monday afternoon, June 19, the discussion was held, the vote was taken, and the majority report—offering classis the opportunity to determine candidacy for office—passed. Once again a number of delegates wanted their negative votes recorded, and Rev. Roger Sparks affixed this protest: "How can the Bible teach two equally valid, contradictory things? Impossible!"

Synod understood that when women elders, preachers, and evangelists began to appear at denominational functions—as they would with the local option in force—their presence would undoubtedly be offensive to those who felt deeply that they were in office in violation of scriptural ordinance. In an attempt to avoid additional controversy and hurt, the delegates passed a series of recommendations to deal with such situations, recommendations that allowed elders and ministers, for instance, to abstain from voting on the candidacy of a woman who was looking to gain the office of minister of the Word.

What's more, Synod 1995 declared that the recommendations passed at that session would be "in effect until the year 2000, at which time it will be reviewed."

And that's where we are, for the most part, today. We have begun ordaining women as pastors in the CRC. Ruth Hofman, Mary Antonides, Mary Lee Bouma, and Eleanor Rietkerk have joined the ranks of our clergy, and others will soon join them. Many members of the denomination are thrilled; many others are long gone.

Rev. Ruth Hofman

That Ruth Hofman had the desire to be a minister is in some senses not surprising. For more than half her life, the CRC had been discussing the issue of women in office. And she had a number of ministerial connections in her family: her father, John Hofman, was a minister, as was her uncle Tymen and her brother Marvin.

Ruth graduated from Calvin College and taught effectively for several years before her convictions about the ministry finally jelled. Because all offices were not yet open to women, she began her preparation for the ministry without the assurance that she would find a place to serve in the CRC. She was always very gracious in her desire that the church should allow women to be ordained, avoiding any connection with or allegiance to the radical feminism that could be found in some circles. Her attitude was one of being ready to serve the Lord whenever and wherever he might direct.

Rev. Ruth Hofman, first woman pastor in the CRC.

After seminary Ruth was called to non-ordained pastoral ministry at First CRC of Toronto. It was then that synod gave each classis the option to sanction the ordination of women in its jurisdiction. Ruth was ordained at First Toronto in the summer of 1996, the first woman minister of the CRC. She was closely followed in this by Mary Antonides, the first to be ordained in the U.S.

—TEH

To those who fought hard and lost, the CRC had finally moved decisively in the direction we'd been leaning for a quarter century. To some we'd fallen, just like the Reformed Church of America, the Presbyterian Church (USA), the Evangelical Lutherans, the United Church, and just about every mainline Protestant fellowship in North America, not to mention what some continue to call our "mother" church in the Netherlands. We'd sold out. The conservatives, who'd had visions of the CRC sliding willy-nilly down the slippery slope for a long time, saw their worst fears verified. We had begun the free-fall. Homosexuality was next. Then the divinity of Christ. The map is there for all to see.

Throughout the long ordeal of our wars over women in ecclesiastical office, conservatives, in good CRC tradition, have been leaving—just as their own ancestors had walked away from the Dutch state church during the *Afscheiding* and the *Doleantie,* and just as their earliest American forebears had pulled out of Van Raalte's infant union with the Reformed Church in America. Calvin and Luther had left the Roman Catholic church too, hundreds of years ago, and Abraham Kuyper himself had broken ranks with liberal theology. Undoubtedly, conservatives found it difficult to leave the churches into which many of them had been born and the denomination that had nurtured their families for generations and created a cultural community that included schools, social organizations, and even retirement homes. But the action of the seceders was not in any way, shape, or form, new to the CRC. When those who couldn't live with the decision

---

Coffee Break and Story Hour Evangelism

The Coffee Break program, one of the most creative and successful efforts for evangelism of women, has its genesis in the Peace Christian Reformed Church of South Holland, Illinois. Begun in 1970 under the leadership of Neva Evenhouse and Pastor Al Vander Griend, a small beginning has blossomed into an international program spanning the United States and Canada and even beyond.

Coffee Break, an effective evangelism fellowship.

Christian Reformed study materials are being used today by many churches and groups. More than fifty different studies have been produced to assist Coffee Break leaders in meeting the spiritual and social needs of women, many of whom are unchurched.

Today there are more than 3,700 Coffee Break groups in more than fifty-five denominations. Developments abroad include groups meeting in Romania, Australia, several Central American countries, and Scotland.

Story Hour is geared to the children of mothers attending Coffee Break and provides a marvelous opportunity for child evangelism.

Commenting on the remarkable success of Coffee Break evangelism, Calvin College professor Helen M. Sterk says, "Coffee Break attracts women to the Bible and its message of salvation because its study is regular, systematic, slow, and intimate. . . . It attracts women through the Bible and its message of salvation because it respects women's characteristics of knowing, sharing, and learning."

—WDB

---

to open the doors to women walked out the door, they did so as only the latest seceders in a long tradition, sometimes glorious, sometimes not.

Nearly 10 percent of the fellowship has departed, most of it within the last five years. The losses total somewhere in the area of thirty thousand—more than the total membership of most of the North American Presbyterian denominations with which the CRC, until recently, maintained ecclesiastical fellowship. For that organization, NAPARC, also walked away from our fellowship.

In 1925, after their leaders were deposed, somewhere in the vicinity of thirteen hundred CRC members left to establish the Protestant Reformed Church—a fraction of the total who've now left. Today the United Reformed Church, the denominational fellowship created by a majority of those who've seceded in the past decade, has forty-three churches and totals almost fifteen thousand members. Another group, the Christian Presbyterian Church, has six thousand members and is composed entirely of Korean congregations, most of which left under the leadership of Dr. John E. Kim, who once pastored the second-largest CRC. Add to those figures the thousands more who left for more liberal fellowships because they were tired of the bickering and indecisiveness in the CRC.

These losses are staggering. The exultation some feel over the ordination of women in the CRC has to be muted by the departure of so many of our former members, members who were brothers and sisters—by confession and even blood.

How did it happen? We've already reviewed at least some of the causes for the divisions. We've already told the story of the synodical record, blow by blow. But how did it happen in the minds and hearts of individual members of the

CRC? How did we—how do we—those who stayed, suffer the wars and still find our place to stand? Maybe the only way to answer those questions is story by story.

A FEW CRC PORTRAITS

Sherri Tweddale

Sherri Tweddale was three years old when her family moved to suburban San Francisco and joined Walnut Creek CRC, which was at that point still a Home Missions outreach church. Sherri's was the sixth family to join. Her mother was born and reared in Ripon, California; her father, a medical doctor, grew up in a CRC parsonage.

Sherri attended Calvin, where she met and married Dave Tweddale, who'd been raised a Lutheran but, she says smilingly, "became a member of the CRC only to please me." Today they have two children, both boys: Trent, a fourth grader, and Jordy, who's in first.

After graduation, Sherri and Dave went back to California. While Dave attended graduate school at the University of California-Davis, Sherri's loyalty to the congregation in which she was reared was so strong that the couple would spend an hour traveling back and forth to Walnut Creek each week to worship and visit her parents.

Sherri says she was not particularly committed to the CRC at that time, but she was committed to the Walnut Creek church. When they moved to San Diego, Sherri and Dave became Presbyterians for a time. But then, on moving back north, they rejoined Walnut Creek.

Sherri, who works today for the Bank of America in a department that services the bank's largest corporate clients, says she is "apolitical" when it comes to the women-in-office issue and other controversies. While she is convinced that women would be a wonderful addition as officebearers, she says she is also sure that the Bible is inspired, and that the apostle Paul was very much a man of his time.

"I have always been a passive liberal," she says. "I thought that the unity of the body of Christ was more important than what I may have believed was right." The disagreements and bickering that erupted in Walnut Creek, she says, "drove me crazy. I preferred to ignore them." She saw the entire congregation as a family in Christ and felt very strongly that families were meant to stay together.

When members of the congregation finally moved out of the fellowship, Sherri never once considered following, even though her own father was one of those who left. What was most distressing, "most painful," in her words, was her parents signing a letter that said Walnut Creek was no longer a "true" church according to Article 29 of the Belgic Confession. "I know that we all serve the same God," she says, "and believe the same Jesus." So she chooses not to believe that her own parents actually meant what they signed.

Sometimes she thinks of God as a frustrated parent, tired of his children fighting. She says she thinks of God sending his children to their respective rooms and commanding them not to come out until they want to get along. But she feels more pain because what is now two churches show little sign of any desire to come out of their

The Tweddale family: Jordy, Sheri, Dave, and Trent.

rooms. She is confident, she says, that someday the two fellowships will look for the things that bind them rather than the things that tear them apart. Meanwhile, she and her husband are very active in the Walnut Creek church. Sherri has taught Pioneer Girls and played in the handball choir for many years. Her husband has been an administrative deacon and treasurer for the past year. Both of them contribute to a monthly newsletter.

They were, she says, part of a fellowship that had nurtured her and embraced them, a fellowship that underwent a divorce. "If one could assign units of pain—let's say, one unit of pain for every family member that became involved in the split," she says, "then I am quite certain that I have experienced more pain than anyone who remained."

For the pain to diminish took an entire year. She says that for a long time she considered herself a "victim" of the wars that tore apart a fellowship she'd always loved. Now she's come to see, she says, that what is important to her may well be something that is not important to certain others. "The message I received from those who left is, 'The differences between us are too great, and we want to separate from you rather than work things out.' We still love each other," she says, "but it's definitely not the same."

Today Sherri is happy. But the pain is still there. She and her own parents worship in different sanctuaries, in different fellowships, in different families. It has not been easy.

Jerry Buteyn

Jerry Buteyn, a hog farmer from northwest Iowa, would agree with Sherri Tweddale: when the church splits, the body of Christ suffers something very much like a divorce. Unlike Sherri the urbanite, however, Jerry lives just outside a small town, Sanborn, Iowa, where it's impossible not to run into those to whom you once were joined, a place where a thriving Christian school is still supported

Jerry and Carol Buteyn and family.

by both churches. "Living in the same house," he says, creates all kinds of discomfort—"chilly hellos, lukewarm conversation, lots of smiley discussions of the weather."

A half century ago, when there was talk of a new college in northwest Iowa, Jerry's father, Henry, was enthused—so enthused, in fact, that he campaigned for its establishment and eventually became part of the Board of Trustees of Dordt College. Later, he and his wife sent all five of their kids there. Today, in rather typical rural midwestern fashion, three of them are gone—two in Michigan, one in Colorado. One sister still lives in Iowa, but Jerry is the only child left in Sanborn.

Jerry didn't necessarily plan on returning to the Buteyn farm. After graduation from college, he took a job teaching German and a little English at Grand Rapids Christian High School, then, later, at Calvin Christian. He loved it, spent eight years in Michigan, as a matter of fact, before his father told him he had decided to retire from his farrow-to-finish hog operation. By then Jerry had married Carol De Vries from Byron Center.

The lure of farming, something he'd always loved, was enough to draw Jerry back, so he and his Michigan wife left the Grand Rapids area and returned to hogs, to five hundred acres of corn and soybeans, and to Sanborn, the town and church where he'd grown up.

In 1985, Jerry was appointed to the classical Home Missions Committee and a few years later to the denominational Home Missions Board. Once the tensions in his local congregation began to turn bitter, those appointments, more than any other single factor, were the reason he stayed Christian Reformed. His regular visits to the local classis meetings often soured him on conservatives, who, he claims, talked much more about loving Scripture than they showed love in their actions. It's much easier, of course, to love principles than people.

While the atmosphere at Sanborn CRC was growing dark, distrustful, and depressing, Jerry's experience with the Home Missions Board was exciting and uplifting. Hearing reports from regional Home Missions directors and meeting people who had been brought to the Lord by programs like Coffee Break, he says, created a dilemma in his mind. On the one hand, locally he was being told that "the CRC had departed from the Lord"; on the other, his board work made very clear that real people had been brought to the Lord through the work of the very institution that some voices in his congregation considered shipwrecked—theologically and spiritually. What was he to believe—the voices or what he saw with his own eyes, the voluminous critics or the new Christians he'd met at Home Missions? Really, there was no question.

What's more, he remembered heated conversations when he was a boy, moments when his father would take on a neighbor in a battle royal about Professor Harold Dekker's views of God's love. He remembers the vehemence of the argument and will never forget worrying, back then, about what was going to happen to his church. "Who is right? Who is wrong? Don't Christians love each other?" Those were the questions that haunted him as a boy, he says. In the middle of the heat of more recent battles, he remembered those old conversations, then looked at his father and his old nemesis—men now well into their eighties—and saw both of them still part of the church, a church he knew from his own firsthand experience was still being used by the Lord.

The Sanborn story is not unlike the stories of splits in other traditional, conservative congregations: there were no factions in the congregation pushing hard for significant change with respect to women in ecclesiastical office. In other words, while progressive forces in the CRC were moving for change elsewhere, there weren't any in Sanborn. "Sure, maybe there was trouble on the neighbor's place," he says, "but in Sanborn nobody was really fighting about anything." In fact, after the split occurred, one former pastor was dumbfounded. "There's not a liberal bone in the church," he said. The questions Jerry Buteyn had to face included this one: why split up this congregation when there is no big problem here?

But those who wanted to leave the denomination were determined. After Synod 1993, before the delegates had their suitcases unpacked, the Sanborn church council reported from the pulpit that they were going to review their relationship with the CRC. Then, a year later, *after* Synod 1994, when the denomination's highest ruling body had moved to reverse the change 1993 had affected and when there seemed less of an immediate reason to pull out, those interested in leaving left. "You would have thought that they might have stayed in at that point," Jerry says. "I couldn't help wondering what the real motive was."

That summer—1994—was the summer Jerry says he will never forget. "For me and my family, the decision came down to a single question: Is God no longer using the CRC to build his kingdom?" he remembers. "When I thought of all the CRC programs that minister to people of all ages and in so many areas, when I remembered the testimony of a young mother who was led to the Lord through a Christian lady from the CRC who had a heart for the lost, when I thought of the way the Lord had used—and still does—the CRC family to build and support Christian education, I knew there was no need to take my family out."

Four years after the split, Jerry says it's possible to see some positive results from all that sadness and trauma. For one, he says, he was "forced to look at my faith in God and how that faith relates to the church and the denomination I am a part of—and that's something I didn't do that much of in the past."

Just a year ago, Jerry and Carol moved his father to the local nursing home. When they sorted through his dad's belongings, they came across a book—*The Assurance of Faith* by Louis Berkhof—which was given to Henry Buteyn upon the occasion of his profession of faith in the Sanborn CRC in 1933. Inside that book, he read Berkhof's words: "The enemy is exerting himself to the utmost to destroy," and "Doubts respecting the most fundamental truth of the Bible are rampant everywhere." If that was true in 1933, he thought, when his father, a pillar of faith, was a kid, wasn't it more or less always true? But what had his father done? For that matter, what had Berkhof done? Had either of them aban-

doned the church? No, Berkhof wrote the book that Jerry's father read.

Jerry and Carol and their four kids stayed CRC.

Eliot Vander Lugt

Rev. Eliot Vander Lugt, pastor of the Stephenville (Texas) CRC, was born in 1966 to Salt Lake City Christian School teachers Allen and Annetta Vander Lugt. He spent his boyhood, however, in Paterson, New Jersey, after his parents moved there and his father began to teach at Eastern Christian Junior High. Deeply rooted in the CRC, the Vander Lugts joined Madison Avenue CRC, an urban church that had fought the urge to flee to the suburbs, as many white fellowships did, when the racial composition of the neighborhood began to change.

"I grew up in an atmosphere of deep Christian faith and social activism," he says, remembering his parents' commitment. His family—including two adopted daughters, one African American, one Hispanic—spent untold hours at work in rescue missions and swinging Habitat for Humanity hammers in urban renewal projects. When in the late seventies the Dawn Treader Christian School—designed for interracial Christian education—was begun, his parents were members of the founding board, and Eliot himself was a student in the school's first class.

He says he cannot remember a time at home or in church when ordination of women to all the offices of the church was not only approved, but assumed. He vividly remembers the anger in most discussions about synod's habitual dithering with respect to the issue. In fact, in the environment in which he was reared, Eliot doesn't remember a single human being who held contrary views. His mother's sister was one of the first female elders at Eastern Avenue CRC in Grand Rapids, Michigan.

"I grew up," he says, "assuming that the people 'out there' who opposed the ordination of women did so for the same reasons they weren't involved in inner-city ministry—they were stuck-in-the mud traditionalists who didn't know what real ministry was." The line between the truly righteous and those hopelessly mired in traditionalism was always sharp and clear for him.

Eliot Vander Lugt, ordained in 1994.

"Discrimination against women was just as evil and wrong as racism," he says. He truly felt that "it was just a matter of time before the entire CRC got with the program."

In 1984, on his very first day as a freshman at Calvin College, Eliot met Brenda Cole, a daughter of Christian schoolteachers from Illinois, and they married two years later. Today Brenda is a nurse in a local doctor's office. They have three children—Kaitlin, ten; Monica, eight; and Lindsey, three.

Eliot Vander Lugt's experience at Calvin College was, however, something different from what he'd expected. While his ideas about women in office didn't change while he was there, he says, he began to meet people and hear discussions that suggested to him for the first time that "the question of the ordination of women to the offices of elders and minister was not first and foremost a question

of 'justice,' or 'the rights of women.'" The idea that there might be something more to the issue than out-and-out bigotry was brand-new to him.

In 1989, entering Calvin Seminary, and eager to serve Jesus Christ as a pastor or missionary, Eliot says he still carried progressive ideas on women's ordination. But at Calvin Seminary he began to understand for the first time specifically what the Belgic Confession clearly states—that believers may not put "custom, nor the majority, nor age, nor the passage of time or person, nor councils, decrees, or official decisions above the truth of God, for truth is above everything else (Art. 7)."

A whole new kind of Christian believer walked into Eliot's life at Calvin Seminary—someone who, in his words, "wished that women could rightly be ordained, but who could not reconcile their wishes with Scripture." That point of view was new and amazing, he says, inasmuch as the only folks he'd known before were those who were quite confident that God agreed with them on this particularly difficult issue.

In May of 1992, at a debate between Calvin Seminary's John Cooper, who'd recently written a booklet describing what he believed to be the best hermeneutical and exegetical case for the ordination of women, and Al Wolters of Redeemer College, Eliot Vander Lugt, then a middler student at the seminary, changed the position he'd grown up with and rarely challenged himself. Wolters, he says, agreed with Cooper's approach to Scripture—his hermeneutics—but disputed Cooper's conclusions—his exegesis. "That debate changed my whole perspective," he says. "I realized at that point that too many people in the CRC *assume* [emphasis his] the correctness of the pro-women-in-office stance based upon their personal experiences." But to Eliot Vander Lugt, nurtured in the CRC's more progressive wing, the whole question became an issue of interpretation of Scripture, not simply a reaction to change in culture and society. He changed his mind.

I suppose one might say that there is in Eliot Vander Lugt still something reflective of his parents' dogged conviction to do the right thing in a racially changing community, even if such a characterization seems far-fetched. "What scares me is what I see and hear from so many members of the CRC who are in favor of the ordination of women—namely, that 'This is the nineties, and we'd better get with the program.'" Brought up in the swirl of community activism and progressive politics, Eliot Vander Lugt now—at least from his point of view—seems, once again, to swim against the currents, just as his parents did when they put him in Dawn Treader School. "We sometimes seem like kids who think that in order to be accepted by the 'in-crowd,' we have to wear the right clothes and say the right (or wrong) words."

His position on women in office notwithstanding, Eliot says he's nowhere near wanting to be out of the CRC. Can he remain in a church that makes exegetical mistakes? "Of course," he says. "That's the only kind of church there is."

So today Eliot Vander Lugt preaches in the middle of cowboy country, on the very northern edge of Texas hill country. His church, ten-year-old, forty-family Stephenville CRC, which has its own unique brand of cultural mix, is one of the CRC's most unusual new churches. About half of the members are California dairy families who've moved to Texas because burgeoning suburbs sprawled into towns like Chino and Ontario. Most of the rest of them, however, are real immigrants, Dutch and Frisian dairy families who came over in the last decade and have become part of a hundred-family Dutch community in north-central Texas. That composition makes the average age of the congregation just a bit over twenty-one years of age; church school is taught in several languages. Eliot says he has parishioners who laughingly tell him he doesn't know how to pronounce his own name.

But those who know anything about life in the Netherlands today will understand that mutual ethnic roots won't begin to create religious solidarity between the most recent immigrants and their fellow parishioners from Southern California. The immigrant families, when they have church roots at all, come from fellowships from just about every point on the doctrinal map in the Netherlands; the ex-Californians, meanwhile, tend to hold steeply defined views on what the church should be, say, and look like. Many of them no longer have relatives in the CRC, since their home churches back in California have left the denomination.

Even though, by last names, the congregation may well appear to be little more than an extended family, differences—profound differences—abound. Many of the more recent immigrants, if they come from church fellowships in the Netherlands at all, have roots in a completely different kind of church experience. Some of them come from congregations, for example, where psalms were the only musical text for worship; they have questions about singing hymns like "Oh, for a Thousand Tongues to Sing." Among other tasks, Eliot's had to continue to work at the idea that the church is not simply a cultural organization—because it isn't.

His congregation, mostly dairy families, is spread over hundreds of square miles, which makes visits difficult. But he says he loves Stephenville, its joys and concerns; and while the church has had its difficulties—people leaving in a huff for both more liberal and more conservative congregations in the neighborhood—many eventually return from those exits because they come to realize that they are not Texas Methodists or Baptists. In that way, he says, the relative isolation of Stephenville on the Texas plains is a definite plus. And the place is unusual—the Hispanic workers on all those dairies wear cowboy hats and wooden shoes, of all things. Not long ago, the whole place was featured in the *New York Times* as well as on National Public Radio.

But Stephenville, Texas, is a long way from the streets of Paterson, New Jersey, where Eliot was reared—a long, long way. And even though Rev. Eliot Vander Lugt, like all of us, has had to find his own place to stand, he ministers in the Christian Reformed Church in North America—and he stays. "I love the CRC," he says, "and my hope and prayer is that all of us can maintain the integrity and faith we so desperately need."

Carol Vanden Bosch Rottman

Carol Vanden Bosch Rottman, of Cleveland, Ohio, a descendant of Koene Van Den Bosch's extended family, was born in Denver in 1938. Her father, Marvin, graduated as salutatorian of Zeeland Public High School in the twenties and proceeded to marry the valedictorian, Cornelia Scholten. He went on to Calvin College and eventually medical school, then did an obstetrics internship in Denver, Colorado. He stayed in the mile-high city, where he was very active in the establishment of Bethesda Hospital and often served as elder and member/president of the local Christian school board. Carol's mother was an active volunteer in the community and worked as an accountant; even today, at eighty-five, she still balances the books of Fort Collins CRC.

But there's more to link Carol to the entire history of the CRC. When Home Missions attempted to recruit medical doctors for month-long residencies at Rehoboth, New Mexico, Dr. Vanden Bosch responded, then stayed—in fact, gave up his practice in Denver for five years and worked in the middle of Navajo and Zuni land to get a hospital built and staffed. That project required a new CRC ministry, and Vanden Bosch was instrumental in creating the Luke Society.

Here is Carol Vanden Bosch Rottman's pedigree—descendent of the Van Den Bosch family, graduate of Calvin College, with familial links to Christian schools, Bethesda Hospital, and the Luke Society.

Carol says she's been CRC "forever." The second of five children, she went to Calvin herself, where she met and married Fritz Rottman, also a lifelong member of the CRC, from Kalamazoo, Michigan. They were married after her junior year, so she finished an undergraduate degree in education at the University of Michigan while

Carol Rottman, leader of women seeking to gain office in the CRC, with her husband, Fritz.

her husband began graduate school in chemistry. Her husband's post-doctoral fellowship at the National Institute of Health in Washington, D. C., brought them to the U.S. capital from 1963-66, at the height of the civil rights movement, in which they were both involved.

In 1970, when her husband was teaching at Michigan State University, Carol completed a masters degree in special education. Her own children at that time were ten, eight, and five. She was teaching handicapped children (infants to kindergarten), and was active in River Terrace CRC, where they were members for sixteen years. In 1981 she and her family moved to Cleveland, where she returned to school at

Case Western Reserve University and completed a Ph.D. in social welfare, then managed inner-city health programs until 1993, when she started her own business to help businesses and institutions write grant proposals, evaluation plans, and program descriptions.

Today, Carol and Fritz's children, all graduates of Calvin College, have married and brought the joy of five grandchildren into Grandpa and Grandma Rottman's life.

When she was seventeen, Carol says, she attended her first classis meeting (Rocky Mountain) and sat through the entire day. Besides being fascinated by how the church works, she witnessed a classical exam and was very moved by the event itself and all the deliberations. She says now that God was calling her to the ministry when she was a girl, but for all sorts of cultural reasons, she never heard the call.

But Carol Rottman, a daughter of the CRC and the civil rights movement, sat in River Terrace CRC one Sunday in April, 1973, and took communion. She says she'd come prepared—"truly sorry for my sins, with a sincere belief in Jesus as Savior, and a desire to lead a godly life"— as the form requires. She watched the elders gather solemnly around the table, receiving the plates of bread and then moving up the aisles of the church. "Before eating my little square of bread, I glanced toward the center aisle as the men marched ceremoniously, two by two, back to the table," she says. She remembers the words of the form she's heard hundreds of times: "Take, eat, remember . . . ," said the preacher, and then again over the wine: "Drink from it—all of you." "That was Christ's greatest symbol of community and inclusion," Carol says, "but I did not feel like one of the 'all.'"

That day, she wrote a note to herself: "I am becoming increasingly uncomfortable in the pews of the Christian Reformed Church because I am a woman. Although women comprise over half the membership of this denomination, they are not permitted to participate fully in the body of believers."

Carol Vanden Bosch Rottman had lived very much in the world of the sixties and seventies, and what she continued to write that day reflects her deep understanding of the world around her.

"While the world of the seventies is gaining a new awareness of the potential of women and their right to equality," she said, "the church is giving only passing notice to the struggles of women as a group and to individuals who are frustrated by their disenfranchised state."

What she saw around her was enough evidence for her conviction. "All-male councils, pastorates, and synods continue year after year, unchallenged." And then, reflecting on her own life and that of other women, she wrote this as a kind of challenge to herself: "The pew has been all too comfortable for women in the past. We have been allowed to remain very passive: listening, obeying, and serving (but only in specified ways). Serve we must, but in active, dynamic, individual ways. The church cannot survive when half its members are passive and unaccountable."

The next day, she says, she went to see her pastor about what had occurred in her mind and soul. And not long after that, she began the "Newsletter" of the Committee

for Women in the Christian Reformed Church by simply appointing herself editor in chief. She says it was an enterprise she couldn't have done without her children, who collated and stapled every one of those early copies.

To many in the CRC, Carol Rottman was an enemy right then, a radical feminist, even something of a revolutionary. She was fudging on scriptural principle. She was hoisting her own desires up against the Word of God. She was not being a servant; she was someone to be feared.

But she was also undoubtedly one of us—not only in pedigree, but in spirit—in the Holy Spirit.

Today Carol Rottman is just as firmly convinced of her position as she ever was. She's an elder in her CRC, and what's more, a Trustee of the Christian Reformed Church of North America.

But today her husband Fritz, a professor at Case Western Reserve, has cancer, and as I type in the words that make up this memoir of sorts, she spends most of her week sitting with her husband in a hospital in Ann Arbor, Michigan, where, at the time of this writing, he has now undergone twenty-two of his thirty-eight treatments.

They're not sure what the future will hold. Fritz would love to be back teaching in September.

But today, Carol says, "Things like women in office take their proper place in the midst of *real* struggles"—the italics are hers.

Carol Rottman's story, just like the others, is one of ours.

CHAPTER 20

Where Are We Going?

Good question. If I had an authoritative crystal ball, I wouldn't be teaching to make a living. Although the apostle Paul lists, among the gifts of the Spirit, the ability to prophesy, I'll claim the Holy Comforter but not that particular gift. No one I know is enough of a visionary to see exactly what shape the denomination will take, say, twenty-five years from today, but all of us understand it won't look like it does today. Nothing will.

What will never change, of course, is what is forever true. Five decades from now each of us may live to be one hundred and fifty years old, most of our work and our play may be done before computer screens in our increasingly technology-enriched domiciles, and the common cold may be sneezed out.

Nonetheless, the twin pillars of orthodox Christianity—and Calvinism's basic truths—will not be altered: the sovereignty of God and the depravity of humankind. Because of our basic, flawed humanity, we stand in dire need of God's all-encompassing love, which is—praise his name!—all-sufficient. That basic scenario won't change. Some computer wizard isn't going to create a debugging program that washes us whiter than snow. We'll maintain our

fallen human nature—you can bet on that. We'll still prefer wandering from God, but his sovereign love will be as all-forgiving as it always has been. Grace will forever be amazing.

We'll dress differently, sing different songs, read different books, watch different shows, down different chow. But I doubt we'll be any wiser than we already are. We'll still have enemies—count on it. We'll still find reasons to get annoyed at our neighbors, and even those with whom we're intimate will get on our nerves. There will be no end to disagreements, feuds, and divisions, at home or in church. Those we have with us always.

We'll never shake Adam's arrogance, after all—we'll still think we stand in the center of the universe. Envy? Sure. Anger? Where two or three are gathered, someone will find a reason to spit fire. If you think the Christian Reformed Church is going to stop arguing about this or that theological matter, you're wrong—unless, of course, there is no CRC. Sloth? Sure, with every convenience at our fingertips, laziness won't disappear. And lust? Plenty of it: check the Internet and see if you can't locate a little sex. My guess is that the more we hole up at home—which is likely to happen—the easier it will be for greed to grow in our

hearts. Gluttony? Likely as not we'll sit on our behinds far too much. The seven deadly sins will still gang up on us.

We're not going to change much, but then, neither is our Lord. For if history teaches us anything—not just CRC history, but the history of humankind—it's this: no matter how badly we mess up, God continues to bring us back. We can't hear this enough, so let's say it again. The gospel's good news is *not* that we're good enough for God's love. Nothing earns us glory but the blood of the Lamb. If we think our dedication to doctrine will win us grace; or our selfless quest for this, that, or the other marginalized group will earn an eternal reward; or our deeper and more moving level of spirituality will truly bring us to salvation, we're deceiving ourselves, and the truth is not in us. From the very beginning those lies are the ones we've loved to tell ourselves.

Our part in the great gospel drama is simply this: failure. We get it wrong—always have, always will.

The gospel's good news includes that reality. It starts there, in fact. We always

get it wrong, but the Lord God Almighty, our personal Savior and dear eternal Friend, always makes it right. The miracle, the astounding and overwhelming miracle of our lives, is that in spite of it all, God loves us. We're dumber than sheep. We're capable of following the strangest impulses; we scatter at a car horn, eat ourselves to death, and stupidly tail along behind most anyone who seems capable of cutting a significant swath, no matter how phony. But the great good news is that the Lord is our shepherd. God is our true wisdom, the salve to our pain. He will lead us beside still waters.

Again and again and again, God restores our soul. That's the same exact story God always told us and we've always told others.

Fifty years from today, when any one of God's sheep falls or wanders into the valley of the shadow, no matter how high-tech our medical care has become, God Almighty, maker of heaven and earth, will be there, so we shall fear no evil. God will be with us, his rod and his staff protecting us.

Some things won't change.

And our mission. Anyone who knows Christ understands the mission—to bring the gospel. Our methodologies will undoubtedly be shaped by the changing voices of the media. Our brochures will change, like our web pages. Who knows? Maybe we'll be using more cartoons. Maybe there will be a Christian (Reformed) newspaper. Maybe our churches will become schools during the week. Who knows?

The gospel story itself always needs repackaging—new wineskins. How the gospel is delivered—how it is preached, sung, acted, written, spoken, worn, viewed, and experienced—will be different than it is today; but the real truth won't budge one iota from what the message always has been. God loves us. God wants us. We are God's people, the sheep of his care. That's the story that gave life and breath to those very first immigrant Dutch folk cutting log homes from Lake Michigan forests or sod houses from the Iowa prairie, and that's the story that will give life and breath to whoever truly worships the Lord fifty or one hundred years hence, in those groups who descend from those early meager efforts.

THE TRAJECTORY OF CHANGE

If anything is certain about the composition of our denomination a quarter or half century hence, it is that its churches will be less Dutch—and, probably as a consequence, less homogenous. Those who sit in the pew will play less Dutch bingo ("your sister's third-grade teacher is my uncle!"), even though locating mutual acquaintances is great fun with anyone, anytime. Individual congregations will look less and less alike as they seek to accomplish their mission in different ways in different parts of the city and country. Once upon a time it was possible to worship at a CRC in Edmonton, Pella, Whitinsville, West Palm Beach, Hamilton, or Denver, and basically praise the Lord in the same liturgical fashion. That era is already long gone. Look for more and more change, more innovation, more flexibility in worship. Look for less homogeneity in ethnicity, but less homogeneity in general as well.

As a denomination, we have never been particularly comfortable with those evangelical brothers and sisters of ours who've

descended from the revivalist traditions—nor have they been all that comfortable with us. We've admired Billy Graham and the whole American evangelical tradition, even sent some of our best students to Wheaton College; but when that tradition of Christian expression suffers its excesses, as it does, we're usually quick to distance ourselves. We don't think of ourselves as kissing cousins with Jimmy Swaggart or Jimmy Baker. But we've never been all that comfy around Pat Robertson either—or Jerry Falwell. Lots and lots of us admire James Dobson, but many of us still understand that down deep we're not cut out of exactly the same cloth.

On the other hand, we've never felt much kinship for the opposite side of the Protestant spectrum either—mainline Protestantism—and for good reasons. Growth isn't the forte of the Presbyterian Church U.S.A. or the Methodists, both of whom speak in grandiose terms about God's love. The virus that seems to have infected those denominations has led to significant, if not terminal, internal deterioration, a malady both we and our old friends in the Reformed Church in America have shown signs of ourselves. Old-line liberal Protestantism does not look particularly appealing to us; for years we've been uncomfortable with preachers who are more vehement about gay rights than they are the virgin birth.

So where are we? From my point of view, here's what's happened. For a half

century at least, Inward-looking CRC folks (the Confessionalists), those who are most conservative doctrinally, have been going to war with the more progressive forces—those we've labeled Outward-looking believers (the Kuyperians). War. At least since Hoeksema and Danhof and the Protestant Reformed split, those two forces have been battling.

It's understandable enough. I know deep and strong Christians on both sides of that ledger. I've 'fessed up to my own leanings—I tend to side with those we've called Outward Christians; after all, I suggested that my son watch movies many Inward Christians would undoubtedly rather burn. Even though I certainly believe that there is a city of God and a city of man, I believe the antithesis strikes most traumatically over the human heart—yours and mine. Some would disagree. It's important to remember that such differences create sometimes unscalable walls.

The result is painfully clear. Today both sides have been decimated, and a sizeable portion of the Confessionalists are already gone. The heat of the battle may have passed, finally, with synodical acceptance of the local option with respect to women in ecclesiastical office and its immediate aftermath, but the smoke has not yet cleared. What's more, thorny issues remain—our denomination's attitude toward homosexuals sits provocatively at the top of the list.

Meanwhile, the Upward-looking believers have, perhaps by default, won the day. From the beginning they've stood above the fray, advocating spirituality and personal evangelism as our thankful response to the gift of grace, as well as an antidote to the problems we've encountered trying to bring a witness to and understanding of the culture of which we're part. With the wholesale departure of many of our most conservative voices and the battle-weary psyches of many left behind (witness the reluctance of many old-line progressives to take up the cause gay members of the CRC are now more openly advocating), those of us who've been least interested in what we've come to call "the cultural wars" and most earnest about personal salvation have discovered themselves least affected by the fighting. Of the three "minds" we've been working with for the last hundred years of CRC history, it seems to me that today the Upward-looking Christians— those most drawn to personal spirituality and the joy and comfort of knowing God intimately—are those who've sustained the battle with fewest casualties.

The result is manifest on our denomination's campuses, as most of those who've been around for awhile will tell you. CRC college-age students have become increasingly pietistic and considerably less enthusiastic about bringing a Christian witness to culture. It doesn't seem all that long ago that it was necessary to cool the jets of students who were absolutely convinced of the necessity of a Christian (and Calvinist) political party. No more. There is presently less and less talk about "the lordship of Christ" and more and more practice of personal spirituality—praise and worship services, small groups meeting for prayer and accountability, frequent testimonies, and even revivals. Those expressions of vital spiritual life, wonderful as they seem, are patterned much more fully from the tradi-

tion of revivalistic Christianity than they are from the tradition of Reformed theology. Students today don't sing hymns like "Onward, Christian Soldiers"; they chant praise choruses.

And who can blame them? After all, they've grown up as "war orphans." Many of them have seen families and friends broken up by ecclesiastical dispute. Can we blame them for looking for deep and enriching spiritual fulfillment after so many years of inhaling the smoke of the howitzers we've been using to blast each other?

In fact, personal spirituality is the rage all around us today. Where revitalization is taking place in mainline Protestant churches, it happens where revival occurs, where a return to fundamentals marks the efforts of the local congregation. Church growth occurs where the gospel's most basic formula is offered most simply and directly. Students today, like their parents, find themselves increasingly interested in fulfilling their own basic spiritual "needs." Perhaps the proximity of the millennium (the calendar change to 2000) has some psychic influence on us—many certainly believe that it does. And there is, after all, the astounding success of our more charismatic brothers and sisters.

The trajectory of change today seems more and more clearly aimed toward some eventual and intimate relationship with the American evangelical world, despite our theological history. For it is the Upward-looking among us who are least concerned with the legacy of our historic creeds, the lessons of our history, or even the nature of the culture around us. Upward Christians tend to fix themselves most securely on the future, sometimes at the expense of the present and the neglect of the past. Being born again often suggests the death of more than the old man of sin.

No one will dispute this thesis: we have become less Dutch. We are moving away from a fellowship whose foundation was once established by a common ethnic and theological past. For better or for worse, we have become more North American.

A WORST-CASE SCENARIO

We've begun to discover that becoming "American" or "Canadian" is not as easy as some old CRC prophetic-types warned it was. What we've come to understand is that today those designations carry dozens of meanings and implications. North America itself is more pluralistic, more diverse than Koene Van Den Bosch or even H. J. Kuiper could have imagined.

We may well take off our wooden shoes—even burn them—but that doesn't mean there's no choice as to what new style of footwear we'll step into. The array of choices is daunting.

The most Outwardly focused elements of the CRC, the most progressive voices, wouldn't mind cozying up to mainline Protestantism, where all church offices are open to women, where doctrine is a good deal less focused, where love is always the answer. The most Upwardly focused elements of the denomination, the most spiritually-minded among us, tend toward fellowship with the culture of today's Christian bookstores. Dobson is their guru; they read Max Lucado and Janette Oke, and they define spiritual warfare in ways Frank Peretti has taught them. Those most Inwardly focused, the toughest conservatives among us, the folks less likely to doff

the wooden shoes, have, for the most part, already left the fellowship. The danger they face is the flip side—one which the CRC itself has faced for years—of creating a fellowship that talks only to itself.

For me at least, it's difficult not to see each faction of the church's "mind" slowly spinning out into its own orbit: the progressives become more mainline, the Upward-looking more evangelical, the conservatives more stubbornly convinced of the old ways. As the gravitational center of all the old orbits appears to fade in reference to the paths of our factions, we'll all spin out. We've lost the center, a shared identity.

Here's the sourest bit of futurism, a worst-case scenario. Hold on. Perhaps we will disintegrate, each of the minds simply slipping out of orbit. With less and less of a sense of what links us, each of the minds will pull out of the old configuration and leave to become parts of fellowships with whom they can more readily *identify*. There are those, after all, who are saying that Protestant America is already undergoing a profound transformation in which like "minds" will reconfigure in new patterns out of the mess of brokenness created by the death of various European legacies. Progressives will join with liberals from all presently existing denominational fellowships; Confessionalists with other Confessionalists; and Expressives (Upward-looking believers) with others of like minds and souls.

Perhaps that scenario will occur because it is somehow the very nature of our own very human endeavors. Movements, especially reform movements (which is the heritage of the CRC), exist to move the church and society. Once they lose their defining essence, once they begin to search (as I am presently searching) for something by which to define themselves, they have probably already lost their social usefulness.

What I fear more than anything as I finish up this history of the CRC is that we've lost something important that once defined us. I know some would say that that defining element was ethnic, but I choose to believe differently—even though we must readily concede that ethnicity once cemented—if, in fact, it didn't create—a very significant bond. I think there was a defining center that was Calvinistic, which was then vitally refined by Abraham Kuyper. Today that defining center, I believe, is almost gone within fellowships that carry the name CRC.

Greater diversity is, of course, a blessing. It's a joy that we're not all alike, that our pews have more Smiths and Kowalskis than Vander Vanders; but the greater our differences, the more difficult it becomes to understand what it is, really, that holds us together. If it's simply a personal commitment to Jesus Christ our Savior, then—it seems to me—there is no further need for a denomination called Christian Reformed. Let me say that again. If what identifies us as a denomination is essentially "no creed but Christ," then I believe we're all better off if individually we throw in our lot with other already existing fellowships and work ecumenically to heal the historic wounds of separation and schism. Let the progressives become mainline Presbyterians, let the upwardly minded folks go Southern Baptist or Assembly of God. And

Gerald Vandezande

Gerald Vandezande is by all odds one of the most remarkable CRC members ever to become involved in civic affairs. He was eighteen years old when he came to Canada in 1951. He left school in the Netherlands when he was fifteen in order to help make a living for his family, and he never went back. But he devoured whatever came his way in the school of life.

After qualifying as an accountant through his work for the Bank of Montreal, Vandezande moved on to work for the Christian Labour Association of Canada. From there he joined the Committee for Public Justice (now called Citizens for Public Justice) in Toronto, where he became the national public affairs director.

It was here that Vandezande found his niche. He

Gerald Vandezande, longtime national public affairs director for the Citizens for Public Justice in Toronto.

became the leading Christian spokesman for this nonpartisan Christian political research and advocacy organization, which develops political and social policies and action programs from a biblical life-perspective. As such he is in regular and ongoing contact with federal and provincial officials and policy makers. He is a confidant of provincial premiers and of Canadian prime ministers, with whom he has developed strong working relationships.

Vandezande has written three books and writes for a variety of publications. He is also involved in the production of the *Cross Currents* program for Vision TV. Because he is a non-partisan, his views and positions are well received and are carefully and responsibly dealt with.

Citizens for Public Justice will miss him now that he is retired. So will Canada.
—TEH

the conservatives? Well, many of them have already voted with their feet.

Last year I gave a speech at Calvin College. The English Department asked me to do the Stanley Wiersma Lecture, an annual event named after its own beloved English professor and folk poet. In that speech, I talked about the end of community, the perception I had that something drastic had changed, something having to do with identity. I said that a world-class Christian artist would not likely come from the Christian Reformed community because

(Top) The King's College, Edmonton, Alberta, youngest member of the Reformed college family, opened in 1979.

Redeemer College, Ancaster, Ontario— the first Canadian CRC-supported Reformed college.

there was precious little community left to nurture that individual. I said I was afraid of where we were bound as a community.

After the speech, a man came up to me in the foyer of Gezon Auditorium. He looked around, then gestured with his hand at the hallway behind him, but meant the entire institution of Calvin College. "Look at this," he said sadly. "It's all at risk."

He was right. If we continue to lose our identity, that which holds us together, much of what we've created as a fellowship is at risk. Unless we discover something more to define us than our shared last names, Calvin College, Trinity, King's, Redeemer, and Dordt are all at risk—as is the Back to God Hour, an international ministry that outside observers look at as one of the most competent and well-run gospel ministries in North America. Also at risk is everything still to be accomplished by World Missions, Home Missions, CRWRC, the Luke Society, a ministry among New Mexico's Navajo and Zuni that is almost a century old, and a substantial booklist put out by CRC Publications. What's at risk is what individuals and groups in the denomination have constructed, brick by brick, for almost one hundred and fifty years. What's at risk is a tradition of thoughtful Christianity that graced the evangelical conversation in North America for a long, long time. What's at risk is our uniqueness, a body of believers who were as convinced of the efficacy of God's gift for us as we were the truth of our mandate to carry that love into every last corner—every last inch—of God's world. What's at risk is a commitment to Christ's kingdom that keeps us busier than beavers doing his work—not only preaching and teaching, but doing every last thing we're privileged to do to make our very lives a mission, our individual careers into kingdom callings. What's at risk is a kingdom vision that really has been our own special gift to North America and its Christians. It's that vision that has built schools and institutions.

Throughout this book, I've not shied away from speaking personally, so let me add this: what's at risk is the view of God and the world that animates me as a Christian writer, that gives me a basis to do my work, a theological vision that not only expects me, but directs me as a reader and a writer to be busy in the world around me. The end of the CRC will not imperil my soul, but it will be a loss, I believe, in the conversations that go on in North American culture, and not only among its evangelicals.

For many, many years in North America, the CRC has been as committed to the truth of the gospel story as any fundamentalist fellowship; yet it has worked tirelessly for the advancement of the kingdom in politics, art, and culture. It has been as dead serious about the gospel as it has been committed to the culture of the world around us. True to its Calvinist heritage, it has tried to be as much a part of this world as the mainline Protestants, yet as stubbornly committed to the truth of the Scriptures as our dear evangelical brothers and sisters. We've never been totally comfortable dallying with either side, in part because we knew ourselves to be different—not just Dutch either. We're not talking about ethnic traditions—wooden shoes and tulips; rather, we are talking

about a tradition that has its roots in a Calvinism other than the American variety planted in New England. We are talking about a vision developed on turf other than our own, an imported theology and philosophy that was lugged along onto this continent by die-hard immigrant faithful. And what we risk in removing the *klompen* is leaving behind that rich theological wisdom.

Let me, once more, tell a story. In 1972, I was a graduate student in English at Arizona State University—intellectually pretentious maybe, a bit too taken with aspirations offered to me by higher education, what some might call "book learning." Somewhere I read about a new book titled *Where the Wasteland Ends,* by Theodore Roszak, a book I thought I should have a look at. It wasn't an easy read, as I remember, but I bought it, read it, and liked it.

Its subject matter was out of my area of literature; it wasn't a novel or a new view of Whitman, Emerson, or Thoreau. But I found the book's vision of American culture to be enlightening—so enlightening, in fact, that I thought I'd try to set down my thoughts about it. So I typed up a review, and I sent it to *The Banner.* I'd never before tried to publish anything. I chose *The Banner* because I thought it was a forum for the ideas the book offered, and I chose it because I wanted, for the first time in my life, to be a voice in that forum. I thought *The Banner* was interested in ideas.

Lester De Koster was the editor back then. He sent me a note several weeks later, along with a check for fifteen dollars, which I still have—well, a copy. It's here on my shelf in the basement, part of my collection of precious things—my very first check from a real publication.

At twenty-five, I was hardly a deeply committed *Banner* reader, even though the magazine was as much a part of my family's life as the Sunday morning, pre-worship Eldersveld Back to God Hour sermon. But when I remember submitting that review now, I have to marvel. I was a young academic, maybe a touch too full of myself and my newly acquired sophisticated education. I was reading a book that has, by the way, now acquired the reputation of being more than a little silly. *Where the Wasteland Ends* was a splash in the early seventies, a splash in a very shallow pan. But what I find amazing is that I believed the CRC should know this book's contents, that I actually wanted to share my feelings about Roszak's ideas with the community I'd grown up in, been educated in—a community this somewhat prodigal son had returned to after some time away. I wanted to contribute to a community's understanding of the culture in which we lived back then.

And what's equally amazing is that Lester De Koster took the review and published it in the tiny print *The Banner* gave to book reviews back then. What is of most interest here is that there was space for my review in *The Banner.*

I say that because there's no room for something similar to happen today—and this is not a shot at current editor John Suk or any of his predecessors. The truth is that no young graduate student anywhere in North America this year, after reading a book like Roszak's, would even think of sending a review of that book to *The Banner*, even consider joining a forum dis-

cussing significant cultural appraisals. Why not? Because *The Banner* doesn't do what it used to—it wouldn't think of running a lengthy review like the one I submitted, in fact. And it certainly wouldn't publish a review of a survey of culture that addresses issues only tangentially related to us. Back then, I saw the denomination as a community interested in new ideas about society and culture; what's more, the denomination's major publication saw itself as a place for that kind of discussion. It doesn't anymore.

Perhaps you don't agree, but I see that change as a loss. It's sad that *The Banner* really can't be a forum for our own developing academics, but what's more tragic is that the readers of *The Banner,* ordinary members of the CRC, have decided—because it has been *our* decision, not simply that of the editors—that what's of greatest interest to us is what *The Banner* does publish today. What all of them would say, I'm sure, is that their questionnaires made very clear that the book review section was the least read copy in the magazine. We have decided—the readership, the denomination itself—that book reviews take up too much valuable space. We have decided that news about our churches is far more important than book reviews. I'm sorry, but I think of that change as a loss—and also a telling fact about our relationship to our world.

The heritage of the CRC—like any Reformed heritage, any legacy emerging from the Calvinist tradition—is a thoughtful one. Our significant, individual contribution to North American culture, whether we live or die, is a world-and-life view that birthed, among other blessings, a system of

Christian schools that are themselves the most obvious tangible witness to the strength and commitment of our theological heritage. What's important to remember is that this "kingdom vision," this "world-and-life view"—call it what you will—is an *intellectual* paradigm, something that must be understood, not just felt or experienced. It is a truth we can adopt with zeal, but it needs to be understood and then assented to intellectually. It's not for children. It's not as simple as "Jesus Loves Me," as absolutely central as that truth is.

At a conference at the University of Chicago, the theologian Karl Barth was once asked to name the most profound truth he'd ever discovered. He answered, "Jesus loves me, this I know, for the Bible tells me so." But Barth, of course, didn't stop thinking about his faith because that truth was central. He kept working at developing a Christian mind, and so have we throughout our history. As important, as definitive as the truth that Jesus loves us is, our unique contribution to the Christian world has been the development of how and why and what that truth leads to in terms of the culture in which we live.

The Calvinist tradition, the Reformed faith, the cultural commitment so well manifest in the heritage we've carried into North America, is something that begins to grow and bear fruit only after one's initial commitment to Jesus Christ.

To my mind, that's what it means to be "Reformed." And to my mind, we've become less interested today in a mandate that includes reforming all of life, while we've become more interested in a more literal interpretation of the Great Commis-sion. Today, we look unapologetically and more universally at a mission of "saving souls" than we have in the past.

We've become more interested in evangelism and less interested in arts, politics, and culture at large. Many of us would say that new vision is an indication of our progress as a fellowship. I'm not so sure.

The new diversity in the Christian Reformed Church is not simply a healthier ethnic and racial mix—although it is that in part. The new diversity in the CRC is a stronger mix of differing mission statements, differing theological foundations, differing individual views of what it means to act as a church and a believer. That new diversity doesn't come simply by way of those new members who carry no Dutch surnames. It has also come from within.

That which held us together in the past—undoubtedly, in part, an ethnic-religious heritage, but also a theological tradition—is fading under the stress of competing interests. If we are to continue as a denominational fellowship, what we will have to muster is some kind of common theological bond. What our leaders will have to work at, what our pulpits will have to preach, what our colleges will have to pledge their allegiance to, what our people will have to believe is something that indeed still sets us apart from other fellowships.

In that sense, I agree with H. J. Kuiper and Peter Eldersveld. In the inevitable change that has made us less "Dutch" and more North American, what we stand to lose is a distinctive and precious commodity—something we've called "being Reformed." That loss—and this cannot be emphasized enough—is not simply ours; for that Reformed, Calvinistic voice will be missed by the North American evangelical Christian subculture, as well as North American culture itself.

A BEST-CASE SCENARIO

Now let's put a good spin on the changes I see occurring around us. But before we do that, let's just run over some impressive statistics, some fascinating information, and a couple of really wonderful stories.

How about this? Last year over one hundred thousand families' lives were improved by contact with our denomination through its various ministries' expressions of Christ's love for the poor.

Don't forget that one hundred thousand *families* is a number larger than our membership. Now hold on. Here's more. Last

---

"Mr. Huu"

Rev. Huu Phu Nguyen is the pastor of the Vietnamese New Hope CRC in Winfield, Illinois. Behind that reality lies a most amazing story of God's gracious providence in the face of unimaginable human evil, bringing forth a life of striking faith and obedience.

When I met Huu Phu Nguyen in 1991 he was simply called Mr. Huu, a slight man even by Vietnamese standards, but a man with an immense heart. Mr. Huu was an evangelical believer who served in the Vietnamese army from 1969-75 as a political-warfare officer, attaining a very important rank. On May 30, 1975, he was taken captive by the Communist forces and spent the next thirty months in a dungeon in total darkness. The prisoners received a bowl of dirty rice and a glass of water twice a day. They caught and ate roaches and other insects to supplement their protein. But Mr. Huu really lived by his faith.

After these thirty months, Huu spent seven years in prison in forced labor. Most of the prisoners died; many were shot. Huu was taken to the wall three times to be shot, but each time he mysteriously escaped; he is sure it was the presence of Christ rescuing him.

After ten years of confinement, Huu was released under house arrest. It was then that he made a miraculous escape to Thailand and eventually came to the United States in 1988, leaving his wife and family in Vietnam.

Through all of these experiences, Huu heard the call of Christ to the Christian ministry. He met Dr. John Kromminga at the International Theological Seminary in California and was soon at Calvin Seminary, where he enrolled as a special student preparing for ordination in the CRC. While he was studying, he worked full time to finance moving his family out of Vietnam. Their reunion in 1992 was a beautiful demonstration of faith and love. Through all the years of work and study for the ministry and providing for his family, Huu often faced mind-boggling problems. But they never got him down. His cheerful response was always, "God got me through everything this far. He will not leave me now!"

Huu was ordained in the CRC in 1993 and called to be the pastor of a group of Vietnamese refugees in Wheaton, Illinois, whom he had ministered to while studying at Calvin Seminary. Recently a generous friend of the church purchased the property of the former Winfield congregation and gave it to the New Hope CRC of Winfield, Illinois. The church is prospering.

The Lord is using this remarkable man with a large faith, who knows himself to be totally caught up in the grace and providence of God. Just to know him is to be blessed.

—TEH

---

year, CRC members gave $8,117,006 in free-will offerings (we're not talking ministry shares here, remember) in support of those denominational ministries. Each year, Peter Vander Meulen, the CRC's Coordinator of Social Justice and Hunger Action, meets with "Hunger Directors" from several mainline denominations. Last year, they were so amazed by CRC contributions that they requested a special workshop from CRWRC on fundraising in an effort to figure out how on earth our denomination achieved and maintained these levels of giving. Keep in mind that I'm not backing away from my "malaise" theory. This level of pure contribution came from a membership which, I'm saying, is not only suffering significant losses but even wondering itself about the future of its own fellowship. If you think CRC people don't care, you're flat wrong.

The number-crunching not convincing? Let's humanize the stats. Amina Yaou, in Niger, West Africa, bought herself a skinny cow last year, fattened it up just as any old-line CRC cattleman would. After Amina fed it millet and bran and bean stalks, that cow got royally plump, Niger-style, fat enough to sell. So she sold the cow at a profit and beefed up her annual income of $200 by about 10 percent, using the additional income to buy millet grain and clothes for her children. Ms. Yaou, along with thirty-three other women living in the Kookari region, has realized an increase in income for the last three years—due, in part, to the efforts of CRC ministries. The women meet together every week and pool some of their resources, putting aside some of their income into a savings fund that will entirely finance their activities

without assistance from CRWRC in just a few years.

Most every North American remembers the images of disastrous flooding in and around Grand Forks, North Dakota, in 1997. The Red River rampaged when it choked back on spring runoff and broadened into a huge lake covering thousands and thousands of acres of normally dry ground. CRWRC responded with relief work in North Dakota, Minnesota, and Manitoba.

The CRWRC is not solely involved in disaster relief. Here a baby receives a DPT shot in a CRWRC-supported vaccination program.

Rev. Don and June Jabaay, of Community CRC in East Grand Forks, Minnesota, sent a note to the denomination indicating their thanks for so much help. "Several volunteers have become our good friends. We'll never forget them," they wrote. "They supported us when we were in great physical, spiritual, and emotional need during this trying time. Both our church and our home are being cleaned and restored because of their tireless efforts. May God continue to bless you as you continue to be His hands in our troubled world."

But it wasn't simply the Jabaays who were the recipients of CRC help. Hundreds of volunteers did everything from scooping mud to finish carpentry in the homes of those ravaged by the Red River, regardless of the victims' denominational loyalties or the nature of their faith. Canadian efforts were coordinated with Mennonite Disaster Services, which provided food and lodging for 120 CRWRC and Service Link volun-

Jan Dykgraaf doing literacy work among the Kambari people of Nigeria.

teers who donated their time and effort to assess, clean up, and assist in the recovery process.

It may come as a shock to you, but there are still over four billion people in the world who do not know Jesus Christ. All around this world, three hundred CRC missionaries in thirty countries continue to work to bring the good news where it hasn't been brought before.

On a remarkable day in March of 1993, during the height of a measles epidemic among the Mamanwa people, some of the earliest inhabitants of the Philippines, but today some of that country's most poor and marginalized, a Christian Reformed World Missions team gathered the entire

community of Gaas to hear the gospel story. After hours of storytelling, public dialogue, and prayer deliberately aimed at the powers of darkness so evident in the region, nearly every Mamanwa there made a simultaneous decision to leave the native religion and follow Jesus. Two months later, forty-seven were baptized into the fellowship of believers. Today, Gaas is a Mamanwa community that continues to experience ongoing transformation. The people have built homes and a church, planted crops, and are beginning to send some of their children to school. They meet weekly for worship and training of church members and leaders.

Even though 95 percent of China's people are unevangelized, the church there is growing explosively, perhaps faster than anywhere else in the world. And yet, officially, it's not supposed to be happening. Officially it isn't happening. "Old thoughts and habits left over from the old society cannot be eradicated in a short period, " says a document published by the Central Committee of the Communist Party in 1992. "Religion will ultimately disappear but will require a long period of development of socialism and communism. When all the objective conditions are in place, then religion will naturally disappear."

Fat chance. Apparently the communists' crystal balls are no more reliable than the capitalists'.

Like the radical gospel it offers, the CRC has found a way of working with the system in an effort to undermine it, a system World Missions calls Gateway Exchanges. "We use the name 'Gateway Exchanges' to make it easier to travel and minister," says

Albert Hamstra, World Missions' missionary in Hong Kong. "It helps us avoid the unfair and unnecessary stigma attached to us if we use Christian Reformed World Missions. It also helps protect Chinese blends."

What Gateway Exchanges does—what the denomination does—is facilitate education and cultural exchanges between the Christian Reformed Church and the needs and opportunities of mainland China. Mission efforts in China don't closely resemble the ministry among the Mamanwa people in the Philippines. Gateway Exchanges made it possible, for instance, for several Calvin College and Seminary professors to attend symposia on Christian philosophy at Peking University.

Strategies may differ, but the end remains the same—the proclamation of the gospel.

But we don't have to go far from home to find the CRC doing good work in ways that are new and powerful. Reggie Smith, the African-American pastor of Roosevelt Park CRC in Grand Rapids, Michigan, grew up in Lawndale, Illinois, where he was mentored by a CRC pastor. He went to college, then seminary, and then became the pastor of a wonderful and bizarre collection of folks at Roosevelt Park. When Roosevelt was formed by the merger of two old Dutch southwest-side churches, what resulted was a hodge-podge of survivors who looked to the community for growth and new life. So today the church has its share of old-line CRC members, as well as some of their own more progressive children, and a growing membership of African American and Hispanic newcomers, all of whom meet in a building that only four years ago ended services in Dutch.

Or how about this? John Algera is a white pastor in a lively and predominantly black CRC in Paterson, New Jersey, that worships, well, "black." Things are going well. A whole number of vital ministries are busily at work in inner cities through-

These kids are part of a Home Missions outreach program of East City Community Church, a CRC ministry in Orleans, Ontario.

out North America—Tony Van Zanten in Roseland, Illinois; Stan Ver Heul and Tom Doorn at Community CRC in Los Angeles, California; Rick Williams at Pullman CRC, another predominately African-American congregation in Chicago. CRC Home Missions claims they want to plant 50 percent of the new churches in urban environments in the next several years. The inner city is where the real action is today, according to many evangelical leaders.

Early one morning, Andrea Mitchell, who had recently lost her job and was feeling depressed, tuned her television to *Faith 20*, where she heard Dr. Joel Nederhood. "Right then and there I rededicated my life to the Lord," she says. "My life seemed to immediately get back on track once I decided I was going to follow Christ."

From that day on, Mitchell tuned her set to *Faith 20,* and in December of 1995 she called the Faithline number on the screen to ask for the nearest church to her own Gary, Indiana, home.

Albertina Vander Weele, the Back to God Hour's coordinator of listener and viewer contact, directed her to Beacon Light CRC in Gary, but it took several months before Andrea visited.

She was scared about going, she says, but decided to attend at night, when she assumed there would be a small crowd. The people who greeted her were friendly, and within the week Rev. James La Grand called her and asked her if he could come over and visit.

In December of 1996, Andrea Mitchell made profession of faith at Beacon Light, and today she attends both the morning and evening services with her children, helps with the weekly church bulletin, and edits the church newsletter.

"*Faith 20,*" Andrea Mitchell says, "has changed my life."

These are reasons—and they are legion—to be optimistic, even proud, of what the CRC is doing today.

As we move from a fellowship at war into one with more solidarity (and the loss of the radical conservatives does, let's remember, make us less splintered), let's assume that in God's own good time we're now to the point where we deeply stand in need of the very kind of revival that is, after a fashion, already occurring around us. We've exhausted ourselves with battles about the pace and direction of culture and our participation in it. We're war-weary.

What we need is to belt out praise to God. What we need more than anything is to replenish the supply of "spiritual" enrichment available from a renewed sense of God's own hand in our personal lives and God's unbounded love. What we need is exactly what we're getting—a new and revived sense of God's glory. We need that love to strengthen us. We need to stop majoring in the minors, as people say, and get about the enterprise that has always been the vital church's real mission.

The changes occurring internally in the church may well be something of a natural phenomenon in a fellowship seeking to define itself. After all, what links us more securely than a commonly held faith in Jesus Christ and his mediating work in our lives? Our identity, now and forever, will be found in our common belief that we have no other comfort in life and death than that we belong to our faithful Savior Jesus Christ. That's what always has unified us and will continue to hold us together as we're nurtured in the deepest source of our greatest joy.

In my opinion, wherever the fellowship continues to believe heartily in God's sovereignty (as articulated in the Contemporary Testimony "Our World Belongs to God"), believers will always be committed to moving down the long and sometimes difficult road of bringing faith into the very culture of our work, of being God's own agents in his world. What links us still to John Calvin himself is that commitment to the Lord's work—not to soft-pedal the importance of a personal relationship with Jesus Christ, but not to emphasize it at the expense of a Christian and Reformed commitment to the world around us. Karl Westerhof, who's worked for years at the

New International Version (NIV)

The genesis of the international best-selling English translation of the Bible goes back to the vision of Peter De Jong and Howard Long, who in 1955 were members of the Seattle CRC consistory. That consistory overtured Classis Pacific to request synod to "join with other conservative churches in sponsoring or facilitating the early production of a faithful translation of Scripture in the common language of the American people."

Classis rejected the proposal, but the Seattle consistory appealed to Synod of 1956. Synod accepted this request and referred it to the teaching staff of the Old and New Testament departments of Calvin Seminary for a thorough consideration and report to Synod 1957.

Synod 1957 approved a recommendation to cooperate with the National Association of Evangelicals (NAE) and the New York Bible Society (now the International Bible Society) in the production of the new translation.

Dr. Edwin Palmer, then pastor of Grandville Avenue CRC, accepted a full-time position as executive secretary of the translation committee in 1968. Christian Reformed scholars involved in the project included John Stek, Marten Woudstra, John Zinkand, David Engelhard, Simon Kistemaker, Gerard Van Groningen, John Timmerman, Richard Wevers, and Elsie Palmer.

They and scores of other theologians and English-language experts from many denominations finished the New Testament in 1973. The Old Testament translation was completed in 1978.

According to Dirk R. Buursma, managing editor of the Bible Department at Zondervan Publishing Company, more than 110 million copies have been printed, and the NIV is the best-selling version in the English language. Approximately fifty different editions geared to a specific audience are available today. From a "day of small beginnings" in that Seattle Christian Reformed consistory room has come an endeavor that has made a significant impact on evangelical and conservative churches in the English-speaking world. The NIV is the Bible of choice for congregations of that stamp throughout the world.　　　　—WDB

Synodical Committee on Race Relations and CRWRC, tells me he has hope in the future of the denomination because he sees the CRC as a "tough, dependable, kingdom workhorse." I like that. We may not be the most beautiful or get the best headlines, but we're in this for the long haul.

We know, better than some, that the fight won't really shut down until the coming of God's kingdom. That's why some

still say that "Onward Christian Soldiers" is a fight song Reformed folks ought to sing more lustily than any of a hundred new praise choruses.

Sanctification, the part of our salvation characterized by the work of the Holy Spirit, is a pilgrimage. It's a journey, the one all of us take throughout our lives, working at actually becoming the very substance of our belief in the world we live in.

That journey doesn't get headlines. It's the workhorse. Initial conversions make great stories because they're dramatic and powerful. Living the new life that flows from it gets ink somewhere near the bottom of the third page. Working out one's salvation, doing the work of the Lord, being a soldier in God's army—whatever metaphor you want to hang on the process—isn't easy because of us. Even though we know God in the very core of our beings, we're still capable of messing up. Sometimes, even our best deeds come off dirty. But slogging along after Jesus day after day is just as important as the dramatic events that put us on that road.

As a people who've come out of the Calvinist tradition, our emphasis—for better *and* for worse—has been on the second half of the regeneration story. Where we've underemphasized the necessity of the experience of the Lord, we've erred. Where we've merely assumed a concrete and vital relationship with God Almighty, we've skipped over something absolutely fundamental. But where we've pressed the claims of God's kingdom in every area of life—as we have—we've made a significant difference in our world and brought our own special flavor of Christian testimony to American evangelicalism.

But that job has not been easy, and it never is. We face issues the culture raises, sometimes shoves into our faces—the place of women, the status of homosexuals in our midst. We don't wish those problems away, or eschew them as if the answers were simply cut-and-dried. We think, and we pray, and we talk, and we argue—too often, we fight. That's what we've been up to for the last twenty years, at least.

And now, as a denomination, to my mind, we've come in from a battering we've inflicted on ourselves, in addition to decades of battling the elements outside our confines. We're tired, we're worn. Right now, we may well need to regain some warmth, some power. We need to be reanimated by a sense of God's glory in our lives. We're in the process of redefining ourselves and beginning at exactly the point where such a redefinition has to occur—in terms of our own individual and

Friendship Ministries

Perhaps one of the most valuable and innovative contributions of the CRC to the wider church fellowship is Friendship Ministries, a program that helps people with mental impairments come to know and love God.

Friendship Ministries began in 1982 when a family with a child with mental impairments requested materials to help them in the spiritual nurture of the youngster. The Board of Publications of the CRC responded to their request and began to publish educational resources. Today Friendship programs are a vital ministry in many different denominations, ranging from the Salvation Army to the Roman Catholic Church.

The core vision of the *Friendship* program is the affirmation that everyone is created in God's image and can relate to God. Proponents believe that the gift of salvation is not dependent on a certain level of intelligence.

Friendship's goal is to encourage and assist students to grow in their relationship to Jesus Christ, to make a public profession of their faith, and to participate in the life and work of the church. Using one-on-one interaction, *Friendship* has dramatically transformed the lives of thousands of men, women, and children with mental disabilities, and it has shared and even lifted the burdens of concerned parents. One of the most significant by-products of the program is an increased sensitivity in the church to the needs and the gifts of those who are mentally impaired.
—WDB

collective relationships with our Savior, Jesus Christ. What's happening on our campuses may be the beginning of something new, something reinvigorated with the profound and eternal blessings of eternal life with the Father. In Bavinck's terms, we may well be becoming converted again for the *first* time—to our heavenly Father. Once we've resubscribed to his eternal promises, we may be in a position to take up the obligations of our second conversion—a movement back to the world, back to the culture at large, back to our mission in the here and now.

In my opinion, that "second conversion" will almost certainly have to occur. Some use the term "postmodern" to define today's society. Although a shelf full of mighty tomes could be written on exactly what that phrase means, it's not difficult to see that a postmodern culture means an open market for more diverse and competing value systems. As modernism slowly fades, any and all avenues to truth will be validated by a culture that accepts, well, everything.

Not long ago in a newspaper I read the story of a man afflicted with AIDS. The story was a testimony to his faith and strength as he faced imminent death. The man claimed that he'd found spiritual strength to go on living with his disease and the reality of his own demise, and found that strength in his acceptance of the tenets of pre-Christian pagan religion, the worship of nature and pagan deities. He'd found happiness and meaning in druids. For the first time in his life, he felt a reason for living, a happiness that emerged from faith and worship.

Who really can doubt that some of those who went up in flames at Waco weren't better off in self-esteem and happiness in the cult nurtured by David Koresh? Heaven's Gate, that strange Internet suicide club, still has devotees who claim that their greatest joy is the anticipation of rejoining the fellowship on some other planet behind some comet yet to be discovered.

Contemporary postmodern culture finds its happiness where it will and licenses just about every medium to that end. Thousands of competing value systems offer and promise personal validation, joy, blessed peace, and assurance for eternity. Some seem even to deliver the kind of peace they offer. Belief in Jesus Christ, in a postmodern world, appears to humanity today as simply one avenue of many thoroughfares all pleasantly offering a destination of joy and personal fulfillment.

In the postmodern marketplace, what Christianity will have to do—or so it seems to me—is define itself not simply by its ability to bring happiness and joy. Lots and lots of folks will be promising deep and personal fulfillment—from druids to crystals to Gregorian chants. We may well be already in an era in which truth will have to be more specifically defined than it has been in recent decades—it may be incumbent on us to define what makes Christianity different from Buddhism, for example, the latest spiritual craze. Individual Christians, their churches, and their denominational fellowships may well have to be more definitively acquainted with truth—and that means a more significant commitment to doctrine and the nature of Christian faith. What I'm saying is that once our period of revival ends—as revivals always do—then perhaps we'll move on our way toward a redefined sense of theology, something that may be increasingly essential to every Christian fellowship. We offer peace, of course, but not crystals or druids.

At that point, a knowledge of our own theological heritage will be crucial, not simply as a weapon to impose upon those who seek something more than material reality, but to guide us in our understanding of the significant issues of our day. Perhaps that's the road we're presently traveling.

If that kind of scenario is the direction of the CRC today, should that moment arise when we need to know what we stand for and what we don't, we will, out of necessity, look substantively at our own story, glean what we can from its history of wins and losses, and thereby find ourselves better prepared to face the conversations and the quarrels that will undoubtedly ensue.

OUR STORY AND ITS RELEVANCE

To that end, I hope this story I've told has made a contribution. We are not what we were—we never will be. It is as specious for us to believe that we can stop the clock as it is for us to assume we can ever go back to something we once were. But it is instructive, I think, to look at those contributions our tradition has made to the ongoing dialogue in the culture at large, to note our strengths and weaknesses, and to become, thereby, more capable of continuing to speak to the issues of our day with the voice of a deeply held and ever zealous commitment to Jesus Christ, our Savior and Lord.

William Faulkner is judged by some to be the finest American writer of the twentieth century, even though his novels appear, at first meeting, nearly impossible to read. Faulkner's vision and prophetic voice is rooted in the American South and its heritage of profound loss—a loss of culture and spirit, a loss created by its own unholy marriage to the evil of institutional slavery.

Often his characters are not so much conscious of that history as they are the infected carriers of its deadly poison. One of them speaks for Faulkner himself, I believe, when he says, "The past is not dead. It's not even the past."

As a specific culture and people, the CRC today certainly does not stand as an inheritor of a legacy as oppressive as Faulkner's characters from the American South. But the truth of that line is not completely off base. We do imperil ourselves and our enterprises by concluding that what's behind us is of no value in the operations of today or the visions we hold for our tomorrows. We are still, in a sense, what we were.

Like ourselves, our history is fraught with sin. We need to remember that the Old Testament decalogue promises a powerful curse when it says that the sins of the fathers will be visited on the generations who follow. American culture's most glorious promise may well be that we can live exuberantly in the present, but we all do well to note that American consumerism does not offer a worldview forged out of scriptural norms. The Bible has a whole different perspective of past, present, and future. And it's the Bible, not progressivism or pragmatism or market

Interchurch Relations and Ecumenicity

The CRC has struggled with interdenominational relations since its birth in 1857. It sought the fellowship of the secular churches in the Netherlands early in its life and was rejected. For its first seventy-five years, the only church the young denomination was in fellowship with was the *Gereformeerde Kerken* of the Netherlands. That relationship eventually brought the CRC into contact with the *Gereformeerde Kerk in Suid Afrika,* another denomination that stemmed directly from the *Afscheiding* in the Netherlands.

These three churches and their mission offspring formed the Reformed Ecumenical Synod, founded in 1946. This association has barely survived the rigors of strife over some very difficult issues. The first was the problem of apartheid in South Africa, an issue in which the RES did some excellent work from 1976 to 1984. The second was the radical change in the doctrinal commitment of the GKN and its position on a number of moral and ethical issues.

In 1974 the CRC's Interchurch Relations Committee took clear steps to create a new day in the denomination's ecumenical life. It changed the former designation of "sister-church relationship" (which held the relationship to be so close that but for the difference in language and geography the two would be one) to "churches in ecclesiastical fellowship" (which allowed churches to have significant differences and still be in fellowship). In so doing it greatly expanded the number of churches with which the CRC has close relations, now including the Reformed Church in America, several Presbyterian groups, and two additional Reformed churches in the Netherlands. The CRC adopted an ecumenical charter in 1987, replacing the old guidelines of 1944.

Reformed Ecumenical Council meeting in Harare, Zimbabwe, 1988.

The committee's next step was to join in on the formation of the conservatively-oriented National Association of Presbyterian and Reformed Churches (NAPARC) in 1975. It also had in view the possibility of joining the World Alliance of Reformed Churches, the oldest ecumenical organization in Western Protestantism. The committee viewed the CRC as a possible bridge to bring the old mainline churches of Reformed heritage into fellowship with the more separatist Presbyterian groups. But its idealism was quickly dashed.

Synod rejected the invitation to join the World Alliance of Reformed Churches and voted to join the National Association of Evangelicals instead, a relationship its Interchurch Relations Committee was not terribly enthusiastic about. To add insult to injury, the CRC was soon expelled from NAPARC over the CRC's new position allowing women's ordination.

Briefly stated, formal CRC ecumenical relationships are not faring well. More hopeful are relationships forming in Canada between the CRC there and both evangelical and mainline churches. These are looser working relationships, not so much geared toward formal union as to expressing the unity we have in Christ as we minister to society as a whole. Perhaps these relationships will serve as a pattern that will help us broaden our ecumenical ties in the future. —TEH

values, that quickens the souls of the family of God.

Finally, no matter where we're going or where we've been, we need to remember that God's love is pure—and more gargantuan than anything our finite minds are capable of imagining. He'll take his own from all of our differing and battling mindsets. Where we fragmentize, he unifies. We may not like each other; but God loves much less circumspectly than we can or do. His grace is amazing, after all. His love is infinite. He is so much bigger than we are. So, so much bigger.

We all know that Jesus Christ did not come to save just us. He came to save the world. "For God so loved the world that he gave his one and only Son, that whoever believes in him shall not perish but have eternal life." As Reformed Christians we have been committed to a view of history and culture that ends in redemption—we know deeply and intimately the delightful promise of our eternal joy. But it has been our legacy to be citizens of this world too. Our strength has been as leaven. Whatever happens in the future—whether we break apart or redefine who we are and go on with a unity of purpose and direction—behind us we have a legacy that is not by any stretch of the imagination divine, but has strengths and accomplishments far beyond our limited numbers. By God's grace alone, what we've accomplished, we've done by deep and abiding commitment—first of all to God, and then back to his world.

Soli Deo Gloria—in this world *and* the next.